DATE DUE

AFTER GORBACHEV

Cambridge Soviet Paperbacks: 3

Editorial board

Dramatic and confusing changes in what used to be the Soviet Union have transformed the world in which we live. Communist rule has given way to multiparty politics; a command economy is being painfully privatised; almost every social and cultural value has been overturned; and Gorbachev's *perestroika* has now been swept away by the reforming policies of Boris Yel'tsin. In turn, these policies are now challenged by a variety of conservative and nationalist forces.

This new edition of Stephen White's best-selling introductory text has been revised throughout and now examines the full cycle of this period of revolutionary change from its Brezhnevite origins to postcommunist disintegration. A new final chapter charts the first turbulent years of Yel'tsin's troubled presidency and the background to his radical policies; and describes both a new role for Russia in the world, and the nature of opposition at home. Professor White pays particular attention to the issues surrounding constitutional reform, and to the confused outcome of the December 1993 elections.

Clearly written but detailed and authoritative, *After Gorbachev*, like its predecessors, will continue to provide an unrivalled guide to the seething processes of transition, upheaval and collapse which now characterise Russia and the post-Soviet republics. It will remain essential reading for students seeking to understand the politics and recent history of Russia and of its Eurasian and East European neighbours.

Cambridge Soviet Paperbacks

1   NICOLA MILLER

Soviet relations with Latin America
0 521 35193 6 (hardback)/0 521 35979 1 (paperback)

2   GALIA GOLAN

Soviet policies in the Middle East.
From World War II to Gorbachev
0 521 35332 7 (hardback)/0 521 35859 0 (paperback)

3   STEPHEN WHITE

After Gorbachev
0 521 45264 3 (hardback)/0 521 45896 X (paperback)

4   PHILIP R. PRYDE

Environmental management in the Soviet Union
0 521 36079 X (hardback)/0 521 40905 5 (paperback)

5   PEKKA SUTELA

Economic thought and economic reform in the Soviet Union
0 521 38020 0 (hardback)/0 521 38902 X (paperback)

6   GAIL LAPIDUS and VICTOR ZASLAVSKY with PHILIP GOLDMAN (eds.)

From Union to Commonwealth
Nationalism and separatism in the Soviet Republics
0 521 41706 6 (hardback)/0 521 42716 9 (paperback)

7   RICHARD STITES

Russian popular culture
Entertainment and society since 1900
0 521 36214 8 (hardback)/0 521 36986 X (paperback)

8   LEWIS H. SIEGELBAUM

Soviet state and society between revolutions, 1918–1929
0 521 36215 6 (hardback)/0 521 36987 8 (paperback)

9   ANNA LAWTON

Kinoglasnost: Soviet cinema in our time
0 521 38117 7 (hardback)/0 521 38814 7 (paperback)

10 CHARLES E. ZIEGLER

Foreign policy and East Asia
Learning and adaptation in the Gorbachev era
0 521 41547 0 (hardback)/0 521 42564 6 (paperback)

After Gorbachev

AAW-6884

Stephen White
Department of Politics, University of Glasgow

CAMBRIDGE
UNIVERSITY PRESS

Published by the Press Syndicate of the University of Cambridge
The Pitt Building, Trumpington Street, Cambridge CB2 1RP
40 West 20th Street, New York, NY 10011–4211, USA
10 Stamford Road, Oakleigh, Melbourne 3166, Australia

After Gorbachev succeeds and replaces four earlier editions:
Third edition *Gorbachev and after* (1992, reprinted 1992) 0 521 43374 6 hardback
43984 1 paperback
Second edition *Gorbachev and after* (1991, reprinted 1992) 0 521 41379 6
hardback 42435 6 paperback
First edition *Gorbachev in Power* (1990, reprinted three times) 0 521 39324 8
hardback 39723 5 paperback

Fourth edition 1993, reprinted with revisions 1994

Printed in the United States of America

A catalogue record for this book is available from the British Library

Library of Congress cataloguing in publication data applied for

ISBN 0 521 45264 3 hardback
ISBN 0 521 45896 X paperback

Contents

Preface

The dramatic changes that have taken place in what used to be the Soviet Union have been at the centre of international attention since they were launched in the mid 1980s. It was certainly a change from the grey uniformity of the later Brezhnev years. The Soviet Union was suddenly under the control of a youthful and imaginative General Secretary with a personable wife by his side. The official ideology came under vigorous assault and a doctrine of 'socialist pluralism' was promoted in its place. Competitive elections were held to the first working parliament in Soviet history. The media began to reflect a variety of points of view. The economy was exposed to private and cooperative ownership as part of a wider transition to market relations. An attempt was made to construct a 'renewed federation' that would take the place of the overcentralised union of the previous seventy years. And 'new thinking' in international affairs led to a series of changes in East–West relations as the Soviet leadership began to construct a cooperative rather than confrontational relationship with the other members of the world community.

The impact of all these changes, by the early 1990s, was still somewhat unclear. Democratisation, for instance, had led to an uneasy combination of party control and democratic accountability, and then, after the end of communist rule and the introduction of a new Russian constitution in 1993, to a strongly presidential republic in which the prime minister – after communist and nationalist successes in the December elections – appeared to be the more powerful figure. The economy hovered between state direction and entrepreneurial capitalism, with many of the worst features of both. *Glasnost'*, still seen as the main achievement of the Gorbachev years, began to be restricted by commercial as well as political pressures. The existing union had collapsed, but its successor, the Commonwealth of Independent States, looked very shaky. Political control, at the same time, had largely broken down as the Communist Party was replaced by a variety of weakly articulated successors, with little sign of the rule of law; and many still looked to the army, the renamed KGB or even Vladimir Zhirinovsky to restore public order, even if a newly established democracy had to be sacrificed.

There were few who thought, by the mid 1990s, that *perestroika* could be said to have succeeded; indeed there were few concepts that were less popular with all sections of political opinion. And yet the Gorbachev experience still generated more questions than answers. Did the General Secretary, for instance, have a long-term strategy, or had he been constantly reacting to circumstances? Was there a political agency, like the CPSU, that could have brought his reforms into effect? Did they enjoy popular support? More generally, could there be some kind of 'third way', combining (as Gorbachev had tried to do) democracy with party dominance and private enterprise with planning and public ownership? And what were the prospects for democratic rule, or even stability, in Russia and the other post-Soviet republics?

An answer to questions of this kind might not be available, in the view of some of Gorbachev's reformers, until the centenary of the revolution itself in 2017 or even later. A considered verdict on the early years of postcommunist Russia may have to wait still longer. In the meantime, the case for at least an interim analysis of the Gorbachev administration and its immediate aftermath is a very strong one. There have been biographies of the Soviet leader and of his wife, and several useful symposia on the process of reform in the Gorbachev era. So far, however, there have been few sustained examinations, not simply of the reform project, but of the experience of *perestroika* over the better part of two British parliamentary terms, and of the early years of postcommunist rule. This book is an attempt to evaluate that experience, covering all major fields of policy, extending – in this new edition – to the Yel'tsin presidency and the confused outcome of the December 1993 elections, and aiming not simply to describe the course of events but also to examine some of the issues of analysis to which the reforms have given rise. It will have achieved its purpose if it contributes to the continuing discussion of a subject that could hardly matter more, not simply to students and academics, but also to a much wider public and international community.

In preparing this study I have been greatly assisted by the UK Economic and Social Research Council, whose two-year grant made possible the employment of a research assistant whose main task was to scan the Soviet press over a wider range than would normally be possible for an individual academic. It also made possible several research visits to the USSR and (later) the Russian Federation for the consultation of sources not normally available in the West, and for discussions with Russian colleagues, most recently in September 1993 (an eventful month) and March 1994. I am grateful also to Hillel Ticktin, my coinvestigator, and to Walter Joyce, our research assistant, for their advice and encouragement throughout this period, and to the Glasgow 'newspaper seminar', which helped to alert me to many items I would otherwise have missed. Mary McAuley, General Editor of the Cambridge Soviet Paperbacks series, has taken an active interest in this project since its inception, and Michael Holdsworth made sure that this new edition as well as its predecessors negotiated the publishing process with despatch as well as professionalism.

Among other colleagues Martin Dewhirst, as always, has been indefatigable in providing quotations and sources both for this new edition and for its predecessors. For their advice and assistance on a number of specific points I am grateful to Rene Beermann, Archie Brown, John Channon, Terry Cox, Juris Dreifelds, Peter Duncan, Peter Ferdinand, Ronald J. Hill, Jyrki Iivonen, Nick Lampert, David Lane, Peter Lentini, Evan Mawdsley, the late Alec Nove, Stephen Revell, Myles Robertson, Ian Thatcher, Michael E. Urban, V. Stanley Vardys, David Wedgwood Benn, Matthew Wyman and several colleagues at the Institute of Sociology and the former Historical Archives Institute in Moscow, particularly Ol'ga Kryshtanovskaya. Dolores de Bromhead, once again, has been my most attentive reader. I also owe a general debt to a larger group of friends and colleagues, too numerous to mention individually, with whom I have discussed the Gorbachev experiment – and now the transition to postcommunist rule – at seminars and conferences over the past six years or more in several countries. Some of us have been 'optimists', some of us have been 'pessimists', and many more have been in between; but all of us have been riveted to our (changing) subject as never before.

Finally, a note on conventions. In respect of transliteration I have used a version of the scheme employed by the journal *Europe-Asia* (formerly *Soviet*) *Studies*, modified in cases where different usages have become established in English (Alexander not Aleksandr, Moscow not Moskva, Zinoviev not Zinov'ev). Sources in the notes are cited in full on their first occurrence in each chapter, and thereafter in abbreviated form.

June 1994   Glasgow

1   From Brezhnev to Gorbachev

In early 1982 Leonid Brezhnev was apparently at the height of his powers. General Secretary of the ruling Communist Party since October 1964 and, since 1977, chairman of the Presidium of the USSR Supreme Soviet or head of state, he had presided over a steady rise in living standards at home and an expansion of Soviet influence throughout the wider world. Under Brezhnev's leadership gross social product had doubled between 1960 and 1970 and more than trebled by 1980. Industrial production had more than quadrupled. Agricultural production had increased much more modestly (in 1981 and 1982 the harvests were so poor that the figures were simply suppressed), but the real incomes of ordinary citizens had more than doubled over the two decades and the wages paid to collective farmers had increased more than four times. Nor was this simply statistics. There were about three times as many members of the society with higher education, for instance, as there had been on Brezhnev's accession. There were more hospital beds, more flats, more motor cars, more refrigerators, and very many more televisions. And despite the disappointments in agriculture, for which climatic conditions were at least partly responsible, there had been considerable improvements in the Soviet diet. The consumption of meat, fish and fruit per head of population was up by about half, while the consumption of potatoes and bread, the staples of earlier years, had fallen back considerably.[1]

By the early 1980s, in parallel with these domestic changes, the USSR had begun to acquire an international influence that accorded rather more closely with the country's enormous territory, population and natural resources. Forced to back down in humiliating circumstances in the Cuban missile crisis of 1962, the USSR had since acquired a strategic capability which gave it an approximate parity with the USA by the end of that decade. The Soviet Union had one of the world's largest armies and one of its largest navies, and it stood at the head of one of the world's two major military alliances. It was the centre of one of the world's major trading blocs, CMEA or Comecon, and an influential member of the United Nations. Its status as a superpower had been enhanced by a series of negotiations and agreements with its major capitalist adversary, particularly SALT I in 1972 and its unratified successor, SALT II, in 1979. The USSR was represented much more widely in international affairs: it had diplomatic relations with 139 countries by the early 1980s, compared with just 74 in 1960.[2] And it traded with over 145 foreign states, compared with just 45 in 1950, with foreign trade as a whole accounting for a modest but steadily increasing share of its national income.[3] The Soviet Union was 'one of the greatest world powers', the official history of Soviet foreign policy was able to boast by the early 1980s, 'without whose participation not a single international problem can be resolved'.[4] This was an exaggeration, but a pardonable one.

Leonid Brezhnev, the symbol of this developing military and politico-economic might, became increasingly the central element in the political system that underpinned it. Originally, in 1964, a 'collective leadership', it had become a leadership 'headed by comrade L. I. Brezhnev' by the early 1970s. The Politburo had been listed in alphabetical order after 1964 to emphasise its collective character, but in 1973, after KGB chairman Yuri Andropov had joined it, Brezhnev's name continued to be listed first although this was a violation of strictly alphabetical principles. In 1976, at the 25th Party Congress, Brezhnev became the party's 'universally acclaimed leader' and *vozhd'* (chief), a term previously used to describe Stalin; he became a marshal of the Soviet Union and a bronze bust was unveiled in his birthplace.[5] In 1977 he added the title of head of state and the Gold Medal of Karl Marx, the highest award of the Academy of Sciences, for his 'outstanding contribution to the development of Marxist-Leninist theory'.[6] In 1978 he received the Order of Victory for his wartime service,[7] and in 1979 the Lenin Prize for Literature for his memoirs, written for him by a literary aide who himself received the Order of Lenin a few days later.[8] At the 26th Party Congress in 1981 Brezhnev was hailed as a 'true continuer of Lenin's great cause' and an 'ardent fighter for peace and communism'; his speech was punctuated seventy-eight times by 'applause', forty times by 'prolonged applause' and eight times by 'stormy, prolonged applause'.[9] Unprecedentedly, the whole Politburo and Secretariat, Brezhnev included, were re-elected without change; Brezhnev's son Yuri, a first deputy minister of foreign trade, became a candidate member of the Central Committee at the same time, and so too did his son-in-law Yuri Churbanov, a first deputy minister of internal affairs.

Brezhnev's seventy-fifth birthday, in December 1981, brought these tributes to a new pitch of intensity. Seven of *Pravda*'s eight pages on 19 December were wholly or partly devoted to the event, and tributes continued to appear in the central press throughout the following week. Brezhnev himself attended a ceremony in the Kremlin where he was invested with a series of distinctions by the leaders of the East European communist states, who had come to Moscow for the occasion. The Soviet awards, which he had himself to authorise as head of state, included a seventh Order of Lenin and a fourth Hero of the Soviet Union citation. Mikhail Suslov, a few years his senior, remarked at the conferment of these awards that seventy-five was regarded in the Soviet Union as no more than the 'beginning of middle age'.[10] Brezhnev's life was turned into a film, 'Story of a Communist';[11] his wartime exploits in the Caucasus, little noted at the time, were presented as all but the decisive turning-point of the struggle against the Nazis; and his memoirs were turned into a film, plays, mime, a popular song and a full-scale oratorio. He had more orders and medals than Khrushchev and Stalin combined, and more military distinctions than Marshal Zhukov, who had saved Leningrad and liberated Berlin during World War II.[12] Even a modest poem, 'To the German Komsomol', written when he was seventeen, received front-page treatment when it appeared in *Pravda* in May 1982.

Brezhnev's personal and political powers, nonetheless, were clearly failing. According to a subsequent and well-informed account, Brezhnev began to suffer serious ill-health at the end of the 1960s and in January 1976 was briefly clinically dead following a stroke.[13] For three months he was unable to work, as his speech and writing had been impaired, and thereafter he was constantly surrounded by doctors, with a fully-equipped ambulance following his car on trips abroad. His speech became increasingly slurred, his breathing laboured, his concentration limited. Unkind anecdotes began to circulate: his eyebrows, in one of these, were 'Stalin's moustache at a higher level'; in another, he was to have an operation to enlarge his chest to accommodate the medals he had been awarded. Perhaps most seriously of all, his grip on affairs of state became increasingly infirm. The death of Suslov, in January 1982, seems in retrospect to have been crucial. One of the Politburo's oldest and longest-serving members with acknowledged authority in both ideology and foreign affairs, Suslov had apparently served as king-maker in 1964, declining the general secretaryship for himself and then backing Brezhnev for the position. With Suslov gone the Brezhnev leadership began to disintegrate rapidly. At the end of the same month the death was reported of Semen Tsvigun, a first deputy chairman of the KGB and a close Brezhnev associate. Rumour suggested it was a case of suicide precipitated by his impending arrest on corruption charges.[14] At the beginning of March 1982 came the arrest of 'Boris the gypsy' and other figures from the worlds of circus and entertainment on charges of smuggling diamonds abroad, bribery and currency speculation. All were close friends of Brezhnev's daughter Galina, and their arrest showed that the general secretary's authority was no longer sufficient to protect them.[15]

Still more significantly, in May 1982 a plenary session of the CPSU Central Committee took place at which Brezhnev (according to Western press reports) was unable to secure the election of his own protégé, Konstantin Chernenko, to the powerful position of Central Committee Secretary with responsibility for ideology which had become vacant with the death of Suslov. In a development widely seen as significant both at home and abroad it was the head of the KGB, Yuri Andropov, who was elected to the position, apparently with the support of the armed forces lobby. The Krasnodar party first secretary and Brezhnev intimate, Sergei Medunov, was dismissed in August 1982; later still came the arrest of the manager of one of Moscow's most famous food shops and his wife, both of whom were close associates of Brezhnev's daughter.[16] All of this suggested that Brezhnev's political authority as well as his physical health were in decline, and reports circulating in the West at about this time suggested that it had in fact already been decided that he would retain the largely ceremonial state presidency, allowing another figure to be elected to the more demanding post of party leader. Brezhnev, in the event, anticipated any changes of this kind by dying suddenly on the morning of 10 November 1982, his health undermined by a two-hour stint in the reviewing box at the anniversary parade in Red Square three days earlier. *Pravda*'s obituary mourned the passing of a 'continuer of the cause of Lenin, a fervent patriot, an outstanding revolutionary and struggler for peace and communism, [and] an outstanding political and government leader of the contemporary era'.[17]

It had widely been expected that a decent interval would elapse before a successor was named as General Secretary, and indeed that a prolonged succession struggle might ensue. On 11 November, however, it was announced that Andropov was to be the chairman of the committee making arrangements for Brezhnev's funeral, and the following day it was announced that an emergency meeting of the Central Committee had elected him to the vacant general secretaryship. Andropov's main rival for the succession, Konstantin Chernenko, had the task of proposing his candidacy to the Central Committee, where it was accepted unanimously. Brezhnev was buried on 15 November, Andropov making the funeral oration, and a week later the new General Secretary made his first speech as party leader to the Central Committee, a brief but effective review of Soviet foreign and domestic policy.[18] In May 1983 it became known that Andropov had succeeded Brezhnev as chairman of the Defence Council of the USSR, the body attached to the Politburo that was responsible for military and security matters, and in June he was elected to the vacant state presidency (chairmanship of the Presidium of the USSR Supreme Soviet), thus concentrating in his hands after only seven months the same combination of posts that Brezhnev had taken almost thirteen years to accumulate. A series of changes in the membership of the Politburo and Secretariat, and at lower levels of the party and state, had meanwhile begun to put in place a coalition of reform-minded technocrats who might be expected to support both the new General Secretary and the policies he intended to promote.

Andropov's own health, however, was far from certain. An elderly man (already sixty-eight when he assumed the party leadership) with a history of heart trouble, there were persistent rumours of incapacity from almost the outset of his period of office. Although a number of members of the 'Brezhnev mafia' swiftly lost their positions, Andropov's rival for the general secretaryship, Konstantin Chernenko, remained prominent, making the opening speech at the June 1983 Central Committee plenum and reportedly chairing the Politburo in Andropov's absence. Andropov's effective authority in fact lasted for only a few months: he was last seen in public in August 1983 and unprecedentedly failed to attend the anniversary parade in Red Square on 7 November and then the Central Committee plenum and the Supreme Soviet session the following month. It became known that Andropov was receiving kidney dialysis treatment at the Central Committee hospital near Moscow and that Mikhail Gorbachev, the youngest member of the Politburo and apparently the one most closely attuned to the General Secretary's own thinking, was maintaining links between him and other members of the leadership. A series of 'interviews' and statements, and an address that was circulated to the Central Committee plenum he was unable to attend, suggested that Andropov's intellectual powers were largely unimpaired. Further changes in the Politburo and Secretariat at the December 1983 plenum indicated that his control over perhaps the most important of all the powers of a party leader, that of patronage, was scarcely diminished. Nonetheless, explanations in terms of 'colds' and 'temporary causes' began to wear thin, and it was not entirely unexpected when on 11 February 1984 the central press reported that Andropov had died two days earlier after a 'long illness'.[19] Once again the party leadership was plunged into the search for a successor.

As before there were two principal contenders: Chernenko, whose political fortunes had revived with Andropov's illness, and Gorbachev, who was evidently Andropov's own favoured candidate for the succession. Chernenko was named on 10 February to head the funeral arrangements committee, which recent precedent suggested gave good grounds for believing that he would shortly be elected the new General Secretary. The formal choice in fact took some time to arrange and appears to have divided the remaining Politburo members into two camps, a 'Brezhnevite' faction supporting Chernenko and composed for the most part of long-serving members of the leadership like Prime Minister Nikolai Tikhonov, Kazakh party leader Dinmukhamed Kunaev and Moscow party secretary Viktor Grishin, and an 'Andropovite' faction consisting of the younger, more reform-minded members who had joined or advanced within the leadership under the late General Secretary, including Vitalii Vorotnikov, Geidar Aliev and Gorbachev himself. The choice fell finally on Chernenko, partly, it appears, because of his seniority and experience, and partly because a Gorbachev leadership would have been likely to last for an unduly lengthy period: Gorbachev at this time was just fifty-two and had been a full member of the Politburo for less than four years.

At all events, on 13 February 1984, four days after Andropov died, another extraordinary meeting of the Central Committee took place at which Chernenko, proposed by Tikhonov, was elected unanimously to the vacant general secretaryship.[20] It emerged subsequently that Gorbachev had also addressed the plenum,[21] and unofficial reports suggested that he had been installed as a *de facto* second secretary with a power of veto, on behalf of the younger 'Andropovite' faction, over leadership decisions.[22] Gorbachev's greater prominence was apparent in, for example, his more advanced placing in the line-up of leaders beside Andropov's coffin, in the ranking he received in pre-election speeches and on other formal party and state occasions. In turn it indicated that the Chernenko leadership was a relatively evenly-balanced coalition, containing both supporters of the late President Andropov's reforming policies and those who believed they had been pressed too far. These sharp internal divisions were sufficient in themselves to slow down the momentum of reform, quite apart from what the new General Secretary might have wished, and they persisted throughout this period of office as neither side could allow the other to gain a decisive advantage by adding to their supporters in the Politburo or Secretariat.

The state presidency and chairmanship of the Defence Council, as well as the party leadership, had become vacant on Andropov's death. It became known later in February 1984 that Chernenko had also assumed the chairmanship of the Defence Council, and in April 1984, on Gorbachev's nomination, the first session of the newly elected Supreme Soviet elected him to the vacant presidency.[23] Chernenko was nevertheless, at seventy-two, the oldest General Secretary ever to have assumed this office, and he had a history of lung disease (emphysema) which caused difficulty in breathing. Perhaps inevitably, it was regarded as a transitional general secretaryship from the outset. Two regular Central Committee plenums were held during Chernenko's period of office: the first, in April 1984, was devoted to the work of the soviets and educational reform, and the second dealt with land improvement. Neither plenum made any change in the membership of the Politburo or Secretariat or even in the membership of the Central Committee itself, and neither could be said to have initiated any major new departure in Soviet public policy (the educational reforms, which were of some importance, had been launched the previous year). Attempts to develop a modest personality cult around Chernenko's service in the border guards in the early 1930s had little success; nor could much be made of his undistinguished wartime service.[24] A series of missed engagements suggested that Chernenko's health was already deteriorating, and official spokesmen had to admit that the recently-elected General Secretary was suffering from a serious cold, or perhaps worse.

Chernenko was last seen in public at the end of December 1984. He failed to meet Greece's Prime Minister Papandreou on his visit to Moscow in February 1985, and failed to deliver the customary eve of poll address to the Soviet people in the republican and local elections later the same month. Although he was shown voting on television on 24 February and was pictured in the central press receiving his deputy's credentials on 1 March,[25] rumours of the General Secretary's physical incapacity were strengthened rather than dispelled by his evident ill-health. Finally, on the evening of 10 March 1985, he died, the medical bulletin stating the cause as heart failure following a deterioration in the working of his lungs and liver.[26] The next day, with unprecedented speed, an extraordinary session of the Central Committee elected Mikhail Gorbachev as its third General Secretary in three and a half years, Gromyko proposing him for the position with the evident support of the KGB, economic administrators and the 'Andropovite' faction within the leadership.[27] Gorbachev, who had just celebrated his fifty-fourth birthday, was still the youngest member of the Politburo and apparently in robust good health, which was in itself a considerable change. As one of the earliest jokes put it: 'What support does Gorbachev have in the Kremlin?' Answer: 'None – he walks unaided'.[28]

A changing policy agenda

Gorbachev told the Politburo meeting that agreed to nominate him to the vacant General Secretaryship that there was 'no need to change [their] policies'.[29] Although he was later concerned to emphasise the decisive break that had occurred with his election and still more with the April 1985 Central Committee plenum at which his programme was first set out, there was in fact a good deal of continuity between the policy agenda that had been established by Andropov and Chernenko and the agenda that Gorbachev came to promote over the years that followed. The decisive break had arguably taken place under Andropov, whose security background tended to obscure his earlier exposure to the Eastern European reform experience while Soviet ambassador to Hungary in the mid-1950s and a penetrating, somewhat puritanical intellect which was completely at odds with the complacency and corruption of the later Brezhnev era. Even Chernenko, despite his background in propaganda and party administration and his long career association with Brezhnev, had a number of special priorities which associated him with broadly 'liberal' opinion in the leadership context of the time, among them an interest in letters from the public, an emphasis upon the consumer sector of the economy and a commitment to detente with the West.[30] There were, in fact, a number of elements in common throughout the reorientation of policy that took place between the death of Andropov and the accession of Gorbachev, although the reformist impetus undoubtedly slackened under Chernenko and acquired a new scope and urgency under Gorbachev.

One element in that reorientation of policy was leadership renewal, which had already begun in the last few months of Brezhnev's term of office and to which Andropov made a major and decisive contribution.

At the May 1982 plenum Andropov had himself become a Central Committee Secretary and Vladimir Dolgikh, the Secretary responsible for heavy industry, had become a candidate member of the Politburo.[31] At the November 1982 plenum, the first after Andropov's election, the Azerbaijani party leader Geidar Aliev was promoted from candidate to full membership of the Politburo (and shortly afterwards became a first deputy prime minister), Nikolai Ryzhkov, a Gosplan official, became a Central Committee Secretary, and Andrei Kirilenko, a longstanding Secretary who was Brezhnev's exact contemporary, retired from the leadership 'for health reasons at his own request'.[32] Further changes took place at the June 1983 Central Committee meeting: the Leningrad regional party leader Grigorii Romanov moved to Moscow to become a Central Committee Secretary and Vitalii Vorotnikov, who had been banished to Cuba as Soviet ambassador by Brezhnev, became a candidate member of the Politburo (and shortly afterwards prime minister of the Russian Republic).[33] The December 1983 Central Committee plenum, the last under Andropov's leadership, saw Vorotnikov consolidate his rapid advance by becoming a full member of the Politburo. Viktor Chebrikov, chairman of the KGB, became a candidate member; and Yegor Ligachev, at this time party first secretary in Tomsk, became a Central Committee Secretary with responsibility for the vitally important area of organisational party work (in practice, appointments and the supervision of local party organs).[34]

During Chernenko's somewhat shorter general secretaryship there were no further changes in the party's leading bodies apart from the loss which inevitably occurred with the death in December 1984 of Dmitri Ustinov, the defence minister and a full member of the Politburo.[35] The change that had already occurred, however, was very considerable. Within the Politburo elected after the 26th Party Congress in March 1981 all but three of its fourteen full members had been born before the revolution, and the average age was over seventy. Arvid Pel'she, born in 1899, had joined the Communist Party during World War I and had been a deputy to the Petrograd Soviet in 1917. In the Politburo that Gorbachev inherited in March 1985 just five of its ten full members were of pre-revolutionary origin, and four (including Gorbachev himself) were in their fifties or early sixties, alarmingly young by recent Soviet standards (the average age had meantime come down to sixty-eight). At least as notable, it had become a leadership of much greater technical and managerial competence. Vorotnikov, for instance, was a qualified aviation engineer who had spent the early part of his career in a Kuibyshev factory. Ryzhkov, before coming to Gosplan, had been the very successful director of the Uralmash engineering works in Sverdlovsk. Ligachev was an engineering graduate; and Chebrikov, also an engineer, had a background in industrial management as well as party work in the Ukraine.[36]

A further priority, associated particularly with Andropov, was social discipline. In part this meant a firm and sustained campaign against the bribery and corruption that had increasingly disfigured the later Brezhnev years. The late General Secretary's family and friends were among the first to feel the effects of the new policy. In December 1982, just a month after Andropov's accession, Interior Minister Nikolai Shchelokov was dismissed from his position;[37] a close associate of Brezhnev from Dnepropetrovsk days, he had enjoyed considerable opportunities for enrichment as head of Soviet law enforcement. His wife and son, according to later reports, had also engaged in illegal activities such as the buying and selling of foreign cars.[38] Shchelokov was replaced as Interior Minister by Vitalii Fedorchuk, an experienced KGB career officer and a trusted Andropov associate, and in June he and another Brezhnev crony, the Krasnodar first secretary Medunov, were dismissed from the Central Committee for 'mistakes in their work'.[39] Although his family reportedly celebrated Chernenko's election with an all-night party, Shchelokov continued to lose favour, being expelled from the party and losing his military rank in November 1984 for 'abuse of position for personal gain and conduct discrediting the military title of General of the Soviet Union'.[40] Shchelokov committed suicide in early 1985; his wife had committed suicide in mid-1983, and his son was dismissed from the bureau of the Komsomol at about the same time.[41]

Brezhnev's own family was also affected. His daughter Galina and her husband Churbanov were banished to Murmansk; Churbanov lost his post as first deputy interior minister in December 1984 and was later arrested on corruption charges.[42] The manager of Gastronom No. 1, the famous food store with whose operations Brezhnev's daughter had been associated, was executed in July 1984.[43] Brezhnev's son Yuri lost his ministerial post and also his Central Committee membership in 1986. An extensive purge took place in Uzbekistan, where nepotism and other corrupt practices had long been notorious.[44] In February 1983 a deputy aviation minister was dismissed for negligence in his supervision of foreign currency dealings; the following month a deputy minister of light engineering who had arranged for the construction of a country house out of state resources was sacked on grounds of corruption and incompetence.[45] The campaign against corruption may have owed something to Andropov's own asceticism: he lived modestly and is believed to have refrained from any attempts to promote the careers of his own children, although his son, Igor, appeared as chief Soviet delegate at the Madrid and Stockholm follow-up conferences on peace and security in Europe and was later appointed Soviet ambassador to Greece.[46] More important, perhaps, was the concern of both Andropov and his successor that corruption, if allowed to go unchecked, might reduce the effectiveness of party control and perhaps ultimately compromise the regime in the eyes of its population, as had clearly happened in Poland in the late 1970s and early 1980s.

The other side of the post-Brezhnev leadership's campaign of social discipline, which also continued under Chernenko, was an attempt to strengthen discipline in the workplace and law and order in the wider society. One of the first clear signs of this new direction in official policy was the series of raids that the police began to make in early 1983 on shops, public baths and even underground stations in order to find out which of those present had taken time off their work without permission. There was certainly some room for improvement. An official report in late 1982 found that of every 100 workers surveyed, an average of 30 were absent 'for personal reasons' at any given moment, in most cases to go shopping or visit the doctor. Another investigation in 800 Moscow enterprises found that in some cases no more than 10 per cent of the workforce were still at their places during the last hour of the shift.[47] A further series of decrees of 'socialist labour discipline' sought to reduce poor quality workmanship, alcoholism and absenteeism more generally at the workplace,[48] and the positive example of Aleksei Stakhanov was again held up for emulation, nearly fifty years after his record-breaking exploits in the Donbass coalmines[49] (rather later, in 1988, it was revealed that the champion miner had been transferred to office work, turned to drink, and died a lonely and disillusioned man[50]).

In terms of politics the Andropov period saw no liberalisation, despite early and perhaps inspired reports that the new General Secretary spoke English, and liked jazz and modern Western literature. There was an open attack, for instance, upon 'alien' and 'decadent' trends in the arts, particularly at the Central Committee meeting in June 1983 which was devoted to this subject, and there were sharply worded attacks upon the Soviet film industry (which had begun to explore some contemporary social ills) and by the board of the Writers' Union upon the literary journal *Novy mir*.[51] Direct dialling facilities with the outside world were ended, apparently at Andropov's behest, in September 1982,[52] and postal and customs regulations became more stringent.[53] Steps were also taken against a number of prominent dissidents. The writer Georgii Vladimov, for instance, author of *Faithful Ruslan* and other works, was compelled to emigrate in early 1983, and the historian and political commentator Roy Medvedev, untouched for many years, was called to the Procurator-General's office and warned that he must cease his 'anti-Soviet activities' or face criminal proceedings.[54] The physicist Andrei Sakharov and his wife, exiled to Gorky by Brezhnev in 1980, continued to suffer harassment, and legal changes in the same year increased the penalties for unauthorised dealings with foreigners.[55] The theatre director Yuri Lyubimov and the historian Mikhail Geller, both resident abroad, lost their Soviet citizenship.[56] The number of Jews allowed to emigrate, another normally reliable barometer of liberalism, also fell sharply, from up to 50,000 a year in the late 1970s to 2,700 in 1982, 1,300 in 1983 and only 896 in 1984.[57]

The immediate post-Brezhnev period, however, saw no reversion to hardline Stalinism. Dissidents and oppositionists, certainly, were harshly treated, but for those who were content to advance their objectives within established channels there was a greater emphasis than before upon consultation and accountability. For the first time in modern Soviet history, for instance, reports began to appear in *Pravda* (and to be read out on radio and television) of the subjects that had been discussed at the weekly meetings of the Politburo (the reports, which were admittedly far from comprehensive, suggested that there was a heavy emphasis upon foreign affairs though domestic issues were usually the first to be considered).[58] Attempts were also made to revive the Khrushchevian practice of meeting members of the public face to face at home or in their workplace. Andropov made a symbolic gesture of some importance by visiting the Sergo Ordzhonikidze machine tool factory at the end of January 1983 for an extended and frankly-worded exchange with its workforce; Chernenko made a somewhat less remarkable visit to the 'Hammer and Sickle' metallurgical factory in Moscow in April 1984.[59] The rights of ordinary workers at their workplace were also strengthened, at least on paper, by a law on labour collectives, adopted in June 1983 after an extended public discussion, which gave workforce meetings greater rights in relation to management and the appointment of leading personnel.[60] The annual plan and budget, apparently for the first time, were submitted to the All-Union Council of Trade Unions for their consideration in late 1984.[61]

In public life more generally there was a greater emphasis upon openness and publicity, or what soon became widely known as *glasnost'*. Reports began to appear in the press, for instance, of the work, not simply of their parent bodies, but of commissions of the Politburo, the Council of Ministers and the Supreme Soviet Presidium (Politburo commissions on educational reform, chaired by Chernenko, and on consumer goods and services, chaired by Geidar Aliev, were the first to be mentioned[62]). The Central Committee resolved, at its June 1983 meeting, to establish a national public opinion centre;[63] and the Khrushchevian practice was resumed (although in only a single instance during these years) of publishing the full proceedings of Central Committee plenums.[64] There was a continuing emphasis, throughout the period, upon the need to take account of the proposals and complaints of ordinary citizens, particularly in the form of letters to party and state bodies and to the press. The harsher penalties that were imposed for bribery, corruption and embezzlement were reported to have been prompted by communications of this kind, and the strengthening of law and order was similarly presented as a response to pressure from citizens in Gorky, who had complained that they were afraid to walk the streets at night.[65] Difficult though it was to assess such matters precisely, these new emphases in public policy appeared to have been well received by the Soviet public: according to an unpublished opinion poll, reported by the Western press in February 1983, fully 87 per cent of those surveyed assessed the first three months of the new regime (and by implication the post-Brezhnev changes) 'positively'.[66]

Still more fundamentally, there was a reconsideration in the Andropov and Chernenko periods of the official ideology from which the regime still claimed to derive its right to rule. One of the most important contributions to a reconsideration of these matters was Andropov's article on 'The teaching of Karl Marx and some questions of socialist construction in the USSR' which appeared in the party theoretical journal *Kommunist* in early 1983. Its sober and realistic tone marked off the post-Brezhnev era from the optimism of Khrushchev, and even from Brezhnev's own somewhat complacent notion of 'developed socialism'. There was a need, Andropov emphasised, for a proper understanding of the stage of development that had been reached in the USSR; any attempt to run ahead of that level of development would simply suggest tasks that were unrealisable. The Soviet Union, he insisted, was only at the beginning of the long historical stage of developed socialism; there should be no exaggeration of their closeness to the ultimate goal of full communism, and there should be a proper acknowledgement of the difficulties that still remained.[67] Andropov's speech at the June 1983 Central Committee plenum, which dwelt extensively with the revisions that would be required in the new edition of the Party Programme for which the 26th Party Congress had called, noted similarly that there were elements of 'isolation from reality' and 'undue anticipation' in the existing text, adopted in 1961. It was vital, he had argued earlier, to proceed from the situation that actually existed and avoid 'ready-made solutions'.[68]

Chernenko, who in turn became chairman of the commission preparing a new Programme, took the same practical and unheroic approach. Addressing the commission in April 1984, he reminded the participants that developed socialism would be an 'historically protracted' period and urged that they concentrate their attention upon the complicated tasks that had still to be resolved rather than dwell upon what Lenin had called the 'distant, beautiful and rosy future'. All 'unfounded promises and prognoses', in particular, should be avoided.[69] These emphases in turn became the basis for a developing specialist literature which acknowledged, more openly than ever before, that socialism had not necessarily resolved complex issues such as environmental conservation, the nationality question or gender inequalities. Still more provocatively, it was argued by a few scholars (notably Anatolii Butenko, a senior researcher attached to the Academy of Sciences) that Soviet-type societies still contained 'contradictions' based upon the different interests of the various groups of which they were composed, and that these could lead to 'serious collisions' of the kind that had occurred in Poland in the early 1980s unless far-reaching democratic reforms were instituted.[70] The debate was suspended in 1984, but two years later it was one of those to which Gorbachev devoted particular attention in his report to the 27th Party Congress.[71]

The Gorbachev administration: building a leadership team

The advent of a new General Secretary had normally meant a significant change in the direction of Soviet public policy, although any change had usually taken some time to establish itself as the new leader gradually marginalised his opponents and coopted his supporters on to the Politburo and Secretariat. At the outset of his administration Gorbachev's objectives, and indeed his personal background, were still fairly obscure even at leading levels of the party. Gorbachev, unlike his two main rivals Grigorii Romanov and Viktor Grishin, had not addressed a party congress, and he had still no published collection of writings to his name. He had made only a couple of important visits abroad, to Canada in 1983 and to the United Kingdom in late 1984, on both occasions as the head of a delegation of Soviet parliamentarians. Andrei Gromyko, proposing Gorbachev's candidacy to the Central Committee, explained what had convinced him personally that Gorbachev would be a suitable General Secretary: Gorbachev, he indicated, had chaired meetings of the Politburo in Chernenko's absence and had done so 'brilliantly, without any exaggeration'.[72] Gorbachev himself, in his acceptance speech, paid tribute to the late General Secretary and then pledged himself to continue the policy of his two predecessors, which he defined as 'acceleration of socio-economic development and the perfection of all aspects of social life'.[73] There were, however, some elements in the new General Secretary's biography which suggested that his administration would be more than a continuation of its immediate precursors.

One of those elements was Gorbachev's own background, particularly his education and more youthful generation. Gorbachev was born, according to his official biography, on 2 March 1931 to a peasant family in the Stavropol territory in southern Russia.[74] He worked first as a mechanic at a machine-tractor station, and then in 1950, with the help of his local party organisation, enrolled in the Law Faculty at Moscow State University. Gorbachev was a Komsomol activist while at university, and joined the CPSU itself in 1952. He graduated in 1955, the first Soviet leader since Lenin to have received a legal training and the first to graduate from the country's premier university. The Czech communist and later dissident Zdeněk Mlynář, who was his classmate and close friend at this time, later recalled Gorbachev's openmindedness and his enthusiasm for Hegel's dictum that the truth was 'always concrete'. Others drew attention to the Soviet leader's early training in amateur dramatics and the ability it appeared to have given him to influence others without revealing his own feelings.[75] After graduation Gorbachev returned to Stavropol where he worked in the Komsomol and party apparatus, later completing a correspondence course at Stavropol Agricultural Institute. In 1966 he became first secretary of the city party committee, in 1970 he was appointed to head the territorial party organisation, and the following year he joined the Central Committee as a full member. In 1978 Gorbachev replaced his mentor Fedor Kulakov in the Central Committee Secretariat, taking responsibility for agriculture. In 1979 he became a candidate, and then in 1980 a full member of the ruling Politburo.[76]

Gorbachev met his wife Raisa, a philosophy graduate, while they were both at Moscow University (if subsequent accounts are to be believed, they met during a class in ballroom dancing[77]). Born, according to her official biography, in the town of Rubtsovsk in Siberia in 1932, Raisa Maksimovna Titorenko was the daughter of a railway engineer and a more talented student than Gorbachev himself. The Gorbachevs married in 1953 and then moved to Stavropol two years later after their graduation. Raisa Gorbachev took the opportunity to pursue some sociological research into daily life in local collective farms, receiving a candidate of science degree (roughly equivalent to a Western doctorate) in 1967. After their return to the capital in the late 1970s she lectured for some years at Moscow University.[78] The Gorbachevs have a daughter, Irina, who is a doctor by profession, and two grandchildren.[79] Previous party leaders' wives had played a very discreet role in Soviet public life: it was not even known that Andropov's wife was still alive until she appeared at his funeral in 1984. Raisa Gorbachev, however, swiftly came to play a prominent part in Soviet public life and especially in international affairs, where she became a Soviet 'First Lady' accompanying the General Secretary on his travels (even when, at Reykjavik, Nancy Reagan stayed at home). Her views were believed to exercise a strong influence upon the General Secretary himself; they certainly discussed 'everything' at home in the evenings, Gorbachev told an NBC interviewer in late 1987 in remarks which were censored for Soviet domestic consumption.[80]

It was not customary for a Soviet leader to discuss his personal affairs with the mass media, but Gorbachev did venture some information on this subject when he was interviewed by the Italian communist paper L'Unità in May 1987. His main weakness, Gorbachev believed, was that he had too many interests. He had enrolled in the law faculty at university, for instance, but had originally intended to study physics. He liked mathematics, but also history and literature. In later years he had turned more and more to the study of economics, while remaining interested in philosophy (this was not, to put it mildly, the intellectual background of his immediate predecessor).[81] Interest in the General Secretary's personal life was hardly satisfied by such revelations and there were further queries in the spring of 1989. Did Mikhail Sergeevich, for instance, like fishing? And why did glasnost' not apply to the person who had introduced it?[82] Gorbachev obliged with some further information in an interview in a Central

Committee journal later the same year. He earned 1,200 rubles a month, he explained, the same as other members of the Politburo. He had a considerable additional income from royalties and other sources (his book *Perestroika* alone appeared in more than 100 countries), but he had donated any earnings of this kind to the party budget and various charitable causes. The General Secretary, it later emerged, had been baptised; one of his grandfathers had been sent to Siberia in 1933 and the other, a collective farm organiser, had spent more than a year in prison (Raisa had also lost a grandfather to Stalinism).[83]

As well as his personal characteristics, there were also clues in Gorbachev's speeches before his assumption of the general secretaryship as to the direction of policy he was likely to pursue. Perhaps the clearest indication of this kind was a speech Gorbachev delivered to an all-union conference on ideology in December 1984. The speech contained positive references to self-management, which Lenin had 'never counterposed to Soviet state power', and drew attention to the various interests of different social groups and to the need for a greater measure of social justice (which had become a coded form of attack upon the Brezhnev legacy). There was enormous scope, Gorbachev went on, for the further development of the Soviet political system, and of socialist democracy. This was partly a matter of developing all aspects of the work of the soviets, and of involving workers more fully in the affairs of their own workplace. It was also a matter of securing a greater degree of *glasnost'* or openness in party and state life. As well as tributes to Chernenko, there were clear and positive allusions to Andropov in his remarks about the 'two previous years' and the need to avoid 'ready-made solutions'.[84] Gorbachev's electoral address of 20 February 1985, made at a time when Chernenko's serious illness was widely known, repeated many of these themes, combining almost populist references to Soviet power as a form of rule 'of the toilers and for the toilers' and to the need for the party 'again and again to check its political course against the rich experience of the people' with more abrasive remarks about the need for self-sufficiency in enterprise management and for greater labour discipline.[85] These speeches, in effect an election manifesto to the Central Committee 'selectorate', made it clear that Gorbachev would continue Andropov's emphasis upon efficiency and discipline but also that they would be placed within a broader framework involving democratic reform and a reassertion of the moral values that were, for Gorbachev, implicit in socialism.

The direction of reform became still clearer at the April 1985 Central Committee plenum, the first that Gorbachev addressed as party leader.

There had been significant achievements in all spheres of Soviet life, Gorbachev told the plenum. The USSR had a powerful, developed economy, a highly skilled workforce and an advanced scientific base. Everyone had the right to work, to social security, to cultural resources of all kinds, and to participation in management. But further changes were needed in order to achieve a 'qualitatively new state of society', including modernisation of the economy and the extension of socialist democracy and popular self-government. The key issue was the acceleration of economic growth. This was quite feasible if the 'human factor' was called more fully into play, and if the reserves that existed throughout the economy were properly utilised. This in turn required a greater degree of decentralisation of economic management, including cost accounting at enterprise level and a closer connection between the work that people did and the payment they received.[86] The months and years that followed saw the gradual assembly of a leadership team to direct these changes and the further extension of what was already a challenging reform agenda.

The formation of a new administration was the easier of these two tasks and the one that advanced more rapidly. The April 1985 Central Committee plenum itself made a start: Viktor Chebrikov, the KGB chairman and an Andropov appointee, moved from candidate to full membership of the Politburo, and Yegor Ligachev and Nikolai Ryzhkov, two Andropov appointees to the Secretariat who had been present when Gorbachev delivered his election address, both became full members of the Politburo without passing through the customary candidate (nonvoting) stage. There had been no promotions of this kind for at least twenty years and it was an early demonstration of Gorbachev's control over the vital power of leadership appointments.[87] There were further changes in July 1985: Grigorii Romanov, Gorbachev's principal rival for the leadership, retired from both Politburo and Secretariat 'on grounds of ill health' (just over sixty, his rumoured weakness for women and alcohol hardly suggested infirmity), and two new CC Secretaries were elected, Boris Yel'tsin, up to this point party first secretary in Sverdlovsk, and Lev Zaikov, previously the party first secretary for the Leningrad region.[88] At the Supreme Soviet session which took place the following day Foreign Minister Andrei Gromyko, rather than Gorbachev himself, was elected to the vacant chairmanship of the Presidium, and Eduard Shevardnadze, the Georgian party first secretary, became foreign minister in his place.[89] In September Nikolai Tikhonov, already eighty and a Brezhnev loyalist, was replaced as prime minister by Ryzhkov; he retired from the Politburo itself the following month.[90]

Two other Brezhnevites, Viktor Grishin and Konstantin Rusakov, retired from the Politburo and Secretariat respectively at a Central Committee meeting early in 1986.[91] A still more extensive restructuring took place at the 27th Party Congress in March 1986. Five new Central Committee Secretaries were appointed, including the veteran ambassador to Washington, Anatolii Dobrynin, and Alexander Yakovlev, a close Gorbachev associate who had previously served as ambassador to Canada and as director of one of the institutes of the Academy of Sciences. The other new Secretaries were Vadim Medvedev, an economist who had previously served as Rector of the party's Academy of Social Sciences; Georgii Razumovsky, a fifty-year-old agronomist who had latterly headed the department of organisational-party work in the Central Committee headquarters; and Alexandra Biryukova, a former Secretary of the All-Union Council of Trade Unions and the first woman member of the leadership since the early 1960s.[92] The Politburo received one new member (Zaikov) and two new candidates (the Belorussian party leader Nikolai Slyun'kov and the new Leningrad regional party secretary Yuri Solov'ev). Remarkably, nearly half the members of this newly-elected Politburo and Secretariat were people who had not served in either body before Gorbachev's election to the general secretaryship the previous year. The Central Committee was itself extensively restructured: some 52 per cent of its membership was entirely new, a rate of turnover much higher than in the Brezhnev years of 'stability of cadres'.[93]

There were more changes in the leadership in the months that followed, all of which tended to strengthen Gorbachev's position still further. The Central Committee plenum which took place in January 1987 brought Alexander Yakovlev into the Politburo as a candidate member; and Nikolai Slyun'kov and Anatolii Luk'yanov, a leading jurist and head of the general department in the Central Committee apparatus, became CC Secretaries (Luk'yanov, it later emerged, had been a member of the Komsomol committee together with Gorbachev when both had been at Moscow University in the early 1950s).[94] Two Brezhnev appointees, Dinmukhamed Kunaev and Mikhail Zimyanin, left the Politburo and Secretariat respectively at the same time; Kunaev, whose resignation was ostensibly 'in connection with his retirement on a pension', was expelled from the Central Committee itself the following November for 'serious shortcomings' in his tenure of the Kazakh party first secretaryship.[95] In June 1987 Slyun'kov and

Yakovlev moved up from candidate to full Politburo membership and another Secretary, Viktor Nikonov, moved straight into full membership. Dmitri Yazov, the new defence minister, became a candidate Politburo member, replacing Marshal Sokolov who had been discredited by the ability of a young West German, Matthias Rust, to land a small plane in Red Square (which soon became known as 'Moscow's fourth international airport').[96]

In September 1988, at yet another remarkable plenum, Andrei Gromyko retired from the Politburo (and also from the presidency, where Gorbachev replaced him). Others retiring included Mikhail Solomentsev, Vladimir Dolgikh and Petr Demichev, all of whom had been members of the leadership since the Brezhnev years or even earlier. Vadim Medvedev, already a CC Secretary, became a full member of the Politburo, Alexander Vlasov, minister of internal affairs and later prime minister of the Russian Republic, became a candidate member, and so too did Biryukova and Luk'yanov.[97] In a further series of changes in September 1989 Nikonov, Chebrikov, Solov'ev, the Ukrainian party leader Shcherbitsky and the former head of Gosplan, Nikolai Talyzin, all resigned from the Politburo. The new KGB chairman, Vladimir Kryuchkov, became a full member, and so too did the recently-appointed head of Gosplan, Yuri Maslyukov. There were two new candidate members of the Politburo, the speaker of one of the chambers of the Supreme Soviet Yevgenii Primakov and Party Control Committee chairman Boris Pugo, and four new Central Committee Secretaries; all were former regional party first secretaries and one of them, the Tatar first secretary Gumer Usmanov, became the leadership's only Muslim.[98]

No additions to the membership of the Central Committee could properly take place until the next congress, which was due to take place after the usual five-year interval in early 1991. In another unexpected move in April 1989, however, ninety-eight of its existing and mostly Brezhnevite membership resigned and twenty-four more reform-minded candidates were promoted to full membership.[99] The 19th Party Conference in 1988 agreed that henceforward up to 20 per cent of the membership of party committees could be replaced during the intervals between congresses; already, however, some 60 per cent of the Central Committee's full members had assumed their positions under the Gorbachev administration.[100] The 28th Congress, which met ahead of time in July 1990, made further changes, indeed the most far-reaching in the entire history of the Central Committee. Some 412 new members were elected; all of them had full voting rights, but only 14.1 per cent had any previous Central Committee experience and only 15.5 per cent had previously held elective party office at the national level.[101] In a related move, a new set of party rules established that up to a third of the members of the Central Committee could in future be replaced before the following congress or any further congresses had taken place.[102]

The party leadership was still more extensively renewed at the 28th Congress in 1990. The Politburo itself was entirely constructed: in future, according to the Party Rules, it would be made up of the General Secretary, a Deputy General Secretary, the first secretaries of the republican party organisations, and such other persons as the Central Committee might decide to appoint.[103] The Politburo that was elected on this basis on 14 July 1990 had twenty-four members. Only two of them (Gorbachev himself and the Lithuanian leader Burokyavichus) had a period of party membership that stretched back to the Stalin years, and only Gorbachev had a Central Committee membership that went back as far as 1971 (half of the new Politburo had joined the Central Committee at the Congress itself). The Secretariat, also elected by the Central Committee, was reconstructed at least as radically. It included Gorbachev himself, as General Secretary, and the former Ukrainian first secretary Vladimir Ivashko, who was elected his Deputy, together with eleven other Secretaries only four of whom had previously held such a position. Taking Politburo and Secretariat together, no fewer than twenty-eight of the thirty-five members involved had never previously held national party office.[104] The Congress also elected five more junior 'members of the Secretariat', reviving an institution that had last existed in the 1920s.[105]

Changes in the party leadership and Central Committee were only a part of a much wider-ranging replacement of leading officials at all levels. All the fourteen republican party first secretaries, for instance, were replaced between 1986 and 1989, some of them on more than one occasion. A fifteenth republican leader was elected for the first time when Ivan Polozkov became first secretary of the newly-established Russian Republican party organisation in June 1990. Some two-thirds of the secretaries of regional, territorial and republican party organisations, and about 70 per cent of those at district and city level, had been replaced by late 1988.[106] There was a still more rapid rate of turnover in the Soviet state structure. No more than twenty-two of the 115 members of the Council of Ministers elected in 1984 were still in their posts five years later, and only ten of these were nominated to the new Council of Ministers in June 1989; none of them survived into the

Cabinet of Ministers, the body which replaced it in December 1990.[107] The diplomatic service was similarly restructured, with new postings to Washington, London, Bonn and other Western capitals; by March 1991 all but two ambassadors had been appointed to their posts since Gorbachev's accession to the party leadership.[108] In the economy, Gorbachev himself reported, more than two-thirds of the country's industrial managers and farm directors had been replaced between 1986 and early 1989.[109]

There was certainly no doubt that, by the end of his first six years of office, Gorbachev had formed a leadership team that reflected his personal priorities. It was younger, for a start: the average age of the Politburo in March 1991 was just 55, compared with an average of 71 in Brezhnev's Politburo of 1982. It was almost entirely of Gorbachev's own choosing, or at least approval: by March 1991 only Gorbachev himself had served during the Brezhnev years, and all but Gorbachev and his deputy Ivashko had joined at the 28th Congress or later. It was a leadership less exclusively male than for at least two decades: Galina Semenova, a journalist, was admittedly its only female member, but she was also a Central Committee Secretary and another woman held junior Secretarial office. It was a much better educated Politburo than its Brezhnevite predecessor: nine of its twenty-four members held candidate or master's degrees, another held a higher doctorate in history, and the editor of *Pravda*, Ivan Frolov, was a full member of the Academy of Sciences. Gorbachev, as President, exercised authority through a further institution, the Federation Council, which (from December 1990) consisted of himself, a vice-president and the heads of state of the union republics. Once again this was a body that consisted almost entirely of figures appointed since Gorbachev had assumed the party leadership: in fact only three of the fifteen republican heads of state had held office of this kind before 1990.

It was one of Gorbachev's central assertions that it had been 'subject-ive' factors, and in particular the quality of leadership, that had led to the degeneration of Soviet socialism over the whole post-revolutionary period. What was the reason for their difficulties, he asked the Central Committee in April 1985? Natural and external factors were obviously important; but the main reason was that the necessary changes had not taken place in the management of a rapidly developing society.[110] For years, Gorbachev explained to the 27th Party Congress in 1986, party and government leaders had lagged behind the needs of the times. The faults he identified, such as inert and bureaucratic management, were 'above all of a subjective character'; their elimination depended upon leaders bringing their methods of work into line with changing circumstances.[111] Speaking to the Russian party congress in July 1990 Gorbachev acknowledged that the mechanical replacement of leading officials was 'not a panacea'; but people mattered more than structures, and the right appointments were of 'decisive' significance.[112] The 'root cause' of their difficulties, he told the Central Committee the following October, was the failure to respond adequately to the challenge of the times, or the 'inertia of old thinking'.[113] And in a speech in November 1990, he declared that the 'most important revolution' was the 'revolution in minds, in our heads, in us ourselves'.[114] There could be little doubt, as the Gorbachev general secretaryship drew to a close, that the Soviet leadership had been renewed more extensively than at any time in postwar history; it was much less clear that the replacement of leading officials with 'conservative thinking' was decisive to the success of *perestroika* and that deeper, more systemic choices could be avoided.

The August coup and the end of party rule

The attempted coup of August 1991, which led to Gorbachev's resignation, was itself a demonstration of the limits of a leadership style that placed its main emphasis upon personal rather than institutional change.[115] Many of the conspirators had been Gorbachev's own appointees, even friends, and he was affected more profoundly by this than by any other aspect of the short-lived emergency.[116] The coup, in fact, had not come without warning. Foreign minister Eduard Shevardnadze, tendering his resignation in December 1990, warned the Soviet parliament that a 'dictatorship' was approaching, although no one yet knew what form it would take.[117] Speaking in early August 1991, he again thought it possible there would be an attempt to resolve the country's difficulties by resorting to a '"strong hand" policy'.[118] An 'Appeal to the People', published in the paper *Sovetskaya Rossiya* in July, called for national and patriotic unity and was signed by two of the conspirators as well as other prominent conservatives.[119] Alexander Yakovlev, in a television interview on 12 August, warned that 'conservative and reactionary forces' had been mobilising and that they would be only too glad to 'turn back the clock'. Speaking a few days later, just before the conspiracy was launched, Yakovlev warned again that a 'Stalinist grouping' had become dominant in the party leadership and that it was preparing a 'party and state coup'.[120]

These warnings notwithstanding, the attempted coup of August 1991 was a shock as well as a surprise to the Soviet leader and to the outside world.[121] August, by a coincidence, was the month in which General Kornilov had attempted to overthrow the Provisional Government in 1917, and it was the month in which the Soviet President normally took his family holidays in the Crimea. In 1987, he spent the time writing his best-selling *Perestroika*. In 1991, he was working on the text of a speech on 18 August when four emissaries arrived unexpectedly from Moscow. All his telephones had been disconnected, so this was clearly no ordinary visit. Gorbachev refused either to resign or to sign a decree instituting a state of emergency, and was thereupon placed under house arrest and isolated from the outside world.[122] In the early hours of 19 August a self-styled State Emergency Committee informed a startled world that Gorbachev was 'unwell' and unable to perform his duties; his responsibilities would be assumed under these circumstances by his Vice-President, Gennadii Yanaev. The Emergency Committee, it later emerged, had eight members. Apart from Yanaev himself there was the KGB chairman, Vladimir Kryuchkov; the Defence Minister, Dmitri Yazov; the Interior Minister, Boris Pugo; the Prime Minister, Valentin Pavlov; and three other members of less prominence, Oleg Baklanov, Vasilii Starodubtsev and Alexander Tizyakov.[123] Yanaev, and four other members of the Committee, addressed a hastily convened press conference later the same day; Gorbachev, they promised, would return to his position as soon as his health had improved.[124]

The Committee, in a series of decrees, meanwhile suspended the activities of all parties (other than those that supported the emergency), banned the publication of all but a small number of newspapers (including *Pravda*), ordered the surrender of firearms, and prohibited meetings, strikes and demonstrations. The Committee's message was not simply a coercive one; it also promised to cut prices and increase wages, and to place food supplies under strict control with priority being given to schools, hospitals, pensioners and the disabled.[125] In a 'message to the Soviet people', broadcast on the morning of 19 August, the Committee offered a more extended justification of its action. The Soviet people, it explained, were in 'mortal danger'. *Perestroika* had reached an 'impasse'. The country had become 'ungovernable'. Not only this: 'extremist forces' had emerged that were seeking to break up the Soviet state and to seize power for themselves. The economy was in crisis, with the breakdown of central planning, a 'chaotic, ungoverned slide towards a market', and famine a real possibility. Crime and immorality were rampant. The Committee, it promised, would reverse these trends, strengthen public order, arrest the fall in living standards and restore the Soviet Union's international standing; it appealed, in turn, for the support of 'all true patriots and people of goodwill', making no reference at all to socialism.[126]

The coup, it soon became clear, had been poorly planned – two of its principal members, Yanaev and Pavlov, appear to have been drunk for most of its duration[127] – and it was opposed from the outset by Boris Yel'tsin, now Russian President, who made a dramatic call for resistance on 19 August standing on one of the tanks stationed outside the Russian parliament building. Yel'tsin denounced the Committee's action as a 'right-wing, reactionary, unconstitutional coup' and declared all its decisions illegal. Gorbachev, he insisted, must be restored immediately to his position, and he called for an indefinite strike until the Soviet parliament had met and constitutional propriety had been reestablished.[128] Huge demonstrations in front of the Russian parliament the following day were addressed by Shevardnadze, Yakovlev, Andrei Sakharov's widow Yelena Bonner and other democrats. The critical moment was the evening of 20 August when about 70,000 Muscovites defied the curfew and assembled in front of the 'White House' to defend it against an expected attack by pro-coup forces. That night, three men were killed – one shot and two crushed by tanks on the Moscow ring road – but the attack on the Russian parliament itself did not materialise.[129] It later emerged that substantial sections of the armed forces had declared against the coup, and that the elite KGB 'Alpha' anti-terrorist group had rejected the order they had been given to storm the building.[130]

On Wednesday 21 August the coup began to collapse. The Russian parliament met in emergency session and gave Yel'tsin their unqualified support. Media restrictions were lifted, and the Ministry of Defence ordered troops to return to their barracks. The USSR Supreme Soviet Presidium declared the actions of the Emergency Committee illegal, and the Procurator General's office announced that criminal proceedings for high treason had been instigated against its members. One of the coup leaders, Boris Pugo, committed suicide; several others went to the Crimea to seek Gorbachev's forgiveness (the Russian parliament sent its own representatives to bring the Soviet President back safely); and still others, such as foreign minister Alexander Bessmertnykh, tried to explain why they had – in his case – suffered a sudden 'cold' while the emergency had been in force (he was dismissed two days later). The most ambiguous figure of all was the Chairman of the Supreme Soviet, Anatolii Luk'yanov, who had refused to denounce the coup at the time and was accused of being its 'chief ideologist' (by the end of the month he was one of the fourteen people involved in the coup who had been arrested and charged with high treason).[131]

Gorbachev was flown back to Moscow in the early hours of 22 August, where he later addressed a crowded press conference. He thanked Yel'tsin as well as the Russian parliament for securing his release, and then described the difficult circumstances under which he had been held. He had refused to accept the conditions his captors had tried to dictate to him, and had refused to eat the food he was brought, but had been able to rig up a makeshift radio on which he had been able to listen to Western radio broadcasts; he had even recorded four copies of a video message to the Soviet people explaining the real nature of the emergency. There was some surprise that the Soviet leader continued to defend the Communist Party, whose role in the attempted coup had been obscure.[132] Later, however, when the complicity of the party leadership became clear, Gorbachev resigned the general secretaryship and called upon the Central Committee to take the 'difficult but honourable decision to dissolve itself'.[133] Yel'tsin had signed a decree suspending the activity of the Communist Party throughout the Russian Federation on 23 August, at a meeting of the Russian parliament that Gorbachev himself attended, and a few days later the USSR Supreme Soviet suspended the activities of the party throughout the Soviet Union; its bank accounts and financial operations had meantime been frozen, and its buildings placed under the control of local soviets.[134]

The Soviet Union itself was a still greater casualty of the coup. Launched to block the signature of a new union treaty, the conspirators – in the end – accelerated the collapse of the state they had sought to preserve. Lithuania had already declared its independence, in the spring of 1990; the other Baltic republics followed immediately; and by the end of the year all of the republics, apart from Russia, had adopted declarations of a similar kind. Several of them had in addition begun to establish their own armies, and had applied to join the United Nations. Finally, in December 1991, the three Slavic republics – Russia, the Ukraine and Belorussia – established a new Commonwealth of Independent States, which was later joined by almost all of the other former Soviet republics. The new Commonwealth was not a state, it had no common parliament, and in particular it had no presidency; the states concerned also agreed that its establishment brought an end to the political union that had originally been established in 1922 (these developments are discussed in more detail on pp. 171–85). With the disappearance of the USSR and of its presidency Gorbachev's position became untenable and he resigned his last remaining public office on 25 December 1991, retaining a salary of 4,000 rubles, a staff of twenty and two motorcars.[135] The post-Soviet era had begun.

2 Democratising the political system

Political reform was not, at the outset, one of the chief priorities of the new administration. Together with a change of leadership at all levels, Gorbachev was much more concerned at the 27th Party Congress in February 1986 to secure an acceleration of economic growth, which he described as the 'key to all our problems, immediate and long-term, economic and social, political and ideological, domestic and foreign', and the only way in which a new kind of Soviet socialism could be built.[1] The Central Committee meetings that took place after the Congress reflected the same emphases: the June 1986 plenum dealt with the 1986–90 economic plan, and the plenum a year later was concerned with the 'radical reform' of Soviet economic management. Addressing the Polish Sejm in July 1988, Gorbachev conceded that he had not, to begin with, fully appreciated the importance of political reform both for its own sake and for the contribution it could make to other social and economic objectives.[2] Speaking to Indian journalists in late 1986, however, he made clear that he intended to secure a political system that functioned 'more effectively',[3] and at the Central Committee meeting which took place in January 1987 political reform became one of the central priorities of the new leadership. The plenum marked the beginning of a second, more broadly reformist stage in the development of the Gorbachev administration; its business proved so controversial that it was postponed three times and met only after the last permissible date under the party's own rules.[4]

Addressing the plenum, Gorbachev made clear that economic reform was conceivable only in association with a far-reaching 'democratisation' of the political system. A 'retarding mechanism' had developed in the economy which had its origins in the shortcomings that existed in the political system, and which had led to the neglect of housing, the food supply, transport and other matters of vital concern to ordinary people. Parasitic and consumerist attitudes had been growing in the society at the expense of socialist values such as labour enthusiasm and Soviet patriotism. Alcohol abuse, drugtaking and crime had become more widespread. The principle of collective leadership in the party had been violated: leaders had placed themselves beyond the reach of criticism, and some had become 'accomplices in – if not organisers of – criminal activities'. Whole republics, regions and ministries had been affected. All of this, in Gorbachev's view, argued the need for a 'profound democratisation' of Soviet society, designed to ensure that ordinary people once again felt themselves to be masters of their own destinies. 'A house can be put in order only by a person who feels that he owns this house', the General Secretary explained; and it was only democratic reform in all spheres of Soviet life that could unleash this powerful 'human factor', combining central guidance 'from above' with new and effective mechanisms of control 'from below'. The further democratisation of Soviet society, accordingly, became the party's 'most urgent task'.[5]

Gorbachev elaborated upon the reasons for these changes in subsequent speeches. Democratisation, he told the All-Union Council of Trade Unions in February 1987, was a 'guarantee against the repetition of past errors, and consequently a guarantee that the restructuring process is irreversible'. There was no choice – it was 'either democracy or social inertia and conservatism'.[6] A Central Committee meeting in June 1987 agreed with the proposal Gorbachev had advanced in January that a party conference – the first for nearly fifty years – should be called in the summer of 1988 to consider further democratising measures.[7] In his address on the seventieth anniversary of the revolution the following November Gorbachev returned to the theme. The better they understood the problems that stood before them, he suggested, the clearer it became that *perestroika* had to be set within a broader political and historical context. Two key issues would determine its future: the democratisation of public life, and radical reform of the economy. Democratisation, he told his audience, was 'at the core of restructuring' and upon it depended the fate of *perestroika* and indeed of socialism as a whole. The changes already agreed represented the 'biggest step in developing socialist democracy since the October revolution'; further change would concentrate particularly upon the soviets, the electoral system, mass organisations such as the trade unions and Komsomol, and the development of a 'culture of socialist democratism' in all spheres of public and social life.[8]

The fullest statement to date of Gorbachev's conception of democratisation was his address to the 19th Party Conference, which met from 28 June to 1 July 1988. In his speech Gorbachev called for 'radical reform' of the political system, not just 'democratisation', and went on to argue that it was crucial to the solution of all the other problems that faced Soviet society. The Soviet Union, he reminded the conference, had pioneered the idea of a workers' state and of workers' control, the right to work and equal rights for women, nations and nationalities. The political system established by the October revolution, however, had subsequently undergone 'serious deformations', leading to political repression and the development of 'command-administrative' rather than democratic structures of management. The role of the bureaucratic apparatus had increased out of all proportion – there were more than 100 central ministries, for instance, and 800 more in the republics – and this bloated administrative apparatus had begun to 'dictate its will' in political and economic matters. Nearly a third of the adult population was regularly elected to the soviets and other bodies, but most of those elected had been removed from real participation in state and public affairs. Social life as a whole had become 'straitjacketed' by governmental controls of various kinds, and ordinary working people had become 'alienated' from public ownership and management. It was this 'ossified system of government, with its command-and-pressure mechanism', that was now the main obstacle to *perestroika*.[9]

The conference, after an extended debate remarkable for its plain speaking and lack of unanimity (there had been nothing like it, Gorbachev suggested, for almost sixty years[10]) duly adopted a series of resolutions calling for the further democratisation of Soviet society and reform of the political system. These proposals were carried further at Central Committee meetings in July and September, and were in turn the basis for a series of constitutional reforms which were approved in November and December 1988. The changes that were agreed included an entirely new electoral law, which was intended to provide for a degree of competition between candidates, and a set of constitutional amendments which established a new state structure including a full-time working parliament for the first time in modern Soviet history. A constitutional review commission – in effect a constitutional court – was also established as a step towards what Gorbachev called a 'socialist system of checks and balances'.[11] These changes, moreover, were no more than the first stage in a process of reform which would later extend to local government, the press, religion, and the trade unions. The animating principle throughout was the control and limitation of executive power in the interests of greater public involvement in all spheres of Soviet life, and it was this 'human factor' that was expected in turn to make a reality of the economic and other objectives of *perestroika*.

Reforming the electoral system

One of the earliest political changes to be directly identified by the General Secretary was electoral reform, which was mentioned briefly in his report to the 27th Party Congress in 1986. The acceleration of socio-economic development, he told the congress, was inconceivable without the further development of socialist democracy. This involved 'necessary corrections' in electoral procedures, as well as changes in the work of the soviets and public organisations more generally. The congress went on, in its resolution on the report, to consider 'correct and timely' the raising of the issue of electoral change, and the Party Programme, adopted in a revised version at the congress, also referred to the 'perfection of the electoral system' and to the development of its 'democratic principles'.[12] None of the speakers at the congress, however, directly raised the issue of electoral reform, and there was no reference to the electoral system in an elaborate Central Committee resolution of July 1986 on the role of the soviets of people's deputies in accelerating socio-economic development in the light of the congress's decisions.[13] There had been a tentative discussion of the possibility of electoral reform in the 1960s. It surfaced in the unpublished letters that were sent to the Constitutional Commission in 1977, and in the autumn of 1986 a number of legal scholars began to raise the issue again in specialist journals.[14] In policy terms, however, the debate on electoral reform was most directly a product of the January 1987 Central Committee plenum at which the broader slogan of 'democratisation' was officially inaugurated.

Gorbachev himself suggested to the plenum that voters should be able to consider several candidacies and that larger constituencies should be formed, each of which would return several members.[15] These proposals were broadly endorsed by the plenum and were then carried forward in the general and specialist press. There was no shortage of evidence, in the discussion, that the existing system had long ago ceased to convince Soviet electors that they wielded effective influence over the institutions that governed in their name. A lack of choice of candidate was perhaps the most widely remarked short-coming. Since the very earliest years of Soviet rule, in fact, there had never been more candidates than seats available, and at the most recent national elections in 1984 not even this degree of choice had been on offer as one of the candidates died just before the poll, leaving 1,499 candidates to fight it out for the 1,500 seats available.[16] The single slate of candidates was often all but entirely unknown to the electorate, not surprisingly as many of them had little connection with the constituency for which they had been nominated. (In a Moscow poll in October 1988 no more than 5 per cent of those taking part in a by-election could name the candidate; in another poll in 1987, only 3.5 per cent thought deputies took any account of their wishes.)[17] Nor could this situation easily be remedied, as the right of nomination was reserved under the constitution for the CPSU and other party-controlled organisations.

Voters could, in theory, delete the name of the single candidate, and at the local level there were usually a number of defeats of this kind in response to particularly unpopular nominations. Such a practice, however, was strongly discouraged by the need to make use of the screened-off booth in the polling station for this purpose. As V. Timofeev, a war and labour veteran, told *Izvestiya* in early 1987:

You pull a pencil out of your pocket – every one can guess your intentions. Young Pioneers or poll attendants are standing by the polling booth. If you go into the booth, it's clear that you voted against the candidate. Those who don't want to vote against go straight to the ballot box. It's the same at plant trade union elections and party election conferences. You can't even go off into a corner by yourself before a curious eye is peering over your shoulder.[18]

The level of turnout was in any case impossibly high, even allowing for absentee ballots and other factors. At the last national elections, in 1984, no less than 99.99 per cent of the registered electorate were reported to have voted – this was an improvement on 1979, when only 99.98 per cent had exercised their democratic rights – and in Turkmenia only a single elector was reported to have abstained out of an electorate of one and a half million.[19] Both press and émigré accounts contained abundant evidence of personation and other abuses;[20] allowing for such factors it appeared that the real level of turnout was about 75 per cent – not very different, in fact, from that recorded in the major industrial democracies.[21]

Several further criticisms were advanced in the debate on political reform which extended throughout 1987 and 1988. In particular, it was argued that the composition of each group of deputies was regulated much too precisely by the central authorities. One local party secretary told *Izvestiya* what his 'programme' was in this respect: 4.6 per cent of the deputies in his area were to be enterprise directors, 1.1 per cent were to be employed in culture and the arts, 0.8 per cent were to be party officials, and 45.9 per cent were to be elected for the first time.[22] The chairman of a rural soviet told the same paper that his 'allocation' was 'so many mechanisers, so many milkmaids, so many with a higher education, and so many with a secondary education'.[23] The need to 'observe the percentages' led to some rather strange scenes. A foundryman who had been elected to the Sverdlovsk regional soviet, for instance, was proposed by his workmates for a second term. '"Stop", the collective was told. "Our thanks to Vasilii Stepanovich, but he's not included on the list because of his age and the need to elect new deputies. What we need is a woman, a Komsomol member and a leading worker. Find one!"'[24] In a still more extraordinary episode, reported by an émigré source, a notorious prostitute had to be nominated to a local soviet because she was the only person in the region who met the relevant requirements – female, single, with two children, aged between thirty-five and forty, and a factory worker.[25]

Gorbachev, in his speech to the January 1987 plenum, promised that the elections to local soviets which were to be held later in the year would be held in an 'atmosphere of broader democracy with the interested participation of the people'. Exactly how different those local elections would be became apparent at the end of March 1987 when it was announced that an 'experiment' would take place under which a choice of candidates would be nominated in a number of enlarged constituencies, each of which would return several members.[26] In the end just over 1 per cent of the constituencies were formed on this new multimember basis, and they returned no more than 4 per cent of all the deputies elected on 21 June 1987. Press reports made it clear that this was none the less a somewhat different exercise from those that had preceded it: there were greater difficulties than usual in securing nomination, and in the election itself there were some notable casualties, including party and state officials, factory directors and collective farm chairmen. For many officials the whole experience was evidently an unwelcome and even distressing one.[27] At the popular level, however, the response was much more favourable: there was a 'real feeling that the people were choosing', according to press reports, and surveys found that while only 55 per cent of those asked took a positive view of the new arrangements before they had been put into effect, fully seventy-seven per cent supported them afterwards.[28]

Gorbachev, in his report to the 19th Party Conference a year later, concluded that competitiveness had made the elections 'more lively, the voters more interested and the deputies more conscious of their responsibilities', and called for the new principles to be extended more widely. It should be possible, for instance, to nominate an unlimited number of candidates, and to discuss them freely; and district election conferences, which decided which of the nominations were entered on the ballot paper, should become 'democratic forums' for a competitive selection of 'principled, vigorous and experienced deputies' who could effectively represent their constituencies and make a real contribution to the work of government bodies.[29] There was no further discussion of the electoral system at the conference itself, but the resolution on political reform with which it concluded committed the party to a 'substantive renewal of the electoral system' in line with Gorbachev's report.[30] A Supreme Soviet by-election in January 1988 had already taken place on the basis of these new principles; so too did republican by-elections in October 1988.[31]

The new electoral law, which was published in draft on 23 October and adopted in its final form on 1 December 1988,[32] made it clear that these practices were to become universal. The right to nominate was extended to voters' meetings of 500 or more (Art. 37), and an unlimited number of candidates could be put forward (Art. 38) (the draft had indicated that 'as a rule' there should be more candidates than seats available; the final text made no specific provision either way). Deputies were not allowed to hold governmental posts at the same time as they exercised their representative duties (how, it was asked, could ministerial deputies be expected to hold themselves to account?[33]), and they were normally required to live or work in the area for which they had been nominated (Arts. 11 and 37). Candidates, moreover, were required to present 'programmes' to the electorate (Art. 45) and had the right to appoint up to ten campaign staff to assist them (Art. 46). Electors, for their part, were required to pass through a booth or room before casting their vote and to make a positive indication of their preference unless (exceptionally) only a single candidate was standing (Art. 53). The new law was to apply to all future elections, beginning with the national elections in March 1989; these, the Central Committee promised at its meeting in November 1988, would be 'unlike all those that had preceded them'.[34]

All power to the Soviets

The process of political reform also extended to the Soviet state. The central objective here was 'All power to the soviets', this time in real rather than formalistic terms, and more generally a shift of executive authority from party to state institutions. The soviets, in Gorbachev's view, had served as the basis of a system of genuinely socialist democracy during the revolutionary years, but very soon afterwards they had fallen victim to bureaucratisation and over-detailed regulation by party committees.[35] One problem identified in the debate that took place in the general and specialist press was the often honorific character of the membership of such bodies. In the Supreme Soviet elected in 1984, the writer Yuri Burtin calculated, something like 39 per cent of the deputies owed their membership to the official positions they occupied, which were such as to ensure an automatic nomination. These *ex officio* deputies, mostly party and state bureaucrats, were balanced by large numbers of manual workers and collective farmers, leaving very few deputies to represent the white collar professions. Would it be so bad, asked Burtin, if there were fewer milkmaids and party secretaries in the new Supreme Soviet, but rather more of the popular and articulate economists, historians, actors and writers who were advancing the cause of *perestroika*?[36]

Another contribution to the discussion came from three prominent jurists, Barabashev, Sheremet and Vasil'ev, writing in the legal journal *Sovetskoe gosudarstvo i pravo*. Surveys, they noted, had found low levels of satisfaction with the work of the soviets, and even deputies themselves appeared to be unsure of their own usefulness. There had been encouraging signs recently, such as the criticism and amendment of legislation that had taken place in the Supreme Soviet, 'probably for the first time in its history', in the summer of 1987. But deputies were allowed access to legislation only in its final stages, and the Supreme Soviet was in any case far less important as a source of binding state decisions than its Presidium and, still more so, the USSR Council of Ministers. The brevity of Supreme Soviet sessions (just three or four days a year) meant that even the annual plan and budget could hardly be seriously discussed. Nor had the Supreme Soviet ever exercised its right to hear a report by the Council of Ministers, which was constitutionally subordinate to it (the last such report, according to a writer in *Pravda*, was as long ago as 1935[37]). There were often violations of the law or of citizens' rights by state bodies, but these had never been considered by the Supreme Soviet, nor could it readily do so when there was no standing commission on socialist legality and hardly any qualified lawyers among its membership.[38]

There was very general agreement among contributors to the discussion, which extended throughout 1987 and 1988, that the soviets should become (as Barabashev, Sheremet and Vasil'ev put it) 'genuine centres for the elaboration and adoption of all major state decisions in the field of legislation and administration'. This meant, for instance, that deputies should be chosen for their professional qualities rather than their social origins, and that they should devote much more of their time to their representative duties. The party, equally, should work exclusively through its representatives in the soviets and make no attempt to discipline them unless – exceptionally – a decision was taken which was directly at variance with CPSU policy.[39] A more radical view, put forward by the jurist Boris Kurashvili in the party theoretical journal *Kommunist* in May 1988, was that nothing less than 'Soviet parliamentarianism' was likely to be sufficient, sustained by a 'separation of powers' which might involve, for instance, a constitutional court with the authority to strike down decisions of the Council of Ministers. Kurashvili favoured a system of smaller, full-time soviets staffed by salaried politicians, and the greatest possible access for the media and members of the public to their proceedings. More controversially, he also suggested that the chairmen of local soviets should be directly elected by the population, not by deputies, and that the local party secretary should normally be nominated to the post. This would, for the first time, allow ordinary citizens to express a view about the party leaders who exercised real authority in the area in which they lived.[40]

This was, in fact, one of the proposals that found a place in Gorbachev's speech at the 19th Party Conference a month later in June 1988. The resumption of full authority by the soviets was indeed the General Secretary's central concern. The soviets, he made clear, must have more adequate, independent and stable sources of revenue, and greater control over local enterprises. Some of the deputies should be freed from their ordinary work and allowed to become full-time representatives; and they should be allowed to choose their executive committees by secret ballot from a plurality of candidates. There should be limitations upon the period of time for which an elected office could be held – two terms, or three in exceptional circumstances. Members of executive committees and leading officials, as several contributors to the debate had suggested, should be ineligible for election to the soviet to which they were themselves responsible. Local soviets should be smaller, and they should be elected for five years (rather than two and a half years) at a time. The most unexpected of all Gorbachev's proposals, however, concerned the central institutions of state. There should, he suggested, be a new 'representative supreme government body', the USSR Congress of People's Deputies, elected by public organisations as well as ordinary voters and meeting annually. This Congress would in turn elect a smaller full-time Supreme Soviet, which would work through an elaborate committee system and scrutinise the work of government much more closely than its predecessors had done. The whole state structure would be headed by a Chairman of the USSR Supreme Soviet (normally the party leader), who would nominate the prime minister and guide the work of a reconstituted Presidium.[41]

The proposals were broadly endorsed by the conference, although several were quite strongly contested. The suggestion that the party leader at each level should become the chairman of the corresponding soviet came in for particularly sharp criticism. Surely, it was argued, party leaders would be overburdened by the demands of the two posts? Equally, was it proper to exclude non-party members from the chairmanship of soviets, as would be the case if such a rule was agreed; and could it in any case be called an election if there was just a single candidate?[42] Most speakers were none the less in favour of the main thrust of Gorbachev's proposals and, in particular, of the decentralisation of political authority that he had proposed. Many of them, indeed, wished to take those proposals further, extending not simply to the decentralisation of decision-making but to more far-reaching forms of regional or republican self-accounting.[43] As the newly-elected Estonian party secretary, Vaino Valjas, told the Conference, more than 90 per cent of the republic's economy was directed by ministries based largely or entirely in Moscow; this made it all but impossible to ensure the balanced development of republican society.[44] The Latvian party leader complained that until very recently Riga bakers had been obliged to secure the approval of Moscow if they wanted to introduce a recipe for a new tart.[45] The Krasnodar (and later Russian) first secretary, Ivan Polozkov, complained similarly that the territorial soviet in his area, elected by five million people, could make no changes in administrative structure or land use, nor could it even establish a new nursing post at the local hospital. He was one of many speakers who supported the call for a 'new, more effective mechanism' for relations between the central government and the Soviet Union's various republics and regions.[46]

The directives approved by the party conference, which broadly reflected Gorbachev's report, in turn found expression in the constitutional amendments that were adopted by the Supreme Soviet, after a month of public discussion, on 1 December 1988.[47] These established, for instance, that all soviets were to be elected for five rather than two and a half years at a time, and that no deputy could serve on more than two soviets at the same time (Arts. 90 and 96). Much more controversially, the Supreme Soviet accepted Gorbachev's proposal (made originally at the Party Conference) that the new supreme state body, the USSR Congress of People's Deputies, should be elected not only by the population at large and by national-territorial areas but also by a wide range of social organisations, including the CPSU, the trade unions and women's councils (Art. 109). The Congress would, as had been suggested, elect a new-style Supreme Soviet which would meet, as a rule, for two three- or four-month sessions every year (Art. 112). A fifth of its members would stand down annually, as would a fifth of the membership of its standing committees (Arts. 111 and 122). Wide-ranging powers were given to the new Chairman of the USSR Supreme Soviet, who was to exercise 'general guidance' over the work of state bodies, report on major questions of foreign and domestic affairs, make nominations to leading state positions, head the Defence Council of the USSR, and issue his own directives (*rasporyazheniya*) (Art. 121). It was also agreed, although not formally specified, that this post would normally be combined with the party leadership (and similarly at lower levels of government).

The party and its role

The reform debate naturally concerned the CPSU itself. In general terms, as *Kommunist* argued in an editorial in January 1988, there should be a more restricted understanding of the party's role, involving a kind of 'division of labour' in which the party would stand aside from direct management of public affairs and confine itself to a much looser coordinating function.[48] The discussion that preceded the party conference saw very widespread support for changes of this kind. There were calls, for instance, for party officials to spend more time working 'with the masses' and less time in their offices, and for all party bodies from the Politburo downwards to present annual reports on their work.[49] It was suggested that there should be party congresses every two years and party conferences during the intervals between them, as in Lenin's time, and that the existing membership, recruited to a large extent during the Brezhnevite years of stagnation, should be reaccredited and if possible reduced.[50] There was also a good deal of concern about the way the party's own finances were handled, with calls for elected bodies at all levels to present proper income and expenditure accounts.[51] They knew more about the finances of the

American presidency and the British royal family, as one speaker at the party conference complained, than they did about the income and expenditure of their own party.[52]

Perhaps the most widely supported proposals, however, were that there should be a choice of candidate at all elections to party office, and that positions of this kind should be held for a limited number of terms. Under the existing system of recommendations from above, wrote one contributor to the discussion, party posts were filled not by election but by appointment, and often for life. Instead of this there should be a 'periodic renewal of elected and non-elected cadres', with maximum periods of tenure.[53] There should, for instance, be a maximum period of continuous membership of the Central Committee and of its apparatus.[54] Other correspondents suggested a normal limit of two terms in the same elected party position, and some called for the restoration of the compulsory turnover rules that had been introduced by Khrushchev but dropped by his successors.[55] Party posts should also be filled by secret ballot from a larger number of candidates than seats available, with replacement possible ahead of time in the case of committees that were working ineffectively.[56] Changes were suggested in the way in which the General Secretary was elected, with either a nationwide vote or a 'kind of party referendum' deciding the matter.[57] There might even be age limits, such as sixty-five for Politburo and Secretariat members.[58] And there should be changes in the party's own bureaucracy: it should be smaller, and less obviously parallel the ministerial hierarchy.[59]

Several more sensitive issues were raised in the discussion, including the operation of the *nomenklatura* appointments system. The present 'closed' system, which too often protected the incompetent and corrupt from the consequences of their actions, came in for repeated criticism.[60] Why, for instance, wrote a labour veteran from Krasnodar, should the politically well-connected have more comfortable flats, better foodstuffs, special hospitals and even their own cemeteries?[61] And why, asked a speaker at the party conference, was there a 'caste of untouchables' who were apparently to bear no direct responsibility for their misdemeanours during the Brezhnev years?[62] There was a strong case, others argued, for separating party membership entirely from the tenure of leading posts in order to avoid membership becoming no more than a 'meal ticket' or a source of privilege.[63] It was also suggested that the 'party maximum' on earnings of Lenin's time should be revived, and that a Committee on Party Ethics along the lines of those that had existed in the 1920s should be reestablished.[64] So far as the party's own members were concerned there was widespread agreement that officials should avoid being hypnotised by the word 'worker' and that more attention should be paid to the moral and political qualities of those that they recruited. Party branches, under existing policies, were becoming dominated by blue-collar staff and pensioners, not by those who were doing most to advance the scientific-technical revolution and the other priorities of *perestroika*.[65]

Most of these themes again found a place in Gorbachev's speech to the Party Conference on 28 June 1988. There had been 'definite deformations in the party itself', Gorbachev told the delegates. Democratic centralism had degenerated into bureaucratic centralism. The rank and file had lost control over the leaderships that spoke in their name. Officials had come to believe that they were infallible and irreplaceable; and an atmosphere of comradeship had been replaced by one of commands and subordination. Party and government had lost their distinctive functions, and the party apparatus had become too closely involved in economic and administrative rather than properly political matters.[66] The conference, in its concluding resolutions, agreed with Gorbachev that a 'profound democratisation' of party life was necessary and insisted that there must 'never again' be a recurrence of the deformations that had taken place during the cult of personality and stagnation periods. Membership should be determined by political criteria rather than centrally-determined quotas; and meetings should be more critical and constructive. Central Committee members should be able to play a more active role in the work of the leadership; more records of party meetings should be published; and – a matter of 'prime importance' – all posts up to the Central Committee level should be filled by secret and competitive ballot for a maximum of two five-year terms.[67]

These reforms, like their counterparts in the state system, gradually began to be implemented over the months that followed. Competitive elections to party office had indeed begun to take place as early as February 1987, when a local party secretary in the Kemerovo region was chosen by secret ballot from two competing candidates.[68] Further changes followed in the autumn of 1988 when the Central Committee approved six new commissions dealing respectively with party affairs, ideology, social and economic policy, agriculture, international affairs and law reform. Each of them was chaired by a senior member of the leadership, and taken as a whole they were intended to involve the Central Committee membership in policy formation at the highest level.[69] The Central Committee apparatus was simplified and reduced in size: from 1988 onwards there were nine departments rather than twenty, and their total staff was reduced by about 30 per cent.[70] A new Central Committee journal, *Izvestiya TsK*, began to appear in 1989; it contained a wealth of biographical and documentary information about all aspects of party life and came out monthly in a large edition. The party's finances were discussed in its first issue, and also in *Pravda*. Members' dues, it emerged, provided the largest part of the party's income, but 19 per cent of expenditure had to be covered by contributions from party publishing houses and other sources. Most of the party's expenditure was incurred on maintaining the party apparatus at local levels; the central party apparatus alone cost just over 50 million rubles a year, which was no more than 3 per cent of the party's total expenditure.[71]

Matters were taken further at a three-day plenum in February 1990 at which the Central Committee accepted Gorbachev's proposal that the party should abandon its guaranteed leading role (in effect, that it should move the deletion or modification of Article 6 of the Constitution). Gorbachev was still concerned that the CPSU should play a 'consolidating' role in Soviet political life, indeed that it should remain a 'ruling' party and the 'political leader' of the society as a whole. Any position of this kind, however, should be won by a competitive struggle for popular support, not guaranteed in advance by the Constitution. The party itself required further reform, and there was broad agreement that this should include a reconsideration of the doctrine of democratic centralism so that lower party organisations and individual members enjoyed a greater degree of autonomy. The proposals that were agreed at the plenum included the idea of 'platforms' within the party, on a group or regional basis, and a new and more decentralised structure for the party's leading bodies, with a committee of party leaders from the republics taking over most if not all of the functions of the Politburo. Some of the proposals that were approved at the plenum, such as an executive presidency with enlarged powers, required a process of constitutional amendment; others, such as a change in the size and function of the Central Committee, required the agreement of a party congress (see below, pp. 249–54). The thrust of these changes was none the less clear: developing democratic practices within the party, and (perhaps not coincidentally) marginalising Gorbachev's opponents within the full-time apparatus.[72]

Law and civil society

Finally, and perhaps most fundamentally, the process of political reform under Gorbachev has involved a reassertion of the rule of law in Soviet society, and more generally a greater place for political activity initiated by individual citizens rather than by the regime itself. Gorbachev, a lawyer by academic training, told interviewers from *Der Spiegel* in October 1988 that *perestroika* was as much a 'legal revolution' as a reform of the political system as such.[73] He set out the main elements of his thinking on this point in his *Perestroika*, published in late 1987. Democracy, he argued, 'cannot exist and develop without the rule of law, because law is designed to protect society from abuses of power and guarantee citizens and their organisations and work collectives their rights and freedoms. This is the reason why we have taken a firm stand on the issue. And we know from our own experience what happens when there are deviations from these principles.' Law, equally, should not be overprescriptive: it was better to follow the principle 'Everything which is not prohibited by law is allowed'. Important steps in this direction had already been taken, including legislation permitting appeals against the actions of officials and establishing a procedure for submitting important questions of public life to a process of national discussion.[74] But much more remained to be done, including the adoption of measures which would guarantee the independence of judges and secure the 'most strictly democratic principles' in the work of the courts.[75]

These principles found expression during 1988 in an entirely new concept, the 'socialist law-based state' (*sotsialisticheskoe pravovoe gosudarstvo*). First mentioned at a meeting between Gorbachev and media workers in May 1988,[76] it was given more prominence in the Theses that were published by the Central Committee in advance of the party conference[77] and in turn became the centrepiece of a resolution adopted at the conference itself. This called for 'large-scale legal reform' over the coming years, including a review of existing codes of law, greater safeguards for the independence of judges, and an extensive programme of legal education for the population as a whole.[78] The process of reform was carried further in the constitutional amendments that were adopted by the Supreme Soviet on 1 December 1988. In perhaps the most notable of these changes, a twenty-three member Committee of Constitutional Supervision was established, elected by the Congress from 'specialists in politics and law', with responsibility for ensuring the constitutionality of governmental decisions and draft legislation (Art. 125). Judges, in addition, were to be elected by soviets at the level immediately above them, and for ten, rather than five, years at a time (Art. 152). All of this, in Gorbachev's view, represented a distinctive 'socialist system of checks and balances', protecting society at large from abuse of power by those who held the highest executive offices of state.[79]

Legal reform was carried further in a number of other changes, among them the adoption of a new criminal code, the first for thirty years. The code, approved in 1991, was intended to contribute to the 'humanisation' as well as modernisation of the criminal law: the number of crimes for which custodial sentences were mandatory was reduced very considerably, better conditions were instituted for the great mass of prisoners, and the scope of the death penalty was very greatly reduced. Legislation on the courts, introduced in 1989, established for the first time the principle of the presumption of innocence of the accused.[80] Another important law enforcement agency, the KGB, sought to bring its work into line with the requirements of *glasnost'*, including the publication of regular bulletins on its work and a more prominent role for its leading personnel in the mass media. It established a public relations department and invited the press to visit its training college; there was even a 'Miss KGB'.[81] Equally, the law as it stood was applied more vigorously than ever before, particularly in cases of organised crime. One of the most spectacular networks of this kind was based in Uzbekistan, fed by the proceeds of a largely fictitious cotton harvest, protected by political contacts at the highest level, and defended by hired assassins.[82] One of those involved ran a personal 'khanate' complete with underground dungeons, concubines, well-guarded villas and a stable of thoroughbreds.[83] Perhaps not fortuitously, many of those involved in these scandals were closely connected with the now discredited Brezhnev administration.

A greater emphasis upon the rule of law helped equally to encourage the growth of a more autonomous citizen-based politics, reflecting what Gorbachev described, from 1988 onwards, as a 'socialist pluralism of opinions'. Gorbachev, in his address to the 27th Party Congress, called directly for the re-establishment of women's councils (bodies of this kind had existed during the 1920s) and for the formation of a war and labour veterans' association.[84] Both organisations were duly established during 1986 and 1987; so too were a Children's Fund, a Designers' Union, a Cultural Fund, an All-Union Music Society, a Union of Theatre Societies, a Red Cross Society and a Journalists' Fund. In 1988 a national society of cinema fans and a society for the protection of animals were founded;[85] more important in political terms were a society for the disabled in the Russian republic (with a potential membership of four million) and an all-union Environmental Fund, which came into existence in December 1988.[86] The following year an advocates' union was established, and an all-union society of cooperators, and the first consumers' association.[87] In 1990 a Peasants' Union was established and also a Scientific-Industrial Union, in effect a kind of national chamber of commerce.[88] New forms of organisation, by the early 1990s, embraced capital as well as labour: there was a League of Commercial Banks, an Insurance Union of Russia and a Russian Union of Industrialists and Entrepreneurs; and an entirely new trade union movement developed, outside the official union structure and often rooted in local strike committees.[89] Some of the earlier associations were granted representation in the USSR Congress of People's Deputies, and their establishment was part of a wider attempt to develop a society based to a greater degree upon citizen initiative rather than state provision and regulation.

Of no less significance, in terms of the development of a Soviet 'civil society', was the formation from 1987 onwards of a range of 'informal' movements, so called because of their distrust of organisational structures and their ambiguous status under Soviet law. The new movements were in part a response to the overly formalised nature of official youth and other organisations, one of the most important of which, the Komsomol, was acknowledged to be in a 'critical' condition in the late 1980s (it disappeared entirely after the coup).[90] Equally, they represented a response to the lack of provision of any kind for a wide range of minority interests – environmental, philosophical, artistic or dietetic. Although it was difficult to establish the number and, still more, the membership of such groups, many of which were ephemeral and few of which kept proper records, it was estimated in 1990 that there were between two and three thousand of them with a national membership of at least two million. On other, more inclusive accounts there were at least 11,000 'independent organisations' by this date.[91] Ecological movements had much more support than those that had directly political objectives; but among those that came into this last category at least four broad tendencies could be identified by the late 1980s.

First of all, there were a number of liberal-socialist associations, including the 'Democratic *Perestroika*' club, the 'Elections 89' committees in Moscow, Leningrad, Khar'kov and elsewhere, the 'Memorial' Society, the Federation of Socialist Clubs and many others. Organisations of this kind, broadly speaking, supported the main principles of *perestroika* but wished to accelerate it in various directions. Memorial, for instance, which was established in August 1988, sought to reconstitute the historical record of Stalinism by collecting oral and other forms of testimony.[92] The Federation of Socialist Clubs sought to revive the democratic principles that were, in their view, inherent in socialism. 'Moscow Tribune', founded in 1988, sought to democratise the election law, to extend the rights of nationalities and to reduce administrative control over the economy; its membership included Andrei Sakharov, Roy Medvedev and Tat'yana Zaslavskaya and, like the other organisations, was largely confined to academics and professionals with a humanistic or social science background.[93] Most of these concerns overlapped with those of a second group, the popular fronts, which came into existence in the Baltic and other republics from 1987 onwards. Although they naturally attached a much higher priority to the national question, the fronts also emphasised issues such as an honest historiography, economic decentralisation and the environment, and they drew upon a very much wider base of public support.[94]

Less easy to reconcile with official policy, in the late 1980s, were two other trends in the 'informal' movement: a liberal, antisocialist tendency centred around the Democratic Union, and an openly chauvinist organisation, *Pamyat'* (Memory). The Democratic Union, founded in 1988, took the view that Gorbachev's *perestroika* was too limited in its objectives; rather more boldly, the Union argued that the sociopolitical order established in October 1917 was a 'system of stagnant totalitarianism in conditions of the omnipotence of the *nomenklatura*', and it openly adopted the role of an oppositional political party dedicated to the overthrow of the CPSU and the socialist order it represented.[95] *Pamyat'* also rejected Soviet socialism, but held it to be Jewish and not simply a Marxist conspiracy. In its early stages a movement in defence of the Russian cultural heritage – historic sites and churches, customs and traditions, even the language itself – *Pamyat'*, from 1986 onwards, became increasingly chauvinist and antisemitic in character, and its meetings became increasingly intolerant of dissenting opinion.[96] The official media, in a succession of warnings, emphasised that there could be no room in the USSR for 'open attacks' on the Soviet order or for 'pluralism on the Western model',[97] and forthcoming legislation on voluntary associations was expected to place strict limits upon those that sought to mount a direct challenge to Soviet socialism or party dominance.

The 1989 elections to the Congress of People's Deputies

The first real test of political reform was the elections which took place in March 1989 to the USSR Congress of People's Deputies.[98] Under the new law the campaign was to proceed in two stages. In the first, nominations were to be made and then approved by a selection conference in the constituency or social organisation for which the candidate was seeking election. In the second, the candidates who had been 'registered' in this way were to compete for the support of their respective electorates: in the ordinary constituencies up to polling day, which was fixed for 26 March 1989, or in the social organisations up to an election meeting at some point during the previous fortnight. This was a new, elaborate and largely unfamiliar set of procedures; it was also one to which many citizens had strong objections. The representation that had been given to social organisations, in particular, appeared to violate the principle of 'one person, one vote', and the holding of selection conferences to approve a final list of candidates was also unpopular.[99] Who needed such 'elections before elections', asked several correspondents during the discussion of the draft law the previous autumn?[100] It was pointed out, however, that some exercise of this kind was necessary so as to reduce a large number of nominations to manageable proportions; and in any case this stage in the proceedings was bypassed in Estonia, most of Lithuania and some districts of Moscow precisely in order to leave such choices to the electorate.[101]

The selection of candidates in the social organisations took a variety of forms. At one extreme was the Council of Collective Farms, which approved fifty-eight candidates for its fifty-eight seats by an open vote in half an hour.[102] The Soviet Peace Committee, similarly, sent a list of preferred candidates to its local branches in December with instructions to approve it and send it back; the list included the Committee's chairman, the journalist Genrikh Borovik, who in the end was nominated by thirteen republics, eleven autonomous republics and fifty-one regions of Russia and the Ukraine. 'I cannot remember such unanimity ever before', wrote a member of the Committee's Presidium to *Sovetskaya Rossiya*. 'No single candidate could get so much support in such a short period of time ... Or did I somehow miss this wave of meetings of peace activists over the New Year period from Sakhalin to Kaliningrad?'[103] The Communist Party itself caused some controversy by nominating no more than 100 names for the 100 seats it had been allocated under the constitution. As well as 'authoritative representatives of the working class and peasantry' the list included most of the Politburo and Secretariat together with a wide range of figures from science, education, culture and the arts (the Bolshoi soloist Yevgenii Nesterenko was perhaps the most unlikely inclusion). The plenum also approved the party's first-ever election manifesto, a lengthy and wide-ranging 'Appeal to the Party, to the Soviet People'.[104]

A somewhat more open process took place in the trade unions, which took seven hours and several rounds of voting to produce a list of 114 candidates for the 100 seats that were available.[105] The Writers' Union also found it difficult to reduce its ninety-two nominations to a final list of twelve official candidates. There was a long argument over whether the voting should be secret, with the danger of taking up too much time, or open, with the embarrassment of people seeing who voted them down. The meeting lasted three days and several rounds of voting were necessary; the leading conservative, Yuri Bondarev, failed in the end to secure a nomination, but so too did liberals such as Yevgenii Yevtushenko and Andrei Voznesensky.[106] The cinema workers' union took two days and a night to agree, eventually, on eighteen candidates for its ten seats; the list included the playwright Alexander Gel'man and the editor of Moscow News, Yegor Yakovlev.[107] There was still greater controversy in the Academy of Sciences, where twenty-three candidates were chosen at a meeting of the Academy's Presidium to contest the twenty seats available. The list did not include Andrei Sakharov, the space scientist Roald Sagdeev and several other well-known reformers, and a vigorous campaign took place in an attempt to secure their nomination at a later stage.[108] The Academy, in an earlier decision which was itself controversial, had allocated ten of its original thirty seats to a group of smaller scientific societies and associations.[109]

The selection of candidates in the constituencies took a still wider variety of forms. A selection conference at Melitopol in the Ukraine, for instance, was packed out by officials to such an extent that it reminded one participant of a conference of party activists. Of the thirty-three who asked to speak, only five were chosen, all of whom supported the Zaporozh'e first secretary, Grigorii Kharchenko; indeed only one of them even raised the possibility that there might be another candidate. The party secretary was duly registered by an overwhelming major-ity.[110] There were many cases of pressure by party secretaries on other candidates to withdraw: so successful were these efforts in Kazakhstan that all seventeen of the republic's first secretaries were unopposed – a 'strange monopoly', as Pravda described it.[111] Alternative candidates found it hard to obtain accommodation for their meetings, or to print their publications; at one of their meetings in Leningrad angry speeches were drowned by 'loud dance music'.[112] One hopeful self-nominee was fired from his work just a month before the election; as work collectives could nominate only their own members he could not, as a result, legally become a candidate.[113] Attempts to nominate *Ogonek*'s controversial editor Vitalii Korotich in Moscow's Dzerzhinsky district led to particularly disorderly scenes. A first attempt to hold a meeting was barracked by *Pamyat'* members and in any case fell below the legal quorum; a second meeting, also attended by *Pamyat'*, was packed out and accompanied by 'din, shouts and chaos' according to Yevtushenko, one of the editor's sponsors.[114] Korotich, in the end, had to seek a nomination elsewhere.

In other constituencies, however, a rather more open atmosphere prevailed. In Moscow's Lenin territorial constituency no. 1, for instance, a 'long and heated struggle' took place to determine which of the thirteen nominations should be placed upon the ballot paper. The candidates considered included Yevtushenko, the economist Gavriil Popov and the cosmonaut Igor Volk. In the end, after eleven hours of discussion, only two of those nominated secured the necessary majority: Valerii Savitsky, a section head at the Institute of State and Law of the Academy of Sciences, and Alexei Emel'yanov, a Moscow University economist.[115] Savitsky, a fifty-eight-year-old lawyer, placed particular emphasis upon human rights in his programme and argued for closer parliamentary scrutiny of the Interior Ministry and the KGB; Emel'yanov (fifty-four) placed greater priority upon an improvement of living standards in the countryside and a reform of agricultural management.[116] Both were interviewed on 'Twelfth Floor', one of central TV's most challenging programmes, and asked all kinds of questions. Did they, for instance, do their shopping in ordinary stores? What had they been doing during the years of 'stagnation'? Could they be trusted to keep their promises (their campaign staff spoke up for them in this respect)? And, in Savitsky's case, was it true that he was connected by marriage to the Brezhnev administration? (He had married the daughter of the deputy president in 1977, Savitsky explained, but divorced her the following year.) Both candidates also spoke at a mass rally at Luzhniki stadium on the eve of the poll.[117]

Nor was this the only exercise of a relatively open kind, according to press reports. In a district in Yaroslavl', for instance, nearly fifteen hours was needed before a final list of candidates could be agreed.[118] In the Siberian countryside the arguments continued, in some cases, until the early morning.[119] *Izvestiya* reported a 'victory over the bureaucracy' in Kishinev in which a popular but unofficial candidate was nominated despite attempts to stop him, while the chairman of the local soviet executive committee was unsuccessful.[120] In Kaliningrad the regional party first secretary failed to get his name on the ballot paper; a factory director and a young party member were registered instead.[121] An interesting contest in Moscow's Tushin district secured the nomination of Telman Gdlyan, the chief special investigator in the case involving extensive fraud in Uzbekistan. The selection conference originally voted him down, but hundreds of local residents kept a vigil outside the building where the meeting was being held and demanded that he be registered. Teams of canvassers recorded interviews with them which were shown inside the hall, while the proceedings of the meeting were relayed to those outside. In the end, at 4 a.m., the conference decided by 312 to 93 to register all five nominations.[122] About half of those interviewed in an extensive national poll considered the selection conferences to have been 'democratic'; the other half thought they had been 'controlled by their organisers'.[123] Allowing for regional variations, this was probably a reasonably accurate reflection of what had taken place.

The most celebrated single contest, that between Boris Yel'tsin and Yevgenii Brakov, director of the Zil factory in Moscow, demonstrated both the changes that had taken place and the extent to which even this reformed electoral system could still be manipulated from above. Although he had been nominated by party branches, Yel'tsin was not one of the 100 candidates recommended for adoption by the CPSU leadership. According to Yel'tsin himself there was strong pressure from party officials not to allow him to be put forward as a candidate anywhere else.[124] Nominated eventually for the Moscow national-territorial seat No. 1 after a thirteen-hour selection conference, Yel'tsin found it difficult to develop an electoral campaign: he appeared only once on central television and production of his election material was hindered by party officials.[125] The Central Committee, unprecedentedly in modern times, established a subcommittee at its meeting on 16 March to determine if his outspoken views were compatible with party membership, and published the record of the October 1987 plenum at which he had attacked the conduct of the party leadership and then had his views declared 'politically mistaken'.[126] Despite (or perhaps because of) these difficulties, an increasingly charismatic Yel'tsin drew enormous crowds for a series of public meetings at which he attacked party privileges, demanded improvements in food and housing, and called for the establishment of an all-union popular front as a means of countering the lack of debate within the CPSU and 'apathy' within the wider society.[127]

The 1989 elections: choosing the deputies

First to vote, on 11 March 1989, were the Society of Inventors and Rationalisers and the Union of Theatrical Workers; directors Oleg Yefremov and Mark Zakharov were among the successful candidates, but not the controversial political playwright Mikhail Shatrov or the Georgian director Robert Sturua.[128] The Writers' Union chose its ten deputies at a two-day plenum; the results were something of a compromise, including conservatives such as Viktor Astaf'ev as well as reformists like Vasil Bykov and Sergei Zalygin.[129] The Journalists' Union, which also had ten seats, filled its places but left out the commentator Alexander Bovin and *Kommunist*'s Otto Latsis as well as *Pravda*'s more conservative Viktor Ovchinnikov.[130] The most vigorously contested of all the social organisation seats were those in the Academy of Sciences, where a campaigning group, 'For Democratic Elections from the Academy of Sciences', was formed to press the claims of the nominees that had been rejected two months earlier. At a meeting of the Academy's general assembly, where voting alone took three hours, only eight of the twenty-three candidates secured a majority and twelve of the seats had to be left vacant.[131] At further elections a month later Sakharov, Sagdeev and several reformist colleagues – including economists Pavel Bunich and Nikolai Shmelev – were eventually successful.[132]

The most important of all the social organisations, the CPSU, conducted its ballot at an enlarged plenum on 15 March to which republican and regional party leaders had also been invited. V. A. Koptyug, chairman of the party's electoral commission, reported that the 100 candidates had held 845 meetings at which 155,000 members had been present, over 4,500 of whom had spoken. Members had also written in with various comments, including the suggestion that none of the party's deputies should be over sixty and that there should be more workers and peasants among them. There had been some criticism of Gorbachev on the grounds that he had, after all, been a member of the now discredited Brezhnev administration, and a more substantial group of correspondents had criticised the nomination of just 100 candidates for 100 seats.[133] All the candidates, none the less, were duly elected, fifty-two of them unanimously; there were twelve votes against Gorbachev and fifty-nine against his liberal ally Alexander Yakovlev but seventy-eight, the largest number, against the leading conservative Yegor Ligachev. This led to one of Yel'tsin's standard campaign jokes: what would have happened if the party had nominated not 100, but 101 candidates for the seats it had available?[134]

Voting in the constituencies began not on 26 March but the previous evening in the Far East, where it was already 7 a.m. by local time. The first results came in from Kamchatka by about midnight on 26 March; Soviet spacemen had already appeared, ballots in hand, on the evening television news. By the afternoon of the following day about half the results had been declared and special telegrams despatched to the Central Electoral Commission, where staff specially deputed from the State Statistical Committee entered them into computers.[135] The first and in some ways most significant result was the turnout. The election legislation and commentaries had made it clear that the abuses of former years would not be tolerated: fathers voting for families, friends for their neighbours, and officials for anyone who stood in the way of a swift and all but universal turnout. Voting took place over a slightly shorter period than had been customary in earlier years (from 7 a.m. until 8 p.m., rather than from 6 a.m. until 10 p.m.); and the date coincided with the introduction of summer time, which meant an earlier start. In some areas, notably Armenia, an active boycotting campaign had been conducted, and the results of the December 1988 earthquake were still in evidence: voting in Leninakan, for instance, had to take place in prefabricated huts or even tents.[136] In these circumstances an overall turnout of 89.8 per cent must be accounted a considerable success, modest though it was compared with the artificially inflated totals of previous years.[137]

The results, constituency by constituency, were still more remarkable. Some 2,884 candidates had been selected to contest the 1,500 constituencies; in 384 of them, despite the intentions of the new law, there was just a single nomination, but elsewhere there was a choice and in one Moscow constituency as many as twelve candidates were competing for the support of voters. In the event, in seventy-six of the constituencies where three or more candidates had been nominated none secured more than half the votes and a run-off (*povtornoe golosovanie*) between the two most successful candidates had to be announced, to be held within the following two weeks. Under the election law the result would be determined by a relative majority, not an absolute one, and there was therefore unlikely to be much difficulty in finding a winner. Unexpectedly, however, even 'sensationally' for

Izvestiya, in 195 constituencies where only one or two candidates were standing none of them secured more than half the vote and no result could be declared. This meant that in these constituencies the whole exercise would have to be repeated (*povtornye vybory*), beginning with the nomination of new and normally different candidates, within a two-month period. In a further three constituencies there would have to be a repeat ballot because fewer than half of the registered electors had voted.[138]

Still more unexpected was the number of defeats suffered by leading party and state officials. A whole series of local leaders, admittedly, were successfully returned, among them the party first secretaries and prime ministers of Belorussia, Estonia, Georgia, Kazakhstan, Moldavia, the Ukraine, Turkmenia, Uzbekistan and the Russian Republic. And there were some striking victories for individual party leaders: the Astrakhan first secretary, for instance, won more than 90 per cent of the vote, the Tambov first secretary won over 92 per cent, and the first secretary in earthquake-stricken Spitak obtained more than 93 per cent of the vote in his constituency.[139] But the defeats that were suffered by local party and state leaders were even more remarkable. The prime minister of Latvia was defeated, and the prime minister and president of Lithuania; so too were some thirty-eight regional and district party secretaries throughout the country.[140] The mayors of Moscow and Kiev were defeated, and the party first secretaries of Kiev, Minsk, Kishinev, Alma-Ata and Frunze. The runaway success of Yel'tsin in Moscow (with 89.4 per cent of the vote) was a particular snub to the party authorities, given the attempts that had been made to frustrate his campaign.[141] The most spectacular defeats of all, however, were in Leningrad, where the list of casualties included the regional first secretary (a candidate member of the Politburo) and the second secretary, the chairman of the city soviet and his deputy, the chairman of the regional soviet and the city party secretary. It was understandably some time before the full dimensions of this rebuff reached the columns of Soviet newspapers.

The Congress of People's Deputies and Supreme Soviet

The representative institutions that emerged from this new-style electoral process were very different from the 'supreme state organs' that had preceded them. There were, in fact, more party members than ever before, despite the setbacks that some of its leading officials had suffered: 87.6 per cent of the new deputies were CPSU members or candidates, well above the previous level.[142] Officials, despite the reform's intentions, were also better represented: 65.2 per cent of the new deputies were paid administrators of some kind, compared with 43.1 per cent in the outgoing Supreme Soviet, and this despite the fact that ministers were no longer eligible for election (the main increase was in lower administrative positions). Equally, however, the scientific and cultural intelligentsia was much more fully represented in the new Congress than in the old Supreme Soviet: apart from Sakharov, Sagdeev, Shmelev and others, the deputies included the eminent literary scholar Dmitri Likhachev, the political commentators Fedor Burlatsky and Roy Medvedev, sociologist Tat'yana Zaslavskaya, economists Gavriil Popov and Oleg Bogomolov, and writers like Valentin Rasputin, Chingiz Aitmatov and Yevgenii Yevtushenko. There were five religious leaders, the first ever elected to a Soviet legislative body; rural leaseholders and commercial cooperators were also represented for the first time; and there was a substantial detachment of pensioners.

In line with the new doctrine that deputies should be chosen for their political qualities rather than their social characteristics, the Congress was also less representative in a sociological sense of the population that had elected it. The proportion of women deputies, most notably, was down by more than half, from 32.8 to 15.7 per cent,[143] and would have been lower still but for the seventy-five seats specifically reserved for women's councils. This, complained a feminist academic, was 'manocracy', not democracy.[144] The proportion of workers and collective farmers, equally, was down by about half: workers from 34.3 per cent in the outgoing Supreme Soviet to 17.9 per cent in the new Congress, and collective farmers from 10.6 to 4.9 per cent.[145] At least one candidate in the run-off elections suggested to his opponent that both should stand down in favour of a worker,[146] and party officials also drew attention to the matter at Central Committee level.[147] The proportion of workers and collective farmers (and of women), in the event, was still lower among the candidates that were successful in the run-off and repeat elections than it had been among those successful in the first round on 26 March.[148] 'Now the workers will understand they have been fooled', a party secretary in Odessa is reported to have remarked;[149] and if this was too simple a verdict, the 1989 elections did nonetheless mark the end of the USSR as a state where policies were at least nominally determined by ordinary working people rather than by white-collar professionals claiming to speak on their behalf.

The Congress of People's Deputies, which held its first session on 25 May 1989, made a number of further innovations in Soviet political and constitutional practice. Gorbachev, as expected, was elected to the newly-established post of Chairman of the Supreme Soviet; what could hardly have been predicted was that two candidates were nominated to stand against him and that he secured election, after a series of searching questions from the deputies, by a less than unanimous vote (2,123 in favour, but 87 against).[150] Anatolii Luk'yanov, who was elected First Vice-Chairman of the Supreme Soviet four days later, faced a still more extended inquisition from deputies, including questions about his responsibility, while in the Central Committee apparatus, for the rapid increase in reported crime.[151] Gorbachev addressed the Congress on 30 May, and Prime Minister Ryzhkov on 7 June; most of the remainder of the session, which lasted until 9 June 1989, was given over to speeches, initially on procedural issues, but latterly on all aspects of party and state policy, and often of a sharply critical character.

The head of the Soviet women's committee, Zoya Pukhova, complained that the USSR was lagging behind many developing, not to speak of developed, countries in its attention to women's rights, and called for 'more profundity' in the speeches of Gorbachev and other leaders on these matters.[152] Yel'tsin, in an explosive contribution, complained that power was still monopolised by the party and state apparatus and warned that the head of state had accumulated so much authority that a 'new dictatorship' was possible.[153] The economist Emel'yanov, supporting him, argued that a one-party system represented a monopolisation of power and that making the leader of that party the head of state extended the monopoly still further. He was one of those to call for the rights of the party to be defined by law and for it to be constitutionally subordinated to the Soviet state, which represented the people as a whole.[154]

Another target was the KGB. Yuri Vlasov, an Olympic weightlifter, in an astonishing speech, listed the sites in which its victims had been buried and accused it of crimes 'unknown in the history of humanity'.[155] Andrei Sakharov, himself criticised for his remarks about the conduct of the war in Afghanistan, read out an alternative programme which included the removal of the CPSU and its leading role from the Constitution.[156] The writer Yuri Karyakin called for Solzhenitsyn to be given back his Soviet citizenship, and went on to propose that Lenin be reburied in Leningrad and that the names of all the victims of Stalinist repression be engraved on the Lubyanka.[157] Moscow University economist Gavriil Popov pointed out that Marx's *Capital* had been written in the nineteenth century and asked when their economic administrators were going to study neo-Keynesianism;[158] another deputy, TV commentator Yuri Chernichenko, asked why responsibility for agriculture had been given to someone (Ligachev) who knew nothing about it.[159] Other issues that were repeatedly aired included the national question, the ecological situation, and the food supply. The Congress established a constitutional commission to prepare a replacement for the document adopted in the Brezhnev era; it also set up a commission to investigate the 1939 Nazi–Soviet pact, and another commission to review the circumstances which had led to the brutal suppression of a peaceful demonstration in Tbilisi on 9 April.[160]

One of the Congress's first acts was to set up the new-style Supreme Soviet, a much smaller body which was expected to remain in session for most of the year. The elections were based in part on a regional quota system; Boris Yel'tsin, nominated for the Russian Republic, failed at first to secure election but then obtained a place when another deputy stood down in his favour.[161] Despite historian Yuri Afanas'ev's criticism that it was a 'Stalinist–Brezhnevite' body with an 'aggressively obedient majority',[162] the new Supreme Soviet when it met for the first time on 3 June soon showed that it would be a very different institution from its unlamented predecessor. One sign of this was the elaborate committee system that was set up, including committees of the Supreme Soviet as a whole and commissions attached to each of its two chambers. One of the Supreme Soviet's new committees dealt with defence and state security; another with *glasnost'* and the rights of citizens.[163] Some 928 deputies, about half of whom were members of the Supreme Soviet itself, were elected to serve on the new committees and commissions; and at least two-thirds of the work of the new parliament was expected to take place under their auspices.[164] Another promising sign was the establishment of an organisational base for the new parliament in central Moscow, with a library and electronic services (together with the expenses of deputies, the new parliament was expected to cost about 40 million rubles a year as compared with seven million rubles for its predecessor).[165] Yet another, potentially much more important, was the formation of an inter-regional deputies' group, in effect a radical caucus, under the effective leadership of Boris Yel'tsin. Nearly 400 deputies attended its inaugural meeting at the end of July 1989 and some 260 agreed to join it.[166] The group, which had its own funds and newspaper, was at least potentially the beginning of a form of parliamentary politics unprecedented in the Soviet period.

Much of the business of the first session of the new Supreme Soviet was concerned with the consideration of Ryzhkov's nominations to the Council of Ministers. It was a very different team, at least in terms of personnel. Only ten of Ryzhkov's nominees had served in the Soviet government elected in 1984, and fewer than half had served in the outgoing Council of Ministers. Nearly a third were entirely new to government service, six were members or candidate members of the Academy of Sciences, and the average age was a modest fifty-five (the final list included the Soviet Union's first non-party minister, a biology professor who was to head the Committee on Nature Conservation). The structure of government was also revised. There were to be no more than fifty-seven ministries and state committees altogether; twenty-five existing ministries were to be wound up; and those that remained were to be 'ministries of a new type', exercising general rather than detailed guidance within their sphere of competence.[167] What was certainly new was the attention with which these nominees were received: both in committee and later in the Supreme Soviet itself the candidates were intensively questioned, and about a third of Ryzhkov's original nominations were rejected.[168] This 'parliamentary marathon' took about three weeks; Ryzhkov later suggested it had been the most unusual process of government formation that had occurred in the history of Soviet rule.[169] The Leningrad deputy Anatolii Sobchak, for the radicals, declared the Congress a 'victory for a nascent democracy' and noted that its 'whole course' had been against the party-state *nomenklatura* and its manner of operation.[170]

Republican elections and party formation

The experience of partly competitive national elections in March 1989 led to further consideration of the system under which they had been conducted. There was strong support, in the discussion, for dispensing with some of the arrangements that had given rise at the time to the greatest number of objections, particularly selection conferences and the representation of social organisations. Selection conferences (or 'constituency pre-election meetings') were still defended by Barabashev and Vasil'ev, two of the jurists most closely involved in devising the new law. Despite fears that the conferences would be used to exclude more controversial candidates, 'excesses' of this kind had been infrequent; more positively, the conferences had given voters a chance to compare the candidates at first hand and to reduce the number of names on the ballot paper to manageable proportions. The representation of social organisations had been equally unpopular, and some candidates had promised, if elected, to campaign for the removal of this provision from the legislation. Barabashev and Vasil'ev, once again, thought the innovation had been justified by its results: the elections had encouraged a greater degree of activism in the organisations concerned, and they had acted as a 'compensation mechanism' helping (for instance) to improve the representation of women and young people.[171]

Arguments of this kind, however, hardly disposed of the central issue, which was that members of social organisations enjoyed additional representation in a way that was quite inconsistent with the principle of 'one person, one vote'. And it was arguments of this kind that appeared to carry the greatest weight with the Soviet public. Letters in the press certainly supported the view that candidates should be nominated exclusively by other citizens, with no rights of this kind for social organisations.[172] A national poll conducted by the All-Union Centre for the Study of Public Opinion, similarly, found strong support in most parts of the country for the view that the CPSU and other social organisations should be required to nominate candidates in the ordinary way. Far fewer (17.2 per cent in the RSFSR) thought the organisations concerned should have a guaranteed number of places in the national legislature, and a substantial minority thought organisations of this kind should take no part at all in the elections. Overwhelming majorities, again, thought a choice of candidate should be compulsory, and very substantial pluralities thought selection conferences were unnecessary (although in Russia and Armenia, as compared with the Baltic and Ukraine, they had more supporters than opponents).[173] These and other views were clearly taken into account when the election law and constitution were revised once again towards the end of 1989.

Speaking to the Supreme Soviet in October 1989, Anatolii Luk'yanov explained that this reconsideration involved both changes in general procedures and a greater tolerance of local variation in practices and institutions. Russia and the Ukraine, for instance, both intended to convene Congresses of People's Deputies from which a working Supreme Soviet would be elected; the other republics intended to elect a Supreme Soviet by direct and popular vote. The formation of presidia would also vary from republic to republic (some would be entirely elected, some entirely *ex officio*, and others still a combination); and there were differences on the question of social organisations, with some republics proposing to retain direct representation and others to abandon it. Different views had similarly been expressed about the idea of selection conferences, and this would be left to the republics to decide (in the end, four Central Asian republics retained a provision of this kind). Equal conditions should be created for all candidates – 'far from all' had competed under such circumstances in the election earlier in the year. On the question of electoral choice, finally, the existing constitutional provisions would be left unchanged, allowing but not requiring the nomination of more candidates than seats available. This, thought Luk'yanov, was 'more democratic'.[174]

These and other changes were passed into law at the Second Congress of People's Deputies in December 1989.[175] Congresses of People's Deputies, it was made clear, would not be obligatory at the republican level (Art. 91); there had been some objection to arrangements of this kind from the Baltic republics at the time of their original adoption, and in the event only the Russian Republic introduced the complicated two-level parliamentary institution that remained in existence at the national level. It was decided to make no reference at all to the representation of social organisations in the USSR Constitution; the Congress of People's Deputies, Luk'yanov explained, would continue to be composed in the same way, but republics would be free to make their own arrangements. In the event, two of them – Kazakhstan (where a quarter of the seats were allocated on this basis) and Belorussia (where disabled and veterans' organisations were given 50 of the 360 seats) – decided to retain such representation in their republican parliaments; the Ukrainian law retained the principle in draft but discarded it in the final version.[176] The reference to selection conferences, equally, was dropped from the Constitution, allowing republics to make their own decisions. Despite further suggestions for a change, finally, the number of candidates that were to be nominated remained as before: there could be any number, leaving the decision (at least in principle) to the electorate.[177]

The republican and local elections that took place upon the basis of this amended law were held over a period of months and often on different dates – a further deviation from established practice, which left republican parliaments in some cases to vote themselves an extended period of office.[178] The elections in the Baltic were among the first: in Estonia, for instance, elections to local soviets took place in December 1989 and to the republican Supreme Soviet in March 1990. More than twenty organised groups took place in the elections to the republican parliament; the Communist Party took 55 of the 105 seats, but it was the Popular Front, with 46 seats and allies in other groups, that headed the largest group of deputies and provided the new prime minister.[179] The outcomes in the other Baltic states were broadly similar, with sweeping successes for nationalist candidates. This was particularly true of Lithuania, where 90 of the 141 seats in the elections of February 1990 went to supporters of Sajudis; the Communist Party's leading role had been removed from the republican constitution the previous December and these were, in effect, the first genuinely competitive elections in Soviet history.[180] Latvia, like Estonia, held its local elections in December 1989 and its parliamentary elections the following March; here again the Popular Front was overwhelmingly successful, although more so in the countryside than in the largely Russian-speaking capital. Candidates claiming membership of the Popular Front took 111 of the 210 seats, and allies brought the total to 131 – close to the two-thirds majority needed for constitutional change.[181]

The Slavic republics voted in early March 1990. Over 6,700 candidates competed for the 1,068 seats that were available in the Russian Republic, with up to 28 nominations for a single seat.[182] The turnout was 77 per cent, substantially lower than the corresponding figure a year earlier; it was lower still in Moscow and Leningrad, and less than half in a Noril'sk constituency where no valid result could be declared.[183] Only 121 seats could be filled after the first round of voting; among them, once again, was Boris Yel'tsin, chosen by over 80 per cent of the electorate in his home town of Sverdlovsk.[184] In the second round, later in the month, turnout was down to about 70 per cent and a 'whole series' of seats could not be filled because the turnout fell below 50 per cent.[185] The 'Democratic Russia' bloc of candidates enjoyed considerable success, taking 20–23 per cent of the vote in the republic as a whole and a considerably larger share in the cities,[186] and after several inconclusive votes its candidate, the former Moscow party secretary Boris Yel'tsin, was elected to the chairmanship of the republican Supreme Soviet on 29 May.[187] Another radical, the economist Gavriil Popov, became mayor of Moscow, and Anatolii Sobchak, up to this point a law professor, became head of the city administration in Leningrad.[188] All three announced their resignation from the Communist Party later in the year.[189]

In the Ukraine only 112 of the 450 constituencies were able to declare a result after the first round of voting, although turnout was relatively high at 85 per cent.[190] In one Kiev constituency there were as many as 33 candidates; the republican average was seven.[191] Large numbers of seats were won by candidates associated with the nationalist movement 'Rukh' and the Greens; Rukh, for instance, took control of Kiev and of much of the west of the republic (a nationalist heartland).[192] In the L'viv region, in the western Ukraine, voters elected not the first secretary of the regional party committee but the Goryn brothers, who had spent many years in prison for their 'anti-Soviet activities'. Another of the successful candidates was the Metropolitan of Vinnitsa and Bratslav; the Ukrainian head of state, Valentina Shevchenko, withdrew from the electoral contest 'because of a number of circumstances' when its outcome began to seem doubtful.[193] In the third Slavic republic, Belorussia, 1,473 candidates fought it out for 310 seats, only 20 of which were uncontested.[194] There was an 87 per cent turnout, but (as elsewhere) only a minority of seats were filled on the first ballot. In one particularly outstanding case a journalist defeated a member of the Belorussian Central Committee Secretariat; Pravda described the result as 'sensational'.[195]

Elections in the other republics took place at various times: in Armenia, for instance, in May 1990, and in Georgia the date was first postponed and then set for November 1990.[196] In Armenia the turnout, already the lowest in 1989, was lower still – 'just over 60 per cent'; nationalist candidates enjoyed considerable success and a member of the Karabakh committee, Levon Ter-Petrosyan, was elected president in early August.[197] In Georgia, the elections which finally took place at the end of October led to the clear victory of a nationalist coalition, Round Table/Free Georgia, which took 54 per cent of the vote as compared with the Communists' 29.6 per cent. Shortly afterwards the veteran dissident Zviad Gamsakhurdia was elected republican president on a programme of transition to full independence.[198] As before, there was least competition in Central Asia. In Uzbekistan, for instance, about a third of seats in the February 1990 elections had only one candidate, and a 'good half' of all the candidates were managers or executives.[199] Elections to the 250 places in the Kirgiz parliament also took place in February 1990;[200] so too did the elections to the Tajik parliament, where 1,035 candidates completed for the 230 seats available. The turnout here was close to the Central Asian norm, at 91.2 per cent.[201]

The republican elections in the spring and autumn of 1990 had a number of common characteristics. In the first place, turnout levels were down on those that had been recorded a year earlier, particularly in the later rounds of voting and in the towns as compared with the countryside. Turnout levels, as in March 1989, were higher in Central Asia than in the other republics; Armenia, on both occasions, recorded the lowest figures. Secondly, there was a greater degree of electoral choice than in the elections to the Congress of People's Deputies, although the level of competition remained much lower in Central Asia and in the elections to local rather than republican levels of government. As a result, larger numbers of seats remained unfilled after the first round of balloting than ever before; the whole exercise became a lengthier and, inevitably, a more expensive one (Estonia, the only republic to employ the single transferable vote system, was able to avoid most of these difficulties). The candidates, in the third place, remained overwhelmingly CPSU members, but a greater share of seats than ever before went to managers, executives, academics and clerics, and the representation of workers, collective farmers, women and young people declined even further (Moscow and Leningrad, for instance, each returned a single worker[202]). And finally, there was a significantly higher level of party or organised group activity, with the beginnings of coordinated platforms across or within republics. This was particularly true of the Baltic and the major cities.

Party formation, in the early 1990s, was still at a rudimentary level, with no clear association between a candidate's programme, his organisational affiliation and his subsequent behaviour in the legislature. There were, however, at least 20 parties in operation on an all-union basis by this time, with a membership ranging from a few dozen to some tens of thousands. In addition, about 500 parties were active at the republican level.[203] Membership figures were difficult to establish: some of the parties kept no central register of members or regarded them as confidential, and almost all of them exaggerated their own numbers considerably. The new parties fell into two main types: 'vanguard parties' (which had adopted some of the organisational forms of the CPSU and were in some cases successors to it), and 'movement parties' (which were similar to the broadly-based popular coalitions that had been formed in Eastern Europe in the late 1980s). The Democratic Party, an example of the first of these, based itself on democratic centralism and exercised strict discipline over the activities of its members; the Democratic Union, which fell into the second category, did not impose the decisions of its leadership upon the mass membership and allowed the formation of organised factions (even of communists) within its ranks.[204] All of these parties operated within the framework of a Law on Public Associations, approved in October 1990, which laid the formal basis of a multiparty system.[205]

There was certainly no shortage of parties, with or without the law that gave them a legal basis: a reference guide published in late 1991 listed over 300 of them, including nine anarchist parties, 17 different monarchist groupings and no fewer than 53 'national-patriotic' parties.[206] Some restored the names of pre-revolutionary parties, like the Constitutional Democrats or Kadets; other took more obvious labels, such as the Liberal Democratic or Social Democratic Party; and others still were more inventive. There was a Humour Party, founded in Odessa, and an Idiots' Party of Russia, certain of victory in a 'land of fools', with its persuasive slogan 'Give the people beer and sausage!'[207] The USSR Ministry of Justice, which was responsible for registering the new nationally-based parties, had at least two thousand applications from bodies of this kind. By August 1991, however, only two parties had completed all the necessary formalities: the Liberal Democratic Party and the Communist Party, whose registration had obviously no practical effect after its suspension.[208] As late as November 1991 only twelve parties had been formally registered under Soviet and Russian law, although the deadline for doing so was the end of December;[209] a new and multiparty system had, nonetheless, clearly come into being, and it represented a recognisable spectrum of opinion.

On the 'right' (in the sense that it sought generally to return to the pre-Soviet order) there were a number of business parties including one that openly entitled itself the Bourgeois Democratic Party, representing the interests of small and medium entrepreneurs.[210] There was an Order of Orthodox Monarchists, and several Christian Democratic parties. More significant, among the new parties, were the Liberal Democratic Party and the grouping collectively known as 'Democratic Russia'. The Liberal Democratic Party, established in 1990, was formally dedicated to the idea of a state based on law and a market economy. In practice, however, it became identified with the extravagant views of its leader, Vladimir Zhirinovsky, who came third in the Russian presidential elections in the summer of 1991 with over six million votes. Zhirinovsky called for the re-establishment of the Russian state within the boundaries of the USSR, or if possible those of January 1917, or 'ideally' those of 1865;[211] after the coup, which he openly supported, he suggested that the LDP might form part of a 'bloc of patriotic parties' in opposition to democrats and radicals.[212] 'Democratic Russia', whose founding congress was held in Moscow in October 1990, was a more loosely structured coalition of political forces originally formed to contest the republican elections of that year in opposition to the CPSU;[213] it was able to mobilise enormous numbers of demonstrators in support of Boris Yel'tsin in early 1991, but its effectiveness was seriously damaged when three member parties withdrew at its second congress in November 1991.[214]

About twenty different parties and movements constituted the 'centre' of the political spectrum, including the Russian Popular Front, the Democratic Reform Movement and the Democratic Party of Russia, led by former CPSU member Nikolai Travkin.[215] This, according to most estimates, was the largest of the new parties, with about 50,000 members in the early 1990s.[216] Founded in May 1990, the Democratic Party declared its aim to be the restoration of an independent Russian state within a voluntary union of republics. State power was to be decentralised, and a 'society of equal opportunities' was to be created on the basis of market relations and equality of all forms of property.[217] Travkin, a national and Russian people's deputy, was the party's most prominent public spokesman; another, until his departure in early 1991, was the chess player Gary Kasparov (splits and leadership struggles were a common feature of many of the newly-formed parties).[218] The Democratic Reform Movement, formally established in December 1991, saw itself as a 'third force' between authoritarianism and anarchy; its leaders included many former members of the Gorbachev administration, including Alexander Yakovlev and Eduard Shevardnadze, and its membership was disproportionately drawn from scientific staff, academics and professionals. Yakovlev, speaking at its founding congress, suggested that the 'most dangerous crisis' in the society was the 'loss, the erosion of all morality'.[219]

Finally, there was a 'left' grouping based upon the Socialist and Social Democratic parties, the Greens and an anarcho-syndicalist confederation.[220] These groups were joined in November 1990 by the Republican Party of the Russian Federation, a 'left centrist party of the parliamentary type', which occupied an intermediate position between the CPSU and the Democratic Party. The Republican Party consisted largely of former members of the CPSU who had been members of the Democratic Platform, a group that had been active in pressing for party democratisation before the 28th Congress.[221] Estimates suggested that this was, by the early 1990s, the second largest of the new parties, with about 20,000 members; the Social Democrats and Christian Democrats had about 10,000 members each, and other parties 'significantly less' (some were known as *divannye* or 'sofa parties').[222] Further to the left were the political groupings that claimed the political legacy – and often the property – of the former CPSU. These included the Soviet Communist Party of Bolsheviks, headed by Nina Andreeva, which accused Gorbachev of 'betrayal of the cause of

Lenin'; the Russian Communist Workers' Party; the Russian Communist Party, which was based on the former Marxist Platform within the CPSU; the Socialist Workers' Party, which included the historian and deputy Roy Medvedev; and a re-established Menshevik Party.[223] Rather more influential was the People's Party of Free Russia, originally a 'Communists for democracy' grouping in the Russian parliament, led by then Vice-President Alexander Rutskoi; on some counts this was the largest of the new parties, with an estimated 100,000 members.[224]

Gorbachev, speaking to American Senators in 1990, described the USSR as the 'most politicised society in the contemporary world';[225] but there were clearly weaknesses in the new party system that had developed beside and (later) in the place of the CPSU. One of these was their limited memberships, even allowing for double counting and exaggeration (Zhirinovsky, for instance, had included all those who attended its inaugural congress as members of the Liberal Democratic Party, and had apparently added the members of some national minority movements without their knowledge; some reports suggested the party's entire membership was largely fictitious[226]). Another weakness was a recurrent tendency to divide: the Peasant Party, for instance, formed in the spring of 1991, had split less than a year later, and even *Pamyat'* contained several different tendencies.[227] More serious than this, perhaps, was a general failure to articulate a clear and distinctive political position apart from opposition to the CPSU, and a related failure to establish a social base. Without this anchor in enduring patterns of interest the new parties became obsessed with leadership intrigue, failed to develop participatory structures of membership, and displayed little cohesion in the legislature (there were 'as many parties as deputies', Anatolii Sobchak pointed out with some impatience[228]). The existence of the new parties had transformed the Soviet political scene; but it would certainly be some time before a structure developed that would be capable of sustaining a coherent government into the post-communist era.

The executive Presidency

The converse of this process of pluralisation, party formation and republican assertiveness was a strengthening of central authority, above all through the establishment of an executive Presidency in 1990. The creation of the new presidency had been among the radical proposals announced by Gorbachev at the Central Committee plenum in February 1990 at which the constitutionally guaranteed 'leading role' had been relinquished. The idea of presidential government, it appears, was under discussion in Gorbachev's immediate circle from late 1987 onwards as a means of circumventing the central party bureaucracy, who were seen as the main obstacle to reform. There was some uncertainty, in the discussion, as to whether the chief executive should be popularly elected or not, and Gorbachev's own intentions remained unclear.[229] The idea of a Soviet presidency, in fact, was a good deal older than this. It had been under discussion at the time of the adoption of the 1936 Constitution (Stalin, however, had opposed it and the idea made no further progress), and had also been considered in 1964 during preparatory work for the constitution eventually adopted in 1977.[230] The idea of presidential government surfaced once again in 1989, when it was suggested in the press and was formally proposed to the Second Congress of People's Deputies – provided the choice was made by direct and competitive elections – by Andrei Sakharov.[231]

The introduction of a presidential system of this kind, for which there was no obvious precedent in Soviet or Russian political practice, was justified by Gorbachev as a means of ensuring that swift executive action could be taken in circumstances that required it, particularly where the economy, ethnic relations and public order were concerned.[232] Anatolii Luk'yanov, who presented the proposals to an extraordinary Congress of People's Deputies in March 1990, argued that an institution of this kind would facilitate dialogue among the sociopolitical movements that had been brought into being by democratisation and decentralisation, and that in turn it would strengthen consensus and mutual understanding. The President could act quickly in the event of wars, disasters, social disorders or other circumstances, and he could help to resolve the impasse that had developed between the Soviet government and the Congress and Supreme Soviet. Nor, he went on, was there any reason to fear that the new presidency would lead to a new form of authoritarian rule; there were several safeguards against this, including limits on age and tenure and the ability of Congress – if a sufficiently large majority decided accordingly – to recall the President and overrule his decisions. What they needed, and what the law provided, was 'authoritative legislative organs, and a powerful President, and an energetic government, and an independent legal system'.[233]

Understandably, perhaps, there were misgivings in some quarters that – whatever assurances were given – this was a step towards

personal dictatorship. Historian Yuri Afanas'ev, on behalf of the Inter-
Regional Group, insisted that the changes were premature – in the
absence of a new constitution – and dangerous in their implications. As
another speaker put it, they trusted Gorbachev, 'but who of us is sure
that four or five years from now someone won't come along who
wants to create a tsarist-style socialism in the USSR?' Speakers from
the union republics were concerned about the possible exercise of
presidential power to suspend the operation of their own parliaments;
and there was a majority, though not a sufficiently large one, in favour
of a formal separation between the presidency and the party leadership.[234] Other speakers, however, accepted the proposals as a means of
ending what was described as a 'vacuum of power', and in the end the
establishment of the Presidency was approved by 1817 votes to 133,
with 61 abstentions.[235] Gorbachev was duly elected to the new post on
15 March, although he received no more than 59 per cent of the votes
of all the members of the Congress (or 71 per cent of those who took
part) in an uncontested ballot.[236] Anatolii Luk'yanov was elected
chairman of the USSR Supreme Soviet in Gorbachev's place, and by a
similar margin.[237]

Any citizen aged between 35 and 65 could be elected to the Presidency for a maximum of two five-year terms. The President was
normally to be elected by universal, equal and direct suffrage,
although in the difficult circumstances that obtained it was agreed that
Gorbachev – exceptionally – would be elected by the Congress itself
(the 'father of the house', literary scholar Dmitrii Likhachev, carried
the day on this point with an impassioned warning that if they did not
elect a President without further delay – and he was old enough to
have experienced the revolution of 1917 – there was a real danger of
civil war[238]). The President, under the terms of the legislation, was to
report annually to the Congress of People's Deputies and would brief
the Supreme Soviet on the 'most important questions of the USSR's
domestic and foreign policy'. He would propose candidates for the
premiership and other leading state positions; he had a suspensory
veto over legislation; and he could dissolve the government and
suspend its directives. He could also declare a state of emergency, and
introduce direct presidential rule. The President headed a new
Council of the Federation, consisting of the presidents of the fifteen
union republics, with responsibility for inter-ethnic and inter-republican issues; he also headed a new Presidential Council, which was
responsible for the 'main directions of the USSR's foreign and domestic policy'.[239]

In September 1990 these already impressive powers were extended by parliamentary vote, giving Gorbachev the right to institute emergency measures to 'stabilise the country's sociopolitical life' for a period of 18 months.[240] Several further changes were made by the Fourth Congress of People's Deputies in December 1990, completing the move to a fully presidential administration. The Council of Ministers was replaced by a more limited 'Cabinet', headed by a prime minister who – together with his colleagues – would be nominated by the President and accountable to him (the former finance minister, Valentin Pavlov, was elected to this position in January 1991). The President became head of a new Security Council with overall responsibility for defence and public order (he himself appointed its other members). He also appointed a new Vice-President, responsible for carrying out the functions that were entrusted to him (Gennadii Yanaev, a member of the Secretariat who had formerly worked in the trade union movement and Komsomol, was elected to this position on 27 December[241]). The Presidential Council, formed the previous March, disappeared entirely, and a reconstituted Council of the Federation headed by the President became, in effect, the supreme state decision-making body.[242]

There was some concern among Soviet liberals that these extensive powers, greater even than Stalin had commanded, could open the way to a new dictatorship. For the Inter-Regional Group, once again, the new proposals represented an 'usurpation of power', leaving too much authority in the hands of a single person. Yel'tsin went still further, complaining that the centre was 'seeking to constitutionalise an absolutist and authoritarian regime which could ultimately be used to provide a legal pretext for any high-handed act'.[243] Gorbachev himself drew attention to a cartoon in which he had been shown with a tsar's crown in his hands, trying it on for size.[244] There were, in fact, considerable limitations upon the powers of the new President, extensive though they undoubtedly were. He could be impeached by a two-thirds vote of the Congress of People's Deputies; his ministerial nominations required the approval of the Supreme Soviet, which could force the resignation of the Cabinet as a whole if it voted accordingly; and he had himself to report annually to the Congress of People's Deputies upon the exercise of his responsibilities. Explaining his position to a gathering of miners in April 1991, Gorbachev pointed out that he had voluntarily surrendered the extraordinary powers of the General Secretary of the CPSU, powers which at that time were greater than those of any other world leader. Would he have done so if he had been seeking unlimited personal authority?[245]

Gorbachev's real power, in any case, was far less than his formal prerogatives might have suggested. Indeed by the early 1990s he was, politically, the least powerful leader the Soviet Union had yet experienced. He was, for instance, the first Soviet leader to face an open call for his resignation, not only as President (at the Congress of People's Deputies in December 1990) but also as General Secretary (at the Central Committee meeting that took place in April 1991). His presidential decrees, moreover, were ignored or even rejected by the bodies that were responsible for implementing them. A decree banning illegal military formations was rejected by the Armenian government in August 1990;[246] Armenia also rejected a presidential decree on economic sabotage,[247] and a presidential decree establishing a joint military and police structure for the maintenance of public order was repudiated by the Georgian and Moldavian as well as Armenian parliaments.[248] Most fundamentally of all, the authority of the central government, for so long unchallengeable, was undermined by the decision (during 1990) of all fifteen union republics to declare their laws sovereign over those of the USSR as a whole. The Soviet Constitution, adopted in 1977, insisted upon the opposite; but its effective force had by the early 1990s become so limited that the illegality of the republics' action was not even a subject of public discussion.

Political change and the Soviet public

If Gorbachev's central objective was to unleash the 'human factor' it was clearly essential to engage the interest and approval of the mass public for political changes of the kind that had now been implemented. The survey evidence that is available certainly suggests that the process of political reform commanded widespread public attention and that, at least initially, the broad principles of democratisation enjoyed substantial popular support. The First Congress of People's Deputies, according to a series of telephone polls conducted as it was meeting, was followed closely throughout the country: from 61 per cent, in the Kazakh capital Alma-Ata, up to 92 per cent, in the Georgian capital Tbilisi, claimed to be watching or listening to its proceedings 'constantly' or 'more or less constantly' (Moscow and Leningrad came in between, with 87 and 78 per cent respectively). Between 79 and 88 per cent of those polled, in various republican capitals, thought the Congress was operating 'completely' or 'more or less democratically'.[249] Between 52 per cent (in Kiev) and 80 per cent (in Tallinn) of respondents were largely or entirely in agreement with the views that had been expressed by the deputies from their area at the Congress; and the overwhelming majority in all cases (from 81 to 93 per cent) supported the election of Gorbachev as Chairman of the Supreme Soviet.[250] Over 141,000 members of the public, prompted no doubt in part by the continuous television transmission of its proceedings, were sufficiently moved to send telegrams or other communications to the Congress as it was meeting.[251]

Still more exhaustive efforts were made to determine the response of the citizenry at large to the new-style elections that had brought the Congress into existence in the first place. According to a survey conducted by the All-Union Centre for the Study of Public Opinion in urban areas throughout the USSR,[252] over 80 per cent of respondents were familiar, at least in part, with the new electoral procedures. Some 48 per cent approved of the new arrangements, 13 per cent were against, and most of the remainder thought it was still too soon to offer an opinion. Asked to choose which methods of influencing state decisions were likely to be the more effective, 14 per cent suggested election campaigns and voting: this came well behind appearances in the mass media and participation in public opinion polls (49 and 38 per cent respectively), but just ahead of meetings and demonstrations (13 per cent) and well ahead of participation in the newly-established informal groups and organisations (7 per cent). A national poll conducted under the auspices of the Academy of Sciences found that a 'majority' approved of the new electoral law, for the most part (57.3 per cent) because it afforded a choice of candidate.[253] In a further poll of about 4,000, conducted in eight different regions by scholars from the party's Academy of Social Sciences, more than two-thirds of respondents expressed the view that the electoral law required further improvement, but 60 per cent thought the nomination of candidates had taken place in a democratic manner and there was substantial if not unqualified support for the view that the elections would accelerate the progress of *perestroika*.[254]

The level of turnout, in the absence of the usual pressures to take part and of falsification on the scale of previous years, was certainly consistent with the view that the 1989 elections had engaged a widespread degree of public interest and support (even in the run-off and repeat elections turnout was still 75 and 78 per cent respectively).[255] Newspapers reported that complete strangers struck up conversations about their voting intentions, and on polling day itself there were queues in some places to enter the premises and then to enter the voting booth, where candidate choice was finally made. In one

Moscow constituency extra voting booths had to be constructed as matter of urgency on the day itself, so great was the pressure to make use of them,[256] and reports from other constituencies spoke of the sick and disabled coming to the polling station in person rather than waiting to be visited by officials. The new elections also received unprecedented coverage in the media, particularly on television where two regular programmes, 'Power to the Soviets' and 'Towards the Elections', gave candidates and voters an opportunity to air their views. In a few areas, such as Estonia and Moscow, there were actual 'telestruggles' between the candidates themselves; the local Moscow programme which aired such contests was the most popular source of election information for 70 per cent of the Muscovites who were interviewed in a telephone poll.[257] National surveys suggested that television was the main source of election information for most respondents (70.1 per cent), followed by the local and national press (54.3 and 53.4 per cent respectively).[258]

It was nonetheless far from clear, by the early 1990s, that this new-style Soviet political system represented a stable and workable combination of centralised direction 'from above' with democratic control 'from below'. There was considerable opposition, in the first place, to the shortcomings that still remained in the new electoral system, with strong pressure for an obligatory choice of candidates, no representation for the social organisations, and a direct and competitive popular vote for the working Supreme Soviet and for the newly-established Presidency. For many voters these were still 'elections without choice' all too reminiscent of the practices of earlier years; some single candidates were opposed simply because of these circumstances, and in a number of cases, such as the Kiev mayor and the Leningrad first secretary in the 1989 elections, the candidates concerned may have been defeated at least in part because of their attempt to avoid a contest.[259] If Pravda's soundings among a group of Moscow voters were representative, only direct, secret and competitive elections to the new Soviet parliament would satisfy public sentiment; or perhaps two rounds of voting, the second of which should take place between the two candidates with the largest number of votes in the first ballot (the union treaty that was published in 1991 acknowledged the force of these objections by abolishing the Congress of People's Deputies and replacing it, for the future, with a directly-elected Supreme Soviet in which no seats at all were reserved for public organisations such as the CPSU).[260]

The early experience of 'democratisation' was also a somewhat disillusioning one. The new-style soviets, it emerged, had rather limited powers, and often made little use of them in any case. Deputies were long on speech-making, but short on practical suggestions; and some of the newly elected democrats (such as the Moscow mayor, Gavriil Popov) aroused a good deal of controversy by travelling abroad extensively on public business. By early 1992, according to a Moscow poll, only 13 per cent had any confidence in the deputies they had elected, and only 16 per cent in the Russian Supreme Soviet; and just 4 per cent connected their hopes for the future with the new political parties or movements.[261] Increasing numbers refused to vote at all, making it impossible to fill vacant seats, and popularity ratings fell sharply at all levels (Leningrad city soviet, for instance, dropped from a 74 per cent level of approval in June 1990 to just 20 per cent the following January[262]). The main characteristic of public opinion on matters of government, according to a detailed examination published in 1990, was in fact 'political alienation'. Some 45 per cent thought that the people they elected to the soviets 'soon forget about our concerns, pay no attention to the interests of the people in their work'; another 31 per cent thought the society was managed by an 'elite that looks after its own interests'; and only 14 per cent thought state institutions took proper account of the needs of those that elected them. Evidence of a 'general distrust of power structures' also emerged in other investigations.[263]

The system of linkage that had been established between Soviet voters and the making of public policy was an unsatisfactory one in several other respects. Deputies, for example, had relatively few opportunities to press the popular demands on the basis of which they had been elected, as only a small minority of them could serve as full-time legislators at any time. The others, people's deputies but not members of the Supreme Soviet, were able to attend meetings of the Congress of People's Deputies once or twice a year, and perhaps an occasional committee meeting, but had otherwise little more to do than members of the discredited Supreme Soviet of old. There was, in any case, no obvious mechanism to connect public concerns with the conduct of government. Candidates at the election put forward individual programmes, and could hardly offer a coordinated programme of action for the country as a whole. Nor could they, as isolated legislators, put forward a list of deputies who might form an alternative administration. For purposes of this kind the experience of Western nations has devised an effective instrument: the political party, which sponsors candidates in all or most constituencies and presents a coherent and notionally workable programme of government for the forthcoming period. If Soviet elections were to provide a meaningful choice it was likely to be difficult to resist the logic of a choice of parties, not just of individuals; and it was this that appeared to have inspired the growth of electoral blocs and the rapid, even chaotic growth of new parties in the early 1990s.

The logic of an organised choice of political alternatives, however, left no obvious role for the Communist Party, supposedly the instrument uniquely capable of articulating the real interests of all working people. Communists, it emerged, took different positions on different issues, once the monolithic facade had been abandoned. They competed with each other on the hustings; some called for demonstrations to be banned, and others took part in them; some advanced what were basically nationalist demands, and others called for the reassertion of central control. The party as a whole, moreover, was implicitly challenged by the principle of the popular mandate that the reforms had introduced into Soviet political life. What, for example, was to be made of the rejection of so many leading officials at the polls in 1989? It could hardly be represented as a 'victory for *perestroika*', as Gorbachev rather optimistically described it;[264] the response of many Central Committee members at the meeting which took place shortly afterwards was rather that it had placed the whole principle of party rule in jeopardy. How, for instance, could the party continue to justify its guaranteed block of seats, and how could it justify a share of the seats reserved for social organisations which substantially exceeded its claims in terms of total membership? How could the party resist a challenge to its monopoly of policy formation by a group of deputies who had secured a convincing mandate from their electors? What, in particular, if elections at lower levels of government produced clear majorities for candidates committed to the separation of their territories from the rest of the USSR, as they did in several republics in 1990?

Political reform, by the early 1990s, had certainly succeeded in dismantling a largely Stalinist inheritance; but it had not yet succeeded in replacing it with a viable combination of Leninism and democracy, of central party control which yet allowed the voters to be sovereign. Even in the view of Soviet reformers an accommodation of this kind was unlikely to be achieved without an extended period of 'learning democracy'. Kurashvili, for instance, spoke of moving from a harshly authoritarian to a democratic-authoritarian regime, at best, in ten or fifteen years; and a group of specialists from the Institute of State and Law pointed out that the rule of law in capitalist countries, with all its pluses and minuses, had taken 'hundreds of years' to establish.[265]

Indeed in some ways the partly reformed political system that had been established by the end of the 1980s combined the worst of both worlds. Voters could reject party officials, but not, at least nationally, effect a change of regime. Deputies, reflecting the wishes of their electors, could resist unpopular policies such as the reduction of subsidies on food, but, elected as individuals, they could hardly put forward an alternative programme of government. The new representative system, with its inclusion of a range of organised interests, lent itself to the articulation of grievances rather than solutions. Most fundamentally of all, there was an unresolved tension between the 'will of the people', expressed through open and competitive elections, and the 'will of the party', based ultimately on the doctrine of Marxism–Leninism.

There were two ways forward in the political practice of the communist world in the early 1990s. One was a continued insistence on the leading role of the party, leaving representative institutions in a basically dependent state (China and Cuba were the leading examples). The other was a commitment to popular sovereignty above all else, even if this led (as in Poland, Hungary and elsewhere) to the formation of a largely or entirely non-communist government. In the USSR itself the party and state apparatus, for the most part, remained firmly committed to the principle of party dominance. Figures such as Boris Yel'tsin, however, acknowledged that the old relationship between party and state was no longer viable; Yel'tsin's election address in 1989 called for the party and all other public bodies to be legally accountable to the Congress of People's Deputies, and he called elsewhere for the removal of the leading role of the party from the Constitution as this gave twenty million CPSU members a quite improper share of political influence among a population that was very much larger.[266] Gorbachev, for his part, insisted that a multiparty system was not a 'panacea', and the reforms that were introduced in early 1990 extended no more than a cautious welcome to 'healthy forces' elsewhere in the society that were willing to cooperate with the CPSU on the basis of the Soviet Constitution and the social order it embodied.[267] The tension between party and state, between Leninism and popular sovereignty, was not a new one: it went back as far as the revolution itself, in which political power had been taken by the Second Congress of Soviets in the name of working people but in fact by the Bolshevik party on behalf of a small but organised minority. Decades later, it was a tension that went to the heart of Gorbachev's 'revolution from above'.

3   *Glasnost'* and public life

Secrecy is a very well-established Russian tradition. In Tsarist times not only military but also quite harmless social information was withheld from the population at large, and especially from foreigners.[1] The Bolsheviks briefly abolished secret diplomacy and other customs of the past when they came to power, and indeed there was consternation in Allied capitals when they published the annexationist secret treaties on which the conduct of the war had been based. Older practices, however, soon reasserted themselves, and for many Western students of Soviet affairs control over the flow of information came to represent a basic element in the communist system of power (it was, for instance, one of the issues about which Soviet negotiators were most concerned during their dealings with the Czech reformists in 1968[2]). Western journalists have generally been compelled to live within a separate foreigners' compound and operate under great restrictions; Soviet official statistics, until recently, left out whole areas of social and economic life, from crime and mortality rates to balance of payments and road accident data; and the official media, at least until the early 1980s, typically presented an almost unvarying diet of champion milkmaids and heroic shockworkers marching forward to a fully communist society in contrast to the unemployment, poverty and hopelessness of the capitalist West.

Although this picture was already beginning to change in the 1960s, it was not until Gorbachev's accession that shortcomings in the official media – and indeed in the quality of Soviet public life in general – became the object of close attention at the very highest levels of the leadership. From the outset Gorbachev committed himself to a policy of openness or *glasnost'*, embracing not only the printed media but also radio, television and all areas of the creative arts. There were several reasons for this change. In the first place, Gorbachev appears to have believed that *glasnost'* would of itself help to bring about a more energetic and constructive atmosphere in the Soviet workplace and thus to reverse the economic stagnation of the later Brezhnev years. 'Broad, up-to-date and honest information', he told a conference in December 1984, 'is a sign of trust in people, respect for their intelligence and feelings, and their ability to make sense of developments'. Equally, it raised the level of labour activism, reduced bureaucracy and helped to avoid errors in party and state work.[3] 'The better the people are informed', he told the Central Committee that elected him, 'the more consciously they act, the more actively they support the party, its plans and programmatic objectives'.[4] People, he wrote in his *Perestroika*, 'should know what is good, and what is bad, too, in order to multiply the good and combat the bad'; *glasnost'* would help them to gain a better understanding of the Soviet past and present, and 'on the basis of this understanding, to participate in the restructuring effort consciously'.[5]

The monotony and other failings of the official media had in any case attracted a lot of public criticism. The daily paper *Sovetskaya Rossiya* reported the case of V. D. Polyakov of Kaluga, a well-read man who followed the central and local press and never missed the evening TV news. He knew in detail what was happening in various African countries, Polyakov complained, but he had 'only a very rough idea of what was happening in his own city'. After studying a file of the local paper *Sovetskaya Rossiya*'s correspondent had to agree: he could not find an answer to a single one of the questions of public interest that Polyakov had raised.[6] Nor was this an isolated case. In the Black Sea resort of Pitsunda, for instance, the peace of an August evening had suddenly been broken by a series of explosions. Frightened holiday-makers tried in vain to find out what had happened, and rumours spread rapidly. But not a word of explanation appeared in the local paper, though it did find the space to cover an unprecedented flood in South East Asia, a volcanic eruption in Latin America and a train collision in France. It eventually emerged, from a Moscow rather than a local publication, that Soviet sailors, at considerable risk to their lives, had been disarming some German bombs that had been left behind after World War II.[7] In October 1985, another correspondent wrote in the same paper a few months later, there was a major earthquake in Tajikistan in Soviet Central Asia, but no details were made known other than that 'lives had been lost'. At about the same time there had been an earthquake in Mexico and a volcanic eruption in Colombia; both were covered fully with on-the-spot reports, including details of the casualties that had been suffered. Was Tajikistan further from Moscow than Latin America?[8]

Readers and journalists also began to complain that when information was provided, particularly from abroad, it was too often partial and inaccurate. Soviet journalists, as Fedor Burlatsky pointed out in early 1987, had allowed a series of 'gaps' to appear in their reporting of such matters. They had had little to say, for instance, about the 'new technological revolution' that was taking place in Japan and the West based upon advanced electronics, or about the emergence of newly industrialised states in the developing world. There would, he believed, be no industrial revolution in the USSR itself so long as Soviet people compared their efforts, not with the best that had been achieved elsewhere, but with what earlier Soviet generations had accomplished as long ago as 1913.[9] Soviet reporting on the Third World was particularly unhelpful, wrote D. Vol'sky, another contributor to the debate. The developing world had turned out to be far more complicated and heterogeneous than Soviet journalists had depicted it, although the truth of this fact tended to become apparent only after the event. Only then, complained Vol'sky, did it become known that the 'national patriotic forces', on coming to power, had behaved like feudal or even prefeudal princes, that 'important industrial projects' had been undertaken to indulge their vanity, and that 'progressive transformations' had often led to economic catastrophe and in turn to their own downfall.[10]

The point was not simply that the official media were silent or one-sided on many issues of the day. The truth, as *Sovetskaya Rossiya* pointed out, would eventually emerge. The problem was that if those who were responsible failed to explain the real state of affairs at the earliest opportunity, it would be replaced by gossip, conjecture and exaggeration.[11] The shortcomings of the official media, in particular, encouraged a greater degree of interest in Western radio and TV broadcasts than would otherwise have been the case. Perhaps two per cent of the Soviet population were able to listen to foreign radio broadcasts in 1940 and about eight per cent could do so by 1950, it has been estimated, but about 50 per cent of the population were able to do so by the 1970s. The BBC alone was estimated to have at least 18 million regular listeners in the USSR in the late 1980s, when jamming was suspended; the foreign radio audience as a whole was estimated at about 67 million, a significant proportion of the adult (and still more of the urban and better-educated) population.[12] Viewers in the Baltic and some other peripheral areas had direct access, in addition, to foreign television programmes, which they generally preferred to domestic ones. The danger of failing to report fully and promptly on the whole range of foreign and domestic developments was that, increasingly, the information deficit would be satisfied by 'foreign voices with anti-Soviet overtones', as *Sovetskaya Rossiya* put it.[13]

The poor quality of official information contributed towards a still more serious outcome: inadequate discussion of policy alternatives, ill-considered decisions and in some cases wasteful and damaging 'projects of the century', such as the Baikal–Amur mainline railway across Siberia, completed in 1985, or the ambitious plan to divert the Siberian rivers southwards, finally abandoned in 1987 (the same ministry, *Izvestiya* reported, had even made plans to irrigate the Sahara desert[14]). Some of these issues were taken up in an article on Soviet sociology by the head of its professional organisation, Tat'yana Zaslavskaya, early in 1987. The problem, Zaslavskaya wrote, was not simply the poor state of Soviet sociology in comparison with the position in Eastern Europe, let alone the USA. Still more serious was the quality of public information: the census had become a steadily less useful source of data on social development since the late 1950s, and whole areas – crime, suicide, the distribution of income, drug abuse, alcohol consumption and environmental pollution in the major cities and republics – were omitted from official sources. If people, she argued, were denied information on the conditions under which they lived, they would hardly assume a more active role in public life; and if sociological 'feedback' was ignored there would be many more mistaken decisions by the authorities.[15] It was considerations of this kind – to activate the 'human factor' and to avoid costly errors – that appear to have contributed most directly to Gorbachev's commitment to *glasnost'* in all fields of public and cultural life.

Re-examining the Soviet past

One of the first tasks of any new Soviet administration is to define its attitude to the Soviet past and, by implication, to the tasks that still lie ahead. The Gorbachev leadership was no different in this regard; indeed, not least because of its reformist objectives, it brought about a debate on the Soviet and Russian past and their relationship to the system of the 1980s which was more far-reaching than any seen since the 1920s. In the first instance this led to a reassessment of the Brezhnev era, hailed at the time as one of 'developed socialism' but increasingly derided, under Gorbachev, as a time of stagnation, corruption and moral decline. For Gorbachev, addressing the 27th Party Congress in February 1986, the Brezhnev era was one of postponed decisions and missed opportunities, when a 'curious psychology – how to change things without really changing anything' – had been dominant.[16] By the end of the year, on the anniversary of Brezhnev's 80th birthday, the charges had become much graver and more personalised. Brezhnev's wartime career, especially the 'brilliant episode' at the Malaya Zemlya beachhead in 1943, was warmly praised; and the early years of his general secretaryship were seen as a time of economic, social and cultural advance, including the attainment of strategic parity with the United States. In the later years of his life, however, there had been too much reliance on 'habitual patterns and formulae', and a lack of openness in public life had made it impossible to identify difficulties in time to deal with them effectively.[17]

Criticism of the Brezhnev era became still more uncompromising over the years that followed. Brezhnev, Gorbachev explained in his address on the 70th anniversary of the revolution in 1987, had helped to bring about a change in methods of economic management soon after his accession. A programme of economic reform had been devised, and major schemes for the development of new parts of the country and new branches of industry had been elaborated. The country's scientific potential had increased, its defence capacity had been strengthened, and living standards had risen. Many developments in foreign policy had enhanced the Soviet Union's international prestige. The promise of these achievements, however, had been dissipated by a failure to carry the reforms through to their logical conclusion, and still more so by a failure to make the changes that had become necessary in social policy and political leadership. The gap between words and deeds had steadily widened, and a pre-crisis situation had developed in the economy. In the society at large, an unequal distribution of benefits had undermined public support for socialist principles and encouraged the growth of social alienation and immorality.[18]

Brezhnev's faults of character were spelt out more fully in press commentaries. He had awarded himself four gold stars as a Hero of the Soviet Union for bravery in World War II when he did not deserve them, *Pravda* charged; and he had added the Order of Victory, which was formally speaking reserved for army commanders who gained important wartime victories. Such was his love of decorations, Roy Medvedev reported, that when he died more than 200 awards and other distinctions had to be carried behind his coffin.[19] He was also greedy for applause, and had arranged for 'organisational measures' to be taken to ensure that his speeches were greeted with prolonged ovations.[20] The corruption of Brezhnev's immediate circle was exposed in other stories: Brezhnev's daughter Galina, for instance, was customarily addressed as 'Madam' and speculated in diamonds, the price of which more than doubled during her father's administration.[21] Readers of *Literaturnaya gazeta* were regaled with accounts of the private life of Nikolai Shchelokov, Brezhnev's close associate who had also been minister of the interior. Shchelokov, it emerged, had a fleet of foreign cars for himself and his immediate family, a set of private flats, a private photographer, an architect, a 'masseur', a cook and a biographer. He 'acquired' old books from a library; he even had a film made about himself for his own private viewing at a cost to the state of about half a million rubles.[22] For such people, it was remarked, full communism had already arrived.

There were few in the Brezhnev entourage, in fact, whose records could withstand scrutiny. His son-in-law Yuri Churbanov, already dismissed from his post at the interior ministry, was arrested in 1987 and brought to trial on charges of bribe-taking on a massive scale. He was sentenced to twelve years imprisonment in a harsh-regime labour camp at the end of December 1988 and stripped of his state honours.[23] Galina herself, together with other family members, lost her special pension and other privileges earlier the same year, and Brezhnev's widow had to return his decorations to public custody.[24] The city of Brezhnev, formerly Naberezhnye Chelny, reverted to its original name in January 1988; so too did Brezhnev Square in Moscow and the Brezhnev – formerly Cherry Tree – district in the capital (unkind humorists suggested that the Brezhnevs would soon become 'Cherry Tree family').[25] Matters were taken further at the end of the year when it was decided that Brezhnev's name should be removed from every town, street, factory and institute that had been named after him following his death, and his Order of Victory was retrospectively cancelled; later still there was a paint attack on the bronze bust in his birthplace.[26] Brezhnev's secretary, G. D. Brovin, was separately identified as connected with a major crime ring and was sentenced to nine years' imprisonment for bribetaking.[27] Brezhnev, according to opinion polls, was already more unpopular than Stalin.[28] The very name had become a curse, Brezhnev's grandson Andrei told *Moscow News*; people connected with the family had been forced out of their jobs, and their families and friends had deserted them.[29]

Brezhnev's predecessor Khrushchev, by contrast, came to be seen in increasingly favourable terms as a courageous reformer who had exposed Stalin's crimes and raised the living standards of ordinary people (in a 1989 opinion poll, for instance, 51 per cent of respondents took a positive view of his administration, compared with 10 per cent for Stalin and only 7 per cent in the case of Brezhnev[30]). A brief but complimentary reference in Gorbachev's speech on the 70th anniversary of the revolution helped to initiate this reconsideration.[31] For Fedor Burlatsky, writing in *Literaturnaya gazeta*, Khrushchev was a representative of the 'NEP' trend in the party, never quite extinguished, which supported democratisation and was opposed to the use of coercion in industry and agriculture, still more so in the cultural sphere. At the 20th Party Congress, in 1956, he had risked his life in making an attack on the Stalinist personality cult – an attack of which no other member of the leadership of the time would have been capable. For Burlatsky, Khrushchev had indeed crushed the personality cult and raised living standards; his fatal weakness was that he was unable to distinguish between genuine supporters and flatterers, which left him unprotected when his opponents mobilised against him in 1964.[32] Reflecting this different and more positive view, Khrushchev's secret speech was finally published in the USSR in 1989; extracts from his memoirs, originally disowned, began to appear in the weekly *Argumenty i fakty* and later in other publications; and there was a call to rebury him with full honours in the Kremlin wall (in 1991 his name was given to a square in the city of Grozny).[33]

The Stalin question, however, was clearly the critical one, as it has been for all Soviet reformers.[34] Gorbachev, to begin with, was reluctant to concede that there was even a question. 'Stalinism', he told an interviewer from the French Communist paper *L'Humanité* in February 1986, was a 'notion made up by opponents of communism and used on a large scale to smear the Soviet Union and socialism as a whole'. The 'personality cult' had been condemned by the 20th Congress of the CPSU in 1956, and the appropriate lessons had been drawn; that, it appeared, was that.[35] By the following February, however, Gorbachev was insisting that there must be 'no forgotten names [or] blank spots' in Soviet history or literature, and in July 1987 he told a group of media workers that they could 'never forgive or justify what happened in 1937–38. Never.'[36] By November 1987, when he came to give his address on the 70th anniversary of the revolution, the terms of the debate had advanced still further. Trotskyism remained a 'leftist pseudorevolutionary rhetoric' which was hostile to the very nature of Leninism; Bukharin and other Politburo moderates, equally, had underestimated the need for urgency in the construction of socialism at that time. The command-administrative system that had been established for the management of the economy, however, had been allowed to extend into socio-political life, choking off its democratic potential, and this had led to the 'wanton repressive measures' of the 1930s – 'real crimes' in which 'many thousands of people inside and outside the party [had been] subjected to wholesale repression'.[37] This was a lesson that subsequent generations must not be allowed to forget.

Gorbachev was able to announce that the Politburo had established a special commission to investigate the crimes of the period, and that a new textbook on the history of the CPSU would be prepared. The textbook, in the end, was never completed; but the Politburo commission, chaired initially by Mikhail Solomentsev, set to work immediately and had cleared more than 600 purge victims by the following August.[38] The most notable victim of the purges, Nikolai Bukharin, was one of the first to be rehabilitated through this process. In February 1988, fifty years after his show trial and a hundred years after his birth, Bukharin and eighteen other members of the 'anti-Soviet right-Trotskyist bloc' were officially cleared of the charges against them by the USSR Supreme Court.[39] In July Bukharin was posthumously restored to party membership, and in October he was reinstated as a member of the Academy of Sciences.[40] The same month a Bukharin exhibition opened in the Museum of the Revolution in Moscow, and in the Lenin Library; a film of his life was reportedly in preparation. Bukharin's articles and books also began to reappear: his eulogy on the fifth anniversary of Lenin's death appeared in the party theoretical journal *Kommunist* in January 1988, and his collected works were issued later in the year.[41] The standard Western biography, by Professor Stephen Cohen of Princeton University, appeared in extracts during the year and in full in early 1989.

The rehabilitation of Bukharin was followed by the judicial and political rehabilitation of those involved in the 'Leningrad affair' of 1950, and in July 1988 by the rehabilitation of Lev Kamenev, Grigorii Zinoviev, Karl Radek and other old Bolsheviks who had been sentenced to death in 1937.[42] In October the 'Workers' Opposition' group was cleared of all charges, followed in December by the 'Jewish Anti-Fascist Committee' and in December 1990 by the 'Leningrad Centre' that had supposedly instigated the murder of Kirov in 1934.[43] Trotsky's son Sergei Sedov, another victim of the purges, was rehabilitated in November 1988,[44] and Trotsky's own contribution to the revolutionary cause began to receive a more balanced historical assessment (some of his works were even republished) although there was little indication that he would – or perhaps ever could – be restored to full political respectability.[45] The Politburo, immediately after the 19th Party Conference had concluded, decided that a monument to the victims of the purges should be constructed (in October 1990 a publicly funded monument 'to all the victims of the totalitarian regime' was finally inaugurated in Moscow opposite KGB headquarters).[46] A presidential decree of August 1990 moved beyond individual cases and provided for the rehabilitation of all victims of political repression from the 1920s to the 1950s. By this time about a million sentences had been reviewed and repealed, and more than two million more had been 'given back their good name'.[47]

Just as the victims of Stalinism were to be rehabilitated, so too the instruments or beneficiaries of Stalinism were exposed and dishonoured. One of the first to be denounced was Pavlik Morozov, the fourteen-year-old schoolboy who had informed on his parents for expressing anti-Soviet views in the early 1930s and had then been killed by a group of peasants, one of them his uncle. Pavlik Morozov was not a symbol of dedication and class consciousness, an article in the youth magazine *Yunost'* explained, but a 'symbol of legalised and romanticised treachery'.[48] A much more important figure, Stalin's chief prosecutor Andrei Vyshinsky, was denounced in January 1988 in a full-page article in *Literaturnaya gazeta* as a 'monster whose claws still defile our criminal procedure and legal system'. Vyshinsky, whose prosecution speeches had typically ended with the words, 'Shoot the mad dogs!', had been 'hand-picked by Stalin to be the blood-soaked director of the purge trials'. Vyshinsky, it emerged, not originally a member of the Bolshevik party, had actually signed an order for the arrest of Lenin as a German spy while acting for the Provisional Government during 1917; this made a mockery of his claim twenty years later that Lenin's closest allies, the victims of the purge trials, had been plotting to do away with Lenin himself.[49] Stalin's cultural commissar, Andrei Zhdanov, was stripped of his posthumous honours in early 1989; Leningrad University, which had been given his name, was one of the principal beneficiaries.[50] Beria's shortcomings, including his sadism and depraved sexual appetites, were also exposed to public censure.[51]

An adequate account of Stalinism and the Soviet past had necessarily to involve the historical record itself, and not just judgements about it. In this respect also the Gorbachev years made some significant contributions. The Nazi–Soviet Pact of 1939 with its secret protocols providing for the annexation of the Baltic republics was one such document: for many years unmentionable in Soviet writings, what purported to be an authentic text was published on the Baltic press in the summer of 1988 and in 1989 its existence was acknowledged by the Kremlin leadership.[52] An extended discussion took place of the numbers that Stalin had killed: for some it was about a million by the end of the 1930s, while for others such as Roy Medvedev the total was at least 12 million, with a further 38 million repressed in other ways (the KGB itself reported a figure of 3.8 million victims in the period 1930–53, of whom 786,098 had been shot).[53] Perhaps still more significant, a number of mass graves of the victims of Stalinist repression began to be discovered and reported in the local press. One of the most important of these was in the Kuropaty forest near Minsk, where what was described as a 'human slaughterhouse' was discovered in 1988. Both archaeological and eye-witness evidence indicated that the victims had been shot during the period 1937–41; most were peasants, but latterly some had been members of the NKVD itself. The total number of victims was estimated at 30,000 or even more.[54] More victims of the purges were found buried in a mass grave near Kiev, near Donetsk in the Ukrainian coalfields, and just outside Leningrad.[55] There was an 'Altai Kuropaty', and still further graves were found near Tomsk, outside Chelyabinsk and in Moscow itself.[56] This grisly record, still expanding in the early 1990s, was in itself a critique of Stalinism more powerful than anything historians could muster.

Public information and 'taboos'

As Zaslavskaya and others had remarked, the quality of public information had steadily deteriorated over the Brezhnev period as problem after problem was 'resolved' by simply discontinuing the publication of any information about it. The census, for example, has always been a vital instrument for planners and government officials as well as for social scientists. The first Soviet post war census, in 1959, was published in sixteen volumes in 1962–63. The next, in 1970, appeared in seven stout volumes between 1972 and 1974. The following census, in 1979, produced only a single summary volume, published five years later. The official statistical handbook, published annually since 1956, continued to appear throughout the period; but it became notably slimmer as the 1970s progressed, and by the early 1980s it was down to a positively anorexic 574 pages compared with 880 pages in the early 1970s. Figures on life expectancy, which was evidently declining, were not updated: the latest available figures, in the early 1980s, were those for ten years earlier. Figures on infant mortality were simply discontinued; a sharp rise in alcohol consumption was disguised by merging the figures for sales of drink with those for foodstuffs. Given an information base of this kind, it was difficult to disagree with official claims that the USSR had entered a qualitatively new phase of social development in the late 1960s and that these and other shortcomings of capitalism had long since been left behind.

A very different approach to the provision of information began to emerge in the Gorbachev era under a central statistical administration which was given a new name – the USSR State Statistics Committee – and a new head, appointed in 1987.[57] In one of the most notable developments, the annual statistical handbook reversed the diminishing trend of the 1970s and became larger and more detailed. The first 'Gorbachev' issue, published in 1986, was almost thirty pages larger than its predecessor; more important, it contained a wealth of information that had not been available for many years. Figures for infant mortality, for instance, were again reported: at 26 per thousand live births, admittedly with large republican variations, they compared poorly with those for the developed capitalist nations. Life expectancy figures returned, at 64 for men and 73 for women; themselves an improvement on the figures belatedly provided for the late 1970s, they were still up to ten years less than those for other industrial nations.[58] Later issues continued this improvement in the quality and quantity of data provided; particularly welcome was a more rigorous approach to definition and an attempt to secure greater international comparability. The annual handbooks were followed from the late 1980s by a series of sectoral volumes dealing with population, labour, industry and so forth, some of them containing data last reported in the 1920s.[59]

The handbook on population, for instance, contained the first-ever systematic data on abortions in the USSR. The figures reported were, by international standards, remarkably high. There were 101.2 abortions for every thousand women aged between 15 and 49 in 1986, it emerged, and still more in the RSFSR and other European republics.[60] As an article in the weekly paper Nedelya pointed out, the rate of abortions in the Russian Republic was about 25 times higher than it was in West Germany, and several times higher than the rate in Britain and the USA. The USSR, in fact, ranked first in the world for the number of abortions that were carried out annually per thousand women; for every 5.6 million births a year there were 6.8 million abortions.[61] The average woman had between two and four abortions over her lifetime and about 15 per cent had several abortions in a single year, some of them carried out privately and often unhygienically (up to 1,000 women lost their lives annually in such operations). Abortion was so widely availed of that it had become a social problem rather than a personal and medical matter.[62] Many other commentaries pointed out shortcomings in the health services as a whole: the health minister, Yevgenii Chazov, himself told the 19th Party Conference in 1988 that the USSR held 32nd place in the world in terms of life expectancy and 50th in terms of infant mortality. The share of national income devoted to the health service was one of the lowest in the world, and there were shortages of even the most basic equipment and supplies.[63]

The first figures on suicide for many decades appeared in early 1989;[64] so too did new figures on Soviet crime. Previously all but closed to public discussion, the data, drawn from the files of the Ministry of Internal Affairs, were the first of their kind to appear since the 1920s. Absolute levels of crime, the figures suggested, were lower than in most developed capitalist countries. The rate, however, was increasing sharply. The overall level of reported crime, per head of population, rose by 17.8 per cent in 1988 compared with 1987; violent murders were up 14 per cent, grievous bodily harm was up by 32 per cent, and robbery in various forms was up by a massive 43 per cent.[65] There were further increases in 1989 and 1990, and in 1991 crime in Russia alone rose by a further 18 per cent, with an increase of nearly half in burglaries and a further fall in the detection rate. Altogether, over the years of *perestroika*, reported crime more than doubled.[66] The police in fact received reports of crime with no great interest, *Izvestiya* discovered, and they were investigated without undue haste; there were two million complaints a year against the police themselves, and they were involved every year in about five million rubles' worth of theft. It seemed as if it was not so much that they were combatting crime but that crime was combatting them, and with some success, Nikolai Ryzhkov remarked in 1990.[67]

Abortion, suicide and crime were only a few of the 'forbidden themes' that became open for discussion in the late 1980s. Another was prostitution. Previously held to be, in principle, a phenomenon confined to capitalist societies, it came to be acknowledged under Gorbachev that this was an 'integral part of Moscow's tourist "service"'.[68] One of the earliest articles on the subject was in the paper *Sovetskaya Rossiya*, which carried a story in March 1987 on the 69th police district of Moscow in which three of the capital's most important railway stations were located. The paper's correspondent interviewed the local police chief, who had made a special study of the 3,500 or so prostitutes who had come to the attention of his department. They were of various ages and origins, but the typical case was a 'dynasty' of mother, daughter and grandmother, all working the same patch, and all displaying the same physical attributes, 'the vacant look, the puffy and unwashed faces and tousled hair'.[69] According to a study conducted in Georgia, nearly all of the 532 prostitutes surveyed were employed or had recently been in employment, and three-quarters of them had obtained at least a secondary education. They engaged in prostitution, it emerged, not necessarily because of economic necessity, but because of a 'discrepancy between their aspirations for self-affirmation and self-fulfilment and the reality of their lives'.[70] Legislation was introduced in June 1987 to deal with the problem; the fines that were involved, however, were hardly enough in the view of most correspondents to constitute an effective deterrent (two Moscow prostitutes who had been involved in foreign-currency operations and who were arrested at about the same time had nearly half a million rubles in bonds alone in their possession). Some, even in the Ministry of Internal Affairs, were prepared to argue in favour of the legalisation of prostitution under these circumstances.[71]

A further subject to emerge from obscurity thanks to *glasnost'* was the drugs problem. One of the earliest articles was by the then minister of the interior, Alexander Vlasov, who admitted in early 1987 that it was a serious and growing concern. The number of registered addicts – 46,000 – was tiny compared with the American total of about 30 million. But 80 per cent of Soviet addicts were less than twenty-one years old, their number was increasing, and some had been supplied (in violation of the law and of their Hippocratic oath) by doctors and hospitals.[72] Another report revealed that over 40,000 drug-related crimes were committed every year;[73] the number of crimes, and of registered addicts, was steadily increasing, and the number of addicts was itself likely to be a significant underestimate of the real extent of the problem (some enterprising addicts concentrated upon the wild hemp that grows in parts of Central Asia and tried to pass themselves off as 'botanists'[74]). A related problem was AIDS, originally seen as a feature of capitalist society or at any rate of foreigners, but increasingly acknowledged as a major public health challenge in the USSR itself. The first Soviet AIDS death occurred in 1987; despite preventive legislation in 1990, it was estimated that at least 1.5 million would be HIV-positive by the year 2000.[75]

Only a tiny minority of drug abusers were women, but women constituted more than half of the population as a whole and their particular concerns were dealt with more openly under Gorbachev than at any time since the 1920s. The physical burdens of Soviet women were an important part of the picture. As Zoya Pukhova, head of the Committee of Soviet Women, told the 19th Party Conference in 1988, nearly three and a half million women worked in conditions that contravened the labour law, and four million were employed, supposedly on a temporary basis, on night shifts (this was twice the number of men who were employed at such times). Wage rates were formally equal, but women's pay was actually less than that of men because they were concentrated in less well paid occupations and at lower levels of seniority. The economic reforms had added to their difficulties, as under conditions of self-financing enterprises were less willing to take on women with small children or to grant them the shorter working day and longer holidays to which they were entitled.[76] Some sociological research on women's 'double burden' was presented by a deputy culture minister in early 1989. Women, it was found, spent an average of 40 hours a week on domestic duties, while men spent just 6. An average woman brought home 2.5 tonnes of shopping a year, and walked about 12 kilometres about the house every day in carrying out her domestic duties. This left, on average, just 17 minutes a day for the upbringing of her children.[77]

Findings of this kind were not entirely unexpected, given the research that had been carried out and published since the 1960s.[78] Perhaps more important and certainly more novel was a discussion on women's social roles, a discussion prompted to some extent by Gorbachev's own 'conservative' views on such matters. Addressing the 27th Party Congress in 1986 Gorbachev took a fairly orthodox position, emphasising the need for a shorter working week and longer periods of maternity leave in order to allow women to combine motherhood with employment.[79] In his book *Perestroika*, published the following year, Gorbachev was equally concerned to encourage the active involvement of women in working life and politics; at the same time he insisted that more attention should be paid to women's 'specific rights and needs arising from their role as mother and home-maker, and their indispensable educational function as regards children'. While they were out working, women no longer had enough time to devote to their 'everyday duties at home – housework, the upbringing of children and the creation of a good family atmosphere'. Many social problems had arisen from the weakening of family responsibilities; there was also the problem of women working in strenuous occupations which were a danger to their health. All of this, in Gorbachev's view, had led quite properly to a discussion of 'what we should do to make it possible for women to return to their purely womanly mission'.[80]

These were not necessarily the views of Soviet women themselves, more than 80 per cent of whom wanted to work even if there was no economic necessity for them to do so,[81] and perhaps the most distinctive element in the debate on the 'woman question' in the Gorbachev period was the cautious articulation of a specifically feminist perspective. An Irkutsk professor, for instance, asked why women party officials were always given secondary and unimportant posts. Why, in their society of supposedly equal opportunities, had they no Indira Gandhi or Margaret Thatcher? And why were there no new women's organisations or movements, as in other countries? Despite 'male *perestroika* eloquence', another writer pointed out, it was women who had to deal with the long queues, undeclared but runaway price increases, poorly stocked chemists' shops and illegal night work. Again, was it not time for a 'really serious women's movement, with its own programme, its own ideas, its left and right, even its hecklers'?[82] Most far-reaching, perhaps, was a discussion of the whole question of gender roles by three feminist academics writing in the party theoretical journal *Kommunist*. Most Soviet work on the subject, they suggested, was biologically determinist in character. They argued rather for a view in which the sexual division of labour was social, rather than natural, in character, leading in turn to a much freer and more egalitarian choice of occupation, domestic and other roles. Equally, the emancipation of women made no sense without the emancipation of men, involving them, for instance, to a greater extent in the care of their children, and endowing them with 'paternity rights' as in the Scandinavian and other countries.[83]

The fall in female representation in the local and national elections in 1989 and 1990 led to a still more energetic discussion of women's social roles. The number of women, it emerged, had fallen from 32.8 to 15.7 per cent of the deputies in the USSR Congress of People's Deputies and to just 5–8 per cent in the republican parliaments, where no seats had been specifically reserved for women's organisations. The letters that came into the Central Committee reflected some concern about these developments. Why, for instance, were there no women in Gorbachev's Presidential Council, established in 1990? And why were they so poorly represented in other institutions of government? Women themselves suggested several responses in the early 1990s. One was to return to a quota-based system of representation; another was to establish a specifically women's political party; still another was to ensure that a woman was nominated as a candidate in the next presidential elections. More promising, perhaps, was what were described as 'politological courses' for the training of the women leaders of the future. Organised by the women's commission of the CPSU Central Committee and the party's Academy of Social Sciences, they involved instruction in politics, sociology and public speaking and a range of meetings with officials, 'American sociologists' and others.[84]

Social issues of all kinds, in fact, came to be more widely reported under conditions of *glasnost'*. The youth paper *Komsomol'skaya pravda*, for instance, launched an investigation into Soviet mental hospitals in late 1987 under the heading 'A Closed Subject'. Apart from incompetence, bribe-taking and the incarceration, in a few cases, of perfectly sane dissidents, the paper also found that diagnoses could be alarmingly erratic: 'The same person might be declared officially schizoid in Moscow, a psychopath in Leningrad, and perfectly sane in Khar'kov'.[85] Road deaths began to be reported fully for the first time in 1988: it emerged that more than 40,000 a year were killed in this way, and more pedestrians lost their lives, despite much lower levels of car ownership than in the UK, USA, France and West Germany put together.[86] Violent crime was covered more extensively than ever before: cases like the cannibal caretaker who had been responsible for the deaths of at least seven young girls, or the locksmith (and party member) who strangled thirty-six women in the Belorussian city of Vitebsk and for whose crimes fourteen innocent people had already been arrested, which was reported in *Literaturnaya gazeta*.[87] The same paper reported the case of the nude black marketeers who patronised naturist beaches in Lithuania which were out of bounds to the militia. 'And even if naked policewomen had tried to raid the beaches', the paper pointed out, 'how could they prove their identity when they had no clothes on?'[88]

There were revelations of many other kinds in the Gorbachev years. The first useful figures for Soviet and Warsaw Pact troop and weapon numbers, for instance, were reported in early 1989.[89] Gorbachev, speaking to the Congress of People's Deputies in May 1989, provided the first meaningful figure for Soviet defence expenditure: at 77 billion rubles, or 15 per cent of the state budget, it was four times higher than the figure previously published. Prime Minister Ryzhkov, speaking to the same gathering, gave the first-ever official figures for the cost of the war in Afghanistan and the extent of Soviet foreign debt.[90] The worst-ever rocket disaster, in 1960, was finally reported in early 1989; so too was the nuclear disaster in the Ural mountains in 1957, much of the area of which was still contaminated.[91] The brutal suppression of demonstrations in Novocherkassk in 1962 – there had been twenty-four deaths – was officially acknowledged in 1989; the 1937 census, suppressed at the time, began to be published in 1990; and so too did an honest account of the (essentially political) Ukrainian famine of the early 1930s.[92] The first official figures for the exercise of the death penalty were made public in 1991; so too were a series of secret cities, unmarked on ordinary maps, where nuclear and other weapons had been produced.[93] 'Openness', moreover, meant that the Soviet population was given unprecedented access to the discussion of issues of this kind. The Party Conference in 1988 was covered by the media only in part, but the first Congress of People's Deputies in 1989 was carried in full and in March 1989 central TV carried its first broadcast from a Central Committee plenum. In 1990 two journalists were invited, for the first time, to attend a meeting of the Secretariat.[94] Innovations of this kind were paralleled by the development of a more extensive network of opinion polling organisations, the most important of which was the All-Union Centre for the Study of Public Opinion, established in 1988 under trade union auspices.[95]

The creative arts and the wider world

Glasnost' led to a further series of changes in literature and the creative arts, although at least in the 1980s the main sensations were produced by work that had been completed anything up to twenty years previously. Perhaps the most important of these publications was Boris Pasternak's *Doctor Zhivago*, written originally in the 1950s, which was published in the first four issues of the literary journal *Novy mir* in 1988 (some excerpts had already appeared in the enterprising weekly *Ogonek* the previous December). Pasternak was posthumously restored to membership of the Writers' Union in 1987, and his house at Peredel'kino, after a lengthy struggle, was finally turned into a museum the following year.[96] Other notable publications in 1988 included Yevgenii Zamyatin's *We*, Vasilii Grossman's *Life and Fate*, Fazil Iskander's *Sandro of Cheghem*, Yevgeniya Ginzberg's *Into the Whirlwind* and extracts from Nadezhda Mandel'shtam's two volumes of memoirs *Hope against Hope* and *Hope Abandoned*. Grossman's *Forever Flowing*, written in the late 1950s and early 1960s, finally appeared in *Oktyabr'* in 1989; at least implicitly it held Lenin to blame for the despotic system that had been established in his name. Anatolii Marchenko's prison-camp memoirs, *My Testimony*, appeared in *Novy mir* in December 1989. Andrei Sakharov's 'Thoughts on Progress, Peaceful Coexistence and Intellectual Freedom', written in 1968, finally appeared in *Voprosy filosofii* in 1990; his *Memoirs* were published in *Znamya* in 1990 and 1991.[97]

The work of émigré writers of various generations also began to appear in central and local literary journals. One of the most notable was Vladimir Nabokov, whose autobiography, poems, short stories, essays and selected novels appeared in 1987 and 1988. His *Lolita* was published by the government publishing house in 1989. Other émigré writers to reappear in Soviet journals included the Nobel prize-winning poet Joseph Brodsky, Vladimir Voinovich, Vasilii Aksenov, Viktor Nekrasov and Naum Korzhavin. The most controversial of Soviet émigré authors, Alexander Solzhenitsyn, was the last to be published in the USSR; despite the overt hostility of CC Secretary Vadim Medvedev some minor works appeared in 1989, and then in the latter part of the year the *Gulag Archipelago* itself was serialised in *Novy mir*. His *Cancer Ward* and *First Circle* both appeared in *Novy mir* in 1990, and his *March 1917* came out in the Leningrad journal *Neva*. Solzhenitsyn was readmitted at the same time to the Writers' Union, from which he had been expelled in 1969, and in 1991 his Soviet citizenship, withdrawn in 1974, was formally restored.[98] Among foreign books previously suppressed George Orwell's *1984* was particularly noteworthy: it appeared in the main literary journal *Novy mir* in early 1989, while the author's still sharper *Animal Farm* appeared in the Latvian journal *Rodnik* in 1988. Extracts from Hitler's *Mein Kampf* were published in *Voenno-istoricheskii zhurnal* in November 1990, and in 1992 another historical journal, *Novaya i noveishaya istoriya*, began to publish the diaries of Joseph Goebbels.

Soviet 'political fiction' also achieved some notable successes in the late 1980s and early 1990s. Perhaps the most important individual publication was again a work of the late 1960s which appeared for the first time in the spring of 1987, Anatolii Rybakov's *Children of the Arbat*. Hardly a work of the first importance in purely literary terms, it described the darkening world of the early 1930s through a child's eyes and featured an attempt to reconstruct the psychological world of the Leader of Leaders himself.[99] Rybakov's *1935 and Other Years*, published in 1988, extended the narrative into the later period. Sergei Antonov's *The Ravine*, also published in 1988, depicted peasants' resistance to forced collectivisation. Chinghiz Aitmatov's *The Executioner's Block*, published in 1986, dealt openly with a youth gang that gathered wild hemp in Kazakhstan to sell as narcotics and argued for a reassertion of traditional religious values as the only means of overcoming such practices. Daringly, a Soviet journal even published a satire on Gorbachev himself, casting him as the inventor of a mysterious but totally meaningless doctrine known as *pablosurzhik* (i.e. *perestroika*) which was none the less embraced enthusiastically, reported upon, fulfilled and overfulfilled, all in response to the leadership's changing directives.[100]

Cinema made several distinctive contributions to the new era, above all Tengiz Abuladze's 'Repentance' (*Pokayanie*), which had been comleted in 1984 but which was released only in late 1986. Set in Soviet Georgia, the central figure, Varlam, was a dictator who combined the features of Hitler, Stalin and Mussolini with the face and pince-nez of the Georgian police chief, Lavrentii Beria. In a series of surreal flashbacks it conjured up the sufferings of the millions of Soviet citizens who had lost friends or family during the Stalin years. It was seen by 700,000 Muscovites in the first ten days after its release, and later by a worldwide audience.[101] Alexander Proshkin's 'Cold Summer of '53', released in 1988, broke new ground by dealing in unsentimental terms with political prisoners in the period just after Stalin's death. 'Little Vera' (1988), directed by Vasilii Pichul, was perhaps less remarkable for its occasional nudity than for its portrayal of the bleakness of life in a Soviet industrial city. Petr Todorovsky's 'Intergirl', released in 1989, dealt with prostitution in tourist hotels and was one of an increasing number of films made by younger directors. The sensations of 1990 were Yevtushenko's 'Stalin's Burial', with Vanessa Redgrave playing an English journalist, and Stanislav Govorukhin's 'We Can't Go On Living Like This', a savage indictment of the whole record of Soviet rule.[102] In theatre, the most notable or at least controversial developments were the political documentaries of Mikhail Shatrov, a committed reformer. Among the first to present Bukharin, Trotsky, Martov and others in a relatively objective manner, Shatrov's plays – 'The Brest Peace' (1987) and especially 'On, and On, and On' (1988) – centred around a dialogue between the original ideals of the revolution and contemporary Soviet realities.

The visual arts were also affected by the new atmosphere, and again some of the most important developments were connected with the rediscovery of a past that had been suppressed in the Stalinist years. There were major Soviet exhibitions in the late 1980s of previously disfavoured artists such as Filonov, Malevich, Chagall and Kandinsky. Among foreign artists, Francis Bacon and Salvador Dali held successful Soviet exhibitions. Contemporary Soviet art was auctioned by Sothebys in Moscow in 1988, and began to enjoy a ready sale abroad for reasons that were more than purely aesthetic. Here again rediscovery of the Soviet past was a central theme, and particularly of the past that had been suppressed during the Stalinist period. One example of the relaxation of taboos was a painting by Isaac Brodsky, 'The Ceremonial Opening of the Second Congress of the Comintern', completed in 1924, which had been kept in the basement of the Lenin Museum for more than sixty years because the artist had included, among others, Zinoviev, Bukharin, Radek and Bela Kun. In 1989 the painting was finally restored to its rightful place.[103] A similar work of restoration took place with the photographs of the period. A picture of Lenin on Red Square on the second anniversary of the revolution, for instance, was reproduced in its authentic form with Trotsky on Lenin's left and Kamenev on his right; and anti-Bolshevik posters of the civil war years, last seen in the late 1920s, began to reappear in public exhibitions.[104] Libraries were affected by these developments: fewer books were to be held in closed stocks, and access to those that remained was greatly simplified; so too were archives, which began to apply a 30-year rule and to allow access to the records of the CPSU itself.[105]

In an associated change, both the creative arts and more especially the printed and electronic media became more open than ever before to a variety of philosophical viewpoints, including those of a non-socialist and even frankly antisocialist character. An archbishop of the Russian Orthodox Church, for instance, was able to complain in *Pravda* in late 1987 that a commercialised culture was turning young people away from reading serious literature, especially the Russian classics. Apart from uncontrolled access to TV, the archbishop wrote, the worst problem was pop music, which was played at a deafening volume in parks and railway carriages and even in children's holiday camps and rest homes.[106] Ecclesiastical writers began to appear in other contexts as well: one, for example, in the main sociological journal in 1987 with an article on the current state of Russian Orthodoxy.[107] A group of Soviet émigrés, including Vladimir Bukovsky, Yuri Orlov and Leonid Plyushch', was allowed to publish a manifesto deeply sceptical of *perestroika* in *Moscow News* in early 1987; the paper, now under the vigorous editorship of Yegor Yakovlev, published responses from its readers in a subsequent issue.[108] The party daily, *Pravda*, began a new series 'From different positions' in February 1987, in which prominent Westerners were allowed to set out their views in full, without any kind of editing, beside a Soviet commentary of equal length. The first such article featured Robert Dole, then the Republican leader in the US

Senate.[109] *Moscow News*, which appeared in Russian as well as foreign languages, included interviews with Zbigniew Brzezinski and Richard Pipes, two spokesmen hardly known for their sympathy with Soviet or socialist viewpoints. Foreign newspapers, among them the *Guardian*, *Financial Times* and *International Herald Tribune*, themselves began to be sold in several hundred copies daily at Soviet newsstands in early 1989; in 1992 the *New York Times* began to appear in a Russian as well as an English-language edition.[110]

Perhaps the most dramatic changes of all, however, took place on Soviet TV with the institution in late 1986 of the practice of interviewing visiting Western politicians and other figures, and of 'spacebridges' which brought together groups of ordinary citizens in Soviet and foreign cities. Soviet TV began to feature studio discussions involving Western politicians such as Helmut Schmidt and David Owen, and visiting ministers – Margaret Thatcher and George Shultz, for example – were interviewed live with simultaneous translation (Thatcher's interview in 1987, in which she clearly discomfited three Soviet journalists, led to an urgent postmortem within the Soviet TV service[111]). Taking advantage of satellite technology, a series of spacebridges linked members of the public – and in the case of 'Congressbridges', parliamentarians – in the USSR and various foreign countries, particularly the USA. The first such broadcast, connecting Leningrad and Seattle, was compered jointly by Vladimir Pozner and Phil Donahue; it is estimated to have attracted a Soviet audience of 270 million (virtually the entire population) on its two showings.[112] Spacebridges have connected the USSR with the United Kingdom, West Germany, Japan and many other nations; they have dealt with sport, music and other subjects as well as politics. Spacebridges have also been employed in Soviet domestic television, particularly on the popular youth programme 'Twelfth Floor', and there has more generally been a shift towards prompter responses, audience interaction, studio discussion and investigative journalism.[113]

The dilemmas of *glasnost'*

Asked in a poll in 1989 what had been the most important outcome of *perestroika*, the largest single group of respondents cited '*glasnost'*, truthfulness of information in the press, radio and television'. Economic reform – the transfer of enterprises to self-financing and new forms of management – came second with 54 per cent, and changes in the government and electoral system came third with 46 per cent.[114] It was, of course, much easier to allow the publication of (for example) *Doctor Zhivago* than to fill the shops with foodstuffs. And yet the scale of the change, in just three or four years, was remarkable. As Andrei Sakharov – whose release from administrative exile at the end of 1986 was in itself a notable development – put it, the authorities themselves were now publishing things for which people would a short time previously have been arrested. The new changes were clearly popular – Soviet newspapers and journals, for example, put on circulation, some at a spectacular rate, and there was an estimated fall of about half in the number of Soviet citizens who regularly listened to Western radio broadcasts.[115] The Soviet censor, interviewed for the first time in November 1988, confirmed that the list of official secrets had already been reduced by about one-third and that it would be reduced still further in the future; indeed censorship as such was nominally abolished in 1990.[116]

These changes notwithstanding, there was much about the operation of *glasnost'* in the late 1980s and early 1990s that was precarious, ambiguous and incomplete. *Glasnost'*, in the first place, did not and was not intended to mean an unqualified 'freedom of the press'. The word itself meant 'publicity', or an explanation of the decisions that had been taken, at least as much as 'openness', or the ability to challenge them; it was possible to be controversial in support of *perestroika* but not (broadly speaking) against it. Indeed it was sometimes easy to forget the extent to which the press, radio and TV continued to conform to longstanding Soviet conventions. The front page of *Pravda* on a random date (21 November 1987) was reasonably typical of at least the earlier Gorbachev years. The top right-hand corner carried a report of the previous day's Politburo meeting. The main feature, under the heading 'Continuing the cause of October', pictured a veteran party member enrolling a new recruit, a statue of Lenin and a champion furnace-worker from Western Siberia. Another lead story, 'They light the creative sparks', dealt with a family of metal workers in Kaluga, three of whose members had received medals for their production achievements. 'News from Orbit' dealt with the scientific spacecraft 'Peace' on which Yuri Romanenko and Alexander Alexandrov were continuing their work and 'feeling fine'. At the bottom of the page, 'Universal Interest' described the reception of Gorbachev's book *Perestroika* in London, Ottawa and Brasilia. For at least one Soviet citizen, writing in *Pravda* at the end of 1986, there was nothing in the papers apart from leaders' speeches that could not have appeared some ten or twenty years earlier.[117] And it was certainly difficult to find, until the very end of the 1980s, any direct criticism of Lenin, the October Revolution, the party's leading role, or of its leaders individually.[118]

There were several other areas in which press discussion and criticism, though it existed, was muted and intermittent. The then editor of *Pravda*, Viktor Afanas'ev, speaking to the 6th Congress of Journalists in March 1987, singled out several of these continuing '"forbidden zones" for criticism' in his address. One of them was the Soviet space programme (in common, it may be remarked, with its counterparts in some Western countries). The spaceships were invariably 'working normally', the cosmonauts were always 'feeling fine'. And yet work in space was well known to be dangerous and heroic. Another 'forbidden zone' was the environment, where a great many meetings were necessary before articles could be cleared for publication. Only with great difficulty and with the personal intervention of a member of the Central Committee Secretariat, Afanas'ev revealed, had *Pravda* been able to 'push through' its articles on the pollution of Lake Baikal and on the scheme to divert the Siberian rivers southwards. All kinds of methods were used to preempt criticism. The local party secretary, for example, might take the earliest possible opportunity to criticise the central press so that any subsequent publications could be presented as revenge. Articles in the press might also be ignored. The most common response, however, was a purely formal one, acknowledging the substance of the criticism but failing to take any practical steps to deal with the problem that had been identified. And 'preventive measures' were also practised, including phone calls to the editor and threats of dismissal to the journalists in question.[119]

Several other topics proved particularly controversial in the early Gorbachev years. One of them was the 'special schools', in which a particular emphasis was placed upon the sciences or (more commonly) a foreign language. In many of these schools, *Moskovskaya pravda* discovered, there was a very high concentration of the children of officials, and the schools themselves were concentrated in certain districts of the capital where the bulk of the population was made up of senior government employees and white-collar professionals. The children came to school in official cars, and the schools themselves were sometimes 'palaces' with fountains and swimming pools. The paper came under very heavy pressure from 'influential papas' to drop its investigation, and the subject largely disappeared from newspaper columns after this particular episode had been concluded.[120] Another difficult subject was the related issue of privilege. One of the earliest sensations in the press in the period after Gorbachev's accession was an article entitled 'Cleansing' which made it clear that there was widespread concern about the abuses of position that had become particularly marked during the later Brezhnev years. He had become convinced, wrote one of *Pravda*'s correspondents, that an 'immobile, inert and viscous "party-administrative stratum"' had formed between the party and the working class, which was by no means interested in radical change. Another reader pointed out that social inequalities had been deepened by party, state and other officials who had taken advantage of 'all kinds of special canteens, special shops, special hospitals and so forth'. By all means let managers earn more than ordinary workers, if they deserved it; but they should stand in line for goods like everyone else.[121]

The whole issue surfaced at the Party Congress later in the month. Boris Yel'tsin, at this time Moscow party secretary, argued that if officials lost their conscience and began to enjoy benefits incommensurate with the work that they performed they became a source of corruption and should be removed. Yel'tsin's own opinion was that 'whatever benefits for officials at all levels are not justified must be abolished'. CC Secretary Ligachev took a rather different view, not supporting privilege as such but deploring the way in which *Pravda* had dealt with the matter,[122] and party officials at other gatherings, such as the 19th Party Conference in 1988, were very scathing about the manner in which the whole issue had been raised. The Kemerovo first secretary, for instance, complained about the 'fantastic privileges' that officials were supposed to enjoy. In his own area a miner could earn over 3 rubles an hour and a worker in light industry more than a ruble, but a party official was paid no more than 38 kopeks.[123] The Komi first secretary, who addressed the same subject, declared that the only privilege party officials had was to work a 10–12 hour day without regard to their health or leisure time.[124] The issue of privilege, again, has been raised fairly infrequently over the subsequent period, and it remains one of the matters on which politicians and officials at all levels – not without some justification – believe the press has deliberately exaggerated a small number of abuses.

If officials did object to media reporting they had a number of means of influence at their disposal, quite apart from the range of mechanisms identified by Afanas'ev in his address to the Journalists' Congress. Gorbachev, speaking in Krasnodar, brought up the case of a party secretary in the Kurgan region whose sharply critical report had been published in a 'sanitised' form that could have appeared in the

Brezhnev era. More than thirty cuts had been made, precisely at the points where there had been specific criticism of individuals or institutions. In Kurgan, it seemed, there were two kinds of *glasnost'*, 'one for a narrow circle and another for everyone else'.[125] A more remarkable case occurred in the Pskov region, later the same year, when the whole print run of a local paper was destroyed because it had unwisely exposed the efforts that officials had made to create a false impression when delegates from a conference on public catering had visited the town. In classic 'Potemkin village' manner the foodshops were over-flowing, the bakery was producing only the best quality loaves, *kvas* and ice cream were being sold by street vendors and the shop fronts had all been freshly painted. After a splendid reception in the 'Forest' restaurant the visitors had called for the comments book and thanked the staff for their 'cultured service, hospitality and tastily prepared lunches and dinners'. The whole exercise had cost many thousands of rubles. Local officials, however, had decided that now the Party Congress was over the time for criticism had passed. They first of all held up the issue in which the deception had been reported, and then destroyed it and printed another issue in its place with a large photograph instead of the tactless story. *Pravda*, which managed to obtain a copy of both editions, described the whole affair as 'unprecedented'.[126]

Glasnost' also registered some signal failures. The failure to report fully and promptly on the nuclear explosion at Chernobyl' was an early example. The explosion, the world's worst nuclear disaster to date, took place early on the morning of Saturday, 26 April 1986. On the Monday morning Swedish monitoring stations reported heightened levels of radiation and traced the source to the Ukraine. The first official Soviet response was the Monday evening TV news, which included a brief announcement that an 'accident' had taken place at the Chernobyl' plant, that one of the reactors had been 'damaged', and that aid was being given to those who had been injured. A longer bulletin the following evening gave a fuller version of the events and reported for the first time that lives had been lost. The first press reports referred similarly to 'dangerous conditions' rather than radiation, and it took more than a fortnight for the story to reach the front page of *Pravda*. Gorbachev's first public response was a TV broadcast on 14 May, nearly three weeks after the explosion had occurred. The full facts, including the detailed report that was presented to the International Atomic Energy Agency, have still to be made available to the Russian and post-Soviet public.[127] The media response to the Nagorno-Karabakh conflict in 1988 was also incomplete and belated: the first reasonably full picture was given in an extended TV documentary on 26 April 1988, itself incorporating some of the amateur footage that had been seen for at least two months on TV screens in the West. The first stories on the Georgian demonstrations in April 1989, reporting what appeared to be an unprovoked attack on peaceful demonstrators, were blocked by newspaper editors. 'Who keeps deciding that every time there are sharp clashes, *glasnost'* is turned off like electricity?', demanded a group of newly-elected Soviet deputies.[128]

Glasnost' was accordingly, at best, in its early stages by the end of the Gorbachev era. Some taboos remained, although many fewer than had been the case under his predecessors. The central press was much more enterprising than its local counterparts, where officials preferred a 'pocket editor' to one inclined to challenge their decisions.[129] *Glasnost'* was very popular among intellectuals, less so among ordinary workers, and not at all to the taste of party and state officials at all levels, nearly all of whom complained of 'sensationalism' and 'irresponsibility' and some of whom pressed for journalists to be made legally answerable for the accuracy of their stories.[130] More fundamentally, an increasing flow of 'bad news', after the emphasis on successes of the recent past, tended to convey the impression that official policies were failing and that problems were getting worse, even if all that had happened was that difficulties that had always existed were being more honestly reported. Gorbachev personally enjoyed a close relationship with the press, and frequently drew editors and others into his confidence. The relationship, however, steadily deteriorated, and there were still no guarantees against political interference of a kind that would protect the media if they began to incur the displeasure of the authorities. Gorbachev himself accused the media of 'abuse of *glasnost'* for the purpose of incitement' at a Central Committee plenum in October 1990, and he called directly for the suspension of the law on the press, adopted the previous year, at a meeting of the Supreme Soviet in January 1991.[131]

The press law, published in draft in December 1989 and then adopted in final form in June 1990, established the right of all Soviet citizens to 'express opinions and beliefs [and] to seek, select, receive and disseminate information and ideas in any form'. Censorship was abolished, at least in principle, apart from a limited number of cases including the disclosure of state secrets and appeals for the violent overthrow of the state and social system. Any media monopoly was prohibited (again in principle), and individuals and political parties as well as state bodies were given the right to establish their own publications.[132] All means of communication, however, had to be registered with the authorities, and there were criminal penalties for the 'abuse' of freedom of speech or for the dissemination of information that did 'not correspond to reality'. State control over printing presses and stocks of paper meant in any case that many of the rights provided in the law were somewhat academic. The new law, nonetheless, did provide a formal basis for a wider range of opinion in the Soviet media than had ever existed previously: there was *Tema*, the 'voice of Soviet lesbians and homosexuals', and *Ekos*, the first Soviet Green journal,[133] as well as many others that catered for business, religious and other interests. About 8,000 newspapers and journals had been registered under the new law by the spring of 1991; of these, about half were entirely new. And there were over a thousand private publishing houses by the end of the same year, compared with only 300 that were still owned by the state.[134]

The press and electronic media, notwithstanding these developments, entered a new and much more difficult decade in the early 1990s. Paper costs had increased substantially, and subscription rates rose accordingly. Delivery became increasingly uncertain because of industrial action by the postal service, and sometimes the papers themselves failed to appear because of shortages of newsprint. There were hardly any taboos left that had not been broken, and hardly any forbidden masterpieces of Soviet or foreign origin that had not been published (the lack of new writing in the journals had already led to charges of 'necrophilia'). There was some public disenchantment with politics, and subscriptions to political journals fell more sharply than any others; but almost all newspapers and magazines were losing readers in the early 1990s. *Pravda*, for instance, was down to 1.4 million subscribers in 1992 compared with the ten million or more it had enjoyed in the late 1980s; in the end it was forced to cease publication for an extended period. *Izvestiya* fell to 3.8 million; and the trade union paper *Trud*, once the best seller, was down from eighteen million or more in the late 1980s to 4.3 million.[135] The eighteen most popular Soviet newspapers, by January 1992, had lost nearly 20 million subscribers in a single year; and the output of books had fallen to its lowest level since the war.[136] The chairman of the State Publishing Committee, reporting on these trends in the early 1990s, warned that even the best-established central newspapers could hardly survive in such conditions and that children's books and many other branches of publishing faced extinction.[137]

More ominously, there were signs that the central authorities and particularly Gorbachev, annoyed by a steady and sometimes exaggerated stream of criticism, were beginning to reassert the control they had earlier seemed willing to relinquish. The State Radio and Television Committee was reconstituted in late 1990 and given a new head, Leonid Kravchenko, formerly director of the official news agency TASS.[138] Almost immediately the popular television programme 'Vzglyad' (Viewpoint) was taken off the air because of an interview it was proposing to run with the former foreign minister Eduard Shevardnadze.[139] Central coverage of the Baltic events of early 1991 was blatantly biased, the miners who struck in sympathy with them were accused of financial links with the United States, and then three presenters of the late-night television news were suspended from their duties on Kravchenko's direct instructions.[140] Kravchenko, on his own admission 'the most unpopular man in the USSR after Saddam Hussein', was dismissed after the coup and replaced by the liberal editor of *Moscow News*, Yegor Yakovlev. The media law that was adopted by the Russian parliament in December 1991, however, at least in its initial version, made it illegal for journalists to withhold their sources of information and contained other provisions that were held to represent a 'real threat to the freedom of the press'; the Russian government, meanwhile, began to subsidise its own press organs and appointed a Yel'tsin loyalist, Vyacheslav Bragin, to head state television, which he was accused of running 'like a district party committee in the good old days'.[141] Developments of this kind were a clear sign that *glasnost'*, under Gorbachev and even under his successors, was still some distance from an unqualified 'freedom of the press'; its meaning in any instance depended upon the changing and precarious balance between authoritarian and reformist sentiment at every level of the society.

4   Reforming the planned economy

Historically considered, the record of Soviet economic management is one of impressive achievement. Russia in 1913 was a backward country by the standards of the time, 'the poorest of the civilised nations' in the words of a contemporary but still authoritative account.[1] There was a small but active manufacturing sector, and levels of production in some areas, such as oil and textiles, were fairly high by world standards. The overwhelming majority of the population, however, were engaged in agriculture, only a quarter of them were able to read and write, levels of infant mortality were high, and living standards were very low in comparison with those of other Western nations. National income per head in pre-revolutionary Russia is estimated to have been about 15 per cent of that in the USA and 22 per cent of that in the United Kingdom, and manufacturing output was similarly well below the levels that had been achieved elsewhere at the same date. The United Kingdom, for instance, produced about ten times as much coal and twice as much iron and steel in 1913 as did Russia, with its vastly greater population and natural resources. Labour productivity in industry, according to Soviet official sources, was only a tenth of the level achieved in the United States. And although living standards were improving, they appear to have been improved less rapidly than was the case elsewhere in Europe.[2]

Seventy years later, the contrast could hardly have been greater. The USSR was one of the world's economic superpowers, with a level of industrial production that was exceeded only by that of the United States (and perhaps Japan). In many areas – oil, gas, cast iron, steel and tractors, for example – Soviet levels of production were the highest in the world. The USSR pioneered the exploration of outer space, and led the world in the number of its scientific staff. The Soviet natural gas distribution system was one of the largest in the world, and Soviet oil wells were the deepest. The USSR maintained one of the world's largest merchant marines, and deployed one of the world's most formidable and technologically advanced concentrations of military might. According to official sources, Soviet national income increased 149 times between 1917 and 1987, and over 18 times between 1940 and 1987. The rate of growth between the late 1920s and 1950s was 6 per cent a year, nearly twice the level that had been achieved in late tsarist Russia. National income, 58 per cent of that of the USA in 1960, had increased to 67 per cent by 1980; industrial production had increased to more than 80 per cent, and agricultural production was about 85 per cent of the US total. Soviet industrial production, about 3 per cent of the global total in 1917, had increased to about 20 per cent by 1987; the USSR by this date produced more than the whole world had done in 1950. Other indicators of development, less dependent on methods of calculation, showed a broadly similar picture: in numbers of students, hospital beds, circulation of newsprint or consumption of calories per head of population the USSR was clearly one of the world's leading nations.[3]

These achievements, moreover, had taken place in historical circumstances that could hardly have been more difficult. As Gorbachev reminded interviewers from *Time* magazine in 1985, the old regime had left Soviet Russia with a 'grim legacy: a backward economy, strong vestiges of feudalism, millions of illiterate people'. To this had to be added two devastating world wars, which had ravaged a large part of the USSR and destroyed much that had been created by the Soviet people. There had also been 'irreparable losses', particularly of personnel: more than 20 million Soviet citizens had perished during World War II, and many millions more had been maimed and wounded (Gorbachev, too young himself to have fought in the war, saw the damage it had wrought during his railway trips from southern Russia to Moscow in the late 1940s). It was asserted by the West at the time, Gorbachev went on, that fifty to a hundred years would be needed to make good what had been destroyed by the Nazi invaders. By doing so in a much shorter period the Soviet people had achieved what had been thought to be impossible. The fact remained that, since the revolution, something like two decades had had to be devoted to wars and reconstruction, leaving barely fifty years for more constructive endeavours.[4] The arms race, after World War II, placed a further burden on the domestic economy: first the atomic and the hydrogen bomb and then a whole series of delivery systems had to be developed, preempting resources that could otherwise have been devoted to the improvement of living standards.

Yet if the economic achievements of the USSR over the longer term

Table 4.1. *Soviet economic growth, 1951–1985 (average annual rates of growth, official data, %)*

	Produced national income	Gross indust. prodn	Gross agric. prodn	Labour prod'y in ind.	Real incomes per head
1951–55	11.4	13.2	4.2	8.2	7.3
1956–60	9.2	10.4	6.0	6.5	5.7
1961–65	6.5	8.6	7.2	4.6	3.6
1966–70	7.8	8.5	3.9	5.8	5.9
1971–75	5.7	7.4	2.5	6.8	4.4
1976–80	4.3	4.4	1.7	4.4	3.4
1981–85	3.6	3.7	1.0	3.4	2.1

Source: Based upon *Narodnoe khozyaistvo SSSR 1922–1972 gg.* (Moscow: Statistika, 1972), p. 56, and *Narodnoe khozyaistvo SSSR za 70 let* (Moscow: Finansy i statistika, 1987), pp. 58–9.

were clear, particularly when war and other factors were taken into account, it was equally apparent by the late 1970s that there were deep-seated difficulties that still had to be resolved. The most striking indicator of these difficulties was the rate of economic growth, which fell consistently from the 1950s to the early 1980s with only a slight reversal in the late 1960s (see table 4.1). Levels of economic growth in the late 1970s and early 1980s, in fact, were the lowest ever recorded in Soviet peacetime history. In 1979, for instance, national income rose just 2.2 per cent, and living standards per head of population a bare 1.9 per cent. Some Western scholars were prepared to argue that Soviet economic growth, in real terms, had altogether ceased during these years.[5] The 11th Five Year Plan, covering the first half of the 1980s, was in turn substantially underfulfilled: the 26th Party Congress, in 1981, had approved directives providing that national income should increase 18–20 per cent by 1985, but the actual increase was 16.5 per cent, with both agricultural and industrial production increasing more slowly than had been forecast (the grain harvest, instead of increasing by a fifth, fell by nearly a quarter as compared with the previous five year period[6]). The targets for industrial output, in fact, had not been met in any of the three five-year plans between 1970 and 1985, whereas before 1970 only once (in the very first five-year plan) had it ever fallen short. And each extra unit of output was bought at the cost of an increasing consumption of energy, raw material and investment funds, unlike the experience in other industrialised nations.[7] If this was the legacy of eighteen years of Brezhnevism it was not a happy one.

Even these figures, moreover, tended to exaggerate the real level of Soviet achievement. In the first place, they normally left out the growth of population, about 0.9 per cent annually during these years. They also concealed a steady increase in over-reporting, amounting to 3 per cent of total production by the 1980s or up to a third in the case of sectors such as cotton or road transportation.[8] Nor did they allow adequately for price increases and changes in specification. According to a highly controversial reassessment of official figures published by the economists Vasilii Selyunin and Grigorii Khanin in early 1987, taking such factors into account Soviet national income from 1928 to 1985 increased six or seven times – a highly creditable performance, but far short of the ninetyfold increase claimed by official statistics. This much more modest increase had been bought, moreover, at the cost of an extravagant use of natural resources, and even then, according to Selyunin and Khanin, national income per head of population had actually fallen in the early 1980s.[9]

Much of Soviet industrial output was in any case hardly a contribution to real wealth. More tractors and combine harvesters were produced, for instance, than people were available to operate them, and the quality of farm machinery was such that more than a million people were engaged in repair workshops, more than were employed in the entire agricultural machinery industry.[10] More than twice as much steel was produced as in the USA, but there was a smaller output of finished products. More than twice as many pairs of footwear were produced as in the USA, but many more had to be imported as the quality and design were so poor.[11] Even on Soviet official figures some alarming developments were beginning to occur. Soviet national income, for instance, 67 per cent of that of the USA in 1980, had slipped to 64 per cent by 1988, and labour productivity in agriculture, already low, had fallen from 'about 20 per cent' of the US figure in the 1970s to 16 per cent in the late 1980s. The figures for grain production between 1981 and 1986 were in fact so bad that they were simply suppressed.[12]

Several factors were usually blamed for the Soviet economic slowdown, both in the West and in the USSR itself. One reason, certainly, was that the increase in the size of the industrial labour force was levelling off. Throughout the 1950s and 1960s large numbers of people were leaving the land to work in industry, allowing output to increase through additional labour inputs rather than through higher productivity. By the early 1980s this outflow had become very much less, leaving economic growth much more dependent upon an increase in the efficiency with which existing resources were used. The population had also been aging, meaning that, as in many Western countries, a relatively smaller labour force was required to support a relatively larger group of pensioners and other members of the non-working population. Some 6.7 per cent of the Soviet population was aged sixty or over in 1939; by 1987 the proportion had more than doubled, to 13.5 per cent, and by the year 2000, according to Soviet demographers, the proportion of the elderly could be expected to increase still further, to about 17–18 per cent.[13] All of this meant an increase in the 'dependency ratio', or the burden of social provision that had to be supported by a labour force which had not increased in numbers. In many of the older industrial areas, in fact, it reflected not simply a relative decline but an actual fall in the numbers of the population who were of working age, and the same was expected to be true of the country as a whole up to the end of the century.[14]

A further contribution to the economic slowdown came from the fact that raw materials which were conveniently located and of particularly high quality had gradually been used up, making it increasingly necessary to extract resources from more remote locations and poorer sources of supply. Additional resources of this kind were increasingly costly per unit of production as they required additional outlays upon transport and other costs, and additional expenditure on purification and refinement. In the 1960s, it has been calculated, one ruble of production in the extractive industries required two rubles of investment; by the early 1980s the same level of output required not two but seven rubles of investment. An example was the oilfield at Samotlar in western Siberia, which had provided two-thirds of the country's needs up to the 1980s but was steadily becoming exhausted. The most obvious alternative source of supply was Noyabr'skoe, 300 kilometres to the north; but it was far from roads and rivers and the oil was deeper and more difficult to extract.[15] More attention had also to be paid to quality and design, if goods were to find buyers in an increasingly demanding market, and to 'externalities' such as environmental conservation, which tended to raise unit costs still further. Very poor levels of agricultural production in the late 1970s and early 1980s, caused to a large extent by adverse weather conditions, made a further contribution to reduced levels of economic growth during these years.

It was nonetheless clear, whatever the circumstances involved, that a steadily falling rate of economic growth could not be sustained much further without serious damage to the international standing of the

USSR and to the 'social contract' between the regime and the population, by which, at least notionally, a relative lack of civil liberties was
traded for a tolerable and assured standard of living.[16] Even the
political stability of the USSR could not be taken for granted, Gorbachev (and two other speakers) warned the 27th Party Congress in 1986,
if popular expectations of this kind continued to be disappointed.[17]
Economic growth had traditionally been the central concern of Soviet
leaders, and it is probably fair to say that the improvement of economic
performance and of rates of growth in particular was both the highest
priority of the Gorbachev leadership and the most difficult of all the
tasks it confronted. As Gorbachev put it in a speech in December 1984,
only a highly-developed economy would allow the USSR to enter the
twenty-first century as a great and flourishing power; the fate of
socialism as a whole, not just of the USSR itself, depended upon the
success of their efforts. Other writers argued, in still more apocalyptic
terms, that unless the USSR achieved more efficient forms of economic
management it would 'cease to be a great power' and would enter the
new century as a 'backward, stagnating state and an example to the
rest of the world how not to conduct its economic life' (in the words of
Leonid Abalkin and Nikolai Shmelev respectively).[18]

Gorbachev and economic reform

The broad framework of economic reform was set out in Gorbachev's
address to the 27th Party Congress in 1986. The top priority, in his
view, was to overcome the factors that had been holding back the
country's socio-economic development as quickly as possible and to
resume the growth of earlier decades.[19] Not only was it necessary to
accelerate the rate of economic growth: it must be a new quality of
growth, based upon scientific and technical progress, structural
change and new forms of management and labour incentives. There
had been 'impressive successes' over the previous quarter of a century,
Gorbachev told the Congress; national income and living standards
had risen rapidly, and there had been welcome advances in science,
medicine and culture. And yet difficulties had built up during the
1970s, with rates of growth declining visibly and Five Year Plan targets
not being met. Some of the factors involved were outside their control.
The main problem, however, was that they had 'failed to produce a
timely political assessment of the changed economic situation' and of
the need for a shift from extensive growth, based on additional inputs
of labour and resources, to intensive growth, based on higher levels of

technology and productivity. A change of this kind was not just desirable; there was 'no other way'.[20]

In the light of these requirements, the revised Party Programme and the Guidelines for the new 12th Five Year Plan set out as their central objective the doubling of national income by the year 2000. This in turn necessitated a thorough modernisation of the economy on the basis of the most advanced science and technology, with particular priority being given to the machine-building and electronics industries, to energy-saving technologies and improved methods of construction. In agriculture the chief priority would be to satisfy the country's food requirements on the basis of a greater degree of autonomy for collective and state farms and greater incentives. The management of the economy as a whole was to be decentralised, with Gosplan (the USSR State Planning Committee) concentrating its efforts on long-term objectives and with enterprises guided to a much greater extent by their performance in the market place. The financial system would be reorganised; prices would be more 'flexible'; and cooperatives of all kinds would be encouraged to extend the scale of their operations. The 'human factor' was also emphasised, including an extension of the right of workers to elect their own management.[21]

Most of these objectives were embodied in the 12th Five-Year Plan, covering the period 1986–90, which the Party Congress adopted in the form of Basic Directives and which was passed into law by the USSR Supreme Soviet later in the year. In the form in which the Supreme Soviet adopted it, Soviet national income was to increase 22.1 per cent by 1990: this was a rate of 4.1 per cent per annum, well above the 3.1 per cent that had been achieved during the first half of the decade. Industrial production was to increase by 4.6 per cent, gross agricultural production by 2.7 per cent, labour productivity by 4.2 per cent and real incomes per head of population by 2.7 per cent over the same period, in each case per annum. The draft version, it was reported, had been sent back three times by the Politburo for further work, in particular to raise the growth targets that had originally been proposed.[22] The Directives covered the rather longer period to the year 2000, in the course of which national income was to increase 'almost twofold'. Industrial productivity was to increase by more than this; labour productivity was to increase by 2.3–2.5 times; real incomes were to increase by 1.6–1.8 times; social benefits were to increase by about twofold; retail trade was to increase by about 1.8 times; and paid services were to increase by between 2.1 and 2.3 times over the whole period.[23]

More detailed guidelines for economic reform were approved by a Central Committee meeting in June 1987, at which Gorbachev delivered the key address. There had been outstanding successes in the years after the revolution, Gorbachev suggested, but the centralised and detailed form of economic management that had been established at that time had now outlived its usefulness. Attempts had been made to reform it from the 1950s onwards, but they had all proved ineffective. Now, in the 1980s, the Soviet economy was in not just a difficult but a 'pre-crisis' situation. The rate of economic growth had dropped to a level which 'virtually signified the onset of economic stagnation'. Resources were being wastefully used, and technological levels lagged increasingly behind those of the rest of the developed world. Budget deficits were being covered by the sale of oil and other raw materials on world markets and by tax returns from the sale of alcohol, which had more than doubled over the previous fifteen years. Money belonging to enterprises and organisations had been incorporated into state revenues without any proper justification, which had made it more difficult for them to function normally. Spending on wages had systematically exceeded plan targets, while increases in output and productivity had been less than predicted. This meant that a proportion of the wages bill was not covered by goods and services. Shortages, inevitably, had become worse: indeed there was a shortage of 'everything', from metal and cement to consumer goods and manpower. Nothing less than a 'radical reform' in the whole system of economic management was needed to reverse these alarming trends.[24]

In agriculture, Gorbachev suggested, greater use should be made of the 'collective' or 'family contract', by which a small group of workers obtained the use of an area of land for a fixed price and received in return the right to sell their surplus produce for whatever it would fetch at collective farm markets. There should be much more local self-sufficiency: why, for instance, was 25–50 per cent of the confectionery consumed in four Central Asian republics brought from elsewhere when these republics were themselves well supplied with the necessary raw materials? And why did Kazakhstan produce only 30 per cent of the canned fruit and vegetables that it consumed?[25] Abandoned land should be put to good use; and storage and processing facilities must be improved (up to 30 per cent of agricultural raw materials were currently being lost in this way). More generally, the management of agriculture should be shifted away from the central or local authorities and into the hands of the workers themselves on a long-term contract basis. There were still immense opportunities in agriculture if the resources of large publicly-owned farms were combined in this way with the collective and family contract method.[26]

Comparable changes were needed in housing and construction, where many enterprises and teams were operating at half capacity or less. Still more important, the production of consumer goods should be given a higher priority. Many ministries still regarded them as a secondary responsibility, or even as a burden, and there were shortages, because of problems of distribution, even of goods that were produced in sufficient quantity. Services should also receive much more attention. Was it really normal, he asked, when having housing and household appliances repaired or an item of footwear or clothing made up became a 'big problem'? Gorbachev quoted an official estimate which suggested that the 'shadow economy' amounted to at least 1.5 billion rubles a year; this arose because the individuals concerned were unable to obtain the services they needed from the state sector. Local party and state bodies should give these issues their immediate attention; some of them were lagging behind the 'dynamic processes now developing in the society'. Nor could the central authorities escape their own responsibilities, including many ministers who were individually named.[27]

Above all, an attempt must be made to establish an 'integrated, efficient and flexible system of economic management', allowing a greater role for cooperative and individual enterprise. Rewards should be tied much more closely to the work that people did, and there should be incentives to work harder and better. Equality did not mean egalitarianism, and he deplored the persistence of 'levelling' (*uravnilovka*) in matters of this kind. There would also be major changes in price formation and public finance, involving a reduction in budgetary subsidies and the ending of the 'illusion of cheapness and inexhaustibility of natural resources'. There should be more competition between the different sections of the economy: between state and cooperative enterprises, and between scientific as well as industrial organisations. More generally, there should be a move from administrative or 'command' forms of management to indirect or 'economic' controls based upon financial and other regulators. Enterprises should be more autonomous, with more responsibility for their own production and finances, leaving Gosplan and other bodies with the responsibility for setting out the broad direction of economic development, but not for detailed intervention in the operation of enterprises themselves.

Plans would continue to be produced, but they would be concerned with long-term objectives and major state programmes, not with the day-to-day functioning of ministries and enterprises. These would in future be based to a much greater extent upon state commercial orders (which would be allocated by the central planners) and upon the orders of other enterprises. Equipment and raw materials would similarly be obtained to a much greater extent through wholesale trade between enterprises, rather than from the central authorities. In extreme cases, if an enterprise failed to pay its way it should be liquidated (about 15 per cent of Soviet enterprises were estimated to fall into this category, and the first largely symbolic 'bankruptcies' had already occurred[28]). Measures of this kind should deepen the Soviet Union's participation in the international division of labour, including capitalist as well as other socialist states, and involving joint ventures and other forms of cooperation. These principles, 'the most thoroughgoing and sweeping reform of its kind over the years of building socialism',[29] were reflected in a set of 'Guidelines for the Radical Restructuring of Economic Management', adopted by the plenum, and were carried further in a Law on the State Enterprise, which the Supreme Soviet adopted shortly afterwards.[30]

In later speeches Gorbachev added further elements to his critique of the 'stagnation' years, emphasising the gravity of the problems by which the economy was confronted and at the same time pointing up the need for 'radical reform'. At the February 1988 Central Committee plenum, in particular, he extended his attack on 'levelling', or the practice of paying people for little more than turning up at their place of work rather than for the actual results of their efforts. This was a widely accepted way of proceeding, but had a 'ruinous impact not only on the economy, but also on people's morality and on their entire way of thinking and acting'. Gorbachev added that the economic situation that had developed in the early 1980s was still worse than he had earlier suggested. Not simply were economic growth rates low and declining: they were sustained by unhealthy and short-term factors, in particular the sale of oil on the world market at the high prices that then obtained, and by a 'totally unjustified increase' in the sale of strong drink. If these two elements were removed the economic growth that had been reported over the previous twenty years dropped to zero, and in the early 1980s there had been an actual decline. Summing up, Gorbachev argued that both long-term and short-term tasks had to be accomplished at the same time: not only 'radical economic reform', but also a simultaneous improvement in the current economic situation and in popular living standards, especially food, housing, consumer goods and services.[31]

The central task of his general secretaryship was to deal with these two related objectives.

The strategy of economic reform

The centrepiece of the Gorbachev economic reform strategy was the Law on the State Enterprise (Association), which was published in draft in February 1987 and adopted in its final form the following June. It came into effect on 1 January 1988.[32] The main aim of the Law, as explained by Gorbachev, was to bring 'real economic independence' to the enterprise on the basis of profit-and-loss accounting, freeing it from the dictates of ministries and higher-level economic bodies. This was not the 'end of central planning', as some Western press reports prematurely concluded, but it was certainly intended to represent a significant change in the nature of this kind of guidance, with the plan being drawn up primarily by the enterprise itself upon the basis of 'control figures' issued by the central authorities (which specified the desired level of production and other general objectives) and 'economic normatives', which covered the contributions that were due to the state budget for resources such as land, labour and capital as well as wage-incentive programmes and investment in child-care, recreational and housing facilities. Within this framework the enterprise was to draw up its own plan, based upon 'state orders' (*goszakazy*) placed with it by the central authorities together with commercial orders placed with it by other enterprises and organisations. The income from these activities, in line with the principle of 'self-financing', was intended to cover the costs that were incurred, including wages, scientific-technical innovation, the expansion of production and social and cultural benefits for the workforce.

The new law sought at the same time to bring the 'human factor' into play by democratising the organisation of the workplace, breaking with the Stalinist tradition by which workers were no more than 'little cogs' (*vintiki*) in the enterprise in which they worked. Workers were to elect their managers at all levels, from the director down to workshop head, 'as a rule' on a competitive basis. The factory director, who represented the interests of the state as well as those of the workforce, was to be elected by a general meeting for five years at a time, although his appointment was subject to approval at higher levels and the director himself remained individually responsible for enterprise performance. The law also established a Council of the Labour Collective, elected by the workforce for two or three years at a time, which was responsible for convening factory meetings at least twice a year and for ensuring that the decisions of such meetings were implemented (the trade union committee, a little awkwardly, also retained its place on the shop floor and in management). The aim of these and other changes was to 'enhance the people's labour activity, bring into play hitherto unused resources, raise efficiency and so achieve higher rates of real growth with high quality production'.[33] Enterprises and associations responsible for two-thirds of industrial output were to transfer to these new conditions by January 1988; the remainder of Soviet industry was to follow a year later. There would be a related reform of planning, pricing, finance and credit, and material and technical supply, all of which was to be completed before the introduction of the 13th Five Year Plan in 1991.[34]

The scope for rapid improvement – and the alleviation of the shortages of most immediate concern to ordinary citizens – was probably greater in agriculture than in industry, and this became the object of a wide-ranging package of reforms approved by a Central Committee plenum in March 1989. The reality, Gorbachev explained in his opening address, was that they were still experiencing shortages of all kinds of farming produce. Large quantities of grain, meat, fruit, vegetables, sugar and other staples had to be purchased abroad. The USSR still lagged behind other developed countries in its labour efficiency, yields and livestock productivity, as well as in the diversity and quality of its foodstuffs, and the gap was widening rather than narrowing. Food shortages gave rise to serious social tensions and actual discontent, not merely criticism. Millions of hectares of land had been lost through industrial construction or mismanagement, and the fertility of the land that remained had been falling in most regions. At least 20 per cent of all agricultural produce was lost because of inefficiencies of various kinds, and in the case of some products the losses were as high as 40 per cent. Problems of this kind had long been recognised and the agricultural sector had received massive injections of machinery, fertiliser and other resources. Up to the present, however, no real solution to the problem had been found, despite the country's enormous agricultural potential.

Part of the problem was historical – the premature abandonment of the more balanced approach of the early 1920s, the 'human tragedy' of the 1930s with its famine and victimisation of millions of peasants, and the adoption of a coercive, voluntarist approach to agricultural management (this was not to deny the necessity for socialist change in the countryside at that time, nor the inherent potential of the collective farm system more generally). The war had dealt a further heavy blow to Soviet agriculture, and even afterwards the countryside had been regarded as a resource to be exploited rather than an asset to be husbanded. Taxation levels had been exorbitant, and peasants had been denied basic civil rights such as a pension, a passport and the right to leave the village if they wished to do so. There had been some improvements in the 1950s, but central control remained excessive and there had been occasional campaigns against, for example, individual peasant smallholdings (the 'private plot', which has always supplied a large proportion of Soviet foodstuffs). The reform programme adopted in 1965 had not been carried out consistently, leaving both state and collective farms in overall deficit by the end of the 1970s, and even the much-vaunted 'food programme' of 1982 had been an unsatisfactory compromise. Clearly, no programme which failed to take account of farmers' real needs and interests, and which was based on their direct participation, was likely to be successful.

What could be done? Agricultural investment, in machines, buildings, roads and fertiliser, was certainly important, but recent experience had shown that efforts of this kind were not enough. The kind of change they all desired would not in fact occur without a change in rural economic relations, giving farmers more opportunity to display independence and initiative, and an improvement in rural social conditions. There should be a diversity of forms of economic management – collective and state farms, agricultural firms and integrated complexes, farmers' households and smallholdings, agricultural facilities belonging to industrial and other enterprises, and so forth. Family-run farms and the collective farmers' private plots should be developed more fully, without the prejudice that these were 'lower' forms of economic activity. Above all, leaseholding, by which groups of farmers received areas of land, livestock, buildings or other resources on a contract basis with the right to sell any surplus, should be encouraged, even in farms that were already highly efficient, as this was one of the main ways by which rural economic relations could be restructured. The collective and state farm system should not, as some had advocated, be entirely replaced by leaseholding. State and collective farms, however, should become collectives of leaseholders, all of whom would have to pay their way on a profit-and-loss basis. They would thereby be encouraged to produce more and better farm products at lower cost, and the state would be able to purchase the food supplies it needed in sufficient quantities.

No purely economic changes, however, would be sufficient without the improvement of rural social conditions, which often lagged far behind those in the towns. Rural housing, for instance, had only a half to a fifth of the level of amenities that obtained in urban areas. Death rates were 20 per cent higher, and infant mortality rates 50 per cent higher than in the towns. Industrial development, even food processing, was almost always based in the towns; small dairy factories, brickworks and bakeries had all but disappeared from the rural scene, and schools, medical facilities and shops had been prematurely closed. Employment opportunities had naturally contracted, and there was a substantial population outflow which had exceeded the natural increase in rural population for many years. For the future there must be a doubling of rural housing construction, and much more general access to heating, gas, water and electricity supply systems. A road-building programme would aim to connect all the main rural farmsteads with local administrative centres; schools, hospitals, shopping and other facilities would be expanded, and efforts would be made to reduce seasonal unemployment by the development of handicrafts and by opening branches of industrial enterprises, especially those producing consumer goods. Areas that had found it particularly difficult to attract a settled population would be assisted by housing incentives and various state grants. All of this, in Gorbachev's view, represented a 'drastic revision of the CPSU's agrarian policy', to be carried forward by party and state authorities in the very different local conditions in which they operated, and intended to ensure that farmers were henceforward 'masters of the land they tilled'.[35]

Leaseholding was essentially a development of the 'normless links', 'family contract' and other experiments in small-scale, profit-oriented agricultural management that had been encouraged since at least the 1970s.[36] Other reforms in agriculture included the formation of a massive superministry, Gosagroprom (the State Agro-Industrial Committee), in late 1985, which brought together five existing ministries and two state committees. Its chairman, Vsevolod Murakhovsky (a Gorbachev associate), became a first deputy prime minister. Efforts were also made to encourage vertical integration (the linking of farms with storage, distribution and processing enterprises), a policy favoured by Brezhnev; and there were financial incentives, from 1986 onwards, for production above plan targets, which were to remain stable for a five-year period. Despite these and other changes, many difficulties remained. Nearly 20,000 collective and state farms (42 per cent of the total), in the late 1980s, were operating at a loss or making a negligible profit; in some 3,000 cases the earnings involved were not enough even to cover the cost of labour, and in these and other cases there could be no immediate prospect of a transition to self-financing.[37] There was a serious shortage of minor agricultural equipment, as distinct from the massive combines and tractors that were required for state and collective farms, and political direction at the local level proved very difficult to reduce. The results achieved by decollectivisation in other communist-ruled countries such as China nonetheless suggested that efforts to supplement or even replace state and collective farms with much smaller-scale, profit-oriented production units were likely to continue (the exoneration of Ivan Khudenko, imprisoned in 1973 for his entrepreneurial management of a state farm but now described as a 'talented pioneer', was symbolic of this change of policy[38]).

What also appeared likely to continue was a policy of encouraging a wide variety of forms of non-state economic activity, on both an individual and a group basis. Under legislation which was approved in November 1986 and which came into force in May 1987, a wide variety of forms of private economic activity was specifically legalised. The main aims, as set out by the chairman of the State Committee on Labour and Social Questions, Ivan Gladky, were that such activities should not detract from production in the state sector, and that the income obtained should correspond to the work that had been performed and to the requirements of social justice. Those who were eligible to engage in activities of this kind included housewives, students, invalids and ordinary employees on their days off; the kinds of work they could undertake included car repairs, translation and coaching, photography, typing, souvenirs and handicrafts, and private car rental. This was not, Gladky insisted, in any sense a 'return to any form of private enterprise, as some bourgeois commentators had suggested'; the socialist sector would remain dominant, no one would be allowed to employ anyone outside their immediate family, and all activities of this kind would be closely regulated by local soviets.[39] Deputies who commented on the legislation even claimed to find that it contained 'lofty humanistic purposes', in particular by encouraging non-members of the workforce to make a useful contribution to society.[40] It was nonetheless a clear recognition that the state sector by itself had failed to satisfy popular requirements in terms of a wide range of goods and services.

A further, potentially more significant change was the adoption in May 1988 of a new Law on Cooperatives which has widely been seen as the most radical single economic measure to have been introduced in the first years of the Gorbachev leadership.[41] As Prime Minister Ryzhkov pointed out in proposing the new law, large state-run enterprises had found it difficult to respond to changing consumer preferences, and what was needed was the promotion of small and medium-sized production units with flexible structures geared directly to the market. The new cooperatives were specifically encouraged to draw those engaged in individual economic activities into their operations; they were also intended to absorb workers who had been required to leave other employment because of the introduction of new technology or other changes.[42] The cooperatives were, in principle, exempted from obligatory state plans and state orders, although they were required at least to inform the relevant authorities of their intentions. Cooperatives could fix their own prices, except when producing for state orders or using state-supplied materials (in practice, a very considerable limitation); they were entitled to conduct foreign trade transactions and keep a significant part of the hard currency that they earned, and they could form joint ventures with foreign companies. Cooperative members were to pay taxes on their activities; the steeply graduated rates originally proposed (up to 90 per cent) were blocked by the Supreme Soviet and the matter was eventually left to the discretion of republican authorities.[43] Here as elsewhere there was clearly a tension between reformers, who wished the cooperatives to develop as rapidly as possible, and conservatives, who were more concerned to prevent excessive incomes and an implied threat to the state sector.[44]

By January 1991 there were 245,300 cooperatives of various kinds in operation in the USSR, more than twice as many as a year previously. There were relatively few in the Central Asian republics, despite their labour surpluses, and most of all in the Baltic republics, where the volume of trade per head of population was more than ten times greater. Most cooperatives were small (they had an average of twenty-five employees), but they employed a total workforce of over 6 million (most of them on a full-time basis) and they paid considerably higher wages than the national average.[45] Most cooperatives were involved in domestic services of various kinds (38 per cent); then came catering cooperatives (22 per cent); and then consumer goods cooperatives (21 per cent of the total). There were housing cooperatives, and information cooperatives, and even a cooperative bank.[46] One of the earliest and best-known cooperative institutions was the restaurant that opened in Moscow at No. 36 Kropotkin Street, although its high charges proved controversial (it was visited on one occasion by a student who asked for a portion of sucking pig, and was told it would cost 60 rubles; he returned the next day with a placard demanding 'Down with NEP!'[47]). The cooperative movement, despite these and other difficulties, was expanding rapidly in the late 1980s and early 1990s, and the experience of other communist-ruled countries suggested that it too was likely to expand still further in the future (consumer cooperatives accounted for a third or more of retail trade in many East European countries in the late 1980s, and official spokesmen suggested it could account for 10–12 per cent of Soviet national income by the mid-1990s[48]).

The main elements of the economic reform strategy were completed by a series of changes in the organisation of Soviet foreign trade, designed to encourage more direct links at the level of enterprises and organisations and to deepen Soviet participation in the international division of labour. Prime Minister Ryzhkov, in his address to the 27th Party Congress, indicated that a foreign trade reform was in preparation and that its main aim would be to involve branch ministries and enterprises to a greater extent in trading relations with other countries. Soviet foreign trade, it was hoped, would consist to a greater extent than in the past of finished goods rather than energy and raw materials, and Soviet manufacturers would be forced to raise their level of technical competence and quality in order to compete successfully on the international market.[49] The basic changes were included in a decree on the management of foreign economic relations of August 1986, which became effective on 1 January 1987.[50] Under the decree the Ministry of Foreign Trade lost its monopoly over foreign trade, with the right to conduct relations of this kind being extended to more than twenty branch ministries and seventy large associations. The Ministry, moreover, was placed under the control of a new superministerial body, the State Foreign Economic Commission, headed by a deputy prime minister; later, in January 1988, both the Ministry and the Commission were merged into a new organisation, the Ministry for Foreign Economic Relations. A presidential decree of October 1990, 'On foreign investment in the USSR', meanwhile authorised full foreign ownership of enterprises and guaranteed such enterprises the same legal protection that was extended to their Soviet counterparts.[51]

By January 1990 1,274 joint enterprises had been officially registered, nearly seven times as many as a year before. Only 307, however, had actually begun to operate, and joint enterprises as a whole imported more than three times the value of their exports. Foreign trade still remained at a relatively low level (about 6 per cent of national income, compared with 20 per cent or more in most developed capitalist countries), and imports and exports actually fell in current prices between 1985 and 1989.[52] In practice the effect of the reform was to strengthen the branch ministries rather than the enterprises that were subordinate to them, and in some cases republican or local authorities also attempted to secure the trading rights that had supposedly been given directly to enterprises. The '"monopoly" of the Ministry of Foreign Trade', as one commentator put it, had been replaced by the '"monopolies" of a number of ministries invested with powers to conduct external economic activities'.[53] In parallel with these changes, the Basic Directives that were adopted by the Central Committee in June 1987 indicated that the ruble should become a convertible currency, first of all within the Comecon area, although this would clearly involve a restructuring of domestic prices and devaluation. The USSR joined the raw materials fund established under the auspices of UNCTAD in 1987, and in 1990 assumed observer status at GATT (the General Agreement on Tariffs and Trade) with a view to ultimate full membership. Despite these and other changes, Soviet commentators accepted that 'only the first steps' had been taken towards a closer association between the domestic and foreign markets by the end of the decade.[54]

Economic reform: from policies to practice

If the central objective of the Gorbachev reform strategy was to recover the economy's growth dynamic, it was clear that this had fallen far short of success in its early years. The Five Year Plan adopted in 1986 called for a 4.2 per cent annual rate of growth in produced national income, as compared with the rate of 3.6 per cent achieved in the first half of the decade; the Guidelines adopted by the 27th Party Congress stipulated a still higher rate of growth in the 1990s, 5 per cent annually, in order to double national income by the year 2000.[55] The rates of growth recorded between 1986 and 1989 in fact averaged a modest 3.7 per cent, which was exactly the same as the figures reported in the late Brezhnev, Andropov and Chernenko years.[56] The failure in Soviet agriculture was particularly striking, and over the three years up to 1988 more than 30 billion rubles had to be spent on foreign grain purchases in order to make good domestic shortfalls.[57] Leonid Abalkin, director of the Institute of Economics of the Academy of Sciences (and later a government minister), addressing the 19th Party Conference in

1988, had to point out that economic growth over the two previous years had been below the rate achieved in the 'stagnation' years of the previous Five Year Plan; and economy in the use of resources, a key indicator of effectiveness, had been five times worse. Capital accumulation had grown faster than consumption, exactly the opposite of what the 27th Party Congress in 1986 had determined; the situation in the consumer market had deteriorated; and Soviet technological backwardness had assumed an increasingly threatening character.[58]

The 1988 plan results, published in the central press in January 1989, showed a slight improvement: produced national income rose by 4.4 per cent, and gross national product by 5 per cent (neither figure corresponded precisely to Western definitions and they tended somewhat to over-report Soviet successes). The figure for national income, however impressive, still left economic growth for the three years up to 1988 below the Five Year Plan target (11.1 as against a planned 12.8 per cent increase). Industrial output was significantly below the target for 1988, and grain production, at 195 million tonnes, was 38 million tonnes short of the plan target (it was announced that 36 million tonnes had had to be bought abroad to repair the deficiency). More generally, state expenditure was still increasing faster than revenue, and wages were going up faster than the quantity of goods that were available for purchase.[59] The 1989 results, reported in the central press in January 1990, showed an increase of 3 per cent in gross national product, but there were falls in housing, transportation, oil and coal, and the output of foodstuffs and consumer goods increased by less than had been planned. The economic situation remained a 'difficult' one, the State Statistics Committee acknowledged, particularly in terms of the consumer market.[60]

Reform-minded economists found still more to concern them in the plan results of the late 1980s. As Grigorii Khanin, for instance, pointed out, some figures, previously very representative of the performance of the economy as a whole, had simply disappeared from the 1988 returns: in particular electric motors, but also turbines, industrial robots, harvesters, ferro-concrete parts, window glass, synthetic resin and plastics. This made it 'almost impossible to assess major industries'. Increases elsewhere, such as 8.5 per cent in the value of retail trade, were largely accounted for by higher prices; and some forms of output, such as children's goods, had actually fallen. By Khanin's own calculations the growth of national income had been not 4.4 but probably 0.3 per cent in 1988, less than the rate of population growth.

Table 4.2. *Soviet economic growth, 1986–1991 (official data, %)*

	1986–90	1986	1987	1988	1989	1990	1991
	average (plan)						
National income produced	4.2	2.3	1.6	4.4	2.4	−4.0	−15.0
Industrial output	4.6	4.4	3.8	3.9	1.7	−1.2	− 7.8
Agricultural output	2.7	5.3	−0.6	1.7	1.3	−2.3	− 7.0

Sources: Narodnoe khozyaistvo SSSR v 1989 g. (Moscow: Finansy i statistika, 1990), pp. 8–9; *Ekonomika i zhizn'*, 1991, no. 5, p. 9, and 1992, no. 6, pp. 13–16.

For Khanin, 'All the major indices of efficiency [indicated] that the economy was in decline in 1988'; for another commentator, Alexander Zaichenko, the following year saw a 'virtual decline' in Soviet national income, with industrial production, in particular, recording its lowest level of increase since World War II.[61] In 1990 and 1991 industrial production actually fell (see pp. 130–1), consumption and living standards fell still more sharply, and the economy moved into an open and deepening recession.

Many of the difficulties the economy had experienced, admittedly, were the result of exogenous factors of various kinds. One of these was a change in the terms of trade, particularly a fall in the value of Soviet energy exports (in 1988 Soviet exports increased 4 per cent by volume but fell 1.9 per cent by value, while imports rose only 1 per cent but cost 6.5 cent more than in the previous year;[62] this contributed to a doubling of the Soviet foreign debt between 1985 and 1988[63]). Further heavy losses were incurred by a series of natural disasters of various kinds, of which the most important were the Chernobyl' nuclear explosion of April 1986 and the Armenian earthquake of December 1988. Despite early and alarmist reports, just thirty-three deaths, not all of them from radiation, occurred in the immediate aftermath of the Chernobyl' explosion. Several thousand more, however, were likely to die as a result of the disaster over the years that followed, and a continuous programme of monitoring had to be mounted which was expected to extend into the next century. The economic costs were also extremely high, including the cost of removing the affected topsoil, forgone production from the disaster area, the construction of new housing and other relief measures. Direct losses were estimated by the Soviet finance minister in September 1986 to be at least two billion rubles; later, more inclusive estimates put the total at eight billion rubles, half from direct losses and half from the reduced output of the affected areas.[64] The Armenian earthquake in December 1988 led to nearly 25,000 deaths and to a further 8,500 million rubles' worth of damage.[65]

Nor could the Gorbachev reforms be blamed for a deterioration in economic performance, in many other respects, because like many of their predecessors they remained very largely on paper (was it not time, asked a letter in *Pravda*, for a 'law on laws' which would ensure that government decisions were actually implemented?[66]). Perhaps the most conspicuous example of this kind was the state orders that were supposed to replace ministerial directives under the Law on the State Enterprise. It soon became apparent that the new law was largely a dead letter: ministries continued to issue directives but simply renamed them *goszakazy* (state orders), and these directives in turn continued to account for the overwhelming share of output. Enterprises, for their part, often sought to obtain a high level of state orders so that their sources of supply could be assured. As a result, *val* or gross output, rather than market-based success indicators, continued to determine the pattern of production in much the same way as it had done ever since the command economy had been established. In the absence of a far-reaching reform of retail and wholesale prices and in conditions of shortage and monopoly (about 30–40 per cent of industrial output consisted of products for which there was a single manufacturer[67]), the profitability of enterprises was in any case a poor guide to their efficiency.

More generally, there were tensions between the introduction of structural reforms of this kind while at the same time attempting to accelerate the performance of the economy. Abalkin put this point to the Party Conference: there could be no increase in growth while simultaneously changing the structure of the economy – it was 'either quantity, or quality'. The 12th Five Year Plan had unfortunately preferred the former.[68] Vasilii Selyunin argued similarly that restructuring must take priority over rates of growth, which in any case reflected a traditional orientation towards producer rather than consumer goods. A low rate of growth, even a negative one, was acceptable if it was accompanied by a shift in the reverse direction.[69] Shlemev went so far as to propose the abandonment of the existing Five Year Plan on the grounds that a market balance, higher technical levels and product quality were more important than economic growth in itself.[70] Gorbachev himself accepted that there were difficulties in introducing a package of economic reform 'on the march', in the middle of a Five Year Plan that had been conceived on a different basis, and agreed that rates of growth were not important for their own sake but only to the extent to which they represented the 'actual satisfaction of people's needs'. What was the point of increased production of raw materials and energy, he asked, if it was swallowed up by wasteful usage? And who needed a greater output of agricultural machinery if it was not being bought because of its low efficiency? This was just 'production for the sake of production', 'the plan for the sake of the plan'.[71] For the future at least, radical economists insisted, there must be an end to the 'fetishisation' of economic growth and a shift towards 'new quality' rather than 'old tempos'.[72]

Shortcomings of this kind were apparent even before the state enterprise law had been adopted and they were still clearer after it had come into legal effect. As early as January 1987 *Pravda* was complaining editorially that a number of enterprises were failing to respond 'responsibly' to the new law.[73] Abalkin pointed out in an interview just two months later that only one of the articles in the law which dealt with the state order had actually been implemented: the one that made them compulsory. For the rest, state orders applied to almost the whole of enterprises' production programmes, they were not awarded on a competitive basis, and there was no real interdependence of the contracting parties. In fact, the old centralised administrative methods still held force, despite the new nomenclature that was employed.[74] Many other elements of the new law remained formal: the election of enterprise management, for instance, was heavily influenced (and had anyway to be approved by) the local party and state authorities, and there was often a tendency to vote for easy-going candidates who aimed for lower targets and higher prices rather than for the energetic and purposive executives the law was presumably intended to encourage.[75] Workers, for their part, wrote to *Pravda* asking why the new law had made so little difference to day-to-day economic realities; they seemed to be bound by countless further 'instructions' which effectively frustrated the operation of the new system.[76]

Nor was this the only instance in which the reform package had little real effect. A decision made by the Party Congress in 1986 to reduce the volume of capital construction, for instance, was effectively ignored and the volume of construction in the event increased considerably. Another decision, Gorbachev reported, had been to increase the output of single-use syringes for medical purposes. Not simply was the decision not carried out; the Ministry of Medical Equipment imported 30 million syringes without needles, failed to make arrangements for the production of the needles in the USSR itself, and then sent the syringes by themselves to clinics around the country.[77] Some of the other changes, whatever their potential in the longer term, were very slow to establish themselves. Direct trading links between Soviet and foreign firms, for instance, accounted for no more than 1 per cent of foreign trade turnover in 1988, and the legislation on individual economic activity, even when it was fully implemented, was expected to contribute no more than 0.5 per cent of Soviet national income.[78] Another respect in which the reforms made little difference in practice was the reduction of administrative staff. Gorbachev had frequently criticised the 'bloated administrative apparatus' which accounted for one in seven of the labour force and cost 40 billion rubles to maintain.[79] Attempts to reduce the staffing of central ministries, however, had little effect: *Pravda* discovered, in a careful investigation, that the administrative apparatus had actually increased in number by 122,000 between 1985 and 1988, despite assurances to the contrary.[80] Very few of the staff that were dismissed had moved into blue-collar professions, and in any case where were they expected to go, in their forties or fifties, with families and no obvious qualifications for other careers? Who had anyway established such a ministerial structure in the first place?[81]

A further decision which turned out to be not simply ineffective but, in the event, probably counterproductive was the campaign against alcohol abuse. Levels of alcohol consumption, despite appearances, were in fact rather lower in the USSR than in some of the major wine producing countries like Italy and France. The consumption of strong drink (over 40 per cent proof), however, was until very recently the highest in the world.[82] The problem, moreover, had steadily worsened. Between 1960 and the mid-1980s alcohol consumption more than doubled, reaching a level of between 15 and 16 litres per annum for all those aged over 15; and by late 1987, despite the efforts that had already been made, there were some 4.5 million registered alcoholics of whom 1 million required hospital treatment.[83] The consequences of alcohol abuse were apparent in every walk of Soviet life, but particularly in industry. Productivity was adversely affected, absenteeism and accidents increased, and the health services were placed under a heavy burden. In an effort to bring these problems under control a comprehensive programme of measures was announced in May 1985: the production of alcoholic drink was reduced, its sale was restricted by time and place, and sporting and other societies were urged to develop a wider range of spare-time activities.[84] In the event, alcohol production declined sharply, but consumption, both from state and illicit sources, was hardly affected. The only real difference was that a vast quantity of excise duty was lost.[85] The campaign was subsequently relaxed and the Central Committee accepted (in a resolution of 1987) that the problem could not be dealt with by a 'single stroke [or] by noisy, short-term campaigns'.[86] Some were even prepared to argue that the price of drink should be reduced and a network of state pubs and cafés established so as to undermine what had become a thriving illegal industry and to recover some of the state revenue that had been forgone.[87]

In other respects, however, the economic reform strategy did make a difference, and where this was the case it was often a source of the difficulties that were encountered during the early years of the Gorbachev administration. Giving greater autonomy to enterprises, for instance, allowed them more freedom to choose their output mix in a way that met their obligations in the easiest possible way. One general response was to reduce or discontinue the production of cheaper and less profitable items and to concentrate on other products. This led to shortages of, for example, children's goods, and to a real but unrecorded increase in the cost of living as more expensive goods were substituted for cheaper but often very similar alternatives. The output of children's foods, for instance, fell in 1988 as compared with the year before; no more than 17 per cent of the breakfast cereals were produced that were needed, and no more than a third of the meat products.[88] Nor was this all. In Tambov, for instance, there were 'huge queues' for matches, and salt had practically disappeared from sale.[89] In Saratov there were shortages of soap, washing powder and toothpaste.[90] A farmer in the Far East, awarded the enormous sum of 147,000 rubles for a gold bar he had found on his land, found it impossible to spend the money in the shops of Vladivostok, with simple items like a shaving brush unobtainable anywhere in the city.[91] Even in Moscow salt, soap and matches were disappearing from retail sale and shelves were visibly emptying.[92] Tat'yana Kolomnikova, a metalworker from Zlatoust, shared her concerns with *Pravda*. Her work, she explained, was noisy, dusty and dirty; she came home utterly exhausted, but could find nothing in the shops. Sometimes she could take it no longer and went to the bathroom to cry, turning on the shower so that her husband and children would be unable to hear her. When would the slogans about social justice finally become a reality?[93]

There were complaints of this kind, in fact, from all over the country. The shortage of soap and washing powder, in the late 1980s, was a source of particular and understandable concern. 'What kind of regime is it if we can't even get washed?', asked an indignant group of workers in the Vladimir region.[94] A housewife who lived in the Moscow region threatened to send her dirty linen every week to the ministries concerned: 'if they can't provide us with soap', she reasoned, 'let them do the washing themselves'.[95] In Tula there were half-empty shelves and anxious queues where before there had been no problems of supply; soap was distributed as it had been during the war, and there was not enough meat even to satisfy those who had coupons (in Kaluga even less soap was available than had been the case during the war).[96] Quality was a related concern. An increasing proportion of sausage, for instance, included fat or additives of various kinds; *Litera-turnaya gazeta* tried it out on thirty cats who knew 'nothing of chemistry, bureaucracy or economies of scale' and found that twenty-four refused any of the varieties they were offered, and five more refused most of them.[97] Nor were these isolated and unrepresentative impressions. More than 73 per cent of those who were asked in a national poll in late 1989 reported that they 'often' or 'constantly' had difficulty in obtaining the foodstuffs they required;[98] and the Politburo itself acknowledged, in a resolution of about the same date, that school books, pencils, batteries, needles, razor blades, zip fasteners, electric irons, teapots, shoes and many other commodities had all but disappeared from retail sale.[99]

One result of shortages of this kind was queues. There were 'day and night' queues for sugar, for instance, in some areas, and queues 'like in the war' for bread.[100] In other areas it took 38 minutes to obtain 100 grammes of sausage, and an hour to get a kilo of tomatoes.[101] Mrs Kamlykova from Barnaul had to stand from 4 p.m. until 6 p.m. for toothpaste, when the supply ran out, and then come back the following day from 3 p.m. until 5.40 p.m., when she managed to obtain three tubes and some bars of soap.[102] Services were also in short supply. According to a national survey of train passengers, for instance, it took nearly an hour and a half in the summer months to obtain a railway ticket, and in some towns up to two or three hours.[103] Another result was a burgeoning black market. Gorbachev himself quoted a figure of 1.5 billion rubles in his address to the Central Committee in 1987; the trade union paper *Trud* quoted a rather more plausible figure of 14–16 billion rubles in 1988, roughly 30 per cent of the value of services provided by the state, and reported the existence of 'several thousand' black market millionaires. Illegal transactions accounted for a relatively small proportion of the trade in foodstuffs but for a third or more of medical work, household repairs, dressmaking and automobile servicing.[104]

The official response to difficulties of this kind was, at least in some parts of the USSR, to introduce a system of rationing (as Gorbachev joked at the Congress of People's Deputies in May 1989, people were carrying round cartoons of Brezhnev covered in medals, and Gorbachev covered in coupons[105]). In late 1988 *Pravda* reported that meat was being rationed in twenty-six of the Russian Republic's fifty-five regions, and sugar in all but two of them. Moscow shops were being 'literally stormed' by visitors; people elsewhere were travelling tens and even hundreds of kilometres for foodstuffs, enduring queues and rude remarks, and then forcing their way on to trains and buses on their return journey. Rationing, however, was not necessarily a solution to the distribution of scarce commodities, according to reports in the press: it was unclear where the coupons were to be used, sometimes they ended up on the black market, and in other cases the goods were wasted as they remained unclaimed.[106]

Shortages also led directly to a series of price increases as enterprises took advantages of their ability to dictate prices in a seller's market and to introduce higher-priced goods whose novelty or better quality was often wholly spurious. A Leningrad pensioner, for instance, wrote to *Pravda* to complain that the price of toothpaste had gone up from 35 to 60 kopeks.[107] A Petrozavodsk reader pointed out that bread was dearer but no better.[108] For a worker from Khar'kov, little had changed for the better for ordinary people, whatever the statistics might suggest: there was no more meat in the shops than there had been before, industrial goods were dearer because cheaper ones had been withdrawn, and the state-run café had closed and a cooperative one which was twice as expensive had opened in its place.[109] Again, these were not unrepresentative impressions. Inflation, according to authoritative estimates, had reached 8.4 per cent by 1988, half as high again as during the previous five years, and many individual items had increased still more sharply: a woman's winter coat, for instance, 181 rubles in 1980, cost 285 rubles eight years later.[110]

The greater the shortages, the more shoppers had to resort to collective farm or other markets, where prices were nearly three and for some products up to eight times higher than in the state sector.[111] The prices that were charged and the earnings that were made in the new cooperatives were a source of particular indignation. Women's boots, for instance, were typically twice as dear in a cooperative shop as in a state enterprise.[112] In many cases higher prices were being charged for products that had themselves been bought in the state sector: a Bratsk cooperative, for instance, was found to have been selling state sausage at a higher price, and pies were being sold in Moscow stations at three and a half times their price in an ordinary shop.[113] Cooperatives, for these and other reasons, were able to offer their members enormous salaries: there were cases of cooperatives paying their members a hundred times as much as an Academician or a minister, and other instances when cooperative members were earning twice as much in a day as an ordinary worker was able to make in a whole month. With such earnings, it was calculated, cooperative members could become ruble millionaires in four or five years.[114] There was also some concern that cooperatives were simply a 'convenient means of legalising stolen money',[115] and certainly high proportions of those who engaged in cooperative or individual economic activity were found, in random investigations, to have a criminal background.[116] There was strong public support for the restrictions upon activity of this kind that were imposed at the end of 1988, and it was one of the demands of striking miners in the summer of the following year that catering, medical and processing cooperatives should be closed down (further restrictions were duly imposed, particularly a 'law on speculation' of November 1990).[117]

Some members of the public wrote directly to the Central Committee about their difficulties.[118] There was a case, wrote a pensioner from the Leningrad region, for increasing the price of bread; at its present price children played football with it, and it was fed to cattle. There was even a case for increasing the price of meat, wrote a reader from Tomsk, as everyone paid the subsidy which kept down its price but relatively few were readily able to obtain it. Two pensioners, however, complained that it was more and more difficult to survive on a joint benefit of 160 rubles a month. A Moscow engineering couple with two young daughters found they could manage 'not a life, but only an existence' on their joint income. A Leningrad reader complained of 'chaos' in price formation; even to breathe fresh air in the park had become more expensive as there were charges for admission. The unjustified rise in prices was undermining people's faith in *perestroika*, wrote another Leningrad reader. Any further increase in retail prices would be, 'without exaggeration, a "death sentence" for the poorer sections of the population'. Was this not anyway an excuse for inefficient production? Would it not be better to try to reduce losses in transport and storage, or to cut the bureaucracy? And what about Marx's views on price and value? The situation was getting worse not just from year to year but 'from day to day', wrote other correspondents. Did *perestroika* in the Altai mean bringing back the rationing system that had been abolished in 1947? And why was everything in short supply?[119]

The early Gorbachev years in fact saw a significant increase in the level of absolute poverty. In a remarkable digest of letters in early 1989, the compiler, *Pravda's* Tat'yana Samolis, confessed that in all her time on the paper she had never before read of people who were too poor to make use of public baths, or to prepare *borshch* for their family. A Leningrad pensioner, for instance, a war and labour veteran who received 57 rubles a month, complained that this was not enough even for food. There had been a lot of talk about *perestroika*, but for pensioners daily life had actually become much worse. She couldn't afford to call the electricity repair man, and looked for cast-off shoes in rubbish bins when it was dark. A dress that could have been bought for 82 rubles five years earlier now cost 176 rubles; even gravestones had gone up from 40 rubles to 132.[120] One large group of the poor were veterans: over 22 million received 60 rubles a month or less, well below the poverty line, and ten million of them lived alone without the benefit of family support.[121] Another disadvantaged group were the 7 million handicapped.[122] Large families had special difficulties; so too did pensioners, over ten million of whom received 50 rubles a month or less.[123] There was a great deal of criticism of official statistics and the notion of an 'average' family, purchasing goods at state prices when in practice most families had to obtain them from cooperatives or collective farm markets.[124] Even official statistics, however, recorded that poorer families – up to 43 million of the population – were consuming about a third less meat and milk products in the late 1980s than they had been able to enjoy in 1970.[125]

Greater enterprise autonomy led to increasing difficulties of a different but related kind: it made it easier for management to put up wages more rapidly than would otherwise have been possible, covering their costs by higher prices. The result was a rapid increase in inflationary pressures, as rising incomes chased much less rapidly increasing commodities. In 1988 as a whole the average monthly income of workers and white-collar staff in the state sector rose by 7 per cent, but productivity in the economy as a whole by just 5.1 per cent.[126] In 1989 the same tendencies were even more apparent: money wages rose by 9.5 per cent, but labour productivity by a much more modest 2.3 per cent.[127] As the Komi first secretary told the Central Committee in April 1989, wages were increasing ahead of production at such a rate that soon the whole of the economy would be devoted to printing paper.[128] *Pravda's* economics editor declared that the rapid increase of money in circulation was doing as much damage to the Soviet economy as Napoleon and Hitler had done when they had printed counterfeit currency. The amount of production per ruble was half what it was in 1965, and a quarter of what it had been in the 1950s.[129] A group of leading economists warned in *Moscow News* that so much money was in circulation by early 1989 that it would buy all the goods available in Western Europe if the ruble was accepted at its official exchange rate.[130] There was some evidence of a flight from money in the USSR itself, as rubles were traded for objects of value like jewellery and watches; and restrictions had to be imposed on Soviet tourists visiting the other socialist countries of Eastern Europe and making use of their rapidly depreciating banknotes.

If individuals and enterprises had financial difficulties, so too did the state itself. With increasing levels of consumption and unchanged prices, the subsidies that were paid particularly for foodstuffs shot up from about 3.5 billion rubles in the mid 1960s to 84 billion rubles in the late 1980s.[131] Heavy costs had been incurred by the Chernobyl' explosion and the Armenian earthquake. And there were increasing pressures for particular groups of the population to be protected from inflationary and other difficulties: teachers and medical workers were among the first whose salaries were increased after Gorbachev's accession, and substantial rises in children's benefits and pensions were introduced in 1989 and 1990. Meanwhile, income was reduced with the fall in the world price of oil and the loss of excise duty from the sale of alcohol (about 40 and 36 billion rubles a year respectively).[132] In 1988, the Finance Minister explained to the Supreme Soviet, income had come to only 96.3 per cent of the planned total, but expenditure had been 2.5 per cent above; the difference had been met by borrowing from the state bank. In 1989 public expenditure would exceed revenue by 7.3 per cent, and a regime of 'severe economy' would be needed.[133] Taking borrowing from the state bank into account, the budgetary deficit was of the order of 120 billion rubles or 11–12 per cent of GNP, as compared with 4 per cent in the USA.[134]

Towards a 'socialist market'?

If the late 1980s were difficult years for the Soviet economy, the early 1990s were ones of deepening crisis. The economic results for 1989, reported in the central press in January 1990, certainly made dismal reading. As we have already noted, there was a 3 per cent increase in GNP and a 2.4 per cent increase in the more familiar Soviet measure, national income produced. Industrial output, however, increased by only 1.7 per cent, and agricultural output by just 1.3 per cent; housing construction actually fell, and so too did goods transportation. The State Statistics Committee, in its report, acknowledged that economic development had 'lost momentum', with many of the most important targets not attained; the consumer market, in particular, was 'tense', with demand continuing to outstrip supply. Inflation was running at a nominal 2 per cent, but unmet demand or hidden inflation increased the figure to about 7.5 per cent. Labour discipline had worsened, with losses of working time up by 30 per cent on the previous year's total. Incomes had risen 12.9 per cent, well above the planned level (and one reason, in itself, for the shortages of consumer goods). Only in the private and cooperative sector was there evidence of advance, with over 6,000 factories and state or collective farms operating on a leasehold basis and 4.5 million employed in the cooperative sector alone.[135]

The 1990 results, when they came out in January 1991, appeared in a specialist economics journal rather than in the central press, and for understandable reasons. GNP had actually fallen, by 2 per cent; labour productivity had dropped by 3 per cent, and national income produced by 4 per cent. Industrial output was down, and so too was agricultural production. Foreign trade fell 6.9 per cent by value, housing construction was down again, and there was a fall in the output of oil and coal, iron and steel, tractors and computer technology, fertilisers and paper. The fall in oil output was a particular concern, given its importance as a source of hard currency: 642 million tonnes in 1988, output in 1990 was just 570 million tonnes or barely sufficient to satisfy domestic demand. Nor was it simply a matter of monetary aggregates, as the plan report also made clear. There was more crime; fewer schools and hospitals were built; and environmental conditions worsened considerably. Almost 130 towns had concentrations of harmful substances in their air that were at least ten times the permitted norm; the town of Rubezhniy had no less than 200 times the permitted level of nitrochlorobenzol in its atmosphere, and in another town the concentration of cement dust was 115 times the permitted level. The 1991 results, reported in the specialist press in February 1992, showed a fall of 17 per cent in national income, more than the United States had suffered during the Great Depression.[136] Gorbachev, his spokesman Gennadii Gerasimov explained, had not won the Nobel Prize for economics; anyone who read these plan results would have understood why.

An economic recovery programme had been introduced by Prime Minister Ryzhkov to the Second Congress of People's Deputies in December 1989, aimed at restoring market equilibrium by 1993.[137] By March 1990 the programme was already judged inadequate in the light of deteriorating performance and a government commission headed by the prime minister was asked to prepare a more sweeping package of reform. Ryzhkov presented its conclusions to the Supreme Soviet on 24 May. They involved a gradual transition to a 'regulated' market in three stages up to 1995, incorporating legal changes, pricing and tax reforms, and a reduction in the scope of central planning. Living standards, Ryzhkov explained, would fall initially, but would then begin to improve from 1993 onwards. The price of bread, much lower than its cost of production, would first of all be raised substantially. The plan came in for heavy criticism (the economist Pavel Bunich, in a celebrated phrase, described it as 'shock without therapy'[138]), and the Supreme Soviet, on 13 June, called for the government to submit a more developed and coherent programme by 1 September. There was also to be a more extended discussion, over the summer, of the measures that were to be taken to protect the population at large from the effect of these changes; and the increase in the price of bread, in particular, was deferred for further consideration. The announcement of proposals for increased prices nonetheless led to panic buying and the introduction, in several cities, of regulations prohibiting the sale of goods to non-residents.[139]

Discussion of the way forward for economic reform continued over the summer, concentrated within small groups of ministers and their advisers. A more radical plan, put forward by a group under the chairmanship of Presidential Council member Stanislav Shatalin, advocated a rapid '500 day' transition to the market based upon a massive transfer of state to other forms of property and a 'hard' rouble (the Russian Republic itself adopted this programme in September 1990).[140] The government's original proposals remained on the table, Ryzhkov in particular arguing against a package of reforms that would lead to a significant fall in living standards and (probably) political instability.[141] Another group, chaired by Academician Abel Aganbegyan, was asked to systematise the various proposals for moving to a market economy with the least social and economic costs; its conclusions were presented to the Supreme Soviet and to republican parliaments.[142] Gorbachev reported back on 17 September on the results of the discussion;[143] the Supreme Soviet asked him in turn to prepare a 'unified programme', combining the best elements of all three documents, and these proposals, 'Guidelines for the stabilisation of the economy and the transition to a market economy', were duly approved by an overwhelming vote on 19 October.[144]

The new Guidelines were based upon the principle of 'maximum freedom of economic activity' combined where appropriate with state regulation, and envisaged a transition to a system of this kind in four stages within a 'relatively short time'. The first stage – a 'programme of emergency measures' – was to be devoted mainly to stabilising the economy and beginning the commercialisation of state enterprises. The second stage emphasised the gradual liberalisation of prices, the introduction of various forms of social security and the maintenance of tight fiscal policies. Further structural reforms, including those of the labour compensation system and the housing market, were to be completed in the third stage, while financial constraints would be eased as market conditions stabilised. In the fourth and final stage, the ruble would become fully convertible against other currencies within the Soviet Union and outside it. The logic of the proposals, Gorbachev explained, was the same as in the document he had presented in September, but it now incorporated the views of parliamentary committees and of the deputies themselves, of the republics and regions, and of ordinary citizens. There could be no question of further postponing the move to what would in effect be a 'mixed economy'.[145]

Gorbachev stressed several other elements of the reform programme in his speeches of late 1990 and early 1991. The military burden was one of them: they had 'one of the most militarised economies in the world', he told the Soviet trade unions in October 1990; in Minsk, in February 1991, he described it as 'the most militarised economy in the world'. Spending cuts, by implication, could hardly threaten national security.[146] Speaking in Odessa in August 1990, Gorbachev described the dominance of state ownership as the 'chief cause of the present crisis' and called for the encouragement of small businesses and the 'spirit of enterprise'. He described free enterprise as the 'motor' of economic growth, and – in a remarkable concession – went on to argue that the market and private property were important not only in themselves but also because they alone could adequately guarantee democracy and human rights. It was the first speech in which the Soviet leader referred directly and approvingly to 'privatisation'.[147] His speech to the Party Congress in July 1990 took a rather more cautious line, emphasising the achievements that had taken place during the years of *perestroika* and calling for a 'new model of the economy: a multi-sectoral model, with diverse forms of ownership and management, and with a modern market infrastructure'. The market, however, would not be allowed to determine long-term state programmes for science, education or the environment, and there would be no changes that could provide a basis for the exploitation of working people by a new generation of private owners.[148]

Gorbachev had originally indicated his preference for Shatalin's more radical '500 days' programme;[149] the Guidelines, however, were clearly a compromise document, described by the deputy and economist Oleg Bogomolov as a combination of the form of the '500 days' programme with the substance of the original government proposals.[150] Shatalin himself, increasingly disillusioned by the pace of change, expressed his dismay in an outspoken letter in *Komsomol'skaya pravda* in November 1990. Signed by the various authors of the '500 days' programme, the letter complained that too much time had been lost and insisted that no compromise was possible in any case between their own proposals and those of the central government: 'a choice had to be made'. The agreement originally concluded with the various republics had been lost with the decision to submit the proposals to republican parliaments, and uncoordinated actions were now being taken, such as price rises and export restrictions, which placed the maintenance of a single all-union market in some doubt. The Guidelines were not in any case a practical reform plan, and in parts (such as the plans to reduce the budgetary deficit) the proposals were wholly unrealistic. The most likely outcome was hyperinflation.[151] Leonid Abalkin, speaking from a government perspective, accepted that the changeover to an effective market economy would take at least a decade and perhaps a generation.[152]

Academic economists, as these discussions suggested, had generally little doubt that any meaningful reform must involve a transition to market relations. Planning officials and party leaders took a more cautious view, tending to argue that the market was 'not an end in itself' and that every effort must be made to protect working people from its consequences.[153] Gorbachev himself pointed out in a speech in February 1991 that there were over 100 market economies, but that only 15–20 of them were prosperous.[154] The head of Gosplan, Yuri Maslyukov, complained that the existing situation was 'neither plan nor market' and insisted in his speech to the Party Congress that the central government retain 'strategic' powers in its own hands.[155] Vladimir Kryuchkov, chairman of the KGB, emphasised for his part that they were moving towards a 'regulated', not an 'Adam Smith' market, and he warned that existing policies were creating thousands of underground millionaires who might – if they had the opportunity – mount their own version of an 'October revolution'.[156] Other members of the leadership accepted a transition to the market upon this highly conditional basis, but generally placed more emphasis upon collective rather than private ownership and upon central direction and social discipline.[157] Nor were managers themselves necessarily eager for the bracing disciplines of the market: the directors of state enterprises, brought together in conference in December 1990, certainly took the view that central control was still necessary, at least until more stable economic conditions had been established.[158]

Public attitudes, most important of all, remained cautious and ambiguous. A poll in Moscow in the summer of 1990, for instance, found that 58 per cent thought the Soviet Union should transfer to a market economy, and 56 per cent thought the transition should begin 'immediately'. But 69 per cent thought ordinary workers, pensioners and office staff – the great majority – would be worse off, 52 per cent thought unemployment was 'abnormal' or 'tragic', and many were concerned that a move to market relations would bring about an increase in inflation, crime and social chaos.[159] Other polls found still higher levels of opposition to the idea of unemployment.[160] Those who worked in the public services were particularly apprehensive about a transition to market conditions. Railway workers, for instance, wrote directly to Gorbachev to express their concern; the prospects for the defence industry, the merchant marine and Soviet culture were no more inviting.[161] And although most were in favour of private property in principle, especially for small shops and salons, an equally substantial majority (75 per cent) were against the private ownership of major industries.[162] There was strong opposition to cooperatives, widely seen as parasitic on the state sector and often criminal in their activities;[163] and a particular concern, prompted to some extent by the experience of Eastern Europe, was that privatisation should not lead to the enrichment of officials in a kind of 'nomenklatura capitalism'.[164]

What kind of a society would result from the adoption of market relations? Only 9 per cent, according to opinion polls, though it would be 'capitalism'; many more (37 per cent) thought it would be 'renewed socialism', 15 per cent thought it would be a society with the worst features of both socialism and capitalism, and 36 per cent had no idea.[165] Another poll, in Moscow and the Moscow region, found that 55 per cent expected a gradual synthesis of capitalism and socialism in the Soviet Union and outside it in the foreseeable future. Far fewer (9 per cent) expected the Soviet future would be a socialist one; only

7 per cent thought all countries would become capitalist, and 3 per cent thought all countries would eventually become communist.[166] Support for the market, it emerged, was based upon little more substantial than the belief that the existing system had to change, and almost 60 per cent, in a poll reported at the end of 1990, freely confessed they had no idea what a market actually was.[167]

Most ordinary people, in practice, had more immediate concerns than large, remote and little-understood changes in government policy. There was little expectation of a rapid improvement under any circumstances: 48 per cent, in a national poll at the end of 1990, thought the USSR would emerge from its economic crisis no earlier than the year 2000, and 12 per cent thought it would 'never' do so. By November 1991 44 per cent expected an 'economic catastrophe'.[168] Despite a good harvest, meanwhile, there were growing shortages on the consumer market. The Ministry of Internal Affairs itself reported that in the first half of 1990 no more than 20 types of goods, out of a minimum of 1,100 different items, were regularly available for sale.[169] Milk products were in short supply; so were sugar and cigarettes (there were 'tobacco riots' in Moscow and workers in Karelia went on strike to try to ensure a reasonable supply).[170] Tea was hard to find; so too were children's books.[171] Bread had become a scarce commodity by early 1990: in Irkutsk it took 'half a day' to get a small loaf and in Leningrad, where there were similar shortages, it was noted that the February revolution had begun in this way.[172] Medicines became all but unobtainable, and typhoid, cholera and diptheria made an unwelcome reappearance.[173] Shortages of foodstuffs and medicine were so bad by the early 1990s that 90 per cent of schoolchildren had vitamin deficiencies.[174] In the city of Ufa, in early 1991, there were even shortages of drinking water.[175]

A situation of this kind had several direct consequences. Queues became longer; and some were driven to desperate measures, like the Muscovites who found it so hard to obtain meat they began to steal rabbits from the zoo, or the citizens of Novosibirsk who spent all night in a shop to be sure of obtaining their sausage in the morning.[176] Others went on lengthy searches for what they needed, like the Muscovite with big feet who needed socks of the proper size; he had become sick before because he hadn't been able to find any, and 'without socks I can't participate in *perestroika*'.[177] Another of *Pravda*'s correspondents, from Donetsk, had spent the two previous years looking for a pair of socks.[178] People wrote in to the Central Committee to try to get hold of what they needed, though the party headquarters, it was pointed out, were 'not a department store'. One of the Central Committee's correspondents in early 1991 was unable to find a box of matches or tobacco anywhere in the Ukraine; even after the war things had been better.[179] There were assaults on sales staff by irate would-be customers.[180] Some, unable to bear these difficulties any further, applied to emigrate: only 8,000 had emigrated in 1986, according to official figures, but 235,000 left in 1989, and more than twice as many left in 1990. Opinion polls found that about 12 per cent of the population, and 17 per cent of young people, would leave the USSR altogether if they could.[181]

Increasingly, coupons were resorted to in order to ensure that whatever supplies were available went to those who needed them most. The Ukraine went furthest in this direction, introducing a system in late 1990 by which 70 per cent of earnings were received in the form of tokens that could be exchanged for goods. In Kazan', in 1991, coupons were even being issued for funerals.[182] In practice this was hardly a solution. The coupons, it emerged, were often enough to provide only a week's supply;[183] they had sometimes not even been printed;[184] and the goods were often not available to which they supposedly provided an entitlement.[185] They were also counterfeited. In one northern town, it was discovered, 15,000 fake alcohol coupons had been issued; the general allocation for the following month had to be cut from three to a single bottle.[186] *Pravda* discovered a particularly ingenious scheme, operating in the town of Kokchetav in the Kazakh republic. False coupons had been issued for sugar and washing powder, and something like 12 tonnes of sugar had been sold in the previous two months in exchange for these coupons. Curiously, it emerged that the fakes had been printed in the same works as the one in which official coupons were being printed, with the apparent connivance of the management.[187] And what were people to do with (for instance) a coupon for one pair of shoes every eighteen months? Should they choose summer or winter shoes in these circumstances?[188]

If any group gained from these shortages, it was black marketeers. In 1990, it was estimated, the Soviet population paid 5 billion rubles above list prices for items other than foodstuffs; this was nearly three times as much as the year before.[189] Estimates of the size of the black market in the early 1990s ranged from 5.1 billion rubles (the view of the State Statistics Committee) or 30 billion (according to the Ministry of Finance) up to as much as 500 billion rubles.[190] By this time there were an estimated 100–150,000 underground millionaires as well as 'dozens' of legal ones (the cooperative director, Artem Tarasov, was the most notorious).[191] At the other end of the spectrum an increasing number lived in poverty: at least 70 million, or a quarter of the total population, according to an estimate published in *Izvestiya* in late 1990.[192] About half of the Soviet poor were members of large families, and half of the Soviet Union's low income families lived in Central Asia and Azerbaijan; but even professors' families found themselves below the subsistence minimum.[193] Another social category that was rapidly increasing in the early 1990s was the unemployed: acknowledged for the first time in the 1990 plan report, the figure given (about 2 million) was understood to be a considerable underestimate.[194] A new employment law, adopted in January 1991, began what would almost certainly be the lengthy process of developing a network of training and placement of facilities that would keep this number within acceptable bounds.[195]

The 'anti-crisis programme' that was announced in the spring of 1991 was likely to deepen these social divisions, at least in the short term. The central element in the programme was a sharp increase in state retail prices (beef, for instance, rose from 2 to 7 rubles a kilo[196]), combined with a move towards free or 'agreed' prices for many others. These increases were accompanied by a more limited set of measures for the 'social compensation' of poorer sections of the community.[197] Prices of luxury goods had been increased the previous November. As the new prime minister, Valentin Pavlov, explained to the Supreme Soviet, there would be fixed state prices for basic commodities such as meat, milk, tea and children's goods, and the price of medicines, coffee, energy, vodka and some other commodities would remain at the same level for the time being. About 30 per cent of retail trade, however, would be conducted at market prices, and the general level of retail prices would rise by 60 per cent.[198] The government programme was rounded off by a series of related measures: there were laws on entrepreneurship, privatisation and foreign investment; a transition began to an insurance-based rather than state-funded health service; and labour exchanges, the last of which had closed in 1930, reopened for business in July 1991.[199]

The politics of economic reform

In the last resort, responses to the deepening difficulties of the Soviet economy were political, rather than technical or managerial. By the end of the Gorbachev era at least two distinct approaches had acquired coherent form. For one group of commentators, many of them academic economists, the problems that were being encountered were the result of too little reform, rather than too much, and in particular too little of the market approach to economic management that the 'radical right' had popularised in Britain and the United States. There was, from this perspective, some room for more traditional approaches to economic reform such as the state quality control system (*gospriemka*), which was introduced in early 1987.[200] In the longer term, however, there was 'no alternative' to an economy based to a much greater extent upon market principles. Prices, for instance, would have to rise in order to eliminate 'wasteful' subsidies (no other element of budgetary spending had risen as rapidly, Shmelev pointed out, and by the late 1980s the retail price of meat and bread covered barely a third of their production cost[201]). Public assets should be gradually privatised, to cooperatives if not necessarily to individuals. Firms should compete with each other through the medium of a 'socialist market'. The collective farm system should be broken up and replaced by family-based smallholdings. Wage differentials should be wider. State planning should be restricted to the regulation of the market, for instance through the prevention of monopolies. And the ruble should be traded internationally so as to apply the disciplines of outside competition to domestic producers.

For Pavel Bunich, for instance, the state could not be a universal provider and there should be no lifebelts for enterprises that failed to pay their way.[202] For Gavriil Popov at least half of the economy should be transferred to cooperative and private ownership. Agriculture should be based upon small family units (Marx had been wrong about the benefits of large-scale farming), and free social benefits, which simply provided a justification for a state bureaucracy, should for the most part be eliminated.[203] For Oleg Bogomolov the 'laws of the socialist market' must be dominant;[204] and for Nikolai Shmelev and others, even a modest pool of unemployment might be necessary if this was the price of economic restructuring. Better living standards, Shmelev believed, would come about only through satisfying the market. The way forward in agriculture was through the private and cooperative sector; in industry, enterprises should be compelled to operate in free market conditions. Fears that this would result in massive unemployment were 'greatly exaggerated'; people were continually changing jobs as it was, nor could they close their eyes to the 'great harm being done by our parasitic reliance on guaranteed employment'. If disorderliness, drunkenness and poor workmanship were really to be eliminated, there was probably no alternative to the establishment of a 'comparatively small reserve army of labour'. Foreign firms should be given greater access to the Soviet market so as to force Soviet enterprises to compete with them, the role of Gosplan and the ministries should be greatly reduced, and Soviet prices should be brought into line with those that prevailed internationally. 'Only the market, only the free movement of supply and demand' could properly determine such matters.[205]

There was however another view, linked more closely with the industrial working class and with those who claimed to speak in its name, such as the trade union confederations and political parties that had succeeded the CPSU on the socialist left. Seen from this perspective, the source of the country's economic difficulties lay much more in the distribution of benefits and the relations between social groups on which that distribution was based. The Soviet working class, they pointed out, was poorly remunerated, even in relative terms: Shmelev, in fact, told the Congress of People's Deputies that the Soviet working class was the most exploited in the world, with only 37–38 per cent of national income being spent on wages as compared with 70 per cent or more in other industrial countries. In tsarist Russia the share of wages in national income had been significantly higher, at 54.8 per cent.[206] The share of consumption in national income, again, was unusually low in the Soviet Union: about 54 per cent, using United Nations methodology, as compared with 69 per cent in West Germany and 72 per cent in the United States. Capital investment, defence and especially management, on the other hand, took a rather larger share.[207]

The same was true of particular social programmes. Spending on the health service, for instance, once at a high level, had dropped to three or four per cent of national income as compared with 8–12 per cent in most industrial nations.[208] Education received only 5–6 per cent of budgetary expenditure, as compared with 10–12 per cent in other developed nations; and rates of housing construction, once very high, had fallen below those of Western Europe, the USA and Japan.[209] Children's benefits accounted for a lower percentage of national income in the Soviet Union than in the United Kingdom or France, although the level of spending was similar to that in West Germany.[210] Spending on social welfare as a whole, similarly, accounted for a lower share of national income in the Soviet Union than it did in the United States, Britain and France, and the gap was widening.[211] Income inequalities, even in monetary terms, were rather greater in the USSR than in the USA, according to a number of estimates.[212] Nor were subsidies necessarily regressive. In some cases, such as housing and meat, those with higher incomes also had a higher level of consumption; but in other cases, such as bread and potatoes, the better-off did not on the whole consume more than the poor, and the subsidy which helped to keep the price down was in effect a form of income redistribution in their favour. Many other countries subsidised basic foodstuffs, Soviet food prices were already high, and they often reflected the distorted prices that were charged for machinery.[213]

Not simply, it was represented, were proposals of a marketising kind on shaky ground empirically: they actually represented an attempt to resolve the nation's economic difficulties at the expense of working people, rather than at the expense of the 'bloated administrative apparatus' that was responsible for them. An increasing level of industrial militancy, most spectacularly in the Siberian and Ukrainian coalfields in the summer of 1989 and again in 1991, was one response to the 'monetarist' diagnosis; another was the increasing willingness of deputies, academics and others to relate the country's economic difficulties to the relations that existed between social groups. For Tat'yana Zaslavskaya, speaking to *Izvestiya* in December 1988, the working class was the victim of a kind of 'indirect exploitation' on the part of the full-time party and state apparatus. By 1991 she was prepared to speak of the 'economic exploitation and political oppression of working people by the party-state *nomenklatura*'.[214] Boris Yel'tsin, speaking to the Congress of People's Deputies, put the argument still more forthrightly. There had been no real advance in social justice in the seventy years or more since the October revolution, he charged, and there was every reason to speak of an 'elite stratum' in the society, 'wallowing in luxury' while tens of millions lived in abject poverty.[215] Moscow deputy Alexei Emel'yanov, in another vigorous speech, warned that an 'administrative-bureaucratic apparat' was attempting to defend its 'monopoly position', including special housing: local people, for instance, being moved to the outskirts of town so that the Council of Ministers and Central Committee could build comfortable accommodation for themselves in the city centre.[216] Indeed for some Soviet writers, in the late 1980s, social relations in their society were best understood in straightforwardly Marxist terms, with a bureaucratic 'class' exploiting the labour of ordinary workers.[217]

Gorbachev and the party leadership as a whole distanced themselves both from the more extreme 'monetarist' and from the more radical 'workerist' perspectives. For Gorbachev personally there could be no talk of a transition to full-scale private ownership – did they really want to be employed by capitalists, he asked a group of Lenin-grad workers?[218] – and price increases, where they were allowed to occur, must be discussed widely and introduced in such a way that living standards were not affected. Gorbachev was equally severe, however, on the 'ultra-left', who imagined that their objectives could be accomplished in a 'single stroke', and he gave no encouragement to the radicals within the new Supreme Soviet or to the wave of working-class activism that developed in the summer of 1989 and again in 1991. There was clearly some room for improvement in economic perform-ance without embracing either of these extreme positions. Attempts could be made, for instance, to reduce the volume of state orders. Military spending could be – and was – reduced significantly. Some efforts could be made to assist the most needy – the Communist Party itself made a donation of a third of its annual income in 1989 to allow the earlier introduction of higher pensions.[219] It would be difficult in the longer run, however, to avoid a choice – either a revolution 'from above', made in the name of working people but without their direct participation and possibly against their interests, or a popular move-ment 'from below', in a form which was likely to challenge the power and not simply the (often fairly modest) privileges of the Soviet leadership at all levels.

5 The Soviet multinational state

Gorbachev inherited a Soviet state which was, in a celebrated Stalinist formulation, 'national in form but socialist in content'. The USSR's fifteen union republics, united on a supposedly voluntary basis, formed an 'integral, federal, multinational state', according to the 1977 Constitution. They enjoyed an extensive range of formal powers, including the right to enter into diplomatic relations with other states (Art. 80) and to determine all matters of purely local significance (Art. 76). Under the previous constitution, from 1944 onwards, the union republics had even enjoyed the right to maintain their own armed forces. Emphasising the point that this was a 'voluntary association of equal Soviet Socialist Republics', each of the union republics enjoyed the right to secede from the USSR (Art. 72) and, towards that end, each of them occupied a territory on the periphery of the USSR within which a particular nationality was in principle predominant – Estonians in Estonia, Ukrainians in the Ukraine, and Russians in the Russian Republic, which was by far the largest. Each union republic had its own parliament (or Supreme Soviet) and its own government (or Council of Ministers). Four of them (the Russian Republic, Uzbekistan, Georgia and Azerbaijan) included autonomous republics within their borders, and there were still smaller administrative units, autonomous regions and autonomous areas, to cater for less numerous national groups.

This elaborate state structure, providing in principle for the greatest possible degree of local self-government, was none the less based upon the principle of democratic centralism which meant that, in the last resort, central decisions could be imposed upon levels of government below them. The whole country functioned upon the basis of a unitary and centrally-determined plan and budget, which greatly limited the scope for lower levels of government to choose their own priorities. The functions of government were nominally divided between the centre and the republics, but all-union ministries, based exclusively in

Moscow, produced 57 per cent of industrial output, union-republican ministries based partly in Moscow produced a further 37 per cent, and only 6 per cent of industry was wholly regulated at the republican level.[1] The Communist Party, moreover, was a unitary organisation based upon the same principle of democratic centralism, and there was no constitutional court which, as in a true federation, could have resolved any dispute about the respective powers of the republics and of the USSR as a whole. Workers, in any case, were supposed to have no interests that conflicted with those of working people in any other part of the USSR, and Soviet socialism was held to have 'solved' the national question by establishing a system of rule which substituted a harmonious and dynamic union based on a community of interests for the centralism and oppression of the Tsarist past.

The complicated administrative makeup of the USSR reflected the various and changing ethnic composition of the people that inhabited it. According to the 1989 census, Russians accounted for just over half (50.8 per cent) of the total population; the balance was accounted for by a hundred or more different national groups, ranging from a few hundred Negidals in the Far East to the major Slavic and Muslim groups which occupied the west and south of the country as well as Russia proper. The ethnic variety of the USSR was in fact still greater than these numbers implied. On other, more inclusive counts there were not a hundred or so nationalities in the USSR (the 1989 census recorded 128) but as many as 400, or even 800.[2] The cultural differences among these various nationalities, moreover, were often very considerable, extending to history, language, religion and social customs of all kinds. The largest group of Soviet nationalities were the Slavs – Russians, Ukrainians and Belorussians – who shared a common linguistic and religious inheritance and together constituted about two-thirds of the total population. The traditionally Muslim peoples of Central Asia accounted for a further 15 per cent; and the balance was made up for the most part of the larger national groups in Transcaucasia and the Baltic.[3]

Russians, the 'elder brother' of the Slavic as well as of the other Soviet peoples, were not just the most numerous but also the dominant national grouping in the USSR as a whole. Russians are a Christian people – the millennium of the Orthodox church was celebrated in 1988 – speaking an East Slavic language, and they have represented the core of the Russian or Soviet state since early medieval times. The overwhelming majority of Russians – some 83 per cent in the 1989 census – lived in the Russian Republic, where they accounted for the

Table 5.1 *The major Soviet nationalities, 1989*

	Census popn. (1989, m.)	% of total	Linguistic group	Traditional religion
The Slavs				
Russians	145.1	50.8	East Slavic	Russian Orthodox
Ukrainians	44.1	15.5	East Slavic	Russian Orthodox
Belorussians	10.0	3.5	East Slavic	Russian Orthodox
The Balts				
Latvians	1.5	0.5	Baltic	Protestant
Lithuanians	3.1	1.1	Baltic	Roman Catholic
Estonians	1.0	0.4	Finno-Ugrian	Protestant
The Caucasians				
Georgians	4.0	1.4	Kartvelian	Georgian Orthodox
Armenians	4.6	1.6	Indo-European	Armenian Orthodox
Azerbaijanis	6.8	2.4	Turkic	Muslim (Shi'a)
The Central Asians				
Uzbeks	16.7	5.8	Turkic	Muslim (Sunni)
Kazakhs	8.1	2.9	Turkic	Muslim (Sunni)
Tajiks	4.2	1.5	Iranian	Muslim (Sunni)
Turkmenians	2.7	1.0	Turkic	Muslim (Sunni)
Kirgiz	2.5	0.9	Turkic	Muslim (Sunni)
Other				
Moldavians	3.4	1.2	Romance	Romanian Orthodox

Source: Based on *Vestnik statistiki*, 1990, no. 10, pp. 69–71.

same proportion of the local population. About eleven million lived in the Ukraine, and there were millions more in other republics (in Kazakhstan they almost outnumbered the Kazakhs). Although scarcely under challenge from other national groups, Russians made up a steadily diminishing proportion of the total population over the postwar period and the Russian Republic included many of the Soviet Union's poorest farmland and most dismal cities, creating at least the impression that it was subsidising developments in more prosperous non-Russian areas.[4] For reasons such as these there had been a steadily rising tide of national self-consciousness since the 1960s, expressed particularly in a movement to protect ancient monuments and churches and also in a group of writers and filmmakers who had tried to rediscover the honesty, simplicity and even patterns of speech of traditional village life.[5]

The writer Valentin Rasputin, reflecting some of these concerns, went so far as to complain at the Congress of People's Deputies in 1989 of 'Russophobia' on the part of other nationalities. Rather than continue to carry this burden, he suggested that the Russian Republic might itself consider seceding from the union. Then, perhaps, people could say that they were Russian without embarrassment, and concern themselves with the ecological and other needs of their own republic.[6] Another speaker at the Congress, the communist deputy V. I. Belov, argued that the Russian Republic was in fact in a position of some disadvantage compared with the other republics, since it alone lacked the full range of party, state and scientific institutions. The result was that the all-union bodies which carried out these functions were seen as Russian bodies, and Russians took the blame for their shortcomings; while Russia itself, one of the areas whose numbers had been increasing most rapidly before the revolution, was threatened with depopulation.[7] Concerns of this kind, as *Pamyat'* demonstrated, could sometimes take a xenophobic or anti-semitic form, but they also helped to provide the impetus behind a growing environmentalist movement centred around issues such as the pollution of Lake Baikal in Siberia and the defence of villages that had been declared 'perspectiveless' by central planners. There was similarly a strong movement, in the late 1980s, to restore the historic names of ancient streets and cities (the most spectacular change of this kind was in 1991 when Leningrad reverted to its original name of St Petersburg[8]).

The Ukrainians, the second most numerous Soviet nationality, were more than 44 million strong in the late 1980s, with a distinctive language (also East Slavic) and a culture of their own.[9] Predominantly Russian Orthodox by religion although with a substantial Roman Catholic (Uniate) minority, Kievan Rus had been the origin of the Russian state in the ninth century and enjoyed an extended period of independence, but then came under Lithuanian, Polish and (from the seventeenth century) Russian control. Despite a programme of Russification (including a ban on the use of Ukrainian in schools and publications), a strongly nationalist movement emerged in the late nineteenth century which led to pressure for greater autonomy and a brief period of independence immediately after the October revolution. It then became one of the constituent republics of the USSR in 1922. The Ukraine suffered particularly heavy losses during the 1930s – there was a devastating and, it is now accepted, largely man-made famine during the early part of the decade, and the republican leadership was badly affected by charges of 'nationalism' (in practice, for pointing out the likely outcomes of central policies).[10] There were further heavy losses during World War II, in which a substantial volunteer detachment fought on the German side. The Ukraine included about a third of the Soviet Union's most important industries – coal, iron and steel – and some of its richest agricultural land, and it was traditionally the home of some of its strongest political dynasties (the 'Dnepropetrovsk mafia', which included Leonid Brezhnev, was perhaps the best-known example). There had however been some resistance to what was seen as Russification since at least the 1960s, and in the 1980s the development of nuclear power was a new and very potent source of public disenchantment.[11]

The Belorussians (about 10 million in the late 1980s) also spoke a distinctive East Slavic language and were predominantly Russian Orthodox by religion.[12] Formerly a part of Kievan Rus, Belorussia also came under Lithuanian and Polish control until it passed to the Russian Empire under the partitions of the late eighteenth century. A generally swampy land without significant natural resources, Belorussia suffered greatly during the wars between Russia and Poland, and then again during the Napoleonic invasion and World Wars I and II. After a brief period of independence, Soviet rule was established in 1919 and the larger part of historic Belorussia joined the USSR in 1922. Western Belorussia, under Polish rule between the wars, was incorporated in 1939. Together with the Ukraine and the USSR itself, Belorussia became a founder member of the United Nations in 1945 and was a member of the International Labour Organisation and UNESCO. Moldavia, also a part of the Kievan state, was however a Latin rather than a Slavic community and had originally constituted part of the Roman province of Dacia. After some centuries of independent statehood it became a part of the Ottoman Empire and then came under Russian influence from the early nineteenth century. Bessarabia, a part of historic Moldavia between the Prut and Dniester rivers, came under Romanian rather than Soviet control from 1918 up to 1940 and again from 1941 to 1944, when it was incorporated into the USSR together with other Moldavian territories as a constituent republic.

Of the major non-Slavic groups, the Baltic nations had a particularly distinctive inheritance, having come under strong German, Polish and Swedish influence from early medieval times.[13] The nationalities concerned are generally Lutheran (Estonians and Latvians) or Roman Catholic (Lithuanians) by religion, not Orthodox, and they have been under Soviet rule for a much shorter period of time than most other nationalities, since 1940 rather than the immediate post-revolutionary period (when communist-led governments were briefly established in all three republics). Estonia, Latvia and Lithuania had been conquered from Sweden in the eighteenth century and incorporated as 'Baltic provinces' into the Russian Empire in the early nineteenth century, although a German landowning and commercial class retained substantial influence. The three republics had an extended experience of representative government, which was not the case in other parts of what became the USSR, and feudalism was abolished in the early nineteenth century, decades before its abolition in Russia proper. There was also a thriving commercial capitalism, particularly around the ports of Riga and Reval (present-day Tallinn). The way of life in these republics in the 1980s remained demonstrably much more 'Western' than that in the other Soviet republics, and they were among those most exposed to outside cultural influences (Estonia, for instance, had ready access to Finnish television and 'Dallas' and 'Dynasty' had a devoted following).

Level of literary and education have traditionally been high in the Baltic republics (Estonia, for instance, was 96.2 per cent literate in the 1897 census compared with an average for European Russia as a whole of 28.4 per cent[14]), and there are higher than average levels of media consumption, urbanisation and other indicators of 'modernity'. Estonia, again, published more than a third as many again books as the USSR average in the late 1980s, and museum and theatre visits were between two and three times the national average.[15] These republics had many of the Soviet Union's most modern industries and its most successful farms, and living standards were the highest in the USSR. Estonia, the most prosperous of the three, had the highest levels of car ownership of any of the Soviet republics and the greatest quantity of urban housing in the late 1980s.[16] High living standards had encouraged migration to these republics from other parts of the USSR, and this became one of the issues most central to the development of a powerful and widely supported nationalist movement in the late 1980s, particularly since the Baltic nations were relatively few in number and tended to have low birth and high divorce rates (in Latvia, where golden and silver wedding anniversaries had formerly been celebrated, there were ceremonies in the 1980s for couples that had been together for just a few years[17]).

The Caucasian peoples – Georgians, Armenians and Azerbaijanis – are also very different in their history, religion, language and culture than the Slavic majority, and they have historically been no less conscious of those differences than the Baltic peoples (there were mass riots in the Georgian capital Tbilisi in 1978, for instance, when it appeared that Georgian was about to be dropped as one of the republic's official languages[18]). The Caucasian peoples are renowned for the Mediterranean climate of the areas in which they live, for their fruit and wine, for their feuds and corruption, for their longevity, and for their paternalistic attitude towards women. The peoples of these republics, however, particularly the Georgians and Armenians, are also celebrated for their high levels of educational and cultural achievement, especially in theatre, film and painting. Abuladze's 'Repentance' was produced in Georgia; the same republic's Rustaveli Theatre under its director Robert Sturua enjoyed an international reputation. Armenia is the homeland of the composer Aram Khachaturyan, and the country of origin of the painter Arshile Gorky and of writer William Saroyan. Both Georgians and Armenians have their own independent churches and have been Christian since the fourth century, six centuries before the Russians; their distinctive languages and alphabets also date from the fourth century. The Azerbaijanis, by contrast, are a Shi'ite Muslim community of Persian culture; the territory that presently constitutes their republic came under Russian control in the early nineteenth century and entered the USSR, together with Georgia and Armenia, in 1922.

The greatest cultural division of all, however, is between the Slavs and other European peoples and the predominantly Muslim nationalities of Central Asia.[19] The peoples of these republics – Uzbeks, Kazakhs, Kirgiz, Tajiks and Turkmenis – are the descendants of the great Mongol empires of medieval times and they speak languages that are of Turkic (or in the case of the Tajiks, Iranian) origin. The territories that they inhabit are for the most part inhospitable, with some of the world's highest mountains and large expanses of desert; and levels of literacy have traditionally been low (some of the nationalities concerned had no written language at all at the time of their incorporation into the USSR). Industry is relatively little developed (although there are important iron and coal deposits in Kazakhstan) and there is a heavy emphasis upon cash crops of various kinds, mostly cotton. The peoples of these republics are overwhelmingly Muslim (mostly Sunni) by religion, and their traditional customs and values, with which their religion is inextricably bound up, have been altered relatively little by the experience of Russian and Soviet rule, which has in fact lasted for no more than a century or so (most of what is now Soviet Central Asia came under Russian control in the second half of the nineteenth century).

The Central Asians, for instance, are often reluctant to permit the employment and education of women, at least to an advanced level, and brides with degrees are reported to command a lower 'price' when they get married than those whose education is less advanced.[20] The proportion of female members of political parties and of local soviets in these republics is considerably lower than it is elsewhere in the former USSR (although in 1988, ironically, the first woman regional party first secretary for many years was appointed in Uzbekistan[21]). Fewer pigs are kept in these republics (pork being an unclean meat for Muslims, as it is for Jews) and traditional customs such as the postponement of cohabitation (*kaitarma*), pilgrimages to the graves of local holy men and even abduction are still practised, in some cases with the covert support of local party officials (most tragic of all were the reports of girls who had burned themselves to death after being dishonoured in this and other ways[22]). There is generally little intermarriage between the Central Asians and other non-Muslim nationalities, and a knowledge of Russian is much less common than it is elsewhere in the other post-Soviet republics.[23] Perhaps most alarmingly of all from a Russian point of view, the population of these republics had been increasing very much more rapidly than the all-union average and on some projections was expected to account for 25–30 per cent of the total Soviet population by the end of the century (the USSR was already the world's fifth largest Muslim state).[24]

Patterns of ethnic interaction

Soviet spokesmen generally argued that, considerable though their ethnic differences might be, they would diminish and ultimately disappear as social and economic standards throughout the USSR improved and became more uniform. There was certainly a good deal of evidence, up to the 1980s, that developments of this kind were taking place. The Soviet Union had become a more industrialised society; an increasing proportion of its population lived in cities and were members of the industrial labour force; and educational standards had risen greatly, particularly among the formerly more backward nations. A knowledge of the Russian language had become more widespread (over 81 per cent of the population were fluent in Russian according to the 1989 census, up from 76 per cent in 1970[25]); and the circulation of printed matter had increased considerably and become more evenly distributed between one republic and another.[26] Membership of the Communist Party had also increased and become more uniform between one nationality and another.[27] The CPSU Central

Committee, reviewing these developments in the early 1970s, went so far as to claim that a 'new historical collectivity of people – the Soviet people' had come into existence in the USSR, based upon the 'common ownership of the means of production, unity of economic, socio-political and cultural life, Marxist–Leninist ideology, and the interests and communist ideals of the working class'.[28] The 1961 Party Programme, still valid on Gorbachev's accession, provided that this process should continue until ultimately the 'complete unity' of the Soviet people was achieved.[29]

A good deal of empirical evidence suggested that these perspectives might not be wholly unrealistic. The investigation conducted by Inkeles and Bauer among Soviet émigrés in the 1950s, for instance, found that the nationality of most respondents had less influence upon their political beliefs and values than did other variables such as social class and education. Nationality as such played little part in most respondents' educational life-chances or expectations; and educational attainment in turn was far more important than nationality as a determinant of occupational position, although Russians did enjoy some advantages in applying for minor bureaucratic positions because of their better knowledge of the language in which most state business was conducted. There were relatively few differences between the Russians and Ukrainians who were surveyed in terms of their political attitudes, and relatively few Ukrainians cited nationality policy as an aspect of the system they would like to change compared with the very large numbers who, like their Russian counterparts, were in favour of the abolition of the collective farm system and the ending of police terror. Younger respondents, moreover, tended on the whole to take a more favourable view of Soviet nationality policy and to manifest less hostility towards Russians then did their elders, particularly if they were better educated.[30] Investigations conducted among more recent groups of émigrés suffer from the fact that such groups have been disproportionately Jewish; there has nevertheless been some support for the view that nationality is not a 'primordial' attachment and that its political importance is likely to depend on situational factors such as the degree of competition for employment opportunities.[31]

A variety of investigations conducted within the USSR itself also suggested that Soviet nationalities policy might be achieving at least some of its objectives. Attitudes towards marriage with a member of a different nationality, for instance, were found to be more favourable among the urban population (an increasing proportion of the total) than among their rural counterparts. They were also more favourable among the better educated, who were in turn more likely to know Russian and to have a marriage partner and friends from a nationality other than their own.[32] A particularly detailed investigation into matters of this kind was conducted in the Tatar autonomous republic, whose social and demographic characteristics were reasonably representative of the Soviet population as a whole. Russians and Tatars, it was found, were distributed in a broadly similar manner in the occupational hierarchy, received approximately the same remuneration, and were active in socio-political life in virtually the same proportions. Nationality as such was found to have little bearing upon patterns of friendship, reading of newspapers, watching of television, or attendance at theatres or concerts. There were slight differences between Russians and Tatars (a traditionally Muslim nationality) in terms of religious observance and size of family; but these were largely accounted for by differences in the age structures of the two groups. Education, moreover, was tending to reduce those differences that still remained; the proportion of children receiving their education through Russian was steadily increasing, and Russian-speaking Tatars were found in turn to be more favourably disposed towards inter-nationality contact in their home and workplace.[33]

Similar trends were found in other Soviet investigations conducted in the 1970s and 1980s. A large-scale investigation in five different republics in the late 1970s, for instance, found that there were fewer differences in educational attainment among younger age-groups than among their older counterparts. Occupational patterns were becoming more uniform, and so too were cultural characteristics such as clothing, housing, media consumption and religious observance. There were still some important differences among the nationalities, but these related primarily to the domestic sphere; Central Asians, for instance, lived in larger family groups, and attached rather more importance to the views of their parents.[34] Other studies, using census as well as survey data, found that levels of urbanisation were becoming more uniform from republic to republic, and that rural and urban living conditions were becoming more similar; there was an increasing uniformity of occupational structure and a particularly notable increase in the representation of specialists among the previously less well educated national groups.[35] The percentage of ethnically mixed marriages was also increasing: it rose in every union republic between 1959 and 1989, and for the USSR as a whole from 10.2 to 18 per cent.[36] A number of nationalities, indeed, had altogether disappeared (or become fully assimilated) over the period of Soviet rule: the census of 1926 recorded the existence of 194 ethnic groups but the census of 1959 only 109 and that of 1970 just 104 (although there was subsequently a slight increase).[37]

The overall picture, however, was by no means so clearcut as the data so far considered might tend to suggest. Levels of intermarriage, in the first place, varied considerably from republic to republic and from nationality to nationality; and although the proportion of ethnically mixed families at the national and republican level might have been increasing, it did not necessarily follow that the incidence of intermarriage between each of the major nationalities had been increasing at a similar rate. The main increase in nationally mixed marriages was in fact among the western or Slavic nationalities of the USSR, and to some extent also between Slavs and Balts; intermarriage between the other major nationalities of the USSR, and in particular between Slavs and Muslims, was much less common and provided much less convincing evidence of the formation of a single 'Soviet nation'. It was reported, for instance, that of the nationally mixed marriages in Turkmenia from the 1920s to the 1970s, not a single one had been between a Turkmen girl and a Russian man. Marriages between Muslim men and non-Muslim women, although not specifically prohibited by Islamic law, were also relatively uncommon.[38] Mixed marriages of all kinds in fact declined in three of the Muslim republics, Uzbekistan, Azerbaijan and Tajikistan, during the 1970s; and differences in the incidence of mixed marriages between one republic and another became slightly greater.[39]

A greater knowledge of the Russian language, moreover, by no means necessarily implied a weaker attachment to the native language of the nationality in question. Russian had indeed become more widely known; it served as the language of administration and internationality communication, as well as a means of education and career advancement. Most Soviet citizens, however, appeared to have remained loyal to their native language in their domestic and family life, and there was little sign of the disappearance of at least the major Soviet languages, most of which were still spoken by the great majority of the nationalities in question (the 1979 census found that 62 per cent of non-Russians were fluent in that language, but that 93 per cent of the population identified their national language as their native one; the 1989 census found that the reported level of knowledge of Russian had actually fallen among at least two national groups, the Uzbeks and Lithuanians[40]). The Central Asian nationalities were the most resistant to russification in this as in other respects: no more than 3 per cent of any of the five major nationalities concerned claimed Russian as a native language in the 1989 census, a much lower proportion than for the non-Russian population as a whole, and levels of fluency in Russian were also much lower than among minority nationalities elsewhere in the USSR.[41] Changes in the degree of attachment of the major Muslim nationalities to their native languages have in fact been 'negligible' over the whole Soviet period.[42]

The gradual assimilation of minority nationalities, moreover, has operated less to the advantage of the Russian population as such than to the advantage of the larger nationalities in general, Russians included. Census data, for instance, made clear that an increasing proportion of the more numerous national groups had been choosing to live in their 'own' union republic, with the greatest increases in Central Asia, the Baltic and Armenia (Russians, by contrast, had become more dispersed throughout the USSR).[43] At the same time there was an increase in the proportion of the populations of most union republics that was accounted for by the titular nationality, an increase that was again most marked in Central Asia with its higher birthrates. There had been a steady increase in the ethnic heterogeneity of most union republics between the wars; since then, and particularly since the 1960s, the trend had been in the opposite direction.[44] There was also a good deal of evidence, by the late 1980s, that the cultural self-consciousness of the minority nationalities had not been adversely affected by their increasing urbanisation, industrialisation and ability to use the Russian language. The circulation of native-language newspapers, for instance, was increasing more rapidly than that of Russian-language newspapers in Central Asia; the local languages were being purged of the Russian loan words that had been imported during the 1930s and 1940s; and the indigenous intelligentsia was showing little sign of relinquishing its national self-consciousness.[45] Nor was there much evidence elsewhere, even before the open disturbances of the late 1980s, that non-Russian nationalities were merging their identity into that of a greater Soviet community.

Indeed the evidence, by the late 1970s and early 1980s, suggested that Soviet nationalities policy, so far from reducing national self-consciousness, might actually be increasing it. The development of republican publishing industries, for instance, had helped to bring into being a group of local writers and journalists who tended naturally to operate in terms of the idiom with which both they and their readers were most familiar. The expansion of educational opportunities in the less industrialised republics, again, led to the emergence of a substantial native intelligentsia who saw little reason for responsible positions in their locality to be filled by outsiders. Local political elites, although originally intended to represent the interests of the central government within their area, appeared increasingly to resent their limited control over local appointment and investment decisions and were increasingly willing to employ 'nationalist' arguments as a means of increasing their leverage upon the central authorities in this connection. The very existence of a national-territorial framework in the USSR, indeed, far from providing for the peaceful solution of the nationalities question that was originally envisaged, appeared to have led to precisely the opposite result by establishing a form of representation in which sectional interests, denied any other means of expression, could in practice take only the form of 'nationalism'.[46] It was certainly clear, as the 1970s drew to a close, that the nationalities question was by no means destined for the historical obsolescence to which official spokesmen wished to consign it, and even Brezhnev, recommending the adoption of the 1977 Constitution, warned that it would be not just unLeninist but actually 'dangerous' if the steady convergence of the Soviet nations were artificially accelerated.[47]

The national question under Gorbachev

The first significant expression of nationalist discontent after Gorbachev's accession was in the Central Asian republic of Kazakhstan, following the nomination of an ethnic Russian, Gennadii Kolbin, to replace the Brezhnevite incumbent Dinmukhamed Kunaev as party first secretary. Kazakhstan had a very substantial Russian population – 37.8 per cent of the total according to the 1989 census, almost as many as the Kazakhs themselves – but it was the home of the great majority of the Soviet Union's Kazakhs and it had become accepted that the republic's party and state leadership should be drawn from the national group after whom the republic was named. Not less important, Kunaev was at the centre of an elaborate network of patronage and corruption which was clearly threatened by the imposition of an ethnic and political outsider.[48] The demonstrations that followed Kolbin's appointment may have been covertly encouraged by Kunaev's clients; there was certainly no doubt that, as *Literaturnaya gazeta* reported in early 1987, the news provoked 'inexperienced and politically illiterate youths' to take to the streets, later to be joined by 'hooligans, drunks and other anti-social types'. Nationalist slogans, 'pulled out of the murkiest depths of history', were chanted, and the crowd, armed with metal posts, sticks and stones, then proceeded to beat up local citizens, overturn cars and set them on fire, and smash the windows of shops and other public buildings.[49] Government sources subsequently acknowledged that up to 3,000 people had been involved in the demonstrations, and that 200 had been injured; unofficial sources suggested that as many as 280 students had lost their lives, together with twenty-nine policemen and soldiers.[50]

The next national issue to take the form of open public discontent was in the summer of 1987 when a group of about 700 Crimean Tatars staged an unprecedented demonstration in Red Square.[51] The Tatars had been one of the groups expelled from their traditional homelands in 1944 on grounds of alleged Nazi sympathies (and a certain amount of active collaboration). Five of the seven ethnic groups that were relocated in this way were rehabilitated and partially repatriated to their native territories in 1956–7. The Crimean Tatars, however, were officially exonerated of the charge of disloyalty much later, in 1967, and they were given no general right to return to their former homelands, not least because the territories they had left had now been settled by other nationalities.[52] By the early 1980s only a few thousand of the million or so who lived elsewhere in the USSR had been able to return, despite an active campaign on their behalf by dissidents as well as Tatar activists. In the event, the Tatars, remarkably and unexpectedly, were allowed to hold their demonstration without police harassment, and following discussions with government representatives a commission headed by then President Gromyko was established to 'study the merits of their case'.[53] In June 1988 it reported, recommending the removal of any improper restrictions upon the right of individual Tatars to return to their native land and calling for more attention to be paid to their cultural needs, but also rejecting the Tatars' call for the reestablishment of their autonomous republic.[54] Substantial numbers of Tatars returned to live in their traditional homelands and, following a referendum in which the idea had received overwhelming support, a Crimean autonomous republic was finally restored by a vote of the Ukrainian parliament in February 1991.[55]

In many ways the most significant of all the Soviet nationality disputes began to acquire open and public form in the summer of 1987 in the Baltic republics on the anniversary of the Nazi–Soviet pact which had led to the incorporation of these republics into the USSR. Several thousand Estonians were reported to have demonstrated on 23 August, the date of the pact's signature; still larger numbers, between 7,000 and 10,000, were reported to have demonstrated in Latvia (where substantial demonstrations also occurred in June 1987 to commemorate those who had been deported from the republic by the Soviet authorities in 1941).[56] The secret protocols under which these republics had been incorporated into the USSR were finally published in the Baltic press in August 1988 and in the national press the following year, but the matters under dispute widened into a challenge to the established relationship between the USSR as a whole and its constituent republics. So far from resolving the issues in dispute, indeed, the public acknowledgement that the protocols had existed began to call in question the legal status of the incorporation of these republics into the USSR, which had followed a Soviet military occupation and a clearly coerced vote by their respective Supreme Soviets.[57]

Baltic discontent was the product of several causes. One of them was the very real concern that, with low birthrates and high levels of immigration, particularly of unskilled Russians, the Baltic peoples might become minorities in their own republics. Estonians, for instance, 90 per cent of the population of their republic in 1940, had slipped to 62 per cent by the late 1980s, and to still lower levels in the towns. Latvians, 77 per cent of the population of their republic before the war, had fallen to 52 per cent in the 1989 census, and to about a third of the population of their capital city, Riga.[58] There was also concern about the environmental damage that had been suffered as a result of decisions about economic development taken in Moscow rather than in the republics themselves. Estonia, for instance, had the largest deposits of shale in the Soviet Union, and very considerable deposits of phosphorite and limestone; but their rapid exploitation in the interests of the Soviet economy as a whole had led to serious environmental damage and to water pollution in particular. Bathing, for instance, had to be forbidden along the fashionable coastline; some ecologists even suggested that Estonian drinking water was so polluted it could be set on fire![59] The safety of the Ignalina nuclear power station in Lithuania, based on a similar design to Chernobyl', was raised by the republican party secretary at the 19th Party Conference; the construction of a third reactor, he complained, was proceeding before the details of its design had been approved, and before proper arrangements had been made for its security.[60]

Influenced by developments such as these, substantial public support began to develop for measures which would protect the position of the indigenous nationalities and which would ensure that economic decisions were taken with a greater degree of consideration for local circumstances. Baltic representatives, for instance, associated themselves closely at the 19th Party Conference with the call for 'regional *khozraschet*' or in practice for republican self-sufficiency. The newly-appointed Estonian leader Vaino Valjas complained that more than 90 per cent of the republican economy was in the hands of Moscow ministries, and called for the balance to be reversed in the republic's favour.[61] The Latvian party leader Boris Pugo attacked the 'boundless *diktat* of the union ministries' and called for the establishment of 'genuine sovereignty' for the union republics based upon the principle of self-financing.[62] The Lithuanian party leader complained similarly of the 'administrative *diktat*' of higher bodies and called for more economic, social and especially ecological powers to be transferred to the republics.[63] The idea of regional or republican cost-accounting received no more than a cautious welcome in the resolution on national relations that was adopted at the conference; the resolution did however speak of the 'further development' of the federation, involving the transfer of greater powers to the local level and to the union republics in particular.[64]

More important, perhaps, was the emergence in the Baltic republics themselves of an open, widely supported and coordinated nationalist movement taking the form of 'popular fronts' (or in Lithuania, Sajudis). Ostensibly 'in favour of *perestroika*' and incorporating many party members within their ranks, the new movements were none the less associated with a policy stance which went very much further than the party conference resolution. Their founding congresses in October 1988, for instance, called (in the case of Sajudis) for 'sovereignty' in all areas of Lithuanian life, the formation of a 'pluralist society' with no organisation 'usurping' political power, a partly privatised economy, and the demilitarisation of the republican territory (in effect, withdrawal from the Warsaw Treaty Organisation).[65] The Latvian Popular Front, similarly, called for the 'economic sovereignty' of the republic, and for the ending of immigration and the abolition of special privileges for all high-ranking officials.[66] In a series of related developments the old flags of the independent Baltic states between the wars were legalised, in Lithuania the pre-war national anthem was restored, and legislation was initiated with a view to establishing Lithuanian and Estonian as official languages in their respective republics.[67] In Lithuania the Roman Catholic cathedral, used as an art gallery for forty years, was restored to the faithful in October 1988.[68] Estonia left the Soviet time zone and aligned itself chronologically with Finland; Christmas became a public holiday; and the republican capital, Tallinn, was given its Estonian name (with two ns rather than one) for all-union purposes.[69]

The publication of draft constitutional amendments in October 1988 led to widespread public protests. Baltic opinion, in particular, objected that the changes proposed were centralising in character and that the republics' (admittedly nominal) right of secession had been prejudiced.[70] The Estonian parliament, influenced by these concerns, adopted a constitutional amendment on 16 November providing for the right of veto over all legislation that was intended to apply to the USSR as a whole. The decision was held to be unconstitutional by the Supreme Soviet Presidium on 20 November and the Baltic republics came in for severe criticism from other delegates at the Supreme Soviet session on 1 December which passed the constitutional amendments into law. Some changes, however, were made in the draft to satisfy those who had challenged it in this way: union republics were given eleven rather than seven seats each in the Supreme Soviet's Council of Nationalities and *ex officio* places on the Committee of Constitutional Supervision, and changes of wording were made in order to remove what Gorbachev described as the 'misunderstanding' that the rights of republics had been infringed. Further constitutional changes were promised at a later stage which would place the relationship between the USSR and its constituent republics on a new and more equitable basis.[71]

Relations between the Baltic republics and the central authorities, in the event, became still more strained over the period that followed. A form of economic decentralisation, already approved by the Baltic legislatures, was given a cautious welcome by the USSR Supreme Soviet in July 1989 and was formally adopted at the winter parliamentary session. The legislation applied to the three Baltic republics and (under a separate provision) Belorussia in the first instance; some regions of the Russian Republic indicated that they too would seek to place their relations with the central government on this new basis.[72] Legislation on the position of the local languages in early 1989 aroused more controversy: according the views of some commentators in *Izvestiya*, the new directives, at least in Estonia, placed non-native speakers at a considerable disadvantage and probably infringed their civil rights.[73] Lithuania and Latvia, in May and June 1989 respectively, established a form of republican citizenship.[74] A set of constitutional amendments adopted by the Estonian Supreme Soviet proved most controversial of all. The amendments (which were later rescinded) restricted the right to vote to those who had lived in the constituency for at least two years, or elsewhere in Estonia for five years or more; deputies themselves had to have lived in Estonia for at least ten years.[75] The change provoked an extended strike on the part of the largely Russian speaking blue-collar labour force, and the Supreme Soviet Presidium in Moscow declared the legislation unconstitutional on the grounds that it violated the principle of equal electoral rights (some 80,000, it was estimated, would be deprived of the franchise under the new regulations).[76] The interests of the non-indigenous population were articulated by bodies such as 'Interfront' in Latvia, set up in January 1989, and its counterparts in the other republics; the concerns of the substantial Russian-speaking minority in these republics were also expressed in letters to the central press, and found some reflection in the speeches of members of the party leadership.[77]

The central party leadership, in fact, went so far as to issue a formal statement on the Baltic situation in late August 1989, warning against the activities of 'extremist' and 'anti-socialist' forces that were pursuing a separatist line with 'growing persistence and aggressiveness'.[78] Declarations of this kind, however, no longer had much effect. The stance that local leaderships had taken had enormous public support, expressed both in the number prepared to take part in public meetings and in opinion polls,[79] and openly nationalist pressures became if anything still stronger. On 23 August 1989, the 50th anniversary of the Nazi–Soviet pact, an estimated two million Balts formed a human chain across the three republics in the biggest demonstration that had yet been seen.[80] The popular fronts themselves became still more intransigent in their demands: both the Latvian and the Lithuanian fronts, in late 1989, were openly contemplating the possibility of formal secession from the USSR, not simply a greater measure of autonomy, and the three fronts jointly organised a Baltic Assembly which called for political independence for the republics within a 'neutral and demilitarised Balto–Scandia'.[81] Perhaps most disturbing from the point of view of the central authorities, the party organisations in the three republics, particularly in Lithuania, began to press for a greater degree of independence, establishing direct links with outside ruling parties and adopting their own programme and statute, within or if necessary outside the framework of the CPSU as a whole.[82]

Inter-republican relations in the USSR entered an entirely new stage when in February 1990 supporters of Sajudis won a majority of seats in the republican parliament and then, on 11 March, formally declared Lithuania independent on the basis of its prewar constitution.[83] Gorbachev, addressing the Congress of People's Deputies, described the Lithuanian action as 'illegitimate and invalid' and refused to open negotiations with what remained, in his view, an integral part of the USSR.[84] The central authorities issued an ultimatum demanding the withdrawal of the declaration of independence; when the Lithuanians refused to comply with this an economic blockade was imposed on 18 April.[85] These pressures notwithstanding, the neighbouring republics of Estonia and Latvia adopted more cautiously-worded declarations of independence on 30 March and 4 May respectively.[86] The situation eased, at least temporarily, when the Lithuanian declaration of independence was suspended by parliamentary vote on 29 June, allowing the blockade to be lifted and a negotiation process to begin.[87] Gorbachev, visiting Lithuania in January 1990, had unexpectedly promised that legislation would be introduced allowing republics to become fully independent; but the law on secession, approved on 3 April 1990, specified a two-thirds majority in a referendum on the issue and then a transitional period of up to five years in which territorial, property and other issues would be resolved.[88] Only the Lithuanians accounted for so large a proportion of the population of their own republic, and the measure was widely seen as blocking rather than facilitating a transition to fully independent status.

The resolution of differences in this or any other way became still more unlikely when in January 1991 military force was used to restore central authority in Latvia and Lithuania on the pretext that the Soviet Constitution was being violated (in particular, that the civil rights of the non-indigenous population were being infringed and that the call-up of recruits into the armed forces was being impeded[89]). In Lithuania, 13 died and 112 were injured when troops stormed the television centre in Vilnius; in Latvia, four died in a battle for government buildings in Riga.[90] The Soviet defence minister, seeking to justify the action, claimed that organised attempts were being made to establish a 'dictatorship of the bourgeois type' in the area; the Lithuanian president, Vytautas Landsbergis, saw the conflict as a result of the 'fifty-one year confrontation between Lithuania and the USSR', and the Russian president, Boris Yel'tsin, more forthrightly described it as an 'offensive against democracy'.[91] At least to some observers the action in the Baltic represented an attempt by hard-line party and military officials, organised in a shadowy 'Committee of National Salvation', to seize power and overthrow the nationalist administrations.[92] Whether they had taken such action with the explicit authorisation of President Gorbachev remained unclear, although it was widely agreed that he had failed to respond adequately to the loss of life that had occurred.

The actions of the central authorities, in the event, served to rally local opinion still more closely around the nationalist leaderships, and when the issue of full independence was put to the republican populations in the spring of 1991 it received overwhelming endorsement. The Lithuanian vote, in February, produced a majority of over 90 per cent on an 84 per cent turnout;[93] in Latvia and Estonia, in March, there were majorities for independence of 74 and 78 per cent on a similar turnout.[94] The votes had little constitutional force (although Iceland, for instance, moved at once to establish diplomatic relations with Lithuania[95]). They nonetheless strengthened the authority of the republican leaderships as they gradually extended their effective control over local affairs. All three republics, for instance, had already reformulated Article 6 of their own constitutions so as to end the communist political monopoly.[96] During 1990 and 1991 they steadily withdrew from the work of all-union bodies, including the Congress of People's Deputies and Federation Council, and suspended contributions to the USSR budget.[97] All three republics established their own customs services and began to issue their own stamps and passports;[98] more significant still, they began to adopt their own budgets and to make preparations for the issuing of local currencies.[99] Of all the Soviet nationalities, the Baltic nations looked the most likely to establish (or as they saw it, resume) their independent statehood in the 1990s; their opportunity to do so came soon after the attempted coup when (in September 1991) the USSR Council of State formally approved their independent status and they were admitted into the United Nations and other international organisations.[100]

Communal tensions: Nagorno-Karabakh, Georgia and Uzbekistan

The pressures for independence or at least a greater measure of autonomy that emerged in the Baltic republics were the most serious of their kind that the Soviet leadership had to confront in the early Gorbachev years. In all three republics, with minor local variations, a largely united people with a distinct cultural identity and a previous history of self-rule were seeking to renegotiate the nature of their relationship with the Soviet state and its economic and political system. The ethnic differences that emerged elsewhere in the USSR in the late 1980s were for the most part more traditional, almost 'tribal' in character, in that they sprang from antipathies between ethnic groups with different religious, linguistic and historical backgrounds and expressed themselves in the form of communal clashes rather than pressures for formal independence. The first of these disputes to emerge was in the Caucasus, where the most serious civil disturbances in Soviet post-war history took place between Armenians and Azerbaijanis over the disputed territorial enclave of Nagorno-Karabakh. There were comparable difficulties elsewhere, particularly in Georgia and Uzbekistan, and indeed there were few parts of Soviet territory that did not experience some form of nationalist self-consciousness combined with pressure for a greater degree of cultural and economic autonomy.

Nationalist tensions took a particularly violent and intractable form in the case of Nagorno-Karabakh, an autonomous region which had since 1923 formed a part of the Azerbaijan republic.[101] A mountainous enclave of about 4,400 square kilometres, Nagorno-Karabakh had originally been assigned to Armenia but had then been transferred to the jurisdiction of its traditionally Muslim neighbour. Its 1979 census population of about 162,000 was 75.9 per cent Armenian and only 22.9 per cent Azerbaijani, and there had been pressure for some years for its transfer back to Armenia and for a greater degree of autonomy for its predominantly Christian people.[102] The open conflict of early 1988 was precipitated, it appears, by the rejection by the central party authorities of an appeal for Nagorno-Karabakh to be returned to Armenia which had been signed by 75,000 Karabakh Armenians.[103] Demonstrations began on 11 February in Stepanakert, the regional capital, and led to the adoption of a resolution by the regional soviet on 20 February which called for Nagorno-Karabakh to be transferred back to Armenia.[104] Further demonstrations took place in the Armenian capital, Yerevan, to support the call for Nagorno-Karabakh's reincorporation into the republic. Up to a million Armenians, by late February, were reported to be demonstrating daily in the city's Opera Square.[105] The demonstrations came temporarily to an end after a personal appeal by Gorbachev on 26 February, but a report that two Azerbaijanis had been killed the previous week led to an anti-Armenian riot on 28–29 February in the oil town of Sumgait in which 32 people were killed and 197 were injured, including more than 100 police officers.[106] The party first secretaries of Armenia, Azerbaijan and Nagorno-Karabakh were all replaced in May 1988; the Central Committee meanwhile promised that steps would be taken to improve housing, schools and hospitals in the region, and to extend broadcasts in both Armenian and Azerbaijani.[107]

Despite Gorbachev's assurances to two Armenian emissaries that a 'just solution' would be found, the Supreme Soviet Presidium warned on 23 March that 'self-proclaimed groups' (a reference to the Karabakh Committee, a group of Armenian activists whose activities were made illegal) could not be allowed to call for the redrawing of state and administrative boundaries, and *Pravda* made clear that the transfer of Nagorno-Karabakh to Armenia would be a 'clearly anti-socialist solution'.[108] On 15 June, after further demonstrations, the Armenian Supreme Soviet voted unanimously for the disputed region to be transferred to their republic; the Azerbaijani Supreme Soviet, meeting two days later, was equally unanimous in holding this vote to be in violation of the Soviet Constitution.[109] The Supreme Soviet Presidium, at its meeting on 18 July, adopted a formal ruling which rejected any change in the constitutional status of Nagorno-Karabakh, but called for greater attention to be given to the concerns of ethnic Armenians living within the disputed region; a programme of cultural and economic aid was also approved.[110] The situation temporarily stabilised, but in further unrest in November at least thirty deaths were reported and tens of thousands of refugees were reported to have joined fellow nationals in the other republic (eventually about 130,000 Azeris left Armenia and 200,000 Armenians made the journey in the reverse direction[111]).

Continued tensions led in January 1989 to the establishment of a 'special form of administration', in effect direct rule from Moscow, headed by Arkadii Vol'sky, who had been appointed the previous summer to represent the central government in the contested region.[112] The situation, according to *Pravda*, nonetheless remained 'tense and complicated'.[113] Demonstrations and disorders continued, some of them involving firearms, explosives and loss of life; the decision of the Congress of People's Deputies to elect an Azerbaijani as well as an Armenian to represent the region in the new Supreme Soviet aroused particular indignation.[114] Further disorders were precipitated by the decision to abolish the special administration in November 1989 and return Nagorno-Karabakh to Azerbaijani rule;[115] and in January 1990 the dispute extended into inter-communal violence across both republics, precipitated by an Armenian decision to extend the provisions of their republican budget and electoral law to the disputed enclave.[116] Tens of thousands took to the streets in Baku alone, up to sixty people (mostly Armenians) lost their lives in pogroms, and there were further fatalities when a state of emergency was declared by the USSR Presidium and troops were used to restore order on 19–20 January. At least ninety-three people lost their lives in the first days of fighting.[117] The dispute was still continuing in the early 1990s, despite attempts at international mediation. For Vol'sky, interviewed in the press, the whole area was in danger of becoming the Soviet Union's 'home-grown Lebanon'.[118]

Two further ethnic disputes reached the point of violence and bloodshed during 1989 and 1990: a dispute between Meskhetian Turks and the native population in the Ferghana valley in eastern Uzbekistan, and a complex dispute in Georgia involving both a strong separatist movement and communal tensions between Georgians and Abkhazians, a national minority within Georgia itself. The violence in Uzbekistan, which erupted suddenly in early June 1989, swiftly became the bloodiest in Soviet peacetime history.[119] The riots appear to have been precipitated by an apparently casual incident when a Meskhetian angrily tipped over a table of strawberries being sold by an Uzbek girl. This provoked disorders in which one person died and sixty were injured.[120] A much more serious incident began on 3 and 4 June when gangs of youths appeared on the streets of Ferghana and nearby towns, armed with iron bars and Molotov cocktails, and in search of Meskhetians.[121] In the nearby village of Tashlak about 200 youths armed with weapons and incendiary devices, 'many of them in an alcoholic or narcotic stupor', destroyed over 400 houses and motor vehicles as well as several public buildings. There were already fifty-six deaths, the great majority of them Meskhetians; some 9,000 Interior Ministry troops had to be despatched to the area, and a curfew was imposed.[122]

The Meskhetians, another of the 'punished peoples', had been moved from their traditional homelands near the Turkish–Soviet border in 1944, ostensibly in order to protect them against the possibility of a German advance. In 1968 their rights were restored, but no prospect was extended of their return to Georgia. About 60,000 of them remained in Uzbekistan, some 12,000 in the Ferghana valley.[123] Rela tions between the Meskhetians and the Uzbek majority had been strained for some time, largely as a result of the poor housing and other conditions in which the Meskhetians had been forced to remain (many still lived in shanty towns, and levels of unemployment were higher than elsewhere in the republic). There were also accusations of cultural and other forms of discrimination at their expense.[124] Encouraged by these circumstances, the disorders of early June continued for some days. The Ferghana party secretary was shot and slightly wounded when he tried to address a crowd; and 5,000 men armed with automatic rifles and pistols were reported to have stormed party and government buildings in the ancient city of Kokand (if *Izvestiya*'s report was to be believed, they carried a portrait of Lenin in front of them with a message written on the back of it which called for the slaughter of all Turks and Russians and ended 'Long live the Islamic republic and Ayatollah Khomeini').[125] By the end of the week 11,000 Meskhetians had fled their homes and were living in refugee camps with troops protecting them; even here they were not entirely safe as a motorised column armed with automatic weapons set out for one of the camps and was stopped only by a detachment of helicopter gunships.[126] By the end of the week at least 100 people had died and 1,000 had been injured; *Izvestiya* reported that some of the bodies that had been found were so thoroughly mutilated it was impossible to tell if they were men or women.[127]

Gorbachev was at this time on an official visit to West Germany, which was curtailed somewhat in view of domestic developments. In his absence a deputation headed by Prime Minister Ryzhkov and Viktor Chebrikov visited the area. Tass meanwhile reported that the rioting had spread to the neighbouring Namangan region, with up to 2,000 people involved in riots in its regional capital. A gang also razed the village of Gorsky, in the west of the Ferghana region.[128] Ryzhkov's visit coincided, fortuitously or otherwise, with an uneasy calm, although this was 'still far from a complete normalisation of the situation', according to Tass's report.[129] Gorbachev, interviewed in West Germany, suggested that Islamic fundamentalism might have played a part in the disturbances.[130] Ryzhkov, speaking in Tashkent, described them as a 'carefully prepared action' led by 'extremists', and blamed complacent local officials for allowing the situation to develop; some of them, in fact, had actively encouraged the rioters.[131] Several hundred people were arrested and charged with 'organising pogroms, murder and violence', according to *Pravda*; troops remained on duty and a curfew was still in effect in Ferghana, and there were reports of further disturbances elsewhere.[132] Further intercommunal clashes in the town of Osh, at the eastern end of the Ferghana valley, left over 200 dead and 'thousands' of refugees in the summer of 1990.[133]

Long-standing tensions also emerged in Soviet Georgia during 1988 and 1989, inspired in part by nationalist pressures for a greater degree of autonomy within (if not total separation from) the USSR, and in part by differences of a social and ethnic character within Georgia itself. Georgians were not simply distinctive in their cultural and historical background; they were also the most 'patriotic' of the major Soviet nationalities, as measured by the proportion that lived in their own republic, and their share of the republican population had been steadily increasing, unlike the position (for instance) in the Baltic republics.[134] There had, nonetheless, been open public disturbances in 1956, shortly after the death of Stalin, and in 1978, when the status of the republican language appeared to be under threat.[135] In the autumn of 1988 the publication of apparently centralising constitutional amendments led, as in the Baltic republics, to open public opposition. As *Pravda* subsequently reported, 'anti-social elements' had organised 'noisy meetings and processions', either with the approval of the local authorities or where necessary without it. Self-proclaimed 'leaders' had put forward 'extremist slogans', such as 'Georgia for the Georgians' and 'Long live the independence of Georgia'. An unprecedented hunger strike took place in Tbilisi, the republican capital, in an attempt to block the changes; more than a hundred of the demonstrators had to be taken to hospital. One of the 'leaders' even managed to climb on to the roof of government buildings, where he desecrated the state flag. There were demonstrations and strikes not only in Tbilisi but also in other large towns. And most worrying of all, in *Pravda*'s view, local party leaders, used to commanding rather than persuading, had found themselves unable to keep control of the situation.[136]

Further demonstrations in support of independence took place in early 1989 on the anniversary of the republic's incorporation into the USSR (February 1921). Some 15,000 protesters were involved, according to Western press reports, 200 of whom were detained.[137] Still more substantial demonstrations were organised in April 1989. Reports indicated that more than 100,000 demonstrators had gathered in front of Georgian party and government headquarters; many factories were on strike as well as the local television, and troops and armoured personnel carriers were on duty. The demonstrators held banners demanding both the secession of Georgia from the Soviet Union and the full integration of the Abkhazian republic, which had itself been seeking to secede from Georgia and to resume the union republican status it had enjoyed from 1921 until 1931.[138] An Abkhaz nationalist grouping, Ayglara (Unity), had been formed, and the Abkhaz party secretary (dismissed in early April) was reported to have favoured the idea of secession.[139] The leader of another informal nationalist grouping, the Forum for the Peoples of Abkhazia, was elected to the Congress of People's Deputies and to the new-style Supreme Soviet, where he expressed some reservations about the idea of strengthening the fifteen union republics at the expense, almost certainly, of the smaller national-territorial units that were subordinate to them.[140] Georgians, however, accounted for by far the largest share of the population of the Abkhaz republic (Abkhazians themselves were a small minority), and they were resolutely opposed to any diminution of their links with their own republic, holding rival demonstrations within Abkhazia and within Georgia to make their position clear.[141]

Matters reached a critical stage when the demonstrators in central Tbilisi were attacked by interior ministry troops on the evening of 9 April 1989. At least sixteen people were killed, according to official sources, and a curfew had to be introduced.[142] The demonstration followed a hunger strike and a wave of industrial disturbances, and was led by the National Democratic Party of Georgia, the Party of National Independence and two other nationalist groupings broadly similar in character to the popular fronts established in the Baltic. Some of the demonstrators, Tass reported, had put forward 'nationalist, anti-socialist slogans' and had called for strikes, civil disobedience and the liquidation of Soviet power in Georgia; some 'extremists' had been armed with sticks, stones and metal objects. Local sources insisted that all the dead had been unarmed and that they had been attacked with sharpened spades and a noxious gas, which had itself been responsible for the death of two women.[143] No such brutal suppression of a peaceful demonstration had been seen in the Soviet Union since at least the early 1960s, strengthening rumours that the action, directed by the Ministry of Internal Affairs rather than by Georgian officials, might have been covertly encouraged by Kremlin conservatives intent on discrediting Gorbachev and the policy of perestroika.[144] The foreign minister and former Georgian party leader, Eduard Shevardnadze, cancelled his plans to attend a Warsaw Pact meeting and flew to Tbilisi to appeal for calm while tanks patrolled the city streets. Gorbachev added a personal appeal on 13 April.[145] At a plenum of the Georgian central committee the following day the party first secretary, Dzumber Patiashvili, resigned and was replaced by the former head of the Georgian KGB, Givi Gumbaridze; the Georgian prime minister and head of state also tendered their resignations.[146] A Georgian parliamentary commission which was established to investigate the incident later concluded that the interior troops had carried out a 'punitive action – a planned mass massacre, committed with especial cruelty'.[147]

Nor was this the end of the violence. In July 1989 there were further disturbances in Abkhazia over plans to open a section of Tbilisi University in the Abkhazian capital Sukhumi. An inter-nationality conflict developed on 15–16 July which led, according to official reports, to 11 deaths and 127 hospital cases.[148] Tensions became still greater in late 1990 following the success of the 'Round Table/Free Georgia' coalition at the elections and the formation of a nationalist administration headed by the veteran dissident Zviad Gamsakhurdia. The Georgian parliament, under its new leadership, unanimously adopted a resolution calling for the full restoration of republican sovereignty as it had existed up to 1921.[149] A republic-wide vote was held on 30 March 1991 in which 90.3 per cent of the population were reported to have taken part, 98.9 per cent of whom expressed support for the restoration of Georgian independence; following this, on 9 April, the Georgian parliament adopted a further resolution proclaiming the republic a fully independent state (the act, for the moment, had little practical significance).[150] Gamsakhurdia was elected President with 86.5 per cent of the vote in May 1991; he came under increasing pressure thereafter because of an increasingly authoritarian style of government, and in January 1992 was forced to flee the Georgian capital. The former party leader and foreign minister, Eduard Shevardnadze, became effective head of state in March 1992.[151]

There were strong pressures from still further national minorities for a greater degree of control over their own affairs. A popular front came into existence in the Ukraine in late 1988, influenced by concerns about the environment (and the further development of nuclear power in particular) as well as by enduring linguistic and other cultural issues. The Front, known as 'Rukh' ('Movement'), held its founding congress in September 1989; the local authorities, meanwhile, began to address one of its central concerns by making Ukrainian the official state language in the republic. A declaration of sovereignty, adopted in July 1990, asserted the republic's right to its own armed forces and security as well as natural resources.[152] A Belorussian popular front was formed in June 1989, although its founding congress had to take place in Lithuania because of the hostility of the republican leadership. [153] Soviet Germans, about two million strong, established a new All-Union Society of Germans in early 1989 and called for the restoration of their autonomous republic, which had been abolished at the outbreak of the war in 1941.[154] There were demonstrations in Moldavia (renamed Moldova) calling for greater control over local affairs, and in particular for official status for the Moldavian language; there were counter-demonstrations by the republic's non-Moldavian population, more than a third of the total, against what they saw as a form of reverse discrimination (Russian, in the event, was retained as a means of inter-nationality communication).[155] Both Tatars and Bashkirs claimed full union republican status, in the autumn of 1990, and complained of the management of up to 97 per cent of their oil-rich economy by outside agencies.[156] There were further calls from many of the Soviet Union's 'little peoples' – minority nationalities of relatively modest numbers which generally lacked their own national-territorial areas – about falling populations and the use of their area for unrestricted industrial activity. The most serious problems were in Siberia, where press reports spoke of the 'unregulated and uncontrolled destruction of the very conditions of existence of the indigenous population'.[157]

National assertiveness reached the largest and most important of the Soviet Union's republics, the Russian, in May 1990, following the elections to the republican Congress of People's Deputies in which radical candidates had won a substantial proportion of the vote (see above, p. 59). After several ballots the former Moscow party secretary, Boris Yel'tsin, was elected chairman of the Russian Supreme Soviet or *de facto* republican president on 29 May. His programme had combined calls for radical political reform with a strong appeal for Russia's sovereign rights, including ownership of all the republic's natural resources, an independent foreign policy, and the primacy of republican legislation over that of the USSR as a whole.[158] The Russian Congress of People's Deputies resolved to this effect on 12 June;[159] in a separate development a Russian Communist Party was established on 21 June and Ivan Polozkov, a relatively conservative party leader from Krasnodar, was elected its first secretary.[160] Other republican institutions, including a trade union organisation, a Komsomol, an Academy of Sciences, a union of journalists and a national symphony orchestra, began to be established during the year; a republican KGB was established in 1991, and a Russian radio and television service.[161] The republican constitution was changed (as others had been) to exclude the leading role of the Communist Party,[162] and an entirely new constitution began to be drafted which would itself be 'deideologised'.[163]

The Russian legislators were concerned, in particular, that Russia should resume control over its own economic destinies. About 70 per cent of Russian industry, according to Yel'tsin, was run by all-union ministries, and central rather than republican institutions owned 87 per cent of capital stock in the republic and accounted for more than 90 per cent of Russian exports.[164] Russia, it was widely argued, subsidised the other republics to the extent of 70 billion rubles a year.[165] According to figures made public in 1990, it was one of the few republics to run a positive balance in its trade with other republics. It was in deficit in its trade with the outside world, calculated in Soviet domestic prices, but with its oil and other resources expressed in world market prices it was the only republic to have a positive balance in its trade with non-Soviet partners; and it was the most economically self-sufficient of all the republics.[166] The dispute, however, was also a personal one, between Yel'tsin and his former Politburo colleague, Mikhail Gorbachev. They agreed on the direction of change, Yel'tsin suggested in October 1990, but not about its tempo; Gorbachev, for his part, professed to see the difference not in personal terms but as one between 'two different political lines and programmatic aims'.[167]

Yel'tsin's position had been strengthened by his election to the all-union and the Russian parliaments, and by a high opinion poll rating. His election was generally seen as the 'event of the year' and he himself as the 'man of the year'; his popularity soon moved above that of the President and General Secretary.[168] According to a poll in early 1991 Yel'tsin was already the most important Russian leader of the twentieth century, ahead of Lenin, Bukharin and (a long way behind but with a similar rating) Gorbachev and Trotsky.[169] His position was strengthened still further by the decision, in March 1991, to institute a fully presidential system in Russia itself; when elections to the position were held, in June 1991, Yel'tsin was elected by a convincing majority on the first ballot with over 45 million votes, 57.3 per cent of the total. His popularity, nonetheless, was beginning to fade, he lacked the backing of an organised political party, and there was some criticism in the Russian parliament itself of his performance as leader and of his unduly confrontational approach to relations with the Soviet President, particularly a direct call for the President's resignation in a TV interview in February 1991.[170] Yel'tsin later agreed to take part in the negotiations that led to a '9 + 1' agreement at Novo–Ogarevo, a government dacha near Moscow, between President Gorbachev and nine of the republican leaders, covering a wide range of measures to deal with the crisis that had developed in every sphere of Soviet life but especially the economy,[171] and he was still prepared, after the unsuccessful coup, to negotiate a new political union. In the end, however, the Ukrainian decision to vote for full independence left him with little alternative but to withdraw from the USSR and in effect bring about its demise (see pp. 179–85).

Policy choices and policy dilemmas

The national question was not, to begin with, one to which Gorbachev devoted particular attention. His early speeches did include an address on the fiftieth anniversary of the Karachaevo-Cherkessk

autonomous region, which was administratively subordinate to Stavropol, and in December 1972, on the occasion of the fiftieth anniversary
of the foundation of the USSR, an article on the 'Great union of
friendly peoples' appeared in the regional newspaper.[172] Some years
later, in 1980, Gorbachev represented the central leadership at a ceremony in Vilnius to commemorate the fortieth anniversary of the
incorporation of Lithuania into the USSR. His speech, 'The friendship
of the peoples of the USSR – a priceless asset', was wholly conventional, even by the standards of the time.[173] Gorbachev's otherwise
adventurous address to an ideology conference in December 1984,
shortly before his assumption of the general secretaryship, was again
wholly routine in its reference to the 'real equality of all nations and
nationalities, their further all-round development and convergence,
indissoluble brotherly friendship, deep family identity [and the] formation of a new historical community – the Soviet people' (Brezhnev
could hardly have put it better).[174] Gorbachev's acceptance speech at
the March 1985 Central Committee meeting contained just a passing
reference to the 'steadfast strengthening of the friendship of the
peoples of our great multinational power'; an address on the 40th
anniversary of the Soviet victory in World War II referred similarly to
the 'blossoming of nations and nationalities' in the USSR which was
'organically connected with their all-round convergence'.[175]

Gorbachev's later speeches on the national question were scarcely
more illuminating. His report to the 27th Party Congress in February
1986, perhaps the most important of these, referred to Soviet nationalities policy as an 'outstanding achievement of socialism' which had
'done away for ever' with national oppression and inequalities of all
kinds. An indissoluble friendship among the Soviet nations had been
established, and a Soviet people, a 'qualitatively new social and international community', had come into being, 'cemented by the same
economic interests, ideology and political goals'. A note of caution,
however, began to be sounded in Gorbachev's warning that 'contradictions' were unavoidable in any kind of social development, including relations among the nationalities, and he acknowledged that there
were still tendencies towards 'national isolation' and 'localism'.[176] His
Perestroika, written in the summer of 1987, reflected the same more
careful tone. The nationality question, for Gorbachev, had certainly
been resolved 'in principle'. The USSR, set against an international
background of ethnic strife, was a 'truly unique example in the history
of human civilisation', as he knew from his own experience in the
northern Caucasus. This did not, however, mean that nationality

matters were free of problems, or that they could be isolated from real life with its diversity and difficulties. There were still tendencies towards national rivalry and arrogance, and these could only be countered by a steadfast policy of internationalism.[177]

Gorbachev's speech to the Central Committee in January 1987, made shortly after the riots in Kazakhstan, marked a new stage in his awareness of the complexity of national issues. The events in Alma-Ata, in the General Secretary's view, required a 'serious analysis and a principled assessment'. There were 'negative phenomena and deformations' in relations between the nationalities, as there were in other spheres of Soviet life; and there had been incidents elsewhere not very different from those in the Kazakh capital. Gorbachev still identified internationalism as the policy which could deal most effectively with problems of this kind. But he also mentioned the need to ensure that the various nationalities were properly represented in political and economic life, and he acknowledged that party officials had sometimes handled nationality issues without the degree of sensitivity that they required. Nor was there a satisfactory body of analysis on matters of this kind: too many of the scholars concerned had preferred to write works that were 'reminiscent at times of complimentary toasts' rather than engage in the difficult task of examining the complex nature of nationality relations in real life.[178] Neglect of nationality issues, the General Secretary told media workers a month later, was even 'dangerous'.[179] They could never forget, he told his audience in his 70th anniversary speech later in the year, that they lived in a multinational state. They must be attentive to all the susceptibilities that people might have in this connection, and ensure that all of them played a part in resolving the tasks that arose in a society of this kind. The whole nationality question, he promised, would shortly be discussed more fully in the light of the changes that were taking place in other areas of Soviet life; perhaps, he added in early 1988, this could be the subject of one of the forthcoming meetings of the Central Committee.[180]

The next sustained discussion of nationality issues in fact took place at the 19th Party Conference in the summer of 1988. Gorbachev, in his address, still felt able to claim that the establishment of a union of nations and nationalities enjoying equal rights was 'one of the greatest accomplishments of socialism'. At the same time there were 'omissions and difficulties' and 'occasional failures to reconcile the interests of individual nations with those of the USSR as a whole'. The way forward, in his view, lay in developing economic links of all kinds among the republics, and deepening the domestic division of labour. The economic and constitutional rights of the republics, at the same time, should be increased and defined more precisely; but any changes of this kind must take account of the fact that each of the republics was itself a multinational state in which the interests of all national groups must be properly respected. Any other policy would 'lead to disaster'.[181] The resolution on nationality relations adopted at the conference reflected very similar concerns. A 'new historical community – the Soviet people' had come into existence, based upon a common destiny and an interdependent economy. The various nations and nationalities of the USSR, at the same time, had their specific concerns, and the neglect of these during the Stalin and Brezhnev years had led them to take the form of 'public disaffection, which now and then escalated into conflicts'. To deal with these problems there should be a further development of the democratic principles of the Soviet federation, extending the rights of the union republics and lower levels of government. Local languages and cultures should be fostered, as well as Russian; and a national research centre should be established to examine these and other issues in more detail.[182]

Although there was still no sign of the Central Committee meeting on the national question, the autumn of 1988 and early months of 1989 saw some elements of a rather different nationalities policy begin to acquire form. The party conference, for instance, had called for a series of constitutional changes, particularly in the USSR Supreme Soviet's Council of Nationalities. The amendments agreed in December 1988 duly provided that while the Council of the Union should concentrate upon economic, diplomatic and other matters affecting the USSR as a whole, the Council of Nationalities should particularly concern itself with the interests of all ethnic groups within the framework of the Soviet multinational state.[183] In November 1988 a set of 'Theses' on the national question was issued by the Central Committee with a view to clarifying the issues that would be discussed at the forthcoming plenum.[184] In March 1989 a set of directives on economic relations between the USSR and its constituent republics was published, which called for the transfer of up to 36 per cent of industrial production to local control (the existing figure was only 5 per cent), with much higher levels – up to 72 per cent – in Georgia and the Baltic republics.[185] The somewhat opaque slogan of a 'strong centre and strong republics' began to appear in official speeches from early 1989.[186] And a working group on constitutional reform, established by the Supreme Soviet in late 1988, began – at least in its reported meetings – to develop the notion of 'republican precedence', by which the union republics should have full authority over all matters that had not been specifically transferred to the USSR government.[187]

Finally, and most important of all, the Central Committee published a draft 'Platform' on the national question in August 1989 setting out the basis on which it proposed to conduct the long-promised plenum, which was now to be held in September. The Platform began by acknowledging the damage that had been done to national relations by the repression of the Stalinist years and by later attempts to accelerate convergence on the basis of an allegedly full and final resolution of the national question. Russians, as well as other nations, had suffered from these policies. In the future, the Central Committee suggested, there should be radical changes in state structure leading to a 'renewed federation' with greater devolved powers for the union republics, including their transfer to a cost-accounting basis within what would continue to be a single domestic market. The Russian Republic, in particular, should enjoy greater rights, including its own party organisation. The CPSU as a whole, however, should remain a united, 'consolidating and directing force of social development', based on a democratic centralism, and with a single statute and programme. National languages should be encouraged, but Russian remained the language of inter-ethnic communication and all languages must have equality of status. There could not, however, be prescriptions that were valid for all cases; national policy was a 'continuous creation', and what was necessary above all was a realistic and undogmatic approach, free of national chauvinism but receptive to legitimate expressions of national self-consciousness.[188]

The Central Committee plenum, which met on 19–20 September 1989, approved the Platform with minor changes and more generally sought to define the party's line in an area in which its decisions had been inadequate and for the most part purely reactive. For Gorbachev, opening the meeting, there could be no retreat from Leninist principles, or from the 'internationalist inheritance' of the revolution. There had been enormous economic advances, which had been possible only on a basis of mutual assistance. And excessive centralisation had often been the fault of the republics and regions themselves, which had competed for major investments by offering to reduce spending on social requirements. There must be equality of rights for all citizens regardless of nationality; and there could be no excuse for discrimination against any of them, nor for 'extremist gatherings' which had terrorised local people who were not of the majority affiliation. To applause, he declared that the full force of the law would be used in these and other situations that required it. In economic matters, the strengthening of the independence of each of the republics and regions must be accompanied by the further development of the Soviet economy as a whole. Local languages must become official republican languages, but Russian might become the official language of the USSR as a whole. The party, he concluded, stood for a 'powerful federal state', convinced that this 'corresponded to the interests of all the people that [made] up the USSR'.[189]

The plenum, in the event, made little influence upon the continuing discussion, and by the early 1990s it was clear that only a reconsideration of the very bases of Soviet statehood would be likely to satisfy the aspirations of the various republics and nationalities. Not simply would the future USSR be a 'renewed federation'; it would also, necessarily, be a voluntary association of republics based upon a new union treaty, whose features became increasingly distinct as the Central Committee plenum faded into obscurity. Gorbachev, speaking after his election as President, called for the conclusion of a 'new union treaty' of this kind;[190] and the Federation Council, when it met later in the year, agreed that a union treaty was necessary which would 'guarantee real economic and political sovereignty for the republics'. A working group, with representatives of all the republics concerned, was established to prepare a first draft.[191] Interethnic relations, Gorbachev conceded in his speech to the 28th Party Congress in July 1990, had deteriorated since the congress before it, and especially over the previous few months. There had been considerable loss of life, and thousands had been forced to leave their homelands. What was needed in these circumstances was an updated union in the form of a 'real union of sovereign states', enshrined in a new union treaty which would replace the treaty of 1922 on which the USSR had originally been founded.[192]

Other members of the leadership, at the Congress, placed some emphasis upon the dangers of what Nikolai Ryzhkov called 'economic separatism'.[193] Yevgenii Primakov, at this time a member of the Presidential Council, called the whole idea of regional self-sufficiency 'economically absurd'.[194] Republican leaders, however, were equally insistent upon the greatest possible devolution of authority consistent with the maintenance of a single state. The Kirgiz leader, Masaliev, called for a unitary USSR with a strong centre;[195] most other republican first secretaries, however, called for a renewed federation, and the Armenian leader Movsisyan went for the more radical idea of the

USSR as a union of sovereign states based upon a network of bilateral associations.[196] After some discussion the Congress agreed to include the objective of a 'union of sovereign states' in its Programmatic Declaration.[197] A stream of legislation over the spring and summer meanwhile established some of the guiding principles of the new association: there were laws on the demarcation of the powers of the USSR and of its constituent republics,[198] on the treatment of Soviet citizens outside their own republic,[199] and on economic relations between the USSR, the union and autonomous republics.[200] Over the same period, in a 'revolution of sovereignties', all the union republics claimed primacy for their own laws over those of the USSR as a whole, and some autonomous republics and regions in turn claimed primacy for their laws over those of the republics within which they were located.[201]

The draft union treaty, after an extended discussion, was finally published in the central press in November 1990.[202] Gorbachev, over the summer, stressed the importance of concluding a new agreement of this kind, and equally, of maintaining a common state framework. The Soviet Union as it presently existed, he conceded in a speech in Odessa, had 'exhausted its potential'. But this was not a justification for the dissolution of an association of this kind; the different republics and nationalities were bound together by a common history, by ties of marriage and settlement, and by the trade that they conducted with each other. Any weakening of the USSR, moreover, would weaken the positive influence it was able to exercise in international affairs.[203] Speaking to the Central Committee in October, he deplored any possible 'Lebanonisation' of the Soviet Union, with all the consequences that would follow.[204] The union treaty was considered at some length by the Central Committee plenum in December 1990; it approved a resolution calling for the 'renewal and preservation of a unitary Soviet Union', a renewal that was 'socialist in character'.[205] Gorbachev himself warned of the danger of replacing an overcentralised state with 'something amoeba-like', and called for 'strong republics and a strong centre'.[206] The union treaty was also approved in principle by the Congress of People's Deputies, meeting in December, although the absence of several republican delegations weakened the force of its decisions.[207]

The treaty, after further consideration, was published in March 1991 in a revised draft.[208] It provided for a 'union of sovereign republics', not necessarily of socialist ones; the Congress of People's Deputies, in December, had agreed not to change the name of the state, but there was still some criticism that the world's first socialist state had somehow disappeared with the promulgation of a union treaty that made no reference to its social character.[209] The revised draft committed its participants to a 'sovereign federal democratic state' based upon a voluntary union of republics with equal rights, each of which would have the right to choose its own forms of property and government. There was no direct reference to socialism or communism; the republics that committed themselves to the treaty would rather be bound to respect the principles of democracy, human rights as defined by international agreements, and social justice. The central government would be responsible for security and foreign policy, law enforcement and the all-union budget; the remaining responsibilities of government, including socioeconomic development, energy, transport, social policy and higher education, were to be resolved 'jointly' (whatever this might mean). The union treaty was intended to serve as the basis for a new Soviet constitution; it also set out the structure of government of the new union, including a directly elected Supreme Soviet in which all national areas would be represented.

Speaking at the Congress of People's Deputies in December 1990, Gorbachev proposed an all-union referendum to resolve the future of the Soviet state. Although the Constitution made provision for referenda, there had never previously been any exercise of this kind. The referendum took place on 17 March 1991, when voters all over the Soviet Union were asked to express a view on the following question: 'Do you consider it necessary to preserve the Union of Soviet Socialist Republics as a renewed federation of equal sovereign republics in which the human rights and freedoms of any nationality will be fully guaranteed?' The question, it was widely remarked, embraced a number of different propositions: some voters might be in favour of the maintenance of a single state but not necessarily a socialist one, and there was little guidance – apart from the draft union treaty – about the nature of a 'renewed federation'. The issue was clouded further by the refusal of six republican governments (the three Baltic republics, Moldavia, Georgia and Armenia) to take part, although some voting did take place on their territories, and by the modification or supplementation of the question in four other republics. Only three republics (Belorussia, Turkmenistan and Tajikistan) eventually voted on the single question that had been proposed by the central authorities.[210]

The results, announced a few days later, made it clear that the proposition had been carried by a very large majority. The turnout, across the Soviet Union as a whole, was 80 per cent,[211] and of those who voted, 76.4 per cent declared in favour of the question that had been asked of them. Two million voted in the six republics that had formally declined to participate, among whom the level of support for the continued existence of the USSR was predictably very high.[212] In the Russian Republic, where a further question was put, 69.9 per cent of those who took part also supported the introduction of a directly elected presidency.[213] There were relatively few reports of irregularities: a Moscow journalist, in an experiment, found he was allowed to vote ten times in five different constituencies;[214] and in one of the Moscow districts there were 346 more votes cast than ballot papers that had been distributed.[215] Disappointingly for the authorities, Moscow and Leningrad voted for the 'renewed federation' by tiny majorities; in Gorbachev's own district in Moscow 375 voted against the proposition and 376 in favour, the only uncertainty being whether the General Secretary or his spouse had cast the decisive ballot.[216] Gorbachev, in his response to the results, nonetheless claimed that they had received a mandate for the 'renewal and strengthening of the union state' and promised to press ahead with the conclusion of the union treaty and a new constitution.[217]

From USSR to Commonwealth of Independent States

The '9 + 1' agreement of April 1991 had committed all of the republics concerned, as well as the Soviet President, to the conclusion of a new union treaty within three months. After an extended process of negotiation Gorbachev was able to announce on 24 July that the nine republics had reached agreement on a new treaty of this kind, bringing into being a 'Union of Soviet Sovereign Republics' in place of the overcentralised association of the recent past.[218] As published in the central press, it specified that defence, foreign policy, energy, communications, transport and budgetary matters would be decided 'jointly' by the centre and the republics, but that in all other matters republican laws would have precedence over those of the union as a whole.[219] It was this version of the union treaty that was to have been signed by Russian and other representatives on 20 August, and it was apparently to prevent this weakening of central authority, particularly in military and budgetary matters, that the attempted coup was launched one day beforehand. In the event, the coup discredited the draft treaty and led to a series of declarations of republican independence which, by the end of the year, had brought about the demise of the USSR as such.

Lithuania had been the first of the Soviet republics to declare independence, in March 1990, and during the coup its two Baltic neighbours followed suit, Estonia on 20 August and Latvia on 21 August. Within weeks their independence had been recognised by the international community (see p. 162). The second largest of the Soviet republics, the Ukraine, declared itself an independent democratic republic on 24 August; Moldavia followed on 27 August, and Azerbaijan on 30 August. The Belorussian president, Nikolai Dementei, who had expressed support for the coup, resigned on 25 August, and the republican parliament voted shortly afterwards in favour of the 'political and economic independence of Belorussia'. The Uzbek parliament voted similarly on 31 August. Kirgizia declared itself an independent, sovereign and democratic state on 1 September; Tajikistan voted for independence on 9 September, and Armenia on 23 September. Turkmenia voted accordingly on 27 October, after a referendum in which (as in Armenia) the idea of independence received overwhelming popular support. Kazakhstan voted for independence on 16 December, leaving Russia, by the end of the year, as the only republic that had not adopted a declaration of this kind (Russia did, however, adopt a new state symbol – a version of the imperial double-headed eagle[220]).

The draft union treaty was clearly superseded by these developments, and as the Kazakh president, Nursultan Nazarbaev, told the USSR Supreme Soviet when it reconvened in early September, only a much looser confederation would satisfy the aspirations of the republics that still wished to establish some kind of association.[221] In the end, ten republics – including some that had declared independence – agreed a joint statement which indicated that a loose union would be established based on Russia and the Central Asian republics, and that around it there would be a 'common economic space' that would include most if not all of the republics that had been part of the USSR. Gorbachev, for the time being, would remain as President; but he was to rule through a Council of State on which all the ten participating republics were represented, and management of the economy was to be entrusted to an inter-republican committee headed by the Russian prime minister Ivan Silaev. The old Soviet parliament was to be replaced by a two-chamber Supreme Soviet, and in due course a new Soviet Constitution would be presented for approval leading to presidential and perhaps more general multiparty elections the following year.[222]

These were intended to be interim arrangements only, and further negotiations took place to try to establish the bases of a more lasting political union. Eventually, on 14 November, nine of the original fifteen republics reached agreement on a new 'union of sovereign states'. The agreement, like those that had preceded it, envisaged a directly elected presidency, and a bicameral legislature made up on a republican and a population basis, respectively; central authority would be limited to those spheres of activity that had been specifically delegated by the members of the union.[223] A referendum in the Ukraine on 1 December, however, resulted in a majority of over 90 per cent in favour of a fully independent status,[224] and this appears to have convinced Yel'tsin that it would be unprofitable to pursue the goal of political union any further. On 8 December, at a country house in Belorussia, the leaders of the three Slav republics met and concluded an agreement establishing an entirely new entity, a 'Commonwealth of Independent States', with its administrative headquarters in Minsk. The new Commonwealth was not a state, but it would nonetheless provide for unitary control of nuclear arms, a single currency and a 'single economic space'. The USSR, as a subject of international law and a geopolitical reality, was declared no longer in existence, and the three republics individually denounced the 1922 treaty through which it had originally been established.[225]

The new Commonwealth declared itself open to other Soviet republics, as well as to states elsewhere that shared its objectives, and on 21 December in Alma Ata a further agreement was signed by the three original members and eight other republics: Armenia, Azerbaijan, Kazakhstan, Kirgizia, Moldavia, Tajikistan, Turkmenia and Uzbekistan. The declaration committed those who signed it to recognise the independence and sovereignty of other members, to respect human rights including those of national minorities, and to observe existing boundaries. Relations among the members of the Commonwealth were to be conducted on a multilateral basis, but it was agreed to endorse the principle of unitary control of strategic nuclear arms and the concept of a 'single economic space'. The USSR as such was held to have 'ended its existence', but the members of the Commonwealth pledged themselves to discharge the obligations that arose from the 15,000 or so international treaties and agreements to which the USSR had been a party. In a separate agreement the heads of member states agreed that Russia should take the seat at the United Nations formerly occupied by the USSR, and a framework of inter-state and inter-governmental consultation was established.[226] On 26 December the upper house of the USSR Supreme Soviet, itself

Table 5.2 *The Commonwealth of Independent States, 1994*

Name of state	Population			Chief executive
	m., 1990	% titular	% Russian	
Armenia	3.3	93.3	1.6	Levon Ter-Petrosyan
Azerbaijan	7.1	82.7	5.6	Geidar Aliev
Belorussia (Belarus)	10.3	77.9	13.2	Mechislav Grib
Georgia	5.4	70.1	6.3	Eduard Shevardnadze
Kazakhstan	16.7	39.7	37.8	Nursultan Nazarbaev
Kirgizia (Kyrgyzstan)	4.3	54.2	21.5	Askar Akaev
Moldavia (Moldova)	4.4	64.5	9.4	Mircea Snegur
Russian Federation	148.0	81.5	81.5	Boris Yel'tsin
Tajikistan	5.3	62.3	7.6	Ali Rakhmanov
Turkmenia	3.6	72.0	9.5	Saparmurad Niyazov
Ukraine	51.8	72.7	22.1	Leonid Kravchuk
Uzbekistan	20.3	71.4	8.4	Islam Karimov

Source: Nationality and population data are as reported in the 1989 census returns published in *Vestnik statistiki*, 1990, nos. 10–12, and 1991, 1 and 4–6.

inquorate, voted a formal end to the original treaty of union (which had not, in fact, provided for any procedure of this kind).[227]

The new Commonwealth was at least a genuinely voluntary union, and yet it was far from clear that it provided the answer to nationality differences that had for so long eluded the Gorbachev leadership. There were, for a start, serious difficulties of economic coordination. The economies of all fifteen Soviet republics had been closely bound together in an all-union division of labour; about 20 per cent of their national income represented trade with other republics, as compared (for instance) with the European Community, only 16 per cent of whose trade was with other members.[228] In the case of oil, for example, the raw material was in one republic, the petrochemical plants were in another, the scientific research was conducted in a third and the extracting equipment was in a fourth; and who owned the pipelines that passed from one republic to another?[229] As Gorbachev himself pointed out to the Central Committee, Russian oil and gas provided most of the energy needs of the other republics. The Russian Republic, the Ukraine and Kazakhstan supplied the other republics with metal, and produced 90 per cent of the grain harvest. Central Asia dominated the production of cotton, and the Baltic republics played a comparable role in advanced engineering.[230] How could such an integrated economic mechanism accommodate a variety of currencies, tax regimes and forms of property? And yet how could the non-Russians indefinitely accept a division of labour that left them, in some cases, as 'raw material' republics, exporting their primary produce and importing more expensive manufactured goods?[231]

There were enormous difficulties, equally, in the sphere of cultural policy and minority rights. Virtually all of the republics, by the late 1980s, had adopted legislation which provided for the majority language of that republic to enjoy official status. In the case of Georgia, for instance, the legislation provided for the greater use of Georgian in official business, and for compulsory instruction in Georgian for school pupils of other nationalities. There was equally to be a greater degree of attention, in schools and elsewhere, to Georgian history, archaeology and culture.[232] The legislation that was considered in Estonia, to take another example, introduced a compulsory language requirement for a number of occupations, although this was a violation of Soviet labour law, and provided that court business was to be conducted in Estonian, although this conflicted with all-union legislation on court procedures.[233] In almost every case, in fact, the attempts that were being made to promote the cultural interests of non-Russian nationalities came into conflict with the multinational composition of each of the republics, not just of the USSR as a whole. More than 75 million Soviet citizens lived outside their 'own' republic (Kazakhstan alone contained more than 100 different nationalities), and very often they had little knowledge of the language of the republican majority.[234] How could a policy be devised that satisfied the aspirations of the local majority, but which provided the same rights for other nationalities? How could the Soviet system – and after it, the Commonwealth – function if there was no widely understood common language? And were there, in any case, enough teachers and schoolbooks to turn any policies that might be agreed into a reality?[235]

There were comparable problems in establishing a form of rule that would satisfy the aspirations of republican majorities but at the same time protect the legitimate interests of local minorities. Gorbachev, shortly before his resignation, sent a message to the representatives who were gathering in Alma Ata urging them to consider a form of Commonwealth citizenship so that all the former citizens of the USSR would feel their rights were protected in whichever republic they were resident.[236] Some of the republics appear to have been sympathetic to this idea but in the end no common citizenship of this kind was established, which was hardly reassuring (for instance) to the very large Russian minorities in the Ukraine and Moldavia. Some of these minorities formed their own state institutions, including the Dnestr republic in Moldavia, which was unrecognised by the Moldavian authorities but enjoyed the firm support of the local Russian population. It voted overwhelmingly for continued membership of the USSR in the March 1991 referendum, and elected its own president.[237] The Russian law on citizenship, adopted in November 1991, extended that privilege not only to the population of the Russian Federation but also to those living in other republics who requested it,[238] and the Russian defence minister, Pavel Grachev, made it clear that fellow nationals would be defended 'wherever they live'; Alexander Rutskoi, speaking as Vice-President, called for recognition of the Dnestr republic, and the Foreign Ministry intervened when it appeared that the civil rights of Russian speakers in the newly independent Baltic republics were being infringed.[239] There was clearly some basis here for irredentist disputes of a kind that had become familiar in interwar Europe.

There were further difficulties within most of the republics stemming from demands for local autonomy or even independence. In the Russian Federation, for instance, the Tatar Republic adopted a declaration of independence in October 1991 and declared its intention of affiliating independently to the newly established Commonwealth. A referendum, held in March 1992, confirmed this position by a large majority although it had itself been declared unconstitutional.[240] By the spring of 1993 at least nine republics or regions within the Russian Federation were insisting that their own laws took precedence over those of the Federation as a whole, and the Chechen republic had gone still further and declared itself a fully independent state.[241] In Georgia the South Ossetian autonomous republic was abolished by the Georgian authorities, but when the referendum took place in March 1991, 99.8 per cent voted in favour of continued membership of the USSR and the republic later sought independence within the Russian Federation.[242] In Azerbaijan the Nagorno-Karabakh autonomous region voted to establish itself as an independent republic with the support of 99.9 per cent of those who took part in a referendum on the matter, and applied to join the newly-established Commonwealth of Independent States; Azerbaijan, for its part, voted to abolish the region entirely, renamed its capital city and placed the whole area under the control of a military governor.[243]

Nor was there general agreement on boundaries and territories, whether republics affiliated to the new Commonwealth or not. As

Gorbachev pointed out in an interview in early 1991, only about 30 per cent of the USSR's boundaries had been legally defined.[244] Yel'tsin caused a great deal of concern in this connection by authorising a statement that Russia would not necessarily recognise existing boundaries with states that did not become members of the same political union;[245] this, at least implicitly, raised issues such as the status of the Crimea, transferred to the Ukraine by Khrushchev in 1954 as a political gesture. The Russian parliament, in February 1992, ordered an investigation into the legality of its transfer; the Ukrainians regarded this as a challenge to their territorial integrity, still more so when (in early 1994) a Russian was elected Crimea's first president and its parliament voted for *de facto* independence.[246] Belorussia, in these new circumstances, began to raise territorial claims against Lithuania, which extended as far as the Lithuanian capital Vilnius.[247] The Lithuanians, in turn, called for the withdrawal of Russian military detachments from Kaliningrad, which was formally part of the Russian Federation.[248] Finns began to express an interest in Karelia, acquired by the USSR following the Winter War;[249] and the Estonians and Latvians began to query the status of their boundaries with Russia.[250] It was already clear that national and territorial disputes could involve substantial loss of life: about ten thousand Soviet citizens were killed or injured in this connection during the years of *perestroika*, and at least 600,000 became refugees in their own country.[251]

Nationalities policy was perhaps the biggest single failure of *perestroika*. Part of the problem, certainly, was the slow and inadequate response of the central authorities and of Gorbachev personally to a deepening crisis. Looking back, Gorbachev was prepared to acknowledge 'mistakes in tactics';[252] but although he travelled more widely throughout the country than previous Soviet leaders, he was also guilty of some remarkably insensitive mistakes (as when he twice referred to the Soviet Union as 'Russia' during a visit to the Ukraine[253]). The failure of Soviet nationalities policy, however, was more than a personal failure; it also reflected the failure, over more than seventy years, to devise an official theory that could adequately account for ethnic and national differences, and perhaps a still deeper weakness in a doctrine that insisted working men 'had no country'. Relations among the Soviet peoples, it had to be acknowledged, were no longer a 'zone of universal harmony'; different stages of social development presented different problems, and there could be no 'complete solution, valid for all time, to one of mankind's most complex problems'.[254] Seventy years of Leninist nationalities policy, certainly, had not provided one.

6 The Soviet Union and the wider world

For a country of its size and population, the Soviet Union had often appeared rather isolated from the affairs of other members of the world community. In part, at least, this reflected the influence of Russian history and of the political tradition that derived from it. With its broad and open frontiers, Russia is a country that has been invaded and occupied many times by outside powers. Foreigners, since the earliest times, have been required to live in special residential areas and have been treated with a good deal of suspicion and hostility by ordinary Russians as well as by government officials.[1] Russian nationalism, an official ideology in the late Tsarist period and still very strong today, helped to create an attitude towards the West which combined an admiration for its prosperity and efficiency with a deep contempt for its petty-mindedness and commercialism: a 'peculiar amalgam of love and hate', as Isaiah Berlin has described it, combining intellectual respect and envy with emotional suspicion, hostility and contempt.[2] These feelings were reinforced by the Orthodox Church, which was a part of the Eastern (Byzantine) communion. Much more closely associated with the state than was the case in the Christian churches that owed their allegiance to Rome, Russian Orthodoxy helped to promote both a more communitarian form of politics and a feeling that Russians were a 'special people' with a particular destiny to fulfil in terms of world civilisation.[3]

The Soviet authorities after 1917 could hardly associate themselves with, for example, Russian Orthodoxy and the tradition it represented. And yet many of the attitudes towards the outside world that had flourished in the Tsarist period still play a role in Soviet and now post-Soviet foreign policy today.[4] It was always a Russian (and later a Soviet) ambition, for instance, to acquire warm-water ports to the south, and to develop a network of client states in Eastern Europe to strengthen the country's defences against the other continental powers. There are no obvious geographical barriers along this frontier and a series of invasions, from the Poles in the seventeenth century to Napoleon in the early nineteenth, have borne witness to its vulnerability. The Russian army has always been a large one, much larger than those of other continental states, and military spending has always been a disproportionately heavy burden on public finances.[5] These feelings of isolation and insecurity, combined with a belief in a 'special destiny', were developed further by the Marxist-Leninist ideology with which the Soviet leadership was associated after 1917. This saw the USSR as an embattled champion of world socialism, a feeling strengthened by the attempts that were made by foreign governments to overthrow Soviet rule immediately after the revolution and again during World War II. As late as the 1980s foreign trade accounted for a relatively small proportion of Soviet national income, the Soviet currency was not freely convertible, and the movement of people and information across Soviet borders was closely regulated and very limited.

For all these tendencies towards isolation, however, the post-revolutionary period saw the USSR integrate itself ever more closely into the international community. A network of diplomatic relations with the neighbouring capitalist world came gradually into existence, first of all with the smaller border states such as Finland and Estonia, then, in the 1920s, with Germany, France, Britain and Japan, and finally, in the early 1930s, with the United States, Belgium, Spain and the newly established states of Eastern Europe. The Russian Empire had diplomatic relations with forty-seven powers in 1914. Before World War II the Soviet authorities had diplomatic relations with only twenty-six foreign states, but by the end of the war the number had doubled to fifty-two and by the late 1980s the Soviet Union had diplomatic relations with over 140 foreign governments.[6] The USSR became a regular participant in international conference diplomacy at the Genoa Conference in 1922; initially hostile to the League of Nations, describing it in 1919 as a 'Holy Alliance of capitalists for the suppression of the workers' revolution',[7] the USSR became a member in 1934 and was in turn a founding member of the United Nations in 1945 and a prominent member of its Security Council. The USSR, equally, took part in a widening network of international conventions and associations, from the Universal Postal Union (in 1924) to the Inter-Parliamentary Union in 1955 and to a series of conventions on copyright, hostage-taking, narcotics, patents and arms control in the 1970s and 1980s.

Nor was this simply a matter of formal relations at a state-to-state level. Foreign trade, for instance, increased sixteen times by volume between 1950 and 1987, more rapidly than national income as a whole. Within this total, trade with the developed capitalist countries increased at twice the rate of trade with the other countries of the socialist community.[8] In 1950 the Soviet Union traded with forty-five foreign countries; by the late 1980s it traded with 145.[9] An increasing number of factories and other enterprises were being constructed in foreign countries: by 1989 over 3,500 had been built, most of them in the socialist world but nearly 900 in developing countries.[10] The number of passengers carried on international flights quadrupled between 1960 and 1970, and quadrupled again (to 4.2 million) between 1970 and 1988.[11] Half a million foreign tourists visited the USSR in 1950, but over two million did so in 1971 and over five million did so in the late 1980s.[12] More books were translated from other languages into Russian in the 1980s, including record numbers from English, German and French; and there were more foreign students in Soviet universities than ever before.[13] The level of foreign trade was still low in terms of national income, and the USSR had not become a major trading partner for most of the developed capitalist countries; nor was interpersonal contact particularly large given the population numbers involved. By the end of the 1980s it was nonetheless possible to say that the USSR was more directly involved in the affairs of the world community than at any previous time in her history, not only at a formal intergovernmental level but also through a variety of personal, commercial, sporting, scientific and other channels.

Soviet interaction with the outside world had also increased in ways that were connected with the USSR's standing as the world's leading communist power. The October revolution had been carried through on the assumption that Russia, although a relatively backward country and hardly 'ripe' for revolution in a Marxist sense, could help to bring about a European and later a worldwide transition to a communist social order. The major capitalist countries, Lenin argued in his *Imperialism* (1916), were economically interconnected, and a revolution in any one of them – most obviously in Russia, the 'weakest link' – would necessarily lead to revolutionary changes in the others. At the time this did not appear an entirely unrealistic perspective. Immediately after the war ended, in 1918–19, there were revolutionary uprisings in many parts of the world, and Soviet republics were established in Bavaria and Hungary. To the early Bolshevik leaders it seemed only a matter of months, if not days, before first Europe and later the rest of the world joined the Soviet and other socialist states.

July 1919, Lenin promised, would be the 'last difficult July'; the following July would see the 'victory of the international Soviet republic – and that victory will be complete and final'.[14] Not only the Bolsheviks but their 'worst enemies', wrote Zinoviev, were convinced that 'socialist revolution on a world scale was going to develop at a mad gallop'.[15] The Communist International, founded at an unrepresentative gathering in March 1919, was intended to supply decisive leadership; the 'workers of the world' would do the rest.

The Soviet republics in Bavaria and Hungary, in the event, soon collapsed, uprisings in Germany and Bulgaria in 1923 proved abortive, and in most of Europe right-wing governments came to power which often dealt harshly with local communist parties and trade unions. Some advances were recorded in the colonial world, but the most promising revolutionary movement, in China, was bloodily suppressed by Chiang Kai-shek in 1927. A Soviet-dominated regime was established in the Siberian region of Tannu Tuva in 1921 and a People's Republic came into being in Mongolia in 1924 after Chinese occupying forces had been defeated. In all other respects, however, the USSR was left in a state of 'capitalist encirclement' between the wars, and there was little response from Western governments to Soviet proposals to establish a common front against the Fascist powers, above all Nazi Germany. The Munich Agreement of 1938 was widely interpreted, not just in the USSR, as confirmation that the major capitalist powers intended to offer no serious resistance to Hitler provided he confined his territorial ambitions to the east. The Nazi–Soviet non-aggression pact of 1939, however morally repugnant, did at least provide the USSR with a breathing-space in which military preparations could be accelerated; the pact, however, was broken off in June 1941 when German forces invaded the USSR's western borderlands, and in the four years that followed the USSR lost over 26 million citizens and suffered material damage on an unimaginable scale.[16] Soviet leaders, at the end of the war, were understandably concerned to secure a settlement which would offer secure guarantees against a further invasion of this kind, and at the Moscow, Yalta and Potsdam conferences in 1944 and 1945 these objectives were largely achieved. The cost was the post-war division of Europe.

The extension of Soviet control over Eastern Europe in the early post-war period is conventionally described by Soviet diplomatic historians as the 'establishment of international relations of a new type', cemented by a network of bilateral alliances of which thirty-five had been concluded by the late 1940s.[17] Soviet control was extended by a process of leadership manipulation, including purges and the enforced adoption of Stalinist legal and economic reforms.[18] In some cases there was little domestic support for communist policies and a new administration had effectively to be installed by the Red Army (this was the case in the GDR, Poland and Romania; Bulgaria, where the communists had enjoyed some support, took the German side during the war and here too a communist government was imposed by the Red Army). In Czechoslovakia and Hungary, on the other hand, the communist party had enjoyed a substantial degree of popular support and the Red Army, despite some excesses, was seen by many as the agency by which these countries had been liberated from the Nazis. In both cases coalition governments were established in which communists swiftly assumed a dominant position. In Yugoslavia, Albania, North Korea and China a rather different pattern developed: in all these countries the communist party came to power through its leadership of a popular struggle against foreign occupation, with little or no help from the USSR in doing so. These, on the whole, were 'indigenous' rather than 'imposed' regimes, and they tended to be the most independent-minded in their relations with the Soviet authorities. This was also the case in Cuba, where Fidel Castro led his 26 July guerrilla movement to power in 1959 and declared his formal adherence to Marxism–Leninism in 1961.

There were further extensions of Soviet influence during the 1970s and 1980s. In Vietnam the US-supported regime in the south was defeated in 1975, following an agreement in Paris in 1973 which formally ended outside involvement in the longstanding conflict with the communist-ruled north. National elections were held in 1976 and the two states were formally merged into the Socialist Republic of Vietnam, linked (from 1978) by a twenty-five-year treaty of friendship and cooperation to the USSR. A new constitution, adopted in 1980, declared that Vietnam was a state of proletarian dictatorship which was developing according to Marxism–Leninism. In Laos a people's democratic republic was established in December 1975 following the abdication of King Sayang Vatthana and the formation of a new government led by the Lao People's Revolutionary Party. Brezhnev, speaking at a reception for a Laotian party and government delegation the following year, welcomed their 'heroic victory' and the establishment of a state which was seeking to establish the 'bases of a socialist society'.[19] In Cambodia, similarly, the communist Khymer Rouge took power in 1975 at the end of a civil war and proceeded to establish a harshly dictatorial regime known as Democratic Kampuchea. This was in turn succeeded by a Vietnamese-backed administration in 1979, headed by the Revolutionary Party of Kampuchea, which failed to secure widespread international recognition and more than a decade later had not yet established effective control of the entire national territory.[20]

The countries that were under the control of ruling Marxist–Leninist parties represented, for the USSR, the 'world socialist system', a community of nations that shared the same political, social and economic interests. The USSR and its East European allies constituted the Warsaw Treaty Organisation, founded in 1955 and extended for twenty years in 1985; a somewhat larger group of states, including Cuba, Mongolia and Vietnam, were members of the Council for Mutual Economic Assistance (CMEA or Comecon).[21] A still broader grouping of states, in the late 1980s, could be described as Marxist or (in Soviet terminology) 'revolutionary-democratic' and had close associations of various kinds with the USSR and its allies. In Afghanistan, for instance, a pro-Soviet administration was formed in 1978 under the leadership of the People's Democratic Party; it concluded a friendship treaty with the USSR later in the year. In Nicaragua a lengthy civil war against the Somoza dictatorship ended with the victory of the Sandinista Liberation Front in 1979. A series of regimes in Africa, in the 1970s and 1980s, adopted avowedly Marxist governments. Ethiopia, where the monarchy was overthrown in 1974, inaugurated a People's Democratic Republic in 1987 under the leadership of the Workers' Party of Ethiopia; Mozambique, which became independent in 1975, was headed by a liberation movement of broadly Marxist orientation; and Angola, which became independent in the same year, was governed by the Marxist MPLA-PT (all three countries concluded friendship treaties with the USSR in the 1970s). Benin was declared a Marxist–Leninist state in 1972; and a similar form of administration was introduced in the People's Republic of the Congo in 1970 under the direction of a single ruling party, the Congolese Party of Labour (which concluded a friendship treaty with the USSR in 1981). Between thirty and forty regimes, worldwide, could be classified as Marxist in this sense in the late 1980s, although their domestic and foreign policies often diverged considerably from those of the USSR and its East European allies.[22]

Soviet influence over the non-communist world was exercised through a variety of agencies, among them a network of about 100 non-ruling parties which, in the late 1980s, had a total membership of more than 80 million.[23] Soviet control had originally been exercised through the Communist International and much less effectively through the Cominform, which was established in 1947 and dissolved in 1956.[24] Since that date the main organisational form that the movement had assumed was periodic congresses of communist and workers' parties, three of which took place between 1957 and 1969. One measure of the declining influence of the Soviet party was that at the last of three congresses several ruling parties (the Yugoslav, Albanian, Chinese, Vietnamese and North Korean) did not attend, and only sixty-one of the seventy-five parties present could be persuaded to sign the final communiqué without reservations although it made no reference to Soviet leadership of the movement and contained no explicit criticism of the Chinese.[25] Since then there had been a number of regional conferences of communist parties, such as the meeting of Latin American parties in 1975 and of European parties in 1976 and 1980, but many parties refused to attend even these more limited gatherings in case they compromised their organisational independence. Several parties, particularly the Italian and Spanish, went still further, accepting NATO, a mixed economy and liberal democracy and rejecting the Soviet model and the heritage of Leninism. By the late 1980s the CPSU itself accepted, as Gorbachev put it to the 27th Party Congress, that no single party could have a 'monopoly of truth' and that the movement as a whole would not normally be unanimous on all the issues it confronted.[26]

Gorbachev and 'new thinking'

Gorbachev's early policy pronouncements gave little indication that one of the central features of his administration would be its emphasis on 'new thinking' in international affairs. His important address to the ideology conference in December 1984, shortly before taking office, stressed the 'necessity of a fundamental change through accelerated economic development' and pointed to *glasnost'* as a means of promoting this process. The section on foreign policy, however, was couched in much more orthodox terms, accusing capitalism of resorting to 'wars and terror' in order to further its objectives and of constantly seeking 'social revenge' on a global scale. Having exhausted their historic potential, Gorbachev went on, the major capitalist countries had decided to accelerate the arms race and militarism of all kinds, and were deliberately preparing their populations for nuclear war. A policy of nothing less than 'state terrorism' had been adopted in Central America, the Middle East, Afghanistan and southern Africa.

The military-industrial complex had strengthened its influence on US foreign policy, and so too had the multinational corporations; together they had declared a 'crusade' against communism, which was threatening the future of the world community as a whole. In relations between the two 'opposing systems', conflict clearly took precedence over competition.[27]

A somewhat different tone began to emerge relatively quickly, particularly in an address that Gorbachev gave to British members of parliament later the same month. In the speech Gorbachev expressed a wish for renewed dialogue and cooperation, above all in relation to the threat of a nuclear war in which there could be 'no winners'. This, however, was only one example of the kind of issue that required the concerted action of states with different social systems. Another was the need to resolve regional issues peacefully; others were the fight against famine and disease, protection of the environment and the global supply of energy and natural resources. The atomic age, Gorbachev suggested, required a 'new way of political thinking', above all the recognition that all the peoples of the world lived in a 'vulnerable, rather fragile but interconnected world'. Whatever divided them, they had to share the same planet; and this dictated a 'constructive dialogue, a search for solutions to key international problems, for areas of agreement'. Gorbachev also made clear the reason why he advocated a position of this kind: it was to be found in the interconnection between foreign and domestic policy. A country's foreign policy, he noted, could not be separated from its 'internal life, its economic and social goals and needs'; the Soviet Union, for its part, needed peace so as to be able to achieve its 'truly breathtaking creative plans'.[28] In his electoral address of February 1985 Gorbachev returned to the European theme, regretting the loss of impetus that had occurred since the signature of the Helsinki Final Act ten years earlier and expressing the hope that West Europeans would not allow 'our common home' to be converted into a testing-ground for American doctrines of 'limited' nuclear war.[29]

Gorbachev's speech on his election as party leader laid proper emphasis on domestic priorities, but also called for better relations with the 'great socialist community', particularly China, and for the continuation of 'peaceful, mutually advantageous cooperation' with the capitalist world, leading if possible to an agreement that would provide for the complete elimination of nuclear arms and with them the threat of nuclear war.[30] His address to the Central Committee in April 1985, his first full statement as party leader, called for 'stable, proper and, if you like, civilised inter-state relations based on a genuine respect for international law'. The unity of the socialist states and their military-strategic parity with the NATO countries must at all costs be preserved, as the only secure guarantee against the 'aggressive appetites of imperialism'. The Soviet armed forces, in particular, would be provided with everything that was necessary for them to perform their task. There was, however, no 'fatal inevitability of confrontation' between the USSR and its major capitalist adversaries. On the contrary, none of the nations wanted war, and 'ever new progressive and democratic forces' had appeared in the capitalist countries which were strengthening the common struggle for peace.[31] In his speech to French parliamentarians the following October Gorbachev laid particular emphasis upon the ever-growing 'interdependence between countries and continents' in ecological as well as military and economic terms. He also emphasised the need to develop cultural contacts of all kinds, and to avoid extending ideological differences to the conduct of interstate relations.[32] His address a few days later to the Central Committee in Moscow balanced these remarks with more familiar declarations about the 'further strengthening of the positions of existing socialism' and growing opposition to the 'reactionary, aggressive forces of imperialism'.[33]

Gorbachev's address to the 27th Party Congress in February 1986 was relatively short of surprises in terms of foreign policy; there was nothing, at any rate, to compare with the unilateral moratorium on nuclear testing that had been announced just a few weeks earlier. It did, however, make clear the extent to which the Soviet approach to international affairs had changed as compared with the relatively simple priorities of the Brezhnev era. Gorbachev pointed out that the contemporary world was 'complicated, diverse, dynamic, permeated with contending tendencies, and full of contradictions'. The gradual development of societies from capitalism to socialism, admittedly, was not an accident, but a necessary, law-governed and irreversible process. The socialist world was a 'powerful international entity' advancing along a path which 'reveal[ed] in every way the intellectual and moral wealth of man and society'. Capitalism, for its part, was a system plagued by problems and crises, and one that was aggressive and interventionist by its very nature. It contained its own 'internal antagonistic contradictions', based on the exploitation of labour, and also contradictions as between the various capitalist countries, such as those between the less powerful capitalist states and transnational corporations, and between the United States, Western Europe and

Japan. Relations were worsening, moreover, between the major capitalist nations and the developing countries, which were being robbed of the fruits of their labour and forced to suffer poverty, illiteracy and famine.

Beyond these differences, however, lay a further group of contradictions relating to the pollution of the environment, the air and the oceans, and the depletion of the world's natural resources. These were problems that no single group of states could resolve by itself; and there were many others. No single group of states, for instance, could deal with the problem of 'corruption and vandalisation' in the cultural sphere (Soviet spokesmen at this time generally cited the 'Rambo' films and other examples of 'warnography'). Nor could capitalist or socialist states deal by themselves with the threat of a nuclear catastrophe, or the difficulties that were facing the developing countries. Gorbachev invited the major capitalist countries to undertake a 'sober, constructive assessment' of problems of this kind, based if nothing else on their common need for self-preservation. The course of history and of social progress, he told the delegates, required with increasing insistence the 'establishment of constructive, creative interaction among states and peoples on the scale of the whole planet'. Notwithstanding their competition and confrontation, both capitalist and socialist countries were coming to appreciate that they lived in an 'interdependent, in many ways integral world' in which they must cooperate for their common benefit. There was novelty in Gorbachev's appeal for cooperation with Social Democrats, and even religious organisations, in this connection; but it was his central proposition – that global problems demanded global solutions and that socialism as such provided no solution to them – that was the most distinctive and important element in the address.[34]

This 'new thinking' in Soviet foreign policy was set out more fully over the months that followed. The 'Delhi declaration' of November 1986, for instance, committed the Soviet leader to a 'non-violent' as well as nuclear-free world.[35] An extraordinary gathering, 'the International Forum for a Nuclear-Free World, for the Survival of Humankind', brought West German Greens, clerics, Academician Sakharov and Western film stars such as Gregory Peck and Claudia Cardinale together in Moscow in February 1987. Gorbachev's address emphasised that the USSR and its people were 'part of a world community' and that their goal was the 'humanisation of international relations'.[36] A new defence doctrine began to take shape at the same time: it was intended to be non-offensive in character and to give other states no reason to fear for their security, notwithstanding the immense size of Soviet armed forces and the perceptions of those forces that were entertained particularly in Europe. The Soviet leader had already taken several unilateral initiatives towards this end. The first was the decision, in April 1985, to freeze the deployment of SS-20 missiles in Europe; the second was the moratorium on all underground nuclear testing which began on 6 August 1985, the anniversary of Hiroshima, and was eventually extended until February 1987. Gorbachev added a more elaborate proposal in January 1986, calling for the elimination of all nuclear weapons by the year 2000; a commitment to this objective was written into the new Party Programme, which was adopted shortly afterwards.[37] A new military doctrine, 'reasonable sufficiency', was adopted by Gorbachev at the 27th Party Congress and subsequently by the Warsaw Treaty Organisation.[38] Nor were these simply doctrinal changes: there were substantial cuts in Soviet military spending and troop numbers from 1989 onwards, and much more information was made available on the structure and size of the military budget and on troop and weapons deployments, which themselves became more defensive in character.[39]

The Central Committee's Theses, adopted shortly before the 19th Party Conference in 1988, contained the first official criticism of Soviet foreign policy in the Brezhnev and Gromyko years, suggesting that there had been too much 'dogmatism' and 'subjectivism' at this time and that Soviet policy had lagged behind the important changes that were taking place in world affairs. Too much emphasis had been placed upon the strengthening of security by military rather than political means, and this had placed an undue burden on the domestic economy. The party's 'new political thinking', by contrast, recognised the existence of a complex and contradictory world in which there were threats to the survival of humanity as such but also great opportunities for coexistence and cooperation. The main elements in this 'new political thinking' included the gradual liquidation of nuclear arms by the year 2000, the establishment of a system of comprehensive security, a doctrine of military sufficiency and non-aggression, and improvements in the world economy. This, the Theses made clear, was the 'foreign policy credo' of the Gorbachev administration; already it had begun to become a reality with the establishment of a broad dialogue with foreign governments and ordinary citizens, the recognition of the variety of national forms in the socialist community, and a series of international agreements on nuclear arms and other issues.[40] Other commentaries went further in their criticism of the Brezhnev–

Gromyko legacy, and the new foreign minister Eduard Shevardnadze was one of those who was clearest in his call for a proper mechanism of democratic control so that the mistakes and violations of international law of these years did not recur.[41]

A still more influential statement of the 'new political thinking' in Soviet foreign policy came in the Soviet leader's address to the General Assembly of the United Nations in December 1988. In the speech Gorbachev expressed his personal support for the United Nations, which had 'increasingly manifested its ability to act as a unique international centre in the service of peace and security', and repeated his belief that the most important issues that faced the world community were global rather than regional in character. This had been made clear by the development of nuclear weapons, by new popular movements and ideologies, and by scientific and technical developments. Improvements in communications had brought the world more closely together; the world economy was increasingly a 'single organism'. The French and Russian revolutions had made an enormous contribution in their time to human progress, but they lived today in a different world in which universal human values must have priority. This meant a common search for a new quality of international interaction, less dependent on military force and free of ideological prejudice.

In more practical terms Gorbachev pointed to the need for a greater measure of agreement on the reduction of all forms of armaments and on the elimination of regional conflicts. There should be a 'more intense and open dialogue' between political leaders and their societies (he had himself taken part in more than 200 meetings with foreign governmental and political representatives). The United Nations should itself play a greater role, especially in issues such as Third World development, environmental assistance and the peaceful use of outer space. The UN could also play a greater part in regulating regional conflicts, such as in Afghanistan. More work needed to be done to clarify and strengthen international law, particularly in relation to human rights. Most spectacularly of all, the Soviet leader announced a reduction of 500,000 in the size of Soviet armed forces over the following two years, including reductions in the number of divisions in both Europe and Asia and changes in the structure of the forces that remained (including the withdrawal of a large number of tanks) so that their purposes became more clearly peaceful. Corresponding moves were suggested on an international scale to 'convert the armaments economy into a disarmament economy'. Helpful though such measures were likely to be in domestic terms, the simultaneous resignation of the Soviet Chief of Staff suggested that not all powerful institutional interests had been persuaded of their necessity.[42]

Superpower relations and arms control

The central issue in global terms, for any Soviet leader, was the relationship with the other superpower. The state of those relations, on Gorbachev's accession, was not an encouraging one. The wartime alliance had been followed by an occasionally hot 'cold war' and then, from the 1950s onwards, by a cautious search for a limited *modus vivendi*. The first major step towards what became known as 'detente' was probably the Partial Test Ban Treaty, signed by Britain, the USA, the USSR and eventually 103 other nations (but not China or France) in 1963.[43] There appears to have been some resistance within the Soviet military to Khrushchev's doctrine of 'minimum deterrence' – the USSR, he had complained in 1963, could not produce 'nothing but rockets'[44] – and the Cuban missile crisis and later the Vietnam War delayed the signature of further agreements. But then in 1968 a Nuclear Non-proliferation Treaty was signed,[45] in 1971 a treaty was signed prohibiting the testing or use of nuclear weapons on the sea bed,[46] and in 1972 three related treaties were signed in Moscow by Leonid Brezhnev and Richard Nixon. These were SALT I (Intermediate Agreement on the Limitation of Strategic Offensive Arms), a Treaty on the Limitation of Anti-Ballistic Missile Systems (the ABM treaty) and a set of Basic Principles for the conduct of US–Soviet relations.[47] SALT I, the most important of these, placed limits on the further construction of intercontinental nuclear weapon systems by both sides; it was intended to remain in force for five years or until superseded by a more comprehensive agreement, and it was the first real fruit of negotiations that had been proceeding since the late 1960s. In 1973, during Brezhnev's visit to the United States, an agreement on the prevention of nuclear war was signed together with a set of basic principles relating to the further limitation of strategic nuclear weapons; and in November 1974 Brezhnev and Nixon's successor, Gerald Ford, signed a series of related agreements at Vladivostok.[48]

In June 1979 a further agreement, SALT II (Treaty on the Limitation of Strategic Offensive Arms), was signed by American and Soviet representatives in Vienna, based upon the provisional agreements reached in Vladivostok and earlier.[49] The treaty limited each side to no more than 2,400 intercontinental launching vehicles and heavy bombers until 1981, and to 2,250 thereafter until the treaty expired in

1985. There were certain additional restrictions upon the types of weapon systems that could be deployed within these limits. The treaty, however, was not presented to the US Senate for ratification, following Soviet military intervention in Afghanistan in December 1979. The worsening crisis in Poland during 1980 and 1981, and what was believed to be a Soviet role in the imposition of martial law in December 1981, made matters worse; so too did Cuban intervention in Angola, and US support for the Contra guerrillas in Nicaragua. 'Detente' quickly became a pejorative term, and President Reagan, elected in 1980, referred to the USSR in a celebrated phrase as an 'evil empire'; the Russians, he declared at his first press conference, would 'lie and cheat and pursue their ends of world domination'.[50] Economic, cultural and other relations between the superpowers also deteriorated; the Olympic Games were a notable casualty.

'Detente' had also involved a series of parallel negotiations and agreements on territorial, economic and other matters. An agreement on the first of these had always been an objective of the Soviet leadership, in order to stabilise the situation in Europe and thus secure formal Western acceptance of the post-war settlement in Eastern Europe. Towards this end they advanced the idea of a European security conference from the mid-1960s onwards. After some detailed negotiation about the composition and scope of such a gathering, the Conference on Security and Cooperation in Europe (CSCE) finally opened in 1973 in Helsinki, and in August 1975 the thirty-three participating nations signed a Final Act – an agreement rather than a formal treaty – which recognised existing boundaries in Europe, in effect legitimising the division of the continent into Soviet and Western spheres of influence which had existed since the end of the war. The Soviet and East European participants, however, were obliged in return to give their agreement to the so-called 'Basket 3', which concerned the movement of people and ideas between East and West in areas such as tourism, the reunification of families and access to printed and other media.[51] The Final Act also committed its signatories to a series of follow-up meetings, designed to monitor the fulfilment of the agreement; the first of these was held in Belgrade in 1977, and the second in Madrid in 1980.

With the deterioration in East–West relations more generally in the late 1970s, other sets of negotiations made less progress. MBFR (Mutual and Balanced Force Reduction) talks began at Vienna in 1973 but became deadlocked around questions such as the way in which the forces deployed on both sides should be counted and whether absolute or relative reductions should be made: the first of these suited the East, which had larger totals, but the second was pressed by Western negotiators. INF (Intermediate-Range Nuclear Force) talks began at Geneva in November 1981 but broke down two years later. Geneva was also the location for the START (Strategic Arms Reduction) talks, which began in June 1982 but made no more progress. Although negotiations on arms reductions were about to resume in Geneva when Gorbachev assumed the general secretaryship, Cruise and Pershing-II weapons had already been deployed in Western Europe following the NATO 'dual track' decision of 1979 (this was itself represented as a response to the Soviet decision to replace its ageing SS-4 and -5 missiles in Eastern Europe with more modern SS-20s). Weapons such as the Pershing-II, launched from Western Europe, could reach Soviet territory in about ten minutes and were seen as strategic rather than intermediate in character by Soviet negotiators. For the US, on the other hand, strategic weapons were those that were launched from the USSR (or from nuclear submarines) and which in turn gave greater opportunities for defensive action. The British government's decision to upgrade its Polaris weapons by replacing them with much more powerful Tridents introduced a further tension, since it was unclear whether this or the French deterrent would be included in general East–West agreements. Chemical weapons, and the whole question of verification, raised additional difficulties.

Perhaps most fundamental of all, however, was the climate of hostility and mistrust that existed between East and West during the 'new cold war' of the late 1970s and early 1980s; and it was the dissipation of this climate, above all through a series of face-to-face meetings between the Soviet and American leaders, that contributed most directly to the resumption of progress in arms control and other matters. The first of these summit meetings took place at Geneva in November 1985; it provided an opportunity for an exchange of views on the progress made at the arms talks and on regional issues. The importance of the summit was, above all, that it had taken place, and that the two leaders had been pictured together in amicable fireside discussion. The communiqué that was issued after the meeting noted that the talks had been 'frank and useful' and did not disguise the fact that there were still 'major differences' on a series of key issues; but the two leaders had achieved a better understanding of their respective positions and had agreed on the importance of maintaining a 'constant dialogue'.[52] Gorbachev, speaking at the closing ceremony, acknowledged that there were basic disagreements between the two sides, but thought the meeting had created 'opportunities for progress'; Reagan thought that 'useful preliminary results' had been achieved, and hoped that further progress would be achieved at the meeting that had been arranged for the following year.[53] The Politburo, reviewing the talks, described them as a 'major political event' and thought particularly significant the two leaders' declaration that a nuclear war could not be won and must never be fought; this was at odds with the views of some influential US (and Soviet) strategists.[54]

The joint statement that had been issued by the two leaders at Geneva also addressed some of the issues that had arisen in the arms control negotiations. The statement called for a 50 per cent reduction, 'appropriately applied', in their strategic arsenals, an interim INF agreement and appropriate measures to 'prevent an arms race in space'.[55] This was an allusion to the Strategic Defense or 'Star Wars' Initiative that the American president had unveiled in March 1983. Reagan himself claimed that the SDI was defensive in character, since it was designed to dispose of nuclear weapons before they reached their target, and that it was in any event a programme of research in the first instance. Critics of the programme, who were numerous in the USA as well as in the Soviet Union, maintained that it would violate the ABM treaty and therefore undermine the whole concept of deterrence by allowing a first strike to be delivered from behind a space 'shield' which would prevent or at least reduce the risk of retaliation. There were additional concerns in Europe, given that the SDI programme was designed to ensure immunity for the United States and that it might prejudice the US commitment to European security in the event of nuclear war. Gorbachev, both at Geneva and in his subsequent address to the Supreme Soviet, argued that SDI was in effect a new type of armament, a 'space-strike weapon' which could be used against missiles, satellites or land-based targets. It would certainly give a new twist to the arms race; indeed some of Reagan's advisers appeared to be recommending SDI precisely because they thought the Soviet economy would collapse under the strain of attempting to emulate it.[56] At a conference in Stockholm in late September 1986, nonetheless, a last-minute agreement was reached that each side should give the other advance warning of troop movements, and that on-site verification should be permitted on a limited basis for the first time.[57] It was in these difficult but not unhopeful circumstances that the two leaders met again, at a reputedly haunted house in Reykjavik on 11–12 October 1986.

The Soviet negotiators arrived, as Gorbachev claimed subsequently, with a package of arms reduction proposals that would if accepted have marked a 'new era in the history of humanity'.[58] In the discussions Gorbachev proposed a cut of at least 50 per cent in US and Soviet strategic arms, leading to their total elimination by the end of the century. The whole 'triad' of strategic arms was to be involved, including land-based missiles, sea-launched missiles and heavy bombers. Both US and Soviet intermediate-range missiles in Europe were to be eliminated entirely, without reference to the British and French deterrents (this was a concession as compared with the Soviet position at Geneva); and discussions should start immediately on the elimination of such missiles from Asia, and on shorter-range or tactical missiles. The ABM treaty was to be respected by both sides for at least a further ten years (it was of indefinite duration but both sides had the right to withdraw after due notice). Laboratory research on SDI could continue; but it could not, Gorbachev insisted, be tested, let alone deployed, in space. And it was on this point that the discussions broke down, as Gorbachev was unwilling to allow any element in his package of proposals to be approved without agreement on all the others.[59] The Politburo, at its meeting on 14 October, blamed the breakdown of negotiations on the Americans, but called for further meetings and discussions on the basis of the proposals that the Soviet side had put forward.[60]

The third summit between the two leaders, which took place in Washington in December 1987, was undoubtedly the most significant. Indeed it was historic, in that it provided for the first time for the elimination of an entire class of nuclear arms – land-based missiles of intermediate and shorter range. Although this represented no more than 4–5 per cent of their combined nuclear arsenals, it was nonetheless the first significant agreement of this kind between the two powers since the ABM treaty of 1972, and was held by both sides to presage the conclusion of an agreement the following year which would make cuts of up to 50 per cent in strategic nuclear arms. The agreement, which was of unlimited duration, made no direct reference to SDI; nor did it involve conventional or chemical weapons, although both sides expressed a wish to reach an agreement on such mat' rs at the earliest opportunity. Little progress was apparent on 'regional issues', particularly Afghanistan and Central America, or on human rights, where the final communiqué recorded that a 'thorough and candid discussion' had taken place. The two sides, however, did instruct their negotiators at Geneva to 'work out an agreement that would commit the sides to observe the ABM treaty, as signed in 1972', and to devise measures which would help to 'ensure a predictability in the development of the US–Soviet strategic relationship under conditions of strategic stability, to reduce the risk of nuclear war'. Further measures were agreed to improve Soviet–American bilateral relations; and President Reagan accepted Gorbachev's invitation to visit the USSR the following year.[61]

In his television address to the Soviet people on the results of the summit Gorbachev described the INF treaty as a 'major event in world politics' and a 'victory for the new political thinking', which represented a 'first step towards the actual liquidation of the nuclear arsenal'. Although only a small number of weapons had been eliminated, scientists had calculated that just 5 per cent of the weapons that existed were sufficient to destroy the world. The agreement, moreover, had shown that it was possible to restrain and even reverse the arms race. There were still powerful forces in the West, however, that were opposed to ratification of the treaty and anxious to 'compensate' for it by the modernisation of existing arsenals and the rapid development of SDI. Such 'dangerous tendencies' could undermine the achievement of the summit in helping to bring about the demilitarisation of international relations.[62] The Politburo, meeting on 17 December, welcomed the agreement as 'historic';[63] and Soviet public opinion, according at least to some rapidly-conducted opinion polls, appeared to take the same view. A telephone poll in Moscow, for instance, found that 42 per cent of respondents thought the results of the summit were 'very good', and that a further 44 per cent thought they were 'good'; at the same time only 37 per cent thought the treaty would strengthen the security of the USSR, and 8 per cent thought it might be detrimental to Soviet interests. The fact that more than four times as many Soviet warheads were to be withdrawn as American ones gave rise to particular misgivings.[64]

The fourth and final summit between the two leaders took place in Moscow in May–June 1988; it was the first visit by a US president to the Soviet capital for fourteen years. During the summit talks were held on arms control, human rights, and regional and bilateral issues, with both sides reportedly obtaining a 'better understanding of each other's positions' on all such matters.[65] The INF treaty, agreed at Washington the previous December, was formally signed by the two leaders on 1 June, following its ratification a few days earlier by the US Senate and by the USSR Supreme Soviet (the first Soviet rockets were destroyed, to some publicity, in early August). A joint statement issued by the two leaders described the meeting as an 'important step in the process of putting US–Soviet relations on a more productive and sustainable basis'; in particular, a draft treaty on the reduction and limitation of strategic nuclear arms had been discussed and a series of agreements had been made on the contentious question of the verification of nuclear testing. Nevertheless, 'serious differences' remained on important issues. Gorbachev, at a press conference on 1 June, expressed the view that more could have been achieved, including a joint statement of political principle and some advance in the discussions on conventional arms, and complained of a certain 'contradictoriness' in the American position. But politics, in the end, was the 'art of the possible'. The Politburo, at its meeting a few days later, described the summit as a 'major event in international life' whose main result had been the 'deepening of the political dialogue between the Soviet Union and the USA';[66] and the dialogue did, indeed, continue under Reagan's successor George Bush, first at a storm-tossed 'get to know you' summit off Malta and then more formally in the course of an official presidential visit to the United States in 1990.

This, the first extended Bush–Gorbachev summit, was hailed as a new beginning in US–Soviet relations, despite acknowledged and continuing differences on a number of key bilateral and international issues. Formally speaking, the summit resulted in several agreements, including a convention banning the production of chemical weapons and a series of bilateral agreements on trade, energy, education and cultural cooperation. In particular, the Soviet Union secured 'most favoured nation' access to the US market for the first time for fifty years. A more far-reaching agreement on reductions in strategic nuclear arms, which at the time of the Malta summit had been thought imminent, was deferred for further discussion. Gorbachev, at the two leaders' concluding press conference, described the summit as an 'event of enormous importance for our bilateral relations' and added that one could now speak of a 'new phase of cooperation' between the two countries.[67] A third and, as it turned out, final summit between the two leaders took place in Moscow in July 1991. The most significant single development at the summit was the signing of a Strategic Arms Reduction Treaty which committed each side to a reduction of 30 per cent in its stock of weapons. In separate talks the US President met Presidents Yel'tsin and Nazarbaev, and he also travelled to Kiev to address the Ukrainian parliament; this was a recognition that Soviet foreign policy had become multipolar even before the USSR had been replaced by its constituent republics.[68]

Gorbachev and the communist world

Relations between the communist states had for some time been less amicable than a common dedication to working-class interests might have suggested. The first split occurred as early as 1948 when Yugoslavia was denounced by the Soviet Union and its allies for supposedly giving too much favour to peasants at the expense of the working class and for exercising party authority in an insufficiently decisive manner. In fact there appears to be no doubt that Stalin simply resented the independence that the Yugoslav leaders were displaying and believed they could be brought to heel as easily as communist leaders in other parts of Eastern Europe. If so, he miscalculated badly: the Yugoslavs arrested Soviet supporters within the communist party and weathered the storm with a largely united people behind them. In 1955 Khrushchev and Bulganin made a visit to Belgrade in an attempt to secure a reconciliation, and the following year a Soviet–Yugoslav communiqué was signed in Moscow which brought the dispute to an end. The Yugoslavs were allowed to retain their non-aligned status, and kept to their 'national path to communism' which differed in important respects from that of the other communist-ruled countries. A dispute in Hungary at about the same time was not resolved so amicably, at least in part because Hungary occupied a far more important strategic position in terms of Soviet security than did Yugoslavia. An attempt to establish a 'liberal communist' regime under Imre Nagy which appeared likely to take Hungary out of the Warsaw Treaty Organisation was brutally crushed by Soviet tanks in October 1956, and a new leadership under János Kádár was installed which took a long time to establish any measure of domestic support.[69]

The next crisis in inter-communist relations was a result of the attempt by the Dubček leadership in Czechoslovakia to establish an alternative model of socialism, one that accorded more closely with the humanistic and democratic traditions of their country. There was apparently no Soviet objection in January 1968 when, following economic and other difficulties, Antonín Novotný was replaced as party first secretary by Alexander Dubček, a Slovak who had received part of his education in the USSR. With the publication of the party's 'Action Programme' in April 1968, however, it became clear that relatively far-reaching changes were envisaged, among them the abolition of censorship, restrictions on the power of the secret police, a genuinely independent judiciary and freedom of travel. After direct negotiations with the Czech party leadership proved of no avail, the USSR and four other Warsaw Pact allies intervened militarily in August 1968 and reestablished communist orthodoxy. An authoritative article in *Pravda* entitled 'The defence of socialism is the highest international duty' set out what later became known as the 'Brezhnev doctrine': this insisted that the interests of the communist countries as a whole took priority over the wishes of any individual communist country and that no defection from the communist camp could be permitted. Brezhnev himself, addressing the Polish party congress in November 1968, made it clear that any threat to the socialist order in a given country would be considered 'not only a problem of the people of the country in question, but a general problem and concern of all the socialist countries'.[70]

Difficulties in Soviet relations with its East European neighbours continued into the 1970s and 1980s, particularly in Romania (which had not taken part in the invasion of Czechoslovakia and refused to allow any Soviet troops to be stationed on its territory) and above all in Poland. Stalin is reported to have remarked at the end of the war that to establish communist rule in Poland would be like 'trying to saddle a cow' and Soviet relations with that country (the largest and most populous in Eastern Europe) have borne out these apprehensions. Perhaps the most important single explanation was that Polish political values and practices were rather closer to those of Western Europe than to those of the more authoritarian East. Poland, for instance, unlike Russia, was a participant in and indeed an important contributor to the great movements in early modern European history, such as the Renaissance and the scientific revolution, and the country's legal system, literary forms and religious faith aligned it firmly with the liberal West rather than the more authoritarian East. An estimated 90 per cent of the population adhered to the Roman Catholic faith, and the Church had a massive presence in Polish society, including its own university, large numbers of priests, newspapers and periodicals, and representatives in the armed forces and the Polish parliament, the Sejm. The election of Cardinal Wojtyła of Krakow as Pope John Paul II in 1978 and his visits to Poland in 1979 and subsequently emphasised these attachments and strengthened the historic association between the Catholic faith and Polish nationhood.[71]

The Polish leadership, headed by Edward Gierek, had been experiencing increasing economic difficulties during the 1970s as an over-ambitious expansion programme began to founder and foreign debts began to mount. Efforts to improve matters by raising prices and reducing subsidies led to open resistance and had to be rescinded. The regime became increasingly draconian in its attempts to deal with the problems it was confronting; the society, in turn, began to establish public associations of all kinds, most notably the workers' defence committee (KSS–KOR), which were independent of party and state control. In July 1980 a dispute at the Lenin shipyards in the Baltic port of Gdańsk led to the formation of an inter-strike committee and shortly afterwards to the establishment of Solidarity, the first (and so far the last) genuinely self-governing trade union that has ever existed in a communist-ruled country. Solidarity, at its peak, embraced more than 9 million of Poland's 13 million workers; it prompted the formation of a country counterpart, Rural Solidarity, and profoundly affected the ruling Polish United Workers' Party, about a third of whose members are estimated to have joined Solidarity at this time. The regime (headed by Stanisław Kania after Gierek's resignation in 1980, and then from 1981 by Wojciech Jaruzelski) committed itself to a programme of 'renewal' (odnowa), but the economic situation continued to deteriorate, while Solidarity for its part became increasingly powerful, radical and politicised in its objectives.

Developments of this kind were obviously worrying to the Soviet leadership, which began to speak openly of the dangers of 'internal counter-revolution'. This had normally been sufficient pretext for direct military intervention, and some action of this kind appears to have been under consideration in December 1980 and again in March 1981. The Soviet party also expressed its concern in a letter of June 1981 to the Central Committee of the Polish party. The letter expressed the CPSU's 'deep anxiety for the fate of socialism in Poland', regretted that the necessary measures had not been taken against domestic anti-Soviet and anti-socialist forces, and called upon the Polish party to 'reverse the course of events and channel them in the right direction'.[72] In the end the situation was not restored (from the Soviet point of view) until December 1981, when Jaruzelski declared a state of martial law, suspending Solidarity and interning some of its most prominent members. The Polish–Soviet alliance, he promised in a public broadcast, would remain the 'cornerstone' of Polish foreign policy; Poland would also remain an 'indestructible part of the Warsaw Treaty and a reliable member of the socialist community of nations'.[73] Jaruzelski's action may have pre-empted Soviet military intervention, but it did not, in the long run, resolve the problem of political order, nor indeed the problem of economic reform. It was not in fact until a newly legalised Solidarity had been successful at the polls and formed a majority administration in 1989 that the making of public policy began again to command at least a minimum of public acceptability. The Soviet response, this time round, was to accept the election of a Solidarity prime minister with relatively good grace (Jaruzelski, after all, had become president);[74] more generally, Soviet theorists began to accept that socialist countries could have legitimate differences of interest and that these could be resolved only through discussion, not by the imposition of a Soviet *diktat*.[75]

Soviet relations with the largest of its neighbours, the People's Republic of China, have also been difficult and at times have broken down altogether.[76] The Chinese leaders appear to have been dissatisfied with a number of aspects of the Sino–Soviet treaty of 1950, and at the 20th Congress of the CPSU in 1956 they were reportedly unhappy about the manner in which Khrushchev had denounced the actions of Stalin. The Chinese, as late as 1957, still accepted Soviet leadership of the international communist movement: 'in the socialist camp there must be a head', Mao explained to students at Moscow University, 'and that head is the Soviet Union. Among the communist and workers' parties of all countries there must be a head, and that head is the CPSU'.[77] Soviet support for the Chinese atomic programme, nonetheless, was withdrawn the following year, the USSR was neutral during the Sino–Indian war of 1959, and in 1960 the dispute between the two communist giants came into the open. Khrushchev, speaking at the Romanian Communist Party Congress in June of that year, attacked the Chinese leadership by name. All Soviet technicians were withdrawn; trade between the two countries dropped off sharply; and a series of hostile open letters was exchanged, the Chinese accusing the Russians of 'revisionism' while the Russians accused the Chinese of 'dogmatism' and 'splittism' (or of attempting to break up the world communist movement).

Relations deteriorated still further during the late 1960s. In 1966 both sides recalled their ambassadors, and in 1969 open military hostilities broke out along the Ussuri river, which marks the Sino–Soviet border in Siberia. Since then relations have slowly normalised. Negotiations on matters in dispute were opened in 1969; in 1970 the ambassadors returned to their posts; and trade began to increase substantially. The two sides, however, were still separated by traditional rivalries extending over several centuries as well as by differing interpretations of Marxism, disputed borders and rivalry in their relations with other countries; indeed it was perhaps surprising that their earlier association had lasted as long as it did. So far as the Chinese were concerned, in the late 1970s, there were 'three great obstacles' to the restoration of closer relations: Soviet troops in Afghanistan, the Soviet military presence along their long common border, and Soviet support for the Vietnamese-sponsored regime in Kampuchea. The Soviet leadership, for its part, deplored Chinese policy on many international issues but called for the normalisation of relations 'on the basis of peaceful coexistence'. By 1981, however, in Brezhnev's view 'unfortunately', there was still no sign of an improvement in the relationship.[78]

Gorbachev, in his accession speech, called specifically for closer relations between the USSR and China, and added that this was 'entirely feasible' if there was some reciprocity on the Chinese side.[79] The Chinese deputy premier Li Peng, who was in Moscow for the occasion, publicly agreed that an improvement in relations was desirable;[80] an agreement on educational exchanges and a trade pact followed later in the year.[81] Gorbachev, addressing the 27th CPSU Congress in 1986, was able to welcome the improvement that had already taken place in relations with 'socialist China'. Differences remained; but it was also clear that in many cases the two countries could work together, on an equal and principled basis, without prejudice to the interests of other countries.[82] In a speech at Vladivostok the following July he expanded these remarks to a broad conception of an Asian security zone. The Pacific region, Gorbachev observed, had not been militarised to the same extent as Europe. There was however some danger of developments of this kind given the resources of the powers that were active in the region. The two biggest wars since 1945, the Korean and Vietnamese, had taken place in Asia; and there was no counterpart to the Helsinki Final Act and the framework of dialogue it had established. In these circumstances, Gorbachev explained, the Soviet Union would expand its bilateral ties with all the states, socialist and non-socialist, in the region. He indicated, on a point of particular importance to the Chinese, that the withdrawal of a substantial number of the Soviet troops stationed in Mongolia was under active consideration; and he announced that six Soviet regiments were being withdrawn from Afghanistan. The Soviet Union and China, Gorbachev observed, had the same priority – to accelerate social and economic development; and he suggested specific forms of cooperation in cross-border trade, railways and space exploration. Gorbachev welcomed the broader ideas that were in circulation concerning Pacific economic cooperation and the possibility of a Pacific 'Helsinki'. More significantly, he supported proposals to establish a Pacific nuclear-free zone and to lower levels of troops and armaments to that of 'reasonable sufficiency'.[83]

Proposals such as these went a long way to alleviate Chinese concerns and brought closer the possibility of a summit meeting between the two leaderships for which Soviet spokesmen had for some time been calling. The final obstacles were removed when the Chinese foreign minister visited Moscow in December 1988 and Shevardnadze visited Peking early the following year; both sides agreed on the desirability of 'Chinese–Soviet relations of a new type'.[84] Gorbachev, finally, was able to visit Peking in May 1989, the first Soviet leader to do so for thirty years. The talks, inevitably, were overshadowed by public demonstrations of support for the Soviet leader which in turn contributed to a wave of public resistance to the policies of the Chinese government itself. There was some substance, none the less, to Gorbachev's claim that relations between the two countries were entering a 'qualitatively new stage', and he suggested several ways in which such relations could be carried further, including a new 'liquid coal' pipeline, a new 'silk way' from China to Europe, and various forms of inter-regional cooperation. The joint communiqué with which the visit concluded welcomed the normalisation of relations between the two countries, and between their two ruling parties. Both sides welcomed the Vietnamese commitment to withdraw their troops from Kampuchea; the level of armed forces along the Sino–Soviet border would be reduced to a minimum, and any remaining territorial differences would be resolved on the basis of international law. In the spring of 1991 the reconciliation was sealed when the Chinese party leader Jiang Zemin visited Moscow, the first visit of its kind since the days of Mao Zedong.[85]

Soviet policy and the developing world

Soviet policymakers had generally taken little interest in the colonial or newly independent world during the Stalin years. Under Khrushchev, however, there was a reassessment, and Soviet policy from this time onwards began to seek links of all kinds with the developing nations both at the political level and through trade, investment, arms sales, the training of students and so forth.[86] A particularly close interest was taken in states of 'socialist orientation' in the developing world, particularly in Africa. States of 'socialist orientation', in the Soviet view, were those that were carrying out major social transformations such as the nationalisation of foreign monopolies, redistribution of land and industrialisation, and which were taking steps to further public education and to reduce poverty and unemployment.

Of particular importance from the Soviet point of view, states of this kind were held to be 'objectively anti-imperialist' in that they generally opposed the substantial control over their domestic affairs that had traditionally been exercised by the major capitalist powers.[87]

Some countries of 'socialist orientation', such as Afghanistan, became very close allies of the USSR in the Brezhnev years and indeed all but members of the socialist state system. Soviet intervention in Afghanistan in December 1979 followed a coup in that country in April 1978 which brought a pro-Soviet Marxist government to power headed by Hafizullah Amin.[88] The coup was apparently neither instigated nor expected by the Soviet authorities, and it brought a regime to power which was bitterly divided by factional differences. The new government provoked widespread rebellion by instituting a series of far-reaching reforms in a brutal and disorganised manner. Before December 1979 there were already 7,000 Soviet military and civilian advisers in Afghanistan, but the government called for further Soviet support to suppress the domestic resistance. On 24 December the Soviet authorities, fearing a further change of government and perhaps of political orientation, began to airlift troops into Kabul; it was claimed that they were responding to an appeal from the Afghan government to suppress a counter-revolution which was being fomented from outside the country, and that their action was justified by the Soviet–Afghan friendship treaty.[89] On 27 December Babrak Karmal, who had been a member of the post-coup government but who had subsequently been exiled to the USSR, announced that the former president had been deposed and that he had taken power; the following day it was announced that Hafizullah Amin had been executed for 'crimes against the noble people of Afghanistan'.[90]

The months and years that followed saw the establishment of a much more substantial Soviet presence in Afghanistan than any that had previously existed, including political and economic links as well as a growing military commitment. For at least some Western observers Soviet action was not simply a violation of international agreements but an attempt to establish a greater degree of influence in the Persian Gulf, an area of enormous significance for Western oil supplies and one in which the Western position had already been weakened by the overthrow of the Shah of Iran. Others saw the action in a more defensive light: as Brezhnev explained at the 26th Party Congress in 1981, the situation in Afghanistan posed a 'direct threat to the security of [the Soviet] southern frontier',[91] and it was certainly true that an unstable, possibly militant Islamic government in a state immediately adjoining the USSR's southern borders might have quite serious implications for public order in the traditionally Muslim republics of Central Asia. Whatever the Soviet objectives might have been, it soon became apparent that it would be very difficult to achieve them.

Babrak Karmal, for a start, proved unable to unite the warring Khalq (Masses) and Parcham (Banner) factions of the People's Democratic Party, the organisation upon which his authority depended. Karmal was subsequently replaced as party leader and president by Najibullah,[92] but there was little progress in establishing the broadly-based 'government of national reconciliation' which was his declared objective.[93] There was considerable destruction in Afghanistan itself: between a quarter and a fifth of the population became refugees, perhaps a million Afghans died, and a series of civil and military objects including roads, bridges and airfields were destroyed. Soviet forces were able to employ enormous firepower, including helicopter gunships and SU-25 attack aircraft, but they established firm control only in the major cities and along the major highways, and much of the countryside remained in the hands of the Mujahaddin guerrillas.

The war was an unsatisfactory one for the USSR in several other respects. It alienated world opinion, particularly in the Third World; it was very expensive (according to figures made public in 1989, the cost was about 5 billion rubles annually[94]); and it was very costly in terms of human life (according to figures again made public in 1989, nearly 14,000 Soviet servicemen lost their lives in the course of the war, more than 11,000 of them in combat[95]). The war became a most unpopular one domestically as the toll of dead and injured steadily mounted. Despite attempts to glamorise those who died fulfilling their 'internationalist duty' in Afghanistan, there were many letters in the Soviet press complaining of the one-sided treatment of the war that had been provided in the Soviet media and of the failure to make proper provision for the wounded on their return to the USSR.[96] There were even suggestions, in published letters, that senior officials had used their influence to prevent their own sons being sent to the front line. *Pravda* reported that most of the 'thousands' of letters it had received asked the simple question: 'When is the war going to end?'[97]

Influenced by considerations such as these, successive leaderships had attempted since almost the beginning of the war to extricate their forces from the conflict. Soviet forces were not, at least in the first instance, to be withdrawn unconditionally. Rather, in negotiations that had proceeded under United Nations auspices since 1981, they were to withdraw upon a number of specific conditions. As Brezhnev told the 26th Party Congress in 1981, 'The sovereignty of Afghanistan must be fully protected, as must its non-aligned status'.[98] This meant in practice that all foreign intervention, by the United States and Pakistan as well as the USSR, must come to an end; secure guarantees must be provided that there would be no further intervention in Afghan affairs; and the People's Democratic Party (which remained strongly Soviet-aligned) was to be accorded a dominant position in any future Afghan government. Further negotiations led finally to a series of agreements, signed in Geneva in April 1988, providing for the withdrawal of Soviet forces.[99] The agreements – comparable, in *Pravda's* view, to the INF treaty[100] – included bilateral accords between Afghanistan and Pakistan on non-interference and non-intervention, and on the voluntary return of refugees; a Soviet–US declaration in support of these agreements; and a joint agreement on the settlement of the Afghan situation which provided for the 'phased withdrawal' of Soviet troops, half of them between May and August 1988 and the remainder within the following nine months. Soviet troop withdrawals began on 15 May and were completed on schedule on 15 February 1989; Shevardnadze, addressing the Supreme Soviet the following October, described the original decision to intervene as a violation of 'general human values' and of party and state procedures.[101]

Developments in Afghanistan assumed a greater significance for Western governments than they would otherwise have had because of the place they appeared to occupy in an 'Arc of Crisis' that extended from the Middle East to South-Eastern Asia.[102] The formation of an anti-Western government in Iran after the fall of the Shah, the increasingly explicit Marxist–Leninist orientation of the People's Democratic Republic of Yemen and Soviet involvement in the Horn of Africa, together with the build-up of the Soviet fleet in the Indian Ocean, seemed to offer convincing evidence of a wide-ranging and effective Soviet strategy directed against vital Western interests, not least the supply of oil and the security of major shipping routes. The intervention of Cuban troops in Angola in 1975 and in the Ogaden war between Ethiopia and Somalia in 1977–78 – in both cases, it was assumed, acting as Soviet proxies – appeared to provide further evidence of a new global interventionism. It was in these circumstances that Western governments began to consider initiatives such as a rapid deployment force in the Gulf area and other measures designed to protect their essential interests.

Soviet strategy had in fact been much more reactive and rather less successful than this picture tended to suggest. This was clearly the case in Soviet relations with Egypt, which became the USSR's most important ally in the Middle East after the mid-1950s when Western governments refused to finance the Aswan Dam.[103] The USSR had been one of the first governments to recognise the state of Israel in 1948, but Soviet support was thereafter thrown behind the Arab cause and behind the Egyptian war effort in particular. Soviet–Egyptian relations remained close even after the death of Nasser in 1970, and the following year, under his successor Anwar Sadat, the two states concluded a fifteen-year friendship treaty, the first of its kind to be made between the USSR and an Arab government. Its twelve articles covered military as well as economic collaboration, and the Soviet presence in Egypt in the early 1970s became the largest anywhere outside the communist bloc at this time. In 1972, however, following a number of disagreements, 20,000 Soviet military advisers were ordered to leave the country. In 1976 the friendship treaty was abrogated, Soviet debts (some US$11 billion) were repudiated, and the Egyptians moved closer to the USA, which had played a central role in the Camp David and other peace negotiations in the area. In 1984, under Sadat's successor Mubarak, the two countries again exchanged ambassadors, but there seemed little likelihood that Soviet–Egyptian relations would ever regain their former intimacy.

Rather closer relations were maintained, in the late 1980s, with the People's Democratic Republic of Yemen (South Yemen), which signed a friendship treaty with the USSR in 1979 but remained a very minor power in terms of size and influence. Military cooperation also led to the conclusion of a friendship treaty with North Yemen in 1984. Iraq, with whom a friendship treaty was concluded in 1972, remained a much more important Soviet ally in the region, but relations were sometimes difficult, particularly following the outbreak of the Iran–Iraq war in 1980. The conflict was an 'absolutely senseless' one, according to Brezhnev at this time,[104] and the USSR initially took a broadly neutral position, hoping to retain the alliance with Iraq but at the same time not to alienate the new and anti-Western Khomeini government in Iran. Latterly the USSR appeared to have reverted to its traditional support for Iraq, while calling for a negotiated settlement at the earliest opportunity. The August 1988 ceasefire was warmly welcomed.[105] Close relations were also maintained with Syria (which concluded a friendship treaty with the USSR in 1980), and with India, which signed a friendship treaty as early as 1971 and which remained one of the closest of the USSR's non-communist allies under Indira Gandhi and her successor Rajiv.[106] The USSR became India's main external source of weaponry and rendered extensive economic aid; Soviet support was in part a response to the support that Pakistan received from the Chinese, with whom the Indians had an unresolved border dispute. Gorbachev had made an official visit to India in November 1986, concluding with the signature of a 'Delhi Declaration' in which both sides pledged themselves to the peaceful resolution of international disputes.[107] A further official visit took place in November 1988, in the course of which both sides reaffirmed their commitment to the Declaration and to the elaboration of a long-term programme for economic, trade, cultural, and scientific cooperation to the year 2000.[108]

Relations with the largest non-Arab country in the Middle East, Iran, were rather more complex both before and after the fall of the Shah. Soviet agreements with the Shah included credits for arms purchases and the construction of an oil pipeline. Iran, in fact, was the Soviet Union's largest trading partner in the Middle East during this period. After the overthrow of the Shah in 1979 the USSR ordered the local communist party (Tudeh) to support the Ayatollah Khomeini, and even began to supply the new regime with weapons. As Brezhnev explained to the 26th CPSU Congress in 1981, developments in Iran were 'complex and contradictory' but what had taken place was none-theless an 'anti-imperialist revolution'.[109] Relations were not disturbed even when the Khomeini government arrested Tudeh leaders and dissolved their movement in 1983. Latterly, however, the Khomeini regime began to describe the USSR as the 'greater Satan'; cultural exchanges were ended, the size of the Soviet mission was restricted, Soviet journalists were refused entry visas, and in March 1988 there was an attack upon the Soviet embassy in Tehran.[110] Both Soviet and American leaders, by the late 1980s, had a common interest in a negotiated end to the Iran–Iraq war and in an international agreement guaranteeing freedom of movement in the Persian Gulf, but neither could necessarily manipulate events in the region to its advantage and neither, perhaps, quite understood the nature of a popular movement so far removed from its own cultural assumptions.

This varied picture of successes and reverses suggested that the USSR was not, in the 'Arc of Crisis' or anywhere else, pursuing a long-term strategy based on Marxist-Leninist doctrine. The evidence suggested rather that the USSR was a defensive and sometimes oppor-tunist power, responding to changing circumstances in much the same way that any other government (or its tsarist predecessor) might have done. Nor was it a particularly successful strategy, despite some apparently spectacular advances in Africa and Afghanistan. The Soviet Union, for instance, sometimes backed the wrong horse (such as Nkomo rather than Mugabe in Zimbabwe). The main instruments of Soviet influence were arms sales and direct subsidies, both expensive to maintain, and neither necessarily secured a permanent commitment (Egypt and Somalia, for instance, abrogated their friendship treaties with the USSR in the 1970s, and the USSR was unable to prevent the replacement of a friendly regime in Grenada by American military action in 1983). Local allies, it turned out, were often reluctant to accept guidance from the USSR; some of them (Egypt, Iraq, the Sudan and Ethiopia) persecuted and even executed large numbers of their domestic communist party members, and others took different views on international issues (Iraq, for instance, openly supported Somalia in the Ogaden war). Soviet allies sometimes found themselves opposed to each other (such as the Ba'athist governments of Syria and Iraq, or Ethiopia and Somalia), and others entered into agreements with Soviet adversaries (both Angola and Mozambique, for instance, signed non-aggression agreements with South Africa in 1984, and Soviet clients generally found it difficult to resist the powerful influence of Western governments and corporations, or in the case of Ethiopia, relief agencies).

It was perhaps above all because of this disenchanting experience that the USSR, under Gorbachev's leadership, began to take a more distanced view of the future development of Third World states. Gorbachev's report to the 27th CPSU Congress in 1986 was the first in modern times to make no reference to the need to assist 'national liberation' movements in the developing countries; rather, the Soviet leader appeared to favour a 'comprehensive system of international security' involving 'the use for the welfare of the world community, above all of the developing countries, of part of the funds that [would] be released as a result of the reduction in military budgets'.[111] The Party Programme, adopted at the same congress, promised only that the Soviet Union would 'do what it could' to assist socialist-oriented states in the developing world; and authoritative commentaries made it clear that the USSR preferred the peaceful settlement of regional conflicts rather than the 'export of revolution'.[112] Its policy during the Gulf War of 1991 strongly favoured a political settlement and a wider set of negotiations, including the Arab–Israeli dispute, but in the end remained consistent with United Nations resolutions notwithstanding the Soviet friendship treaty with the Iraqi government.[113] The USSR, as before, remained ready to further its own interests wherever it could, and those interests were not always in agreement with those of Western governments – nor had they been in tsarist times. There was, however, a greater awareness of the need to develop a framework of rules which could operate in the interests of the world community as a whole – against terrorism or narcotics, for instance – and a greater readiness to establish relations with traditionally conservative states, such as the Arab monarchies, as well as with those that claimed to adhere to Marxism–Leninism. How far this reorientation extended was likely to depend at least as much upon the responses of Western governments and the behaviour of the other states concerned as it did upon the Soviet authorities themselves.

Gorbachev's foreign policy: a balance sheet

If Gorbachev enjoyed success in any sphere it was perhaps above all foreign policy. His 'new thinking', admittedly, was not necessarily new: the central propositions had been discussed by Soviet specialists for some time, and the term itself appeared to derive from Bertrand Russell's *New Thinking for the Nuclear Age*, published in 1960. The ideas of a 'common European home', similarly, had first been employed by Brezhnev during a visit to West Germany in 1981.[114] The term 'new thinking' was in any case a 'general framework for policy rather than a detailed plan of action'.[115] Original or not, the application of such concepts under the Gorbachev leadership brought considerable rewards from the point of view of Soviet interests. The conclusion of a major arms agreement with the United States was perhaps the central achievement; but still more important was the restoration of normal relations with the other global superpower after the collapse of detente in the late 1970s. The Soviet Union, under Gorbachev, broadened its relations more generally with the world community – with Latin American states apart from Cuba, with the Vatican, with Israel, and even with South Africa.[116] Relations with the other communist giant, the People's Republic of China, had improved remarkably at both a state and a party-to-party level. In some ways most striking of all, the perception of the Soviet Union as a closed, aggressive society had been largely replaced by one of a changing and liberalising system genuinely committed to peace and headed by a dynamic, Kennedyesque leader and his personable wife.

Gorbachev made a considerable personal contribution to this changing image. He went out of his way to meet foreign visitors from all walks of life – politicians certainly, but also a delegation from a Nobel prizewinners' congress, a group of doctors connected with the medical movement against nuclear war, the Latin American writer Gabriel Garcia Marquez, a group of writers including Arthur Miller and James Baldwin who were attending the Issyl-Kum forum in 1986, and many others. He travelled abroad incessantly, making at least two major foreign visits a year: in 1989, for instance, he carried out official visits to Britain, France, Finland and West Germany, visited Cuba, East Germany and China, took part in the first-ever summit between the Soviet Union and Ireland during a stop-over at Shannon airport, and still found time to meet the new US President George Bush in December after a state visit to Italy and a first-ever meeting with the Pope. Gorbachev was Man of the Year for *Time* magazine in 1987 and for *Der Spiegel* in 1988; in 1989 he was 'statesman of the decade' for independent television in Britain; in 1990 he was Man of the Year in France and received the Nobel Peace Prize. He was trusted, according to opinion polls, rather more in Western Europe than his American counterpart, and the regime he headed was seen as more seriously committed to peace and disarmament.[117] Even in the United States there was a considerable change: in 1984 about 60 per cent of Americans thought of the USSR as an 'evil empire', according to the *Los Angeles Times*, but by late 1987 nearly 70 per cent took a different view. And Gallup found that more than half of Americans polled were 'favourably' disposed towards Gorbachev, the highest rating for any Soviet leader since the Second World War.[118] On some occasions, such as his visit to West Germany in 1989, the popular response was described as 'Gorbymania'.

It was nonetheless closer to the truth to describe Gorbachev's foreign policy as a 'diplomacy of decline'.[119] The agreements with the United States had been bought at the cost of disproportionate cuts in Soviet weaponry and were clearly dictated by the need to reduce military spending, a much heavier relative burden for the USSR than for the United States. The propaganda campaign against the deployment of Euromissiles was lost, despite considerable public opposition in the countries concerned; and the war in Afghanistan was brought to an end, because of its cost as well as unpopularity, on terms that offered no guarantee the Najibullah government would survive or that external intervention in its affairs would cease (it finally collapsed in 1992). More seriously, the Soviet alliance system in Eastern Europe began to disappear as a series of popular revolutions overturned the communist governments in Poland, Hungary, Czechoslovakia,

Romania and the GDR (which became a part of Germany and thereby of NATO under the terms of a treaty signed by the two Germanies, France, Britain and the United States as well as the Soviet Union in September 1990). The Warsaw Treaty Organisation and CMEA, reflecting these developments, were formally dissolved in 1991. Gorbachev, speaking to the Central Committee in December 1989, professed to welcome the 'positive changes' that had taken place in Eastern Europe, but it was difficult to disguise the fact that the sphere of influence acquired at great cost during World War II had disappeared, probably for good.[120] The world communist movement, meanwhile, had virtually collapsed as an organised force, and individual parties had lost ground in nearly all the countries in which they had a legal existence (some had simply disappeared).[121]

Nor did these developments give a misleading impression of Soviet influence on world affairs. According to a careful investigation of such matters which was published in the West in the late Brezhnev years, Soviet global influence was at its height in the 1950s, when about 14 per cent of the world's nations could be described as Soviet-aligned; by the late 1970s, however, the total had fallen to 12 per cent. There was certainly 'no significant Soviet geopolitical momentum in recent years'. Soviet influence, moreover, was overwhelmingly concentrated among the poorest and least important countries in terms of population and GNP, whose support was often more of a liability than an asset; the world's major military and industrial powers, by contrast, were all allied or aligned with the United States. In 1958, according to the same calculations, the Soviet Union influenced 31 per cent of the world's population and 9 per cent of the world's GNP (excluding the USSR itself); by 1979 the USSR influenced only 6 per cent of the world's population and only 5 per cent of the world's GNP, again excluding the USSR itself. 'If these data indicated anything', the authors concluded, 'it is the decline of Soviet world influence since the 1950s.'[122] Perhaps symptomatically, successive Soviet General Secretaries, from Stalin to Brezhnev, had boasted at party congresses that the 'correlation of forces' on the world arena was changing steadily to the advantage of socialism and the Soviet Union. Gorbachev, at the 27th Party Congress in 1986, made no such claim and indeed could not realistically have done so.

In these and other respects, it was difficult to separate the success or failure of Soviet foreign policy from the achievements of *perestroika* as a whole. The weakness of the Soviet position internationally reflected the weakness of the Soviet economy, which accounted for a small and diminishing share of world trade and provided no secure basis for the exercise of global influence. As Shevardnadze put it in a speech to foreign ministry staff in 1987, they represented a country which for the previous fifteen years had been 'more and more losing its position as one of the leading industrially developed countries'.[123] The declining appeal of socialist ideas was openly acknowledged, for instance, by Anatolii Dobrynin, the veteran US ambassador and later Central Committee Secretary, and by the commentator Alexander Bovin, for whom the changes in Eastern Europe were evidence that 'the great socialist experiment that spanned the entire twentieth century had failed'.[124] Justifiably or not, the Soviet Union in the later Brezhnev years had provided no advertisement for socialism, and even communist parties in other countries had felt compelled to distance themselves from the Soviet model and the heritage of Leninism. Gorbachev's response to these developments appeared to be twofold, so far as foreign policy was concerned. His first objective was to restore the authority of Soviet socialism by economic reform and political democratisation; the second, much more ambitious objective was to reposition Soviet communism in relation to the European tradition from which it had originally emerged, seeking to build up a coalition of working class, religious, ecological, youth and other forces which could unite around the slogan of peace and social justice, if not necessarily Marxism–Leninism.[125] At the end of the Gorbachev administration the success of both objectives remained problematic.

7   Gorbachev and the politics of *perestroika*

If economic reform was the 'key to all our problems' at the outset of Gorbachev's administration and political reform increasingly the means by which it was to be accomplished, the ultimate objective remained the achievement of a form of socialism which advanced decisively on those that had preceded it. Gorbachev described this vision at the April 1985 plenum, hardly in the most memorable of terms, as a 'qualitatively new state [*sostoyanie*] of society'.[1] Elsewhere he referred to it as 'developing socialism', differentiating it from the 'developed socialism' that was supposed to have been constructed in the Brezhnev era and still more so from the utopian vision of a society rapidly advancing towards full communism that had been current in the Khrushchev years. Still later, from 1990 onwards, the emphasis shifted to 'humane, democratic socialism'.[2] And yet six years into the new administration, or even after it, the nature of Gorbachevian socialism remained frustratingly elusive. What kind of society did he envisage, beyond some rather vacuous generalities? Was the vision a coherent and convincing one? And how was it to be achieved – was there agreement about it within the leadership and the wider society, and did a political agency exist that could bring it into being? The issues at stake could hardly have been greater, and they concerned the other members of the world community just as much as they concerned the USSR: for it was not only in the USSR that an answer was being sought to the question as to whether there could be a 'third way' – a socialism that ensured a decent and equitable living for all its members and yet avoided monopolistic concentrations of power of a kind that had led to political repression in the USSR and other communist-ruled nations.[3]

Gorbachev and 'Gorbachevism'

Gorbachev's early speeches gave relatively little attention to the longer-term objectives he had in mind for Soviet society. His acceptance speech, in March 1985, promised that the strategy worked out by the 26th Party Congress – over which Brezhnev had presided – and at subsequent meetings of the Central Committee would remain unchanged: a policy of the 'acceleration of the country's socio-economic development [and] the perfection of all aspects of the life of the society'. More precisely, the strategy meant the transformation of the material-technical basis of production, the improvement of social relations particularly in economic matters, and the development of 'man himself' in both a material and a spiritual sense.[4] His first full address to the Central Committee in April 1985 again emphasised the importance of the 26th Congress and called for a 'steady advance' rather than a clear break with earlier policies; the party's general line, as he explained it, involved the 'perfection of developed socialist society', a characterisation that was thoroughly Brezhnevian in tone. Gorbachev did call for 'further changes and transformations' and for the establishment of a 'qualitatively new state of society, in the broadest sense of the word'. It was changes in the economy, however, that would be decisive in any development of this kind, and the speech was largely preoccupied with familiar matters such as growth, efficiency and labour productivity.[5]

The most authoritative statement of the party's longer-term purposes was its programme, first adopted in 1903 and then in further editions in 1919 and 1961.[6] The 1961 Programme, hailed by Khrushchev as a 'Communist Manifesto of the modern era', was best known for its assumption that the achievement of a fully communist society had become an 'immediate practical task for the Soviet people'. By the end of that decade, it promised, the strongest and richest capitalist country, the USA, would be overtaken in total production; by the end of the 1970s a state of abundance would be created and a communist society 'in the main' would be constructed, to be 'fully completed' over the following period.[7] These optimistic perspectives were quickly abandoned by Khrushchev's successors, and under Brezhnev it began to be claimed that the USSR had achieved no more than the construction of a 'developed socialist society', a new and quite distinct stage of Soviet development whose further evolution into full communism would be a matter for the fairly distant future.[8] The Party Programme of 1961 was clearly difficult to reconcile with these rather different perspectives, and the 26th Congress in 1981 approved Brezhnev's proposal that a new edition should be prepared. The essentials of the existing programme, Brezhnev explained, were still valid, but twenty years had elapsed since its adoption and there were many developments it had failed to record, among them the fact that Soviet society was proceeding to communism through the stage of 'developed socialism'. This, Brezhnev pointed out, was a necessary and 'historically extended' period in the formation of a fully communist society.[9]

Brezhnev became chairman of the committee that was charged with the preparation of a new draft, and on his death the following year his successor Andropov assumed the same responsibility. Andropov set out his general approach to such matters in a speech in the spring of 1983 in which he emphasised that the Soviet Union was 'only at the beginning' of the long historical stage of developed socialism; there must be no exaggeration of the country's closeness to communism, and no attempt to minimise the difficulties that lay ahead.[10] Discussing the party programme more directly, Andropov told the Central Committee in June 1983 that many of its directives had in fact been realised: links between citizens and deputies, for instance, had become closer, and national discussion of major items of legislation had become a well-established practice. Some of the assumptions of the programme, however, had not withstood the test of time, and there were elements of 'detachment from reality, undue anticipation and unnecessary detail'.[11] These emphases were repeated by Konstantin Chernenko, particularly in his address to the commission that had been set up by the Central Committee to prepare a revised programme. Chernenko stressed the need to remove the 'oversimplified impression of the means and dates by which a transition to the higher stage of communism' would take place, and argued that the new programme should provide a 'realistic' evaluation of developed socialism, which would be an 'historically protracted period'.[12]

Gorbachev succeeded Chernenko not only as General Secretary but also, it emerged, as chairman of the commission preparing the new programme. He set out his thinking in an address to the Central Committee in October 1985. Gorbachev emphasised the continuity of political principle between the new version of the programme and its predecessors, but also pointed out the need for 'creative development' in the light of changing domestic and international circumstances. His speech reflected his predecessors' determination to avoid 'excessive detail and groundless fantasy', and in particular any 'rushing ahead, introducing communist principles without taking account the level of society's material and intellectual maturity'. The central aim, he explained, was to attain a 'qualitatively new state of Soviet society through acceleration of the country's socioeconomic development'. The economy, as before, would have a 'decisive role', but so too would the widening of socialist democracy, including the active participation of ordinary people in state and public affairs.[13] The draft programme was published in the central press for public discussion in October 1985; altogether, Gorbachev told the 27th Congress the following February, six million responses had been received from ordinary citizens, raising a whole variety of issues.[14]

A number of these correspondents, Gorbachev reported, had in fact suggested that the new text be considered an entirely new fourth Party Programme, rather than a revision of the third, because the changes it proposed were so far-reaching.[15] Perhaps the most striking single change in the new programme was the abandonment of the optimistic perspectives of its Khrushchevian predecessor. The 1961 Programme, for instance, had defined itself as a 'Programme for the building of communist society'; the revised version of 1986 was no more than a Programme for the 'planned and all-round perfection of socialism' and for further advance to communism through the country's 'accelerated socio-economic development'. The dates and stages by which communism was to be reached disappeared entirely; the 1986 Programme, on the contrary, noted that the party did 'not attempt to foresee in detail the features of full communism' and warned that any attempt to advance too rapidly was 'doomed to failure and might cause both political and economic damage'. The collectivist emphases of the 1961 Programme – more and more services such as transport and housing to be provided free of charge, more public catering and shared upbringing of children – found no place in the new text, nor did the promise of a minimum one month paid holiday for all citizens. The 1986 Programme, similarly, contained no reference to the historic goal of the withering away of the state (it had long been predicted that the only thing that would wither away was the *idea* that the state should wither away); its main emphasis was upon practical and short-term objectives, and it struck a disciplinarian rather than utopian note in its references to careerism, nepotism and profiteering.[16]

Both the new version of the Programme and a revised set of party rules, which were also approved at the 27th Congress, included a reference to 'developed socialism'. During the period since the 1960s, as the Party Programme put it, the USSR had 'entered the stage of developed socialism'.[17] Some of those who had commented on the draft of the new programme, Gorbachev revealed, thought the term should have been entirely removed; others, on the contrary, thought it should have been dealt with at greater length. The reference to developed socialism had in the end been retained, Gorbachev explained, partly because it figured in the programmes of other ruling parties, but mainly because the term had been misrepresented. It had, in fact, originally been employed as a reaction against 'simplistic ideas about the means and periods of time for carrying out the tasks of communist construction'. Latterly, however, it had become no more than a framework for the recording of successes, with little attention being paid to problems such as the intensification of production or the improvement of food supplies. It was the earlier, less complacent version of the term that Gorbachev wished to emphasise. Developed socialism, nonetheless, did not subsequently figure in the General Secretary's speeches or in party documents, and it was replaced later the same year by the term 'developing socialism' (*razvivayushchiisya sotsializm*), implying a still earlier stage in the transition towards the communist society of the future.[18]

A fuller statement of Gorbachev's vision of the Soviet future came in the conclusion of his address to the 19th Party Conference in 1988. They were looking, he told the delegates, for a socialism that 'renounced everything that deformed socialism in the 1930s and that led to its stagnation in the 1970s', a socialism that would inherit the 'best elements' of the thinking of its founding fathers together with the constructive achievements of other countries and social systems. Although it was impossible to describe such a society in a detailed way, some of its main features could and should be indicated. Such a socialism, Gorbachev explained, would be a system of 'true and tangible humanism in which man is really the measure of all things'. There would, for instance, be a dynamic and advanced economy with the highest possible labour productivity based upon a variety of forms of property and worker participation. It would combine a broad measure of central planning with a great deal of autonomy for individual enterprises, which would be self-financing and interconnected through a market. The basic needs of all for housing, health care and employment would be satisfied; at the same time the abilities of individuals would be highly rewarded, where this was appropriate, in both moral and material terms. A society of this kind would have a high level of culture and morality, and it would be managed by a system of genuine people's rule, of 'profound and consistent democracy'. This 'new image of socialism' was described by Gorbachev as 'democratic and humane', and in turn an 'important stage in the advance to communism'.[19]

Gorbachev expanded upon this vision of a 'qualitatively new state of society' in an address to senior party functionaries in July 1989. It would, he explained, be a 'society of free people, a society of and for the working people, built on the principles of humanism, socialist democracy and social justice'. It would be based on a variety of forms of public ownership which would enable people to be masters of their own lives and to give full play to their energy and abilities. Economic development would be based on self-regulation, with the centre playing a merely coordinating role. It would be a society in which the people would have 'absolute power and the full range of rights', and it would be based on both the 'finest traditions of Soviet democracy and the experience of mankind's democratic evolution'. Nations and ethnic groups, similarly, would have equal rights, at least within the Soviet federation. This would be a society with a 'rich inner life and a high level of culture and morality', and it would be 'open to the world, to cooperation in the interests of building new international relations based on free choice, equality, security and universal values'. This, however, was no more than a 'general outline' which needed to be developed in detail by the scholarly community; indeed it was 'vitally necessary' that they do so.[20]

Gorbachev himself contributed to this task in an extended statement, 'The socialist idea and revolutionary *perestroika*', which appeared in *Pravda* in November 1989. It drew upon a series of speeches he had made in the late autumn, particularly an address to an all-union student forum. If at first he had thought it would be sufficient simply to eliminate various shortcomings in Soviet life, Gorbachev explained, he was now in no doubt that nothing less than a radical reconstruction of the whole of society was necessary. There was no detailed plan to guide this work, nor could there be; but it would certainly avoid the command-administrative methods of the Soviet past and the capitalist methods of the West. A process of this kind – *perestroika* – would occupy a 'lengthy stage in the historical development of socialism', extending into the twenty-first century. Its ultimate objective would be the establishment of a 'genuinely democratic and self-governing social organism' in place of the authoritarian and bureaucratic system that had come into existence in the Stalinist years. Gorbachev had no doubt that the socialist choice in October 1917 had been the right one; nor could Marx be blamed for subsequent developments he had obviously been unable to foresee. Socialism, in any case, had to be conceived as a 'global process'. The experience of other countries and movements, particularly European social democracy, provided much from which they could learn; and the future lay in a cooperative rather than confrontational relationship between the USSR and the wider world from which both sides could benefit.[21]

Official perspectives of this kind were summed up in the 'Programmatic Declaration' adopted by the 28th Party Congress in July 1990. Entitled 'Towards a humane, democratic socialism', the Declaration insisted, as Gorbachev had done, that the origins of Soviet difficulties were to be found, not in any deficiency of the socialist idea itself, but in the deformations to which it had been subjected in the past. The Declaration included a set of 'urgent anti-crisis measures' to deal with some of these concerns, including the new union treaty and stabilisation of the consumer market. For the longer term it envisaged the strengthening of civil liberties, a 'stage-by-stage transition to a market system', international cooperation and democratisation of the party itself. Gorbachev, in his own contribution to the discussion, spoke of a 'civil society of free men and women' which would replace the 'Stalinist model' of the past; continuing the work of the 20th Congress of 1956, its purpose was to 'profoundly democratise and humanise society, to make it free and create living conditions worthy of a human being'. The Congress agreed to begin work on a new, fourth Party Programme, replacing the document agreed in 1986. According to an early draft, the new Programme would give the CPSU the task of carrying out 'historically progressive aims' (not necessarily communism), and socialism itself was defined as a society of 'economic effectiveness, social justice, political democracy and human solidarity' (but not necessarily of public ownership).[22]

This broad vision of the Soviet and indeed global future was carried forward in the late 1980s and early 1990s by a group of reform-minded academics and commentators, among them Fedor Burlatsky, Boris Kurashvili and Anatolii Butenko. Burlatsky, a people's deputy as well as scholar and journalist, argued in favour of a decentralised, self-managing socialism which drew upon the experience of the New Economic Policy of the 1920s as well as the socialist tradition in other countries. Two different conceptions of socialism, Burlatsky suggested, had been applied in the USSR over the post-revolutionary period. One of these was 'war communism', a centralised model based upon commands and coercion and harking back to the militarised society of the civil war years. The other was the more relaxed model of the New Economic Policy, which was based upon a mixed economy and more democratic norms. The war communism model had enjoyed considerable popularity, in part because of the USSR's 'authoritarian-patriarchal culture', and had later taken the form of Stalinism, with its belief that the state should play the major part in the transition to socialism. This concept, 'state socialism', was however not properly socialist, and in any case it was inappropriate to modern conditions. It should be replaced, in Burlatsky's view, by a different concept, 'public, self-managing socialism', in which many functions presently performed by the state would be devolved to civil society and its institutions.

What would this 'qualitatively new model' of a 'more effective, democratic and humanistic socialism' look like? It would, Burlatsky suggested, be based upon a wide variety of property forms, including state property which would be developed to the higher level of public ownership of the whole people. It would incorporate a variety of forms of enterprise, including individual, family and cooperative as well as state productive units, which would be economically self-sufficient and interrelated through a market. There would be a sharing of power between the party, the state and social organisations, and each of these would be based upon more democratic norms, including the development of self-management, elections, the rotation of office and attention to public attitudes. A wide variety of cultural trends would coexist, and a socialist culture and personality would develop. This form of socialism, based upon the accountability of the state to society rather than vice versa, would take a long time to develop, but it was this form of socialism that supporters of *perestroika* hoped the Party Conference would develop further[23] – as indeed it did.

Another, somewhat bolder version of a Soviet 'tomorrow' was presented to the readers of *Moscow News* by Boris Kurashvili, a senior researcher at the Institute of State and Law of the USSR Academy of Sciences.[24] The future socialist society, he explained, would be one in which state planning would be retained in only a few essential sectors, but which would otherwise rely upon market forces. It would incorporate a variety of forms of property, including joint enterprises in which employees held up to 49 per cent of the shares. The party and state apparatus that was responsible for the management of the economy would be reduced to about a tenth of its present size; and democratic practices would be revived within the CPSU, primarily through party-wide discussions and votes on major issues. 'Real power' would be restored to the elected soviets, and a 'mass public and political organisation' with some similarities to a second party would be set up to run them. In international relations there would be an era of 'growing cooperation' between capitalism and socialism, leading towards a synthesis which would combine the best features of both (Lenin's formulations on such matters, he suggested, were 'not always satisfactory').[25] Writing later on 'models of socialism', Kurashvili looked forward to a further stage of 'democratic socialism' which would include respect for minority rights, a separation of powers, genuine federalism and a 'socialist multiparty system'.[26]

A further contributor to the discussion was Anatolii Butenko, a department head at the Institute of the Economics of the World Socialist System at the USSR Academy of Sciences. In his writings of the early 1980s, which were strongly influenced by the Polish crisis, Butenko argued that Soviet-type societies did not eliminate 'contradictions', in particular those between the sectional interests of managers and the working people they directed. Writing subsequently and at greater length, Butenko set out a vision of the Soviet future that was based upon the concept of 'socialist popular self-management' and which involved the abolition of the *nomenklatura* appointments system and a wide-ranging electoral reform.[27] Interviewed in *Pravda* in 1989, Butenko placed the greatest emphasis upon the emancipation of labour as the goal of socialism. This meant more than the elimination of exploitation, which had already been achieved in the Stalinist period: it meant the elimination of the oppression of man by man, which could be achieved only by the working class itself and not by a bureaucracy on its behalf. Butenko called in particular for the establishment of a socialist civil society, based upon a wide dispersal of ownership (so long as workers depended upon their employers, even under public ownership, they could never become the agents of their own destiny). This meant individual and private as well as state and municipal ownership; and in the political sphere it meant 'genuine popular rule – rule of the people by the people themselves'.[28]

Butenko was one of a group of leading scholars which met regularly from the spring of 1987 under party auspices with a view to formulating an adequate and up-to-date conception of socialism.[29] The results of their labours appeared in the party press in 1989; they summed up the perspectives of the most strongly reformist section of the social science community. Lenin's 'new model of socialism', they argued, had been put into effect during the 1920s, but then replaced by a Stalinist system which had 'created an alienation of the individual from ownership, from power and from the results of his work'. Liberating society from this legacy was no easy matter, because not only officials but wide strata of the population thought this Stalinist model was in fact the very epitome of socialism. The statement distinguished, as Butenko had done, between exploitation (which had been eliminated by public ownership) and oppression, which had continued. More controversially, and following Hayek and other critics of socialist collectivism, the group went on to argue that complete state ownership led to 'totalitarian forms of government', and that a wide variety of forms of property, including private ownership, was necessary if the personal liberties of citizens were to be securely protected. Economic life, more generally, was to be regulated through a 'socialist market', but with an improved system of social benefits to protect the disadvantaged from its worst effects. It would, finally, be a society based upon the rule of law, and upon universal human values such as honesty, decency and a sense of duty.[30]

Scholarly thinking became still more outspoken in the early 1990s. Indeed little of what had been unchallengeable orthodoxy since the 1920s remained untouched. The rector of the party's Institute of Social Sciences, for instance, Yuri Krasin, insisted upon the continuing relevance of Marxist conceptions of social justice and equality, but accepted the obsolescence of the earlier idea that commodity-money relations would be unnecessary in a socialist society. S. S. Alekseev, chairman of the Constitutional Supervision Committee, found most of enduring value in the ideas of the early Marx, particularly his concept of alienation. Georgii Shakhnazarov, head of the Soviet political science association and a Gorbachev adviser, went still further in a series of articles on the 'new model of socialism' in the party theoretical journal *Kommunist*. For Shakhnazarov, socialism would continue as long as mankind pursued a better world; but he rejected the idea of 'stages' of human history and the primacy of economic factors and saw communism itself as a 'hypothesis' or even a 'dream'. Some were even prepared to argue that socialism was not necessarily incompatible with 'capitalist private property'. It was difficult, in any of this, to discover what a future socialist or communist society would be like; if there was consensus about anything it was that it would not be based upon public ownership, would not be dominated by a single ruling party, would not supersede capitalism and might not even offer an alternative to it.[31]

The party's considered response to these and other discussions was a draft Programme, 'Socialism, Democracy, Progress', which was approved by a Central Committee plenum in July 1991 and subsequently published for discussion. Several writers, in the discussion, had urged the CPSU to adopt its own 'Bad Godesberg', after the German Social Democratic Programme of 1959 in which the last vestiges of that party's Marxist heritage had been discarded. The published Programme did still commit the party to communism as an 'historic perspective', but this, as the Leningrad party leader Boris Gidaspov commented, was very much in the spirit of an 'epitaph on a tomb-stone'. The draft Programme was certainly much briefer than its immediate predecessors; it was also very different in character. It committed the party to a set of basic principles including 'all-human values', 'democracy and freedom in all its forms', social justice and international integration, and to a series of more immediate policy objectives. The longer-term aim was the construction of a society based on a mixed economy, political pluralism and 'genuine people's power', which in turn could only be formed in association with a 'new world civilisation'.[32] The new Programme was intended to provide a 'plan of concrete action for today and tomorrow'; it was also, in Gorbachev's words, an admission that the communist ideal was unrealisable in the foreseeable future.[33]

Gorbachevism and the party leadership

Coherent or otherwise, the Gorbachevian vision had relatively few convinced supporters within the party leadership during his early years of office. One of them, certainly, was Foreign Minister Eduard Shevardnadze, who had previously been party first secretary in Georgia. In that capacity he had presided over a campaign against corruption, and more positively over a relaxation of the restrictions upon private trade and local government. The Georgian party organi-sation was also distinctive in the attention it devoted to the study of public opinion, in particular through a professional sociological service attached to party headquarters.[34] Perhaps the clearest expression of Shevardnadze's views was a speech he delivered in April 1986 on the annniversary of Lenin's birth, some months after he had become professionally responsible for foreign affairs. In the speech Shevard-nadze called for the broadest possible democratisation of political and economic life, including greater autonomy for enterprises and the election of management. He emphasised the need for benefits of all kinds to be fairly distributed and attacked the dispensing of *glasnost'* in measured doses; he drew attention to nationality differences and called for the 'perfection [in other words, reform] of the electoral system', a point the General Secretary himself first developed in his speech to the Central Committee the following year.[35] Shevardnadze's speeches as Foreign Minister (until his unexpected resignation in December 1990) showed a similar concern for openness, consultation and democratic accountability.[36]

Another 'Gorbachevian' member of the leadership was Vadim Medvedev, a Secretariat member from 1986 and a full member of the Politburo from September 1988 (he left both posts in 1990). Medvedev was a former rector of the Central Committee's Academy of Social Sciences, and in September 1988 he became head of the newly-established ideological commission of the Central Committee and thus the leadership's most prominent theoretician. Medvedev called, in October 1988, for an 'up-to-date conception of socialism', one that took into account the diversity of experience of the other socialist countries and indeed the lessons that could be learned from the capitalist world. Socialism, in his view, was a logical stage in the development of human civilisation; it should take account not only of the scientific and technical achievements of capitalism but also of its forms of political and economic organisation, including small-scale enterprise and international economic integration. The experience of Western social democracy also deserved attention, particularly for its defence of the social and political gains of the working class. Within the USSR itself there must be a less exclusive emphasis upon state ownership and greater scope for cooperative, leasehold and other arrangements. There must also be a place for 'commodity-money relations', or in other words the market, which was an 'irreplaceable means for the flexible economic coordination of production with growing and constantly changing public requirements and an important instrument of public control over the quality of goods and the costs of their production'.

There was still a role for central economic management, in Medvedev's view, but it should be of a wholly strategic kind, leaving operational decisions to the enterprises themselves as 'socialist commodity producers'. This must be complemented by a political system of a 'socialist pluralist' character, one that would take into account the 'diversity of interests and aspirations of all social groups and communities of people'. Internationally, this system would inevitably interact with capitalism within the framework of 'one and the same human civilisation'.[37] Speaking in early 1989, Medvedev (an economist by training) spoke still more positively of the market as a 'flexible instrument for reconciling production and consumption' which could be adapted to the purposes of a wide variety of social systems. It encouraged a swift response by producers to changing demand, and provided incentives for efficient economic management. Any attempt to evade it for the sake of the 'purity of the "socialist ideal"', he warned, would simply lead to a further expansion of the bureaucratic apparatus and to the dictatorship of the producer.[38] Speaking to the Central Committee later in the year, Medvedev accepted that the process of change in which they were engaged might be complex and even alarming. There was no real alternative, however, to the 'unconditional continuation' and even 'deepening' of democratisation and *glasnost*'.[39]

Perhaps the most intellectually convincing exponent of the Gorbachevian position was Alexander Yakovlev, a Central Committee Secretary from 1986 and full Politburo member from 1987 to 1990. A doctor of historical sciences and corresponding member of the Academy of Sciences, Yakovlev (an exchange student at Columbia University in the late 1950s) had come to Gorbachev's attention while ambassador to Canada and from 1983 to 1985 had directed the important Institute of the World Economy and International Relations of the USSR Academy of Sciences. In September 1988 he became, in addition, chairman of the Central Committee commission on international affairs. Speaking in April 1987, Yakovlev attacked 'dogmatic thinking' and located its social origins in that section of the society that had 'no interest in development, who are personally satisfied with the customary and convenient status quo, who are unable or unwilling to respond to the challenges of the times and to new phenomena in life'. In cultural affairs, for instance, they resolved the question of what films or plays could be seen with 'bureaucratic callousness'. Artistic creativity, in Yakovlev's view, served the needs of society for self-understanding and self-knowledge; without it there could be no moral progress or human development.[40] There could be no proper limits to *glasnost*', in Yakovlev's view.[41] And no one, he argued in terms that could have come straight from John Stuart Mill, could have a monopoly of the truth, either in asking questions or answering them; it could be determined only through the interplay of argument.[42]

Yakovlev's speeches had three central themes: the necessity of the market, international affairs, and, most distinctively, morality. Speaking in Vilnius in August 1988, for instance, he devoted particular attention to 'common human interests', such as the conservation of global resources, in which both East and West could cooperate.[43] Speaking in Perm' in December 1988 Yakovlev emphasised that for Lenin, at least after 1921, socialism was a 'society with commodity production, a market, competition, money [and] democracy', and himself urged the establishment of a 'developed socialist market'.[44] Speaking to Moscow automobile workers in June 1989, Yakovlev argued that Marx's 'utopia' of non-commodity production had simply not justified itself. Not simply was a market the only effective mechanism for the exchange of commodities and services in a large-scale modern society; it was also the foundation of democracy, as it provided the economic independence that made a dictatorship impossible.[45] The larger purposes of *perestroika*, however, were ethical: it must revive moral norms, honesty and decency, without which man was 'merely a consumer of material values rather than a bearer and creator of spiritual values'. This, perhaps, was the most fundamental objective of the reformers: to end a system in which the population was seen as a 'building material from which anything could be moulded' and to create in its place a 'highly moral society of free, creatively thinking, active and independent people'.[46]

A very different view of the Soviet future, however, was put forward by other members of the Soviet leadership, among them Yegor Ligachev and (from 1990) Ivan Polozkov and KGB chairman Vladimir Kryuchkov. For this section of the leadership, the Soviet past was to be seen in a much more positive light, while a much greater emphasis was laid upon discipline and central control in political and economic affairs. Ligachev, for instance, argued in a speech in June 1987 that the 'class enemy' was hoping that *perestroika* would undermine the influence of Marxist–Leninist ideology in the USSR and had been making use of it to spread 'irresponsible demagogy, hostile to the interests of the toilers'.[47] In a further speech in August 1987 he complained that there had been a tendency both in the USSR and outside it to see the socialist construction of the 1930s as no more than a series of mistakes. On the contrary, Ligachev argued, it had seen the collectivisation of agriculture, the USSR's emergence as the world's second-largest economy and subsequently the defeat of Nazi Germany. There had been some among their 'class opponents', Ligachev went on, who had been praising *perestroika*, hoping it represented a departure from socialism in favour of a market economy, ideological pluralism and Western-style democracy. On the contrary, Ligachev insisted, the USSR would never leave the path of Leninism or abandon the achievements of the 'glorious seventy-year history of Soviet power'.[48]

Speaking in the city of Gorky in August 1988, Ligachev again insisted that the CPSU was unapologetically a 'ruling' party. There was no room for multiparty politics or a political opposition, and there could be no place for strikes or other 'antisocialist' phenomena. Nor would there be any copying of Western market and property forms, with the unemployment and inequality that inevitably accompanied them. In foreign affairs, equally, there could be no retreat from 'class' positions, and no 'artificial "slow-down" in the social and national-liberation struggle'.[49] In other speeches Ligachev insisted that the CPSU was 'above all a party of the working class'; and although an 'unrestricted dialogue' was necessary under single-party conditions, *glasnost'* should be 'constructive' and must not be used for 'selfish' or 'anti-Soviet purposes'.[50] He attacked any deviation from 'class positions' in public life, and called for a more vigorous defence of the founders of socialism. And while he acknowledged the losses of the 'cult of personality' period, he insisted (in an address to the French Communist Party) that 'not a year' had been lost in the process of socialist construction – in effect a defence of the Brezhnev as well as Stalinist years.[51] It was, apparently, because of Ligachev's insistence that the Central Committee report to the party congress in 1990 made no reference to private property. Defeated for the deputy party leadership at the Congress, Ligachev remained an open and vocal exponent of 'socialist *perestroika*' and continued to insist upon the priority of planning and party dominance.[52]

Viktor Chebrikov, at this time KGB chairman, made a still more pointed speech in September 1987 in which he declared that Western intelligence services were attempting to subvert Soviet youth and to sow the seeds of nationalist discontent, hoping in this way to undermine socialism morally and politically and to inculcate political pluralism (Gorbachev, by contrast, had spoken strongly in favour of 'socialist pluralism' at a meeting with French public figures the same month[53]). Socialist democracy and discipline, Chebrikov went on, were inextricably connected; so too were citizens' rights and their obligations. It must above all be clear that *perestroika* was taking place under the auspices of the CPSU and that it would be conducted within the framework of socialism. Chebrikov was particularly scathing about the 'informal groups' that had been attracting public attention, warning that 'extremist elements' had worked their way into the leaderships of some of them and that they were encouraging them to engage in actions 'objectively against the interests of our society'.[54] Chebrikov's successor, Vladimir Kryuchkov, went even further, arguing in December 1990 that 'destructive elements' were engaged in an attempt to overthrow Soviet rule and that foreign intelligence services had declared a 'covert war' against the USSR.[55]

The Russian party leader, Ivan Polozkov, was another Politburo member publicly associated with conservative positions. Polozkov's speeches after his election in 1990 took a strongly 'workerist' line. The CPSU, in his view, must represent the interests of 'working people' above all, and must ensure that any transition to market relations reflected their interests and not those of 'neocapitalist elements and the criminal bourgeoisie'.[56] Polozkov saw the two-party system as an attempt to divide and weaken the working class; he rejected anything that would lead to the emergence of divisions between rich and poor in Soviet society, and insisted upon the dominance of state control and ownership.[57] Speaking to the Central Committee in January 1991, Polozkov attached the 'so-called democrats' who had undermined *perestroika* and whose real aim was to re-establish the 'dictatorship of private capital'.[58] The Leningrad party leader Boris Gidaspov, a member of the Secretariat from 1990 onwards, placed most of his emphasis upon central control and discipline; he was openly dismissive of ideas of 'people's capitalism' and 'nonparty *glasnost"* and in 1991 attacked what he described as the 'anti-democratic liquidationist movement' that was taking advantage of the weakness and indecision of the party leadership.[59]

Politburo 'conservatives' hardly had a coherent programme, and their numbers were subject to continual attrition (Ligachev, who left the leadership after his defeat at the 28th Congress, was a notable casualty). They did, however, have a political position, articulated most clearly in a remarkable letter ostensibly addressed to the newspaper *Sovetskaya Rossiya* in early 1988 by Nina Andreeva, a Leningrad chemistry lecturer. The letter, 'I can't forgo principles', was reportedly published at the behest of Ligachev and for some time it was believed that Andreeva was the pseudonym of a conservative member of the leadership.[60] Andreeva began by welcoming the more open atmosphere in which her students were discussing all kinds of issues, but deplored the way in which the Soviet past had become identified with mistakes and shortcomings. There had been a meeting in a student dormitory, for instance, with a retired colonel, who had been asked about political repression in the armed forces. He replied, apparently to the students' dissatisfaction, that he had himself encountered nothing of the kind and indeed that many of those who had started off the war with him and seen it through to the end had become major military commanders. The subject of repression, Andreeva contended, had become 'excessively magnified in the perception of some young people, pushing an objective comprehension of the past into the background'.

There were many other examples of this kind. One of her students, for instance, had told her that the class struggle was an obsolete concept, and an eminent academic had put forward the view that relations between capitalist and socialist states were devoid of class content (he had previously maintained the opposite). Not surprisingly, 'nihilistic views' were intensifying among young people; they were becoming politically disorientated, and some had even argued that it was 'time to call to account the Communists who had supposedly "humanised" the country's life after 1917'. The construction of socialism, as a recent film about the life of Sergei Kirov had shown, was a time of enthusiasm and optimism, not the period of repression and ignorance of which the script had spoken. Andreeva went on to complain of historical plays, such as those of Mikhail Shatrov, which were arbitrary in their interpretation and close to the views that had been put forward by Lenin's opponents, and she deplored the obsessive interest in Stalin among many writers, obscuring the fact that his was a complex and transitional period in which industrialisation, collectivisation and a cultural revolution had brought the USSR into the ranks of the great powers. Andreeva shared the anger and indignation of others in respect of the repression of the 1930s and 1940s, in which her own family had suffered. But common sense could not permit the 'monochromatic colouring of contradictory events' that had begun to prevail in some quarters of the press.

Andreeva called for an assessment of all party and state leaders, including Stalin, from a class and political standpoint, not on the basis of abstract moralising by people who were far removed from the period concerned. There was in fact no shortage of evidence, even by those that were opposed to him, that Stalin had been an outstanding leader (she quoted Winston Churchill to this effect, as well as de Gaulle and others). In the USSR as well as outside it there were those who had an interest in attacking the record of these years; they included the 'spiritual heirs' of Menshevism, of Trotsky and of the kulaks. Indeed these were far from abstract scholarly debates. On the contrary, all kinds of groups and associations representing ideas of this kind had come into existence in the USSR: some of them had openly called for 'power-sharing' on the basis of a 'parliamentary regime', for 'free trade unions', 'autonomous publishing houses' and so forth. All of this unavoidably suggested that the 'central question in the debates now under way in the country is the question of recognising or not recognising the leading role of the party and the working class in socialist construction, and hence in restructuring'. As Gorbachev had himself told the Central Committee in February 1988, in the ideological sphere above all they must be guided by their Marxist–Leninist principles and not forgo them under any circumstances.

Andreeva's letter was in turn attacked in a lengthy editorial in *Pravda* on 5 April 1988, three weeks later and after Gorbachev had reportedly been able to secure the agreement of the Politburo to a considered rebuttal. The editorial, 'The principles of restructuring: the revolutionary nature of thinking and acting', insisted that there was 'no alternative to *perestroika*' and that even its postponement would be gravely damaging to Soviet society and to socialism internationally. Over the previous three years *perestroika* had become a reality; the Soviet people themselves had changed, and were facing facts that had earlier been obscured from them. This, admittedly, was not an easy process; some were inclined to doubt their own strength, and others had failed to understand the seriousness of the task that lay before them. There was also a form of opposition to *perestroika* that stemmed from outdated patterns of thinking and the self-interest of those who had become used to living at the expense of others. Andreeva's letter had echoed such sentiments: indeed it had gone further and was completely incompatible with the principles of restructuring. There were evidently quite a few people who, like Andreeva, had failed to appreciate the seriousness of the task that faced them in April 1985 and the uselessness of applying the command–administrative methods of the past. The time had come, *Pravda* argued, for a return to the essence of socialism, and for a break with the distorted form it had acquired during the 1930s and 1940s. Only this would 'free the best constructive forces for the struggle for socialism, for our values and our ideals'.

A critical examination of the Soviet past, as in Andreeva's letter, was a necessary part of *perestroika* in that it helped to provide a better, clearer picture of the way forward. Historical truth was sometimes bitter. It was known, for instance, that 'many thousands' of party and non-party members had been subjected to mass repression during the Stalin period; this was the truth of the matter, and there was no escaping it. Then there was the role of Stalin. Rather than quoting Churchill (or more precisely, it appeared, the British Trotskyist Isaac Deutscher) *Pravda* reminded its readers of Lenin's assessment of Stalin, and of the verdict of the party congresses of 1956 and 1961. These made clear both Stalin's undoubted contribution to the struggle to achieve and then defend socialism, but also his 'flagrant political mistakes' for which a 'great price' had been paid. It was true that the press gave far more attention to shortcomings than had been the case in the recent past, but those shortcomings were a feature of life itself and would not disappear if the newspapers simply ignored them. *Pravda* noted the heavy responsibilities that party papers had to accept in these difficult times, and charged that the Andreeva letter was in effect an attempt, 'little by little', to reverse decisions the party had already taken.[61] *Sovetskaya Rossiya*, ten days later, acknowledged that publication of the letter had been inopportune;[62] this could not disguise the fact that there were profound differences in approach at leading levels of the party, which had been reflected in both sides of the exchange.

Perestroika and the Soviet public

Public responses to *perestroika* were studied with unusual attention, in part because the success of the strategy was held to depend upon activating the 'human factor', and in part because the techniques of opinion polling advanced rapidly in the USSR during the 1980s. The first reasonably representative surveys were carried out in the 1960s, particularly through the youth newspaper *Komsomol'skaya pravda*; its findings, however, were based upon the written responses of readers, who were clearly a self-selected if fairly numerous sample of the wider population.[63] The surveys of later years were based to a greater extent upon professionally conducted polling; but they suffered from a number of serious deficiencies, among them the limited range of approved responses that was typically offered, and above all their geographically selective nature.[64] In June 1983 the CPSU Central Committee approved the establishment of a national opinion poll centre, based at the Institute of Sociology of the Academy of Sciences.[65] In the event it was not until 1988 that the All-Union Centre for the Study of Public Opinion (VTsIOM) was established in Moscow under the auspices of the trade union council and the State Committee on Labour and Social Questions. Its director was the reform-minded sociologist Tat'yana Zaslavskaya, who told *Pravda* that about 10–12 surveys would be conducted every year into social and economic issues, based upon a national network of researchers.[66] Polls of a professional and nationally representative character were also carried out, in the late 1980s, by the Institute of Sociology, the CPSU's Academy of Social Sciences, and in some cases by foreign polling organisations.[67]

The polls covered a wide range of topics, from assessments of work organisation to the future of *perestroika*, privileges and individual members of the leadership. The earliest indications, according to Professor V. Ivanov, director of the Institute of Sociology, were that there was 'overwhelming support in the country for *perestroika*'. Something like 90 per cent of those polled at 120 enterprises throughout the USSR were in favour; only 0.6 per cent were opposed to any change in the existing system. Professionals – engineers and white-collar workers – were particularly strong in their support (94 per cent, according to a survey of young workers in the town of Orsk); blue-collar workers were also in favour of *perestroika*, but less overwhelmingly so (84 per cent in the same survey, a result, Ivanov thought, of the relatively slow change in living conditions as compared with cultural and intellectual life). There was also some evidence that support for *perestroika* tended to 'fade' the further an enterprise was located from the major metropolitan areas; and while there might be overwhelming support, it was 'quite another thing to take an actual part in changes and to strive for results'. It was also the case that 'the closer to production, the lower the evaluation of the processes taking place': one manager in five interviewed in the Moscow region thought that *perestroika* was advancing successfully in his enterprise, but not a single foreman took the same view.

Ordinary workers were also more likely to take the view that *glasnost'* did more harm than good (about a quarter of the engineering workers interviewed in Kazakhstan took this view), and many thought such negative information was in any case for 'official consumption'. There was considerable apathy and indifference: people still expected *perestroika* to be introduced by decree, without their active participation, and substantial numbers of workers (a third of those interviewed in a Moscow factory, for instance) thought they should wait until *perestroika* took definite form before they committed themselves to it. The changes that were necessary in this respect depended in turn upon a reconstruction of the economic mechanism, and this was proceeding slowly. There was also strong resistance to wider pay differentials: in Kazakhstan, for instance, 40 per cent of the workers who were interviewed wanted the old wage arrangements retained. There was some reluctance to participate in enterprise self-management, which had been extended under the Law on the State Enterprise: 14 per cent of the workers interviewed in Kazakhstan, for instance, openly declared that they took part in such activities only because they were required to do so. Nominations to elective positions in the factory were still 'sent down from above', and there was still a widespread feeling of 'them and us'. Many managers complained of the inertia and indifference of their workforce, while the workers complained of the complacency and indecisiveness of management.[68]

In a further interview, *Izvestiya* spoke to Professor Zhan Toshchenko of the party's Academy of Social Sciences. Some 4,000 workers had been polled in their investigation; 90 per cent believed they could increase the quality and quantity of their work, and the great majority appeared to be motivated by altruistic rather than selfish considerations. None the less, while workers recognised the priority of social interests, they were 'possessed of a certain wariness, harbouring a secret prejudice against change'. People were not yet working to their full capacity, taking the view that 'when it happens, I will be prepared to meet the increased requirements. But not now, not right away'. One in three took the view that even if the quality of their work deteriorated they would suffer no reduction in wages; in fact the majority had the 'dangerous conviction that their wellbeing [had] little or no connection with how they worked'. As in the case of the earlier survey, there was a clear differentiation in the assessment of *perestroika* between management and workers: most managers were confident of their success, but most workers disagreed and thought that the optimism of managers hardly corresponded with their actions. Very few managers in fact took the view that they should take the opinion of the workforce into account when they made their decisions; only 7 per cent of the workers, for their part, thought that any of their suggestions for improving production methods would actually be put into practice. This, unquestionably, bore the 'seeds of future conflicts'.[69]

Later polls, for the most part, bore out these cautious and sometimes pessimistic conclusions. An Academy of Social Sciences poll of over 13,000 in 1989 did find that 71.1 per cent were 'content', and that about half of the respondents were at least 'interested' in *perestroika*. Only a quarter of those polled, however, were actually involved in the restructuring process, and fully three quarters intended to continue working in the old way. They needed restructuring, in other words, 'only if it [didn't] involve any additional effort on their part'. Two thirds of those polled expressed no interest in the state of *glasnost'*, and no more than 28.6 per cent expressed any concern about their responsibilities to the wider society. Another national poll, this time conducted by VTsIOM, found that the environment was the most urgent priority for political action in the view of 87 per cent of respondents: it was followed by the food supply (82 per cent), housing (79 per cent), consumer goods (74 per cent), the abuse of power and unfair distribution of goods and services (73 per cent), low pay and high prices (76 per cent), and the educational and health services (both 67 per cent). It was the shortage of consumer goods that affected respondents and their families most directly; while it was housing that they regarded as the most serious problem for the country as a whole.[70]

The opinion of more educated sections of the community emerged more clearly from a questionnaire published in the weekly paper *Literaturnaya gazeta* in early 1989, to which there were no fewer than 200,000 responses. In terms of living standards only 11 per cent thought they were well off; a third described their lifestyle as 'modest'; 27 per cent said they had a hard time making ends meet; and nearly a third complained they were heavily in debt and obliged to seek help from friends and relatives. Inadequate food supplies and consumer goods were a major concern in terms of the quality of life, and nearly a third of the respondents thought that medical services were on the decline. Heavy drinking, profiteering, corruption and theft were also cited as major social problems. Nearly a half thought that members of cooperatives stood to gain most from *perestroika*, and over a third believed that the USSR was now a 'thief's paradise'. The most important single impediment to the reform process, in the view of respondents, was the party-state bureaucracy, and concern was expressed about the continuation of unjustified privileges and benefits. About half took the view that the USSR's difficulties were attributable to the development strategy it had adopted; a third attributed them to Stalinism, although half of those polled thought too much space had been given in the media to Stalinist malpractices. The great majority, however, were in favour of the freedom of speech and opinion that had been ushered in by *glasnost'*, with 84 per cent taking the view that the press and television had improved as a result. And Gorbachev, personally, was Man of the Year (Woman of the Year was Margaret Thatcher).[71]

Together with opinion surveys, letters to the press and to the party have traditionally served as a means of self-expression for ordinary citizens in the Soviet system.[72] Letters are also sent to the general secretary in person, and Gorbachev quoted from them to justify the 'democratisation' of party and state life that was approved at the January 1987 Central Committee plenum and the economic reform programme that was approved the following June. All the delegates to the 19th Party Conference, in June 1988, were provided with a special digest of the letters that had been reaching party headquarters from members and ordinary citizens throughout the country.[73] Gorbachev was asked, during a visit to Leningrad in October 1987, if letters from ordinary people actually reached him. Yes, they did, he replied; he tried to read as many of them as possible, and took many home with him for further study.[74] Gorbachev referred to the 'wonderful' letters that were appearing in the Soviet press in his book *Perestroika*. Letters and direct communications of other kinds from citizens, he noted, were 'the major "feedback" linking the Soviet leadership with the masses', and they were discussed at regular intervals within the Politburo.[75] Letters reached Gorbachev from foreign as well as Soviet citizens: *Pravda*, for instance, carried a whole page of them in its issue of 5 December 1987, and Gorbachev was able to make effective use of this kind of communication during his visit to Washington for the summit later in the month.[76]

Letters are sent to the political parties, to the Supreme Soviet, to the radio and television and other bodies, and in the largest numbers of all to the newspapers. A particularly large number are sent to *Pravda*, the CPSU's own daily paper: in 1989 there were 473,000 of them, or about 2,000 every working day.[77] The letters department in *Pravda*, not surprisingly, is the paper's largest, with a staff of about a hundred (direct comparisons are hardly meaningful but the London *Times*, for instance, received no more than 70,000 letters a year during the same period[78]). *Pravda* played a particularly prominent role in the discussion that took place about the strategy of *perestroika*; more space was given over to letters than ever before, they often appeared on the front page, and new rubrics appeared such as 'Your position on *perestroika*' and 'Life as it really is'. *Pravda*'s editorial policy remained relatively orthodox; its editor, most unusually, was criticised by name at the 19th Party Conference (he was replaced in 1989) and the paper latterly began to lose circulation to some of its more outspoken rivals (in 1990 it was overtaken by the government paper *Izvestiya*). At the same time it remained the vehicle within which the party conducted most of its open self-examination, and its treatment of privilege just before the 27th Party Congress was sufficiently provocative to earn a rebuke from Ligachev.[79] What did *Pravda*'s letters, and those to other sections of the press, suggest about the public mood?

There were, of course, the statutory plaudits for the party's bold and far-seeing strategy. A teacher from northern Kazakhstan, for instance, wanted *Pravda* to know that *perestroika* had reached the state farm on which he worked; more houses were being built, there were fewer drunks about, and the hairdresser was even paying them a regular visit.[80] Workers from the industrial town of Cherepovets reported that labour turnover had been reduced.[81] An employee from an engineering factory in Simferopol wrote in to say that the suggestions he had made in a letter concerning the Law on the State Enterprise, adopted in June 1987, had been incorporated into the final draft. 'Even now', he wrote, 'I still find it difficult to contain my feelings'.[82] There were compliments for the Soviet health service and its personnel, and praise for the housing officials that had helped a reader obtain a new flat.[83] And there has certainly been no lack of good will. Tell Gorbachev, wrote I. Goncharov from the Tatar republic, that 'all the working class' as well as 'honest' members of the scientific and technical intelligentsia were in favour of the course he was pursuing.[84] 'We are all very satisfied with M. S. Gorbachev and our government', wrote another reader as the General Secretary set off for the Washington summit at the end of 1987.[85]

The new openness, however, also allowed a much wider range of shortcomings to be discussed, some of them of fairly long standing but others more directly connected with *perestroika*. The shortage of sugar was an example of the second of these, stemming as it did from the anti-alcoholism campaign that had been launched in 1985. As A. Shulyachenko reported from the Kiev region, in order to discourage moonshiners it had been decided that sugar would be sold locally only between 4 and 5 p.m. The queues were 'kilometres long'.[86] Another reader, also from the Ukraine, reported that in his local area every shop had been given a limited amount of sugar to sell; people were queuing overnight, and if all the family were working they got none at all.[87] The shortage of drink on sale through the usual channels, until the policy was relaxed somewhat in 1988, also caused a great increase in the price of *samogon* or home brew. As a letter from a group of collective farmers in the Voronezh region reported, *samogon* had actually become more expensive than the real thing: 70 rubles (about £70 or $110 at this time) was being demanded for a three-litre bottle. They could provide a list of the moonshiners if requested, but asked not to be named as '*perestroika* hasn't reached us yet'.[88]

The shift of emphasis from state to private and cooperative trade also had unfortunate consequences, if readers' letters were any guide. The price of fruit and vegetables in the collective farm markets, for instance, increased considerably.[89] Tea became more difficult to obtain, in part because of restrictions on the sale of alcohol.[90] The price of summer holidays had 'shot up', wrote V. Ivanova from the Moscow region. In Sochi, Yalta and elsewhere massive Intourist hotels were being constructed for the benefit of foreigners. When would they start to take account of the needs of their own citizens in such matters?[91] Older problems also persisted, among them the range and quality of consumer goods. Gorbachev had personally criticised the reliability of

Soviet televisions; so too did a distraught pensioner, V. Grybina from Vladivostok. There had been no *perestroika* at all in consumer goods, she wrote. The first television she had bought, at a cost of 300 rubles, quickly broke down; so did the second, approved by the state quality control commission, on which she had lavished the 200 rubles she had managed to save from her pension. 'Now I sit and cry', wrote Mrs Grybina; 'where am I to get the money to buy a third television?'[92] Other correspondents complained of shortages of newspapers at retail kiosks, of overcrowding and delays on public transport, of the lack of children's clothes (from a mother of 11), and of food queues as long as they had been during the war.[93]

There were, of course, some improvements to report, but they were often cosmetic. A worker from Kuibyshev, for instance, wrote to *Pravda* that he had popped into his workshop canteen after he had returned from holidays. He hardly knew it – it had been reconstructed just like a restaurant! The comfortable oval tables beside the buffet, the panels on the walls, the cleanliness – nothing like it had ever been seen before. Then he had a look at the menu – it was no different. It emerged that 'there were changes on the outside, but inside all remained the same'.[94] Other writers reported that the new electoral arrangements for the selection of leading personnel had often been used to eliminate trouble-makers and to replace them with clients of the director.[95] Virtually all *Pravda*'s correspondents were 'for' *perestroika* in principle; the trouble was that it had led to little but words while local conditions had hardly been affected. As a blacksmith from Kuibyshev told the paper, *perestroika* reminded him of a storm in a forest: 'there is a lot of noise up at the top, but down below hardly a puff of wind'.[96] Local officials, it emerged, had responded to the challenge of *perestroika* in all kinds of ways. Some ignored it, and others passed resolutions about it; still others, more inventive, set up commissions on *perestroika* and organised campaigns about it with targets that were noisily overful-filled.[97] One of *Pravda*'s correspondents, a practising Catholic from Lithuania, was so impressed by the resistance Gorbachev was con-fronting that she prayed for him at Mass every Sunday, since in his own way he was helping to save the world from its sins.[98]

In some ways more disturbing than the stories of material difficulty, harrowing though these could be, were the letters that were con-cerned essentially with a loss of faith. A mother in Minsk, for instance, wrote to complain about the lack of positive values on which she could rear her three children. She herself had grown up with socialism as her ideal and purpose in life. But now, with *glasnost'* and unrestrained criticism of all aspects of the society, the socialist ideal was rather discredited. Her own faith was wavering, while her children were swamped by a flood of negative information that denigrated every-thing. How could young people grow up in conditions of 'total criti-cism', in a society where 'nothing was sacred'?[99] Or there was Sergei Slipkov of the Krasnoyarsk territory, who wrote in to the youth paper *Komsomol'skaya pravda*. 'I'm 17', he began. 'I've read *Children of the Arbat* and newspaper and magazine articles about the repressions, about the persecution of Zoshchenko and Akhmatova, about Lysenko's hold over science, and life seems a nightmare to me. There's nothing ahead. I used to believe we'd overcome all hardships, for our history has been so heroic. I no longer do. How do I regain my faith?' (the paper had no obvious answer).[100] Others were confused by the changes in termin-ology. What was 'real socialism', for a start, wrote I. Konyakhin of Gorky; did this mean there could be 'unreal socialism', or a socialism that was neither real nor unreal?[101] And what was 'pluralism', asked another reader: when had this ceased to be a spurious doctrine which was characteristic of bourgeois rather than socialist society?[102]

Still others, even more disturbed by the changes they saw around them, wrote in to complain. Why was the whole of the Soviet past being denigrated, wrote Lev Zhdanov, a party member from Voro-shilovgrad? Why were the works of counter-revolutionary generals like Denikin being prepared for a wide readership, while the writings of Molotov, Malenkov and others were unavailable? And why was there such a rapid increase in all kinds of anti-social phenomena, including embezzlement and rape?[103] 'In the past the press wrote that everything was alright in this country and that everything abroad was wrong. Now it's the other way round: everything is wrong here, and perfectly OK there. Is that reality?', asked Arnold Korolenko from Khar'kov.[104] There was clearly some scepticism, in any event, about the ability of government to make the changes that were so evidently necessary. Only 14.2 per cent, in a national poll in late 1989, thought the institutions of government had the people's interests at heart; 31.1 per cent thought the leadership was an 'elite, concerned only with its own interests', and a further 44.7 per cent thought that the deputies they elected 'quickly forgot the concerns of ordinary people'.[105] Some 55.5 per cent of respondents thought the economic situation was 'critical', but only 17.2 per cent thought the government had a well-considered programme to deal with the situation and only 12.1 per cent thought there would be a significant improvement in living standards in the near future. More than 20 per cent, in separate polls, thought that Soviet economic difficulties were attributable not to 'mistakes' but to the nature of socialism itself; and only 6 per cent thought that Marxism–Leninism could provide any of the answers to the country's problems.[106]

The public mood darkened still further in the early 1990s, reflecting deteriorating conditions in the country at large. When, for instance, did people believe the Soviet Union would come out of its crisis? No earlier than the year 2000, in the view of 48 per cent of those who responded to a national poll in late 1990, and 'never', in the view of a further 12 per cent. Of all the people that would make a difference to the Soviet Union by the same date, Jesus Christ came first with 58 per cent; Sakharov came second with 48 per cent, Lenin was third with 36 per cent and Gorbachev came a poor fourth with 26 per cent.[107] What did people think the Soviet Union lacked most in 1990? The largest number, 53 per cent, thought it was 'real power' and 36 per cent – the second largest group – thought it was 'trust in the leadership'. If they had known in 1985 what *perestroika* would have led to, only 23 per cent would have supported it and twice as many would have opposed it.[108] What did Soviet rule provide for its citizens, the National Public Opinion Centre asked in 1991? A quarter of those who were polled said 'peace', but for 65 per cent – the largest number – it meant 'shortages, queues and poverty', and for 28 per cent it meant 'powerlessness, constant insults and humiliation'.[109] Asked 'what is *perestroika*', 29 per cent found it hard to say; but of those that did have an answer, the largest group (18 per cent) thought it was an 'attempt by the ruling group to hold on to their power by a certain degree of democratisation', and 14 per cent found it an 'out of date and exhausted slogan'.[110]

It did not necessarily follow, however, that there was overwhelming support for capitalism or the institutions of liberal democracy. Asked what they would do if the October revolution took place a second time, 43 per cent told pollsters they would actively or passively support the Bolsheviks, and only 6 per cent would oppose them. The largest group (39 per cent) thought the October revolution 'reflected the wishes of the peoples of the Russian empire', and a majority were prepared to accept the necessity of the use of force at this time and the formation of the Cheka or security police with their wide-ranging powers.[111] Asked in a national poll in 1991 for their views about socialism, the largest group (38 per cent) thought it had been shown to be deficient in principle; but when asked what kind of a society should be constructed in the Russian Federation, 29 per cent said a socialist one, 56 per cent thought it should be a Swedish-style combination of the best features of capitalism and socialism, and only 3 per cent opted for undisguised capitalism.[112] In another national poll in late 1990, 58.6 per cent thought the basic principles of socialism were correct but that they had not been properly implemented; 56.3 per cent connected their hopes for the future of the country with socialism, and only 7 per cent with capitalism.[113]

Nor, according to a wide range of polls, was there much tendency to blame Lenin, founder of the Soviet system, for the multiplicity of ills to which that system had given rise. In a national poll in November 1990, 59 per cent were wholly favourable in their evaluation of Lenin, and 76.1 per cent took a positive view of his actions. More than half of those polled, indeed, believed they had come to evaluate Lenin more positively as a result of *perestroika*, notwithstanding the publication of a letter of Lenin's of 1922 in which he had called for the shooting of as many reactionary priests as possible and new evidence that he might have instigated the murder of the Tsar and his family.[114] In another poll in late 1991, Peter the Great was chosen by 13 per cent as the greatest figure of all times and nations; Jesus Christ came second with 11 per cent; but Lenin and Albert Einstein both came third, with 8 per cent support, and ahead of Sakharov, Alexander Nevsky, the pre-revolutionary prime minister Stolypin and Napoleon Bonaparte.[115] It was still necessary, in late 1990, for Gorbachev to issue a presidential decree designed to protect statues of Lenin from the attacks that were being made upon them, and there were repeated calls for his reburial outside the Lenin Mausoleum in line (it was thought) with his family's own wishes.[116]

Letters to the Soviet press continued to provide less sociologically representative but more first-hand responses to what was acknowledged to be an all-embracing crisis. There was still some praise as well as criticism for the Soviet leader. A veteran from Archangel, for instance, wrote in to *Pravda* to let him know of his support for the 'wise foreign policy' that was being pursued by the Soviet government 'and especially President M. S. Gorbachev'.[117] A Moscow translator, Sergei Svetushkin, pointed out that daily life had become more lively and that international tensions had been reduced under his skilful administration.[118] These, however, were minority opinions. *Perestroika*, in the view of a correspondent from L'vov, was the 'worst they had had to live through since the war (for that matter in peacetime and because of the actions of our own government)'. Not a single foreign enemy had brought the USSR so much sorrow and suffering as *perestroika*, wrote a further correspondent. What had *perestroika* produced for ordinary people? 'Mass unemployment and a rationing system.' For another of *Pravda*'s letter-writers, *perestroika* had led to 'empty shelves in the shops, price rises, the collapse of the union, banditism, violence, hooliganism, interethnic conflict, the disintegration of the CPSU and the collapse of the socialist community'. As another letter remarked, 'Only in hell could you have a life like this'.[119] When, asked a lecturer from Alma Ata, would they at last have achieved *perestroika* and be able to live a normal, human life? When would they be able to be materialists and not idealists who were supposed to be uninterested in soap, tea, sugar, tights and other everyday commodities?[120]

The party and *perestroika*

The public mood was important, and Gorbachev relied upon it more directly than most earlier Soviet leaders. The central question, however, was that of political agency, and this in turn was a question of the role the CPSU was to perform in implementing the reform strategy. The party, under the Constitution, had historically been the 'leading and guiding force' of Soviet society and the 'nucleus' of its political system. Gorbachev, initially, showed no willingness to remove this provision, which privileged a relatively small proportion of the population; the party, in his view, was the initiator of *perestroika* and the only force that could carry it to a successful conclusion, or more generally unite a complex and far from homogeneous society. *Perestroika*, he told the 19th Party Conference in 1988, could 'not be accomplished without the guiding activity of the party, without giving effect to its political course. Without this *perestroika* [would] be doomed politically, ideologically and organisationally'.[121] Speaking to journalists after he had cast his vote at the March 1989 elections, Gorbachev was sharply dismissive of the idea of a multiparty system in the USSR and pointed out that the number of parties that were permitted was hardly, by itself, a measure of democracy. And notwithstanding the abandonment of the party's constitutionally guaranteed position of the following year, he remained convinced that a multiparty system was 'not a panacea' and that the CPSU must properly remain the 'political leader' of the wider society.[122]

The party, of course, would have to restructure its own activities, and it began to do so from the January 1987 Central Committee plenum onwards. A secret competitive ballot was introduced for party office, together with the principle that such positions should be held for a limited period (see above, pp. 38–41). Membership criteria were revised, at least informally, with the aim of encouraging recruitment on the basis of political qualities rather than social background. More information about the party's own operations was made available than ever before, including detailed accounts of its income and expenditure, and opportunities for rank and file participation in its activities were widened, particularly through the establishment of advisory commissions at national and local levels. The number of commissions and the numbers engaged in them were expanded at a Central Committee meeting in October 1990.[123] The 28th Congress, earlier in the year, adopted a new set of rules which increased the rights of ordinary members still further. 'Platforms', if not organized factions, were approved, minority rights were strengthened, and 'horizontal' links between members and branches at the same level were specifically encouraged (they had previously been regarded as incompatible with democratic centralism). All of this was designed to provide the basis, as Gorbachev saw it, for an 'updated CPSU', a tolerant and self-managing party that would combine a parliamentary with its traditional vanguard role.[124]

The outcome of such exhortations, by the early 1990s, was most unclear. There was little doubt, however, that the CPSU was restructuring itself much more slowly than other public organisations. Leon Onikov, a party official, presented some evidence of this 'democratisation gap' in a series of articles in *Pravda*. More than a thousand local secretaries, he wrote in 1989, had been chosen on a competitive basis in the last round of party elections. This, however, was only 8.6 per cent of the total, and at higher levels the figures were even less impressive – just seven regional secretaries, for instance, had been elected on a competitive basis, which was just 1 per cent of the total. No fewer than 74 per cent of the members of the new Congress of People's Deputies, by contrast, had been elected from a choice of candidate – 'a difference hardly in favour of the party'.[125] An open letter to Gorbachev in early 1989 signed by the playwright Alexander Gel'man and five others warned that party officials were attempting to 'sabotage' political reform and that party headquarters were dominated by a 'dictatorship of mediocrities'.[126] Onikov pointed out that the existing party rules, adopted in a modified version in 1986, had largely been formulated in the Brezhnev and Chernenko years. The section on democratic centralism, for instance, had been modified slightly to include a reference to the need for 'collectivism' in the work of all party bodies; but the basic definition was still the one that had been authorised by Stalin more than fifty years earlier, in 1934. It was 'as if the party clock had stopped' in that year.[127]

Not simply was the 'vanguard lagging', as Onikov put it. Still more important, the party began to lose members, particularly among the working class, and began to experience what party officials themselves described as a 'crisis of confidence'. The rate of increase in party membership, first of all, slowed down, and then in 1989 it recorded its first decline for more than thirty years. In 1990 and 1991 the decline was precipitous: over 4 million members left the party in a period of eighteen months, about a quarter of the total, and the great majority of them 'of their own volition'.[128] More than 300 Communist deputies to the Russian and Soviet parliaments left the party, and even members of the party's own Central Committee.[129] The Komsomol, the party's youth wing, fell more sharply still, losing about a quarter of its members in 1990 alone (in 1991, after the coup, it disappeared entirely).[130] There were still recruits (over 108,000 in 1990), but fewer of them were female, working-class or young, and the party's average age increased slightly from 44.6 to 46 years.[131] The circulation of the party press fell dramatically (most party publications lost between two-thirds and three-quarters of their subscribers), and over a million members fell behind with their dues (a phenomenon that had earlier been almost unknown).[132] The party organisation as a whole began to run at a loss, and a regime of 'severe economy' had to be instituted; Gorbachev, speaking in July 1991, himself called it the most serious crisis in the party's history.[133]

Why had members been leaving, or failing to join? A party leader in the Penza region explained that young people were reluctant to join an organisation many of whose members had brought it into disrepute by their actions in earlier years.[134] The party's failure to democratise was another disincentive. It still remained a 'rigid command–administrative structure with a central "headquarters" and a "drive mechanism"', wrote one disaffected Moscow member. Activists were leaving to join 'livelier, more flexible' grass-roots organisations.[135] Perhaps the central reason, however, was the party's failure to establish its moral authority. The party, one member pointed out, had approved the bloody crimes of Stalin, then the 'voluntaristic adventures' of Khrushchev, and then the military and literary '"talents"' of Leonid Brezhnev. How could its support of *perestroika* be taken seriously? He had been promised everything in his lifetime, even communism, wrote T. Gisikhin from the Leningrad region. So far as current policies were concerned he would be honest: 'I don't believe

you, Mikhail Sergeevich!' In his twenty-five years of party membership, wrote another of *Pravda*'s correspondents, he had believed he
was helping to construct communism. Now it seemed the party had
led the nation to the verge of catastrophe.[136] The party's activity was
based upon a 'false and completely discredited doctrine that called for
the reconstruction of society', declared a Moscow researcher,
explaining why he had left. The party was guilty of 'unprecedented
crimes' for which it had yet to show repentance; and it was still
attempting to decide for future generations what kind of society they
would live in, although it had 'no idea what communism – or socialism, for that matter – really is'.[137]

The party's 'crisis of confidence' reflected a deeper uncertainty
about its function under conditions of *perestroika*, and indeed about the
direction in which the society as a whole was meant to be moving.
Gone, for a start, were the days of 'monolithic unity'. Some party
members were leading strikes, and others were opposing them. Party
members in the Baltic republics were joining the popular fronts, and
even supplying their leaderships, while other members were joining
their Russian-speaking counterparts. Party members were competing
against other members at the polls, and on the basis of different
electoral programmes; the party as a whole suffered a shattering blow
in the defeats that were suffered by leading officials, even if its representation among the successful candidates was higher than it had been
before. There were persistent rumours that the leadership was divided
or at least far from unanimous, and the 'braking mechanism' that
members were urged to fight turned out to be another section of the
party itself. Members were certainly divided and disillusioned, if
survey evidence in the early 1990s was any guide. Only 55 per cent,
according to an inquiry conducted by the party's own Academy of
Social Sciences, supported the idea of the 'socialist choice', and only 37
per cent believed in the possibility of implementing communist principles.[138] As for the party itself, as many as 80 per cent of the members
who were surveyed in the summer of 1990 did not believe it was
capable of restructuring itself and leading the country out of its crisis.
There was general agreement, among the membership, that the party
should be 'radically renewed' – but how? And what influence, in any
case, did ordinary members have on matters of this kind?[139]

The most fundamental problem, as delegates to party congresses in
1990 pointed out, was precisely the lack of a coherent and convincing
vision of the manner in which Soviet society was to develop under the
party's leadership. Gorbachev had called, at the 27th Party Congress,

for the party to lose its 'infallibility complex';[140] but for many members, particularly officials responsible for carrying out party policy, it must have appeared that the party had no more positive idea of the public role it was supposed to perform. The Armenian leader Suren Aruty-unyan raised some of these issues at a party meeting in July 1989. What, he asked, was party work supposed to mean in contemporary circumstances; did 'all power to the soviets', for instance, mean that they were not to be guided in their work by party committees? And what about the *nomenklatura*, asked the Kirgiz first secretary Masaliev: how, without it, could the party's leading role be sustained? The Sverdlovsk first secretary queried the weakening of party influence in economic matters, and added that the party's role in respect of ideology was still more unsatisfactory. Working people, for instance, had been almost entirely eliminated from the media, and their place had been taken by prostitutes, narcomaniacs and hooligans. Where was the party's 'firm line' on such matters? More generally, in the view of the party secretaries from Rostov and Chimkent, the party needed to set out a clear model of the kind of society it wished to construct if it was to rally its membership behind it.[141]

Lacking clear agreement on fundamentals, and hardly successful in terms of its performance, the party began to lose the 'monolithic unity' on which it had earlier insisted. Several organised groupings made their appearance in the months before the 28th Party Congress: a liberal 'Democratic Platform' and a more orthodox 'Marxist Platform' among others.[142] By the early 1990s, according to party officials, there were 'at least a dozen' currents of this kind within the party's ranks. They ranged from a 'social democratic' wing associated with the political commentator Fedor Burlatsky, at one extreme, to a hard-line 'Unity' grouping at the other, headed by Nina Andreeva, author of the celebrated letter to *Sovetskaya Rossiya*. Andreeva's group planned a '20th Congress of the VKP (b)', in other words a return to the Communist Party as it had existed in late Stalinist times, in order to counter what they described as the 'bourgeois-reformist political course' of the party as a whole.[143] There were open revolts against local party leaderships, and some regional party organisations, in a rebellion of a different kind, declared themselves of full republican status.[144] A few republican party organisations, in turn, fragmented or seceded from the CPSU altogether: the Lithuanian party was the first to leave, in December 1989, followed by the Georgian party a year later and by the Moldavian party early in 1991.[145] More generally, throughout the USSR increasing numbers of party members elected to the soviets refused to accept any direction of their activities.[146]

The party's uncertainty about its purposes was reflected in a society that appeared increasingly to doubt its right to rule. The CPSU still came first when Soviet voters were asked to express their hypothetical preferences, although it fell short of an overall majority; at the end of 1990, for instance, it could command the support of 34 per cent of the Soviet public, well ahead of the Democratic Party of Russia on 15 per cent.[147] The party's public standing, however, declined sharply. If 37 per cent were prepared to trust the CPSU in February 1989, only 27 per cent were prepared to do so by the following December; support for the Central Committee more specifically fell from 71 per cent in November 1988 to 21 per cent by the time of the Party Congress.[148] By July 1990 only 14 per cent 'completely trusted' the CPSU, as compared with 38 per cent who had 'absolutely no confidence' in it.[149] Fewer people than before wrote to the Central Committee with their problems, fewer people visited party offices, and there were fewer letters to *Pravda* and party committees at all levels.[150] Leading party officials themselves admitted that the party's authority was declining, and that a process of 'deideologisation' was taking place in the wider society. Important as the economic difficulties were, a party secretary told the Central Committee, the most serious of all shortages was the 'lack of popular trust' in the CPSU itself; and it was this mistrust, strengthened by the apparent complicity of its leadership in the coup, that later allowed Boris Yel'tsin first to suspend and then to ban the party altogether (by September 1991, following the coup, only 2.3 per cent were still prepared to give the party their 'full support').[151]

Gorbachev, *perestroika* and socialism

Judged at the end of his first six years of office, the Gorbachev record could hardly be accounted an unqualified success. The General Secretary's own standing, at least initially, was not in doubt. In a national poll at the end of 1989, 43 per cent of those asked found him the country's 'most outstanding political figure'; Yel'tsin came a distant second, with 17 per cent, and Ryzkhov a still more distant third, with 13 per cent.[152] There was overwhelming support, in another national poll in 1989, for Gorbachev's election as the first Chairman of the USSR Supreme Soviet: from 81 to 93 per cent, in Moscow, Leningrad and four republican capitals, approved entirely or almost entirely, with no more than 17 per cent (in the Georgian capital, Tbilisi) in disagreement.[153] A survey based on letters to the popular weekly, *Argumenty i fakty*, found that Andrei Sakharov was by a very large margin the deputy who commanded the greatest public respect; he was followed by the economist Gavriil Popov, Boris Yel'tsin, Yuri Afanas'ev and the weightlifter turned critic of the KGB, Yuri Vlasov.[154] A subsequent and much more representative poll in the same paper found that Gorbachev in fact had the support of 66 per cent of respondents, and that Ryzkhov's standing was also a high one; support for both leaders was still higher among party members than it was among the population at large.[155]

This, however, was the highest point that the Soviet leader was ever to attain. If 52 per cent 'entirely approved' of Gorbachev's activities in December 1989, only 21 per cent did so a year later.[156] In 1988, 55 per cent voted for Gorbachev as Man of the Year; in 1989, 46 per cent did so; but by 1990 he was down to 19 per cent.[157] By the end of 1990 his popularity level, across a variety of Russian towns, varied from 5 to 21 per cent; Boris Yel'tsin's, in the same locations, ranged from 33 up to 65 per cent. By late 1991, in some polls, Gorbachev's approval rating had fallen as low as 3 per cent.[158] Yel'tsin's standing, in fact, improved in inverse proportion to the reputation of the President and General Secretary. In a national poll in January 1991 44 per cent thought Yel'tsin's views were close to their own, as compared with 22 per cent who identified with Gorbachev. Yel'tsin was seen as 'open and straightforward' (34 per cent), 'ambitious' (26 per cent) but also 'resolute' (24 per cent). Gorbachev, by contrast, was seen as 'hypocritical' (28 per cent), 'weak and lacking in self-confidence' (20 per cent) and 'indifferent to human suffering' (19 per cent), although also 'flexible and capable of adapting to change' (18 per cent).[159] There were few, notwithstanding this disenchantment, who thought he would readily surrender his positions, nor could he easily be dismissed as President (two-thirds of a relatively conservative Congress of People's Deputies would have to vote against him) or as General Secretary (following a change in the rules in 1990, only a full congress could elect or dismiss the party leader).

It was much more widely accepted, in the early 1990s, that Gorbachev's programme of *perestroika* had failed to achieve its original intentions (Ryzhkov, indeed, himself volunteered this admission to the Congress of People's Deputies in December 1990[160]). The economic reforms they had promoted had attempted to combine the advantages of central planning with the disciplines of the market, but in many ways secured the worst of both worlds: control over inflationary and other processes slipped out of the hands of government, while market forces had little opportunity to exercise their supposedly beneficial influence in circumstances of shortage and monopoly. The result was 'neither plan nor market'. There were signs of a similar incoherence in other spheres of policy. *Glasnost'*, for instance, perhaps the most significant of the changes that had been introduced into Soviet domestic affairs, remained a highly qualified achievement, as Gorbachev made clear when he attempted to remove two newspaper editors in late 1989 for exercising their powers in a manner he found unacceptable. One of the editors, *Argumenty i fakty*'s Vladislav Starkov, had published the survey of the popularity of deputies in which Sakharov had originally been placed first. The paper had also published a letter from fifty building workers complaining of the construction of a luxurious residence for party officials in central Moscow at a time when local residents were living in squalor. Surely ordinary workers, asked Starkov, were the social group for whom the party leadership claimed normally to speak?[161]

Political life was riddled with similar ambiguities and limitations, exposed perhaps most clearly in the tension that developed after March 1989 between popular sovereignty (as expressed through the electoral mechanism) and the party's continued claim to exercise overall guidance. Why, for instance, should the party and other public bodies have the right to a guaranteed allocation of seats in the country's parliament? (The union treaty eventually dropped any representation of this kind.) Why should the party claim the right to control nominations to key positions – the vital power of *nomenklatura*? (This right, again, was challenged when ministerial candidates began to be rejected and many more posts became genuinely elective.) What was the party's mandate to rule, when so many of its leading officials had been defeated at the ballot box? And why should the party exercise a constitutionally guaranteed 'leading role' when the overwhelming majority of voters and citizens were outside its ranks? Gorbachev, eventually, was persuaded that there was little point in retaining a guaranteed position of this kind when the society as a whole had moved beyond it; but the CPSU was still to remain the dominant force in Soviet political life, accepting the cooperation of other groupings only insofar as they in turn were willing to accept the Constitution and the 'socialist choice' upon which it was supposed to be based (who had made this choice, and when, remained obscure).

The Soviet public, in fact, showed no clear preference for multiparty politics. No more than 27.1 per cent of those who were asked, in a national poll in the summer of 1989, thought a system of this kind 'essential for the natural development of democracy'; but nearly as many (25.2 per cent) thought the CPSU already represented a variety of political positions, 23.1 per cent had no opinion, and 18.8 per cent thought such a development would only increase bureaucracy and hot air.[162] Such evidence as was available of Soviet public values, in fact, suggested that democratic procedures in general did not command overwhelming support. As many as 70 per cent, in a 1991 poll, thought 'Russia's salvation [would] be a person able to lead people and bring order to the country'; only 4 per cent, in a different poll, had any confidence in the ability of the new parties and movements to take the country out of its crisis, compared with 23 per cent who had confidence in the Russian president and 20 per cent in entrepreneurs. These results were broadly consistent with the views of those who had argued that Soviet political culture, formed over centuries of autocratic rule, provided a relatively weak base for the development of pluralistic politics.[163] It was nonetheless difficult to find a coherent position which could justify democratisation and 'all power to the soviets' but at the same time insist (as Gorbachev had done until 1990) on the dominance of a single party that included no more than a tenth of the adult population.

Gorbachev's position on party reform was scarcely more clear-cut. He called, for instance, for a more open and decentralised CPSU with more vigorous internal debate and shared responsibility; at the same time he accumulated a succession of leading posts, including the state presidency as well as the party general secretaryship and the chairmanship of the bureau of the party that was established in December 1989 to cater for the needs of members in the Russian Republic.[164] Democratic centralism was not abandoned in the revised Party Rules that were adopted in 1990, and he exercised every influence that was available to him to persuade party members in Lithuania and elsewhere not to carry out their decision – approved by an overwhelming majority – to seek a greater degree of independence. At the same time it remained unclear, some generalities apart, precisely how the party was to lead the whole society under conditions of *perestroika*: and if Gorbachev himself offered little practical guidance on such matters, for ordinary members the question was even more obscure. It should 'guide' and 'consolidate' – but what if the wider society rejected its advice? And what – a much more immediate prospect – if the party itself was of no clear mind what advice to offer?

Gorbachev's reforming programme, as we have seen, had been premised upon the assumption that the defects of the Soviet system were in no sense inherent in socialism but were rather the result of 'subjective' failings in leadership and policy formation (pp. 22–3). Six years or more into the process of *perestroika* it was perhaps this assumption that had come under the greatest challenge of all. Khrushchev, in the 1950s, had ascribed the repression of the Stalin years to the 'cult of personality': the vanity, paranoia and other character faults of the leader of leaders himself. The Italian communist, Palmiro Togliatti, had at the time exposed that assumption to some searching criticism in a celebrated interview in the magazine *Nuovi argomenti*. Stalin's errors, Togliatti suggested, were not simply personal ones, but went 'deeper into the very roots of Soviet life'. To explain Stalinism in terms of character faults was, in fact, to remain within the terms of the 'personality cult' itself; and the real question was evaded, which was why Soviet society had degenerated in the way that it had. The increasing dominance in party and state life of a bureaucratic apparatus appeared to be part of an adequate explanation; so were the historical circumstances – civil war, and then industrialisation – in which Stalin had come to power.[165] Satisfactory or not, this was at least a diagnosis that located Stalinism within the society of which it was a part, and it took the debate beyond the issue of the personality and thinking of individual leaders to which Khrushchev – and following him, Gorbachev – had largely wished to confine it.

One of the most notable developments in the Soviet debate in the late 1980s and early 1990s, in fact, was precisely the hesitant beginnings of a search for the answers to Soviet problems that went beyond personal shortcomings and if necessary beyond the framework of Soviet socialism altogether. One of these controversies concerned the nature of the USSR itself: was it, in fact, to be considered a socialist society at all? Some of these articles took as their point of departure Gorbachev's slogan of 'More socialism! More democracy!' Socialism, it was noted, had officially been established in the USSR in the late 1930s. If this was the case, how could more of it be needed in the late 1980s? And if what had been established was not socialism, how should it be classified?[166] A related issue was the necessity of the October revolution and, intimately connected with it, the validity of the heritage of Leninism. Had the October revolution, as some were prepared to argue, prevented a normal pattern of peaceful and democratic development after Tsardom had been overthrown? How much blame should be attached to Lenin for the repressive, over-centralised system that had succeeded him? And how much was Marxism itself to blame for the economic inefficiency and political authoritarianism that had characterised at least a substantial part of Soviet history?[167]

For Gorbachev, writing in November 1989, liberal democracy, whatever its merits, was not on offer in October 1917; a far more likely alternative would have been a period of military dictatorship. The Marxist tradition, equally, although it had underestimated capitalism's capacity to adapt, still provided a uniquely valuable insight into societies and their development.[168] For a growing number of academics and publicists, by the early 1990s, these were not assumptions that could be allowed to remain untested. A celebrated series of articles by Alexander Tsipko, for instance, traced the roots of Stalinism back to pre-revolutionary society, and more particularly to Marxism itself. It was from Marx, for instance, that Stalin had taken the principle of collectivising small-scale peasant agriculture; and his hostility to the market was not very different from that of other Marxists, nor indeed from the thinking of Marx, Engels and Lenin themselves. The deformation of socialism, for Tsipko, had doctrinal as well as other origins; it was pointless, for instance, to pretend that there could be firm guarantees of democracy if all were employed by the state, or of liberty if it was believed that the revolution was its 'own justification and its own law'.[169] Another scholar, the sociologist Igor Klyamkin, argued similarly in early 1989 that Stalinism was not the aberration of a single man but the logical result of Lenin's single-party system, which prized unity more than democracy and had remained largely intact ever since.[170]

These, clearly, were more than academic debates: at least implicitly they raised the question of the nature of Soviet society and the claim of the Communist Party to exercise political authority within it. Lenin, in his later writings, had argued that the competition between capitalism and socialism would be won, in the last resort, by the system that provided the higher level of labour productivity.[171] It was difficult, in the early 1990s, to argue that Soviet socialism had provided higher living standards for its people than those that prevailed in the developed capitalist world; the claim was rather, as Gorbachev put it during his visit to the United States in late 1988, that it made available a better standard of social security for all members of society.[172] Yet even this became more and more difficult to defend, in the late 1980s, as the quality of Soviet health care, housing and other services came under increasing scrutiny, and as the social benefits provided in most Western states became more widely known. The writer Chinghiz Aitmatov, for instance, a communist member of the Congress of

People's Deputies, pointed out that workers in countries like Sweden, Austria and the Netherlands earned four or five times the amount that a Soviet worker could obtain; not simply this, their social security and welfare rights were vastly superior.[173] For economist and people's deputy Oleg Bogomolov, writing in late 1989, Sweden and Austria might in fact have found the 'only realistic way to put many socialist ideas into practice in the current world context'.[174]

The USSR entered the 1990s, accordingly, not only a different but also a much more uncertain society than the one that Gorbachev had inherited. *Glasnost'* remained a welcome improvement on what had gone before it, but it had begun to lose some of its appeal and the circulation of many periodicals was falling. Political reform was also welcome, but there had been some disillusionment with speech-making politicians and the republican and local elections were drawing much more modest levels of participation than the national polls the year before. Organised crime was a major preoccupation; so too was the food supply, as bad, it appeared, as at any time since the war. Gorbachev's own popularity was falling, and his energies were being placed under greater strain than ever before by a nationalist challenge to the unity of the USSR itself and by ethnic tensions that came close to civil war. There was some public support for a 'firm hand', or even martial law, to discipline speculators and protect social order; and yet the obvious instrument of such a policy, the Communist Party, was divided in its purposes and losing the support it had earlier commanded. Gorbachev, it was clear, had personally and courage-ously initiated a search for a combination of plan and market, and of popular government and party rule, that was still expected to remain within the boundaries of socialism. As his administration came to an end after more than six turbulent years, it was also clear that he had found no coherent framework for reconciling these often incompatible objectives and that a solution to the problems he had identified was likely to require a reconsideration of the bases of the Soviet system and not simply an attempt to manage that system more effectively.

8   Towards a New Russia?

Gorbachev's resignation as Soviet President appeared to resolve the most important of the dilemmas he had confronted during the last months of communist rule. There was no longer any need to reconcile the competing claims of party power and popular sovereignty as the CPSU was consigned to the 'dustbin of history' to which it had tried to send its opponents more than seventy years earlier. The extended search for a 'socialist market' was replaced by a commitment to private ownership, even before the USSR itself had been superseded by an association of independent states. And the rights of citizens had no longer to be understood within a context of 'socialist pluralism', as first the USSR and then the Russian Federation committed themselves to a wide range of liberal freedoms. The Soviet parliament had already adopted a 'Declaration of the rights and freedoms of the individual' in September 1991, which made it clear that the 'highest value of our society' was the 'freedom of the individual, his honour and worth'. Everyone, under the Declaration, had 'natural, inalienable and inviolable rights and freedoms', including equality before the law, freedom of speech and assembly and the right to own private property, which was described as the 'guarantee of the realisation of the interests and freedoms of the individual'.[1] The Russian parliament, in November 1991, added the presumption of innocence and the right to engage in 'entrepreneurial activities', and the declaration was itself incorporated into the Russian constitution in April 1992.[2]

The man who had replaced Gorbachev as leader of the largest post-Soviet republic was still something of an enigma. Boris Yel'tsin was in fact a month older than the Soviet President; he had been a party member since 1961, and then first secretary of the regional organisation in his native Sverdlovsk from 1976 until 1985, when he joined the central leadership.[3] A hastily written autobiography made it clear that he had been lucky to have reached this degree of prominence: he was nearly drowned by the priest when being baptised, he

lost two fingers in an accident during his schooldays, and later contracted typhoid fever.[4] Yel'tsin was asked, when he took over as
chairman of the Russian parliament in 1990, if he was a socialist. What,
he asked, could this mean? There had been 'developed socialism',
'finally and irrevocably established' socialism, Pol Pot socialism, even
National Socialism; and there were different forms of capitalism. Was
there any point in arguing about definitions, or 'which society is
better'?[5] His speeches and interviews during the campaign for the
Russian presidency were scarcely more forthcoming. He was in favour
of 'radical reform', a transition to the market, and the preservation of
peace and stability – but so was Gorbachev; the only real difference
was his insistence upon the priority of Russian over all-union legislation.[6] Once a month, Yel'tsin told interviewers in 1992, he attended a
religious service, but in general he was happy to rely upon his
intuition.[7] A close analysis of his speeches by three academics found
that the Russian president was 'predictable in only one respect – his
unpredictability.'[8]

Several years into the Yel'tsin leadership, it was still unclear what
kind of society had replaced the Soviet system of the late communist
period. The Russian parliament, during the early post-communist
years, was the one that had been elected in 1990, and Yel'tsin had
himself been elected with a Communist running-mate at a time when
the party was still the dominant political force. Some of the largest
republics, like Ukraine and Kazakhstan, were ruled by men who had
been prominent in the party leadership during the late communist
years. The Communist Party, banned after the coup, was allowed to
reconstitute itself in 1993 and soon became the largest of the new
parties with the most substantial popular following. Local officials
were often – indeed normally – the people who had been party
secretaries in the late communist period.[9] The economy remained
overwhelmingly in the hands of the state, despite a programme of
privatisation that had itself been initiated during the period of communist rule; so too did educational, health, broadcasting and other
services. And popular values were still very supportive of traditional
socialist objectives such as full employment and the comprehensive
provision of housing and social welfare; indeed most Russians were
still in favour of the USSR a year after its official demise.[10] The old
Soviet system, it had to be remembered, had collapsed rather than
been overthrown; and the mix of people and institutions that succeeded it showed a substantial measure of continuity, at least in Russia
and the other states that remained inside the new Commonwealth.

Parliamentary or presidential rule?

Political developments during the early post-communist period centred around the Russian Congress of People's Deputies, the 1068-member 'super-parliament' that had been elected in March 1990 (see above, p. 59). The Congress, led by its increasingly influential speaker Ruslan Khasbulatov, included a substantial representation of former Communists and directors of state enterprises, and it showed little sympathy for the market-oriented and privatising reforms that were promoted by President and government. At the sixth Congress in April 1992, the first since the demise of the USSR, an attempt to debate a motion of no confidence in the government was narrowly defeated, and a resolution was adopted that called for 'basic changes' in the reform programme including substantial increases in public spending.[11] The government promptly resigned, warning that the adoption of a resolution of this kind would prejudice economic reform and jeopardise the assistance that had been promised by the West.[12] The government's resignation, in the event, was not accepted (Khasbulatov explained that 'the boys had lost their heads'[13]), and the Congress subsequently adopted a more moderately worded resolution which supported at least the principle of a 'fundamental transformation' of the Russian economy.[14] The Congress did, nonetheless, require Yel'tsin to give up the acting prime ministership within three months; and on 15 June Yegor Gaidar, architect of reform since the previous November and grandson of a famous children's writer, was appointed to these duties by presidential decree.[15]

The tensions between president and parliament became still more apparent at the seventh session of the Congress in December 1992. Yel'tsin, who addressed the Congress on 1 December, accepted that there had been some mistakes in tactics but insisted that the strategy of reform was not responsible and called for a 'period of stabilisation'.[16] Khasbulatov, in a speech that was more warmly received, pointed out in reply that the reforms had led to a collapse of production and to an 'absolute deterioration' in living standards. Attacking the tendency to 'Americanise our economy', he called instead for the 'socially oriented market' that had operated successfully in Europe, Canada, Israel and China and urged deputies to 'choose between these two models of economic development'.[17] In the end, despite Yel'tsin's public support, Gaidar was forced to step down as acting prime minister; his place was taken by Viktor Chernomyrdin, formerly a deputy prime minister in charge of energy and with a background in the gas industry.[18]

Chernomyrdin told the Congress that he was in favour of reforms, but 'without deepening the impoverishment of the people';[19] he told journalists that the government programme should be reviewed to take account of the 'realities of life';[20] and among his first acts, at the start of the new year, was to freeze the prices of basic foodstuffs.[21] The government announced on 23 December nonetheless included most of the members of the Gaidar team, including foreign minister Andrei Kozyrev (who had been fiercely criticised by hardliners) and privatisation minister Anatolii Chubais.[22]

The Seventh Congress had agreed to hold a referendum on 11 April 1993, at which the basic principles of a new constitution would be placed before the Russian people.[23] An extraordinary eighth session of the Congress, however, took place in March 1993; it stripped the president of the emergency powers he had been granted in November 1991 and ordered him to act in accordance with the Russian Constitution, in terms of which the Congress was itself the 'supreme body of state power' on all questions relating to the Federation and the president merely the 'chief official and head of executive authority'.[24] The Congress, on its conclusion, issued an appeal to the Russian people in which it described all Yel'tsin's initiatives as aimed at the 'preservation of special powers for himself that are not in conformity with the constitution', and explained that they had been rejected because they contradicted Russia's declared objective of 'building a democratic society and a state based on the rule of law'.[25] Yel'tsin and his supporters had talked, on the eve of the Congress, of the possible need for 'emergency measures', which would not necessarily be in line with the Constitution; these were understood to involve a dissolution of the Congress and the institution of direct presidential rule (at least the first of these would certainly have been illegal).[26] The Congress reversed the earlier agreement to conduct a referendum on 11 April, ordering that the funds that had been saved should be spent on accommodating officers returning from Eastern Europe.[27] Yel'tsin's staff, at the conclusion of the Congress, announced that they would nonetheless be conducting a popular vote – which would not have the full force of law – on the date that had originally been intended.[28]

Yel'tsin's personal response to this challenge emerged on the evening of Saturday 20 March 1993, when in a televised address to the Russian people he called for the introduction of a 'special form of administration'. Under these provisions parliament would not be suspended, and the ordinary rights of citizens would be unaffected; but the legislature would be unable to overrule the decrees that president or government might choose to adopt. In the meantime, Yel'tsin promised, there would be a popular vote on 25 April at which the President and Vice-President would ask for an expression of confidence, and which would also provide an opportunity to approve the bases of a new constitution and electoral law.[29] The address was supported by the Russian government[30] but swiftly condemned by the chairman of the Constitutional Court as an 'attempted coup' and denounced by Vice-President Rutskoi, the Prosecutor-General and parliamentary representatives.[31] When the text of Yel'tsin's decree was finally published, on 24 March, it did not in fact make reference to a 'special form of administration' and called for no more than a vote of confidence in the president and an expression of opinion on the draft constitution and electoral law.[32] The Congress of People's Deputies was hurriedly convened in order to consider this new challenge to the authority of parliament. When it met, on 26 March, an attempt to impeach the President was narrowly defeated (nearly 70 per cent of the deputies present voted in favour, but not quite two-thirds of the entire membership).[33] The outcome was that a referendum was agreed, for 25 April, but it would consider different questions from those – including the establishment of a 'presidential republic' and private ownership of land – that Yel'tsin had originally suggested.[34]

The referendum, when it finally took place, did little to resolve the continuing impasse. There were four questions on the ballot paper: (i) 'Do you have confidence in the President of the Russian Federation B. N. Yel'tsin?'; (ii) 'Do you approve the socioeconomic policy that the President and government of the Russian Federation have been conducting since 1992?'; (iii) 'Do you think it necessary to hold early elections for the Presidency of the Russian Federation?'; and (iv) 'Do you think it necessary to hold early parliamentary elections?'[35] The outcome, in most respects, was a victory for the President, although a less dramatic one than exit polls had originally suggested. The turnout over the country as a whole was a respectable 64.6 per cent (voting took place everywhere except the Chechen republic; in Tatarstan the turnout of just 23 per cent was not enough to produce a valid result). Of those who voted, 58.7 per cent supported the President and 53 per cent approved his socioeconomic policies. The other two questions, according to the Constitutional Court, required a majority of the total electorate, not just of voters. On this basis, only 31.7 per cent had called for early presidential elections, and 43.1 per cent for early parliamentary elections.[36] For Yel'tsin and his supporters this was a verdict that justified pressing ahead with a constitution that provided for a presidential republic with a much more limited legislature and judiciary;[37] for his opponents it was a result that owed a great deal to media pressure and in any case exposed the limitations of Yel'tsin's support, particularly outside the large cities and in non-Russian areas.[38]

Several elements were involved in a deepening political stalemate that had begun, by the early 1990s, to threaten the exercise of government itself. One of these, certainly, was the continuing competition for authority between President and Congress. For Yel'tsin himself, without a strong executive there would be 'no reforms, no order and no statehood worth of Russia, its history and traditions'.[39] To reduce the presidency to a figurehead, he told the Congress of People's Deputies in April 1992, would lead to chaos and regional separatism; only a strong executive could preserve the integrity of Russia and with it the continuation of reform.[40] He had received his authority directly from the Russian people, Yel'tsin made clear in early 1993, and he did not necessarily consider he was bound by a constitution that had been repeatedly amended since he had sworn to abide by its provisions as Russian President.[41] The Congress, he complained in December 1992, tended 'just to reject, just to destroy'. Too many deputies engaged in 'cheap populism and open demagoguery ... and, in the final analysis, the restoration of a totalitarian Soviet-Communist system'. The only way forward, in his view, was a direct appeal to the voters who had elected him, and a referendum – similar to the exercise that took place a few months later – on whether they had confidence in the President or in the Congress and Supreme Soviet.[42]

For parliamentarians and their speaker, Ruslan Khasbulatov, the issue was a rather different one: whether government should be accountable to elected representatives, and whether a broadly representative parliament should be allowed to act as a counterbalance to what would otherwise be an overwhelmingly powerful executive. For Khasbulatov, Russian history and then Marxism–Leninism had combined to exaggerate the power of a single 'tsar'. It was crucial, in these circumstances, to establish a secure division of powers and to develop the role of parliament as a 'representative organ' of the whole society. Parliament, in particular, could serve as a 'counterweight' to the executive, exercising its influence over public spending, legislation and the composition of government as parliaments did in other countries.[43] Khasbulatov, an economics professor in his early fifties, had become acting speaker in July 1991 with Yel'tsin's support and had taken part in the defence of the White House but had since emerged as the President's most articulate opponent. Opening the Russian parliament in March 1992, he accused the government of an 'attack on democracy' and complained of the dismissive attitude of ministers towards representative institutions in general.[44] He also insisted, in the confrontation between parliament and presidency, that the Cabinet of Ministers should be accountable to the Congress and Supreme Soviet rather than to the 'collective Rasputin' that surrounded the President.[45] Whatever the merits of these views, Khasbulatov had less public support than the Russian president;[46] he was, after all, a Chechen, not a native Russian, and his main quality (according to opinion polls) was 'cunning' rather than statesmanship.[47] He had been elected, moreover, by the Russian parliament, not by the people as a whole, and at the ninth session of the Congress, in March 1993, his position was directly challenged.[48] His importance was perhaps less as an individual than as a symbol of the principle of representative rather than presidential government.

Other political systems, like the French and American, managed to operate effectively despite the separate election of an executive president and a working parliament. What made the Russian system so peculiarly immobile, in the early 1990s, was the absence of a party system which could have bound together a president and a parliamentary majority. Yel'tsin had spoken, in November 1992, of attempting to establish a 'party or movement' that would support his presidential position,[49] but the proposal made little progress. Nor were other parties any stronger. The Communists, suspended in August and then banned entirely in November 1991, were allowed to reconstitute themselves after the Constitutional Court had ruled the ban illegal (although the Court also found it had been legitimate to suppress the party's central institutions, which had usurped the state itself).[50] The party was duly revived in February 1993, claiming more than half a million members;[51] this made it the largest of the new parties, although still far smaller than the CPSU it had succeeded. Altogether, by the summer of 1992, there were at least 1200 parties or movements in operation across the country as a whole,[52] and 28 of them, by early 1993, had been formally registered with the Ministry of Justice.[53] Surveys conducted in early 1993 suggested that Nikolai Travkin's Democratic Party had the most widespread popular support (17.8 per cent viewed it 'positively' and 16.8 per cent would vote for it); but communist groupings came second and third with about 23.1 per cent between them, followed by the All-Russian Union of Cossacks, the Democratic Reform Movement and the Peasant Party of Russia.[54]

This was still some distance short of a party system that could sustain effective government, still less a pluralist democracy. Memberships, for a start, were very low, and active memberships lower still: about 30,000 altogether, according to an estimate that was published in early 1992.[55] Levels of knowledge and identification were little better. In a Russian survey of late 1993, more than three-quarters of those asked were unable to name a single Russian party or public movement.[56] So far as trust was concerned, a different survey found 'some' or even 'a lot' of confidence in the army (48 per cent), the courts (39 per cent), television and state security (33 per cent each), and even local government and the Supreme Soviet (18 and 11 per cent respectively). Political parties came last of all, with just 3 per cent.[57] And there was a clear distinction, according to the surveys, between verbal support and willingness to attend meetings, carry out party activities, or even vote for the party of one's nominal preference.[58]

For many, in fact, these were proto-parties or leadership support groups, not parties in the commonly recognised sense. And this, it was suggested, was because coherent social interests had not themselves begun to crystallise. Without the formation of interests of this kind, no parties could develop that had a clear and coherent programme; and the parties that did come into existence were based upon a 'small group of intellectuals', with original but also 'abstract' ideas. Much more likely, for the immediate future, was the formation of movements of various kinds headed by popular individuals.[59] There was, indeed, some hostility to the very idea of a political party. Why have two parties, it had been remarked during the years of communist monopoly: wasn't one bad enough? As K. Lozovsky, a teacher from the Vitebsk region, put it in a letter to *Izvestiya*, 'wouldn't it be better to do without parties altogether?' The word itself was deeply compromised after so many years in which it had been a synonym for single-party dictatorship. And what was a party anyway? It was 'always and everywhere a struggle for power, posts and positions', fed by a lust for power that was 'stronger than any narcotic'. Wouldn't it be better to let the 'demagogues and hypocrites, power-lovers and careerists, flatterers and opportunists' fight it out among themselves, while ordinary people sought to strengthen the human qualities that had always sustained them in the past?[60] Or as a 45-year old woman, formerly in the CPSU, explained, 'I don't believe in any of the parties any more ... All the ones we have at the moment are only interested in getting into power, and no-one is concerned about ordinary people. Not even the communists'.[61]

A deepening crisis appeared to ease somewhat towards the end of 1993 when elections were held to a new Federal Assembly, and at the same time a new constitution was adopted that provided for a strongly presidential republic. The elections followed a presidential decree on 'gradual constitutional reform' of 21 September which suspended the Russian parliament and called for elections to the State Duma, the lower house of the new Assembly, on 11–12 December. Yel'tsin claimed in his decree that the Supreme Soviet had blocked the process of economic and constitutional reform, and that the 'security of Russia and its peoples' was a 'higher priority than formal conformity to contradictory norms created by the legislative branch of government'; an entirely new constitution would be presented by the time of the elections, and in the meantime government would be conducted directly by the President and Council of Ministers.[62] In further decrees Yegor Gaidar was brought back as minister of economics and first deputy prime minister; parliamentary property was transferred to the presidency; and the parliamentary newspaper, *Rossiiskaya guzeta*, was suspended.[63] The Constitutional Court, meeting on the evening of 21 September, found Yel'tsin's decree in violation of the Constitution and agreed there were grounds for impeachment; the Supreme Soviet Presidium, headed by Khasbulatov, voted later the same evening to annul the decree and transfer the powers of president to Vice-President Rutskoi.[64] A session of the Congress of People's Deputies, hastily convened on 23 September, condemned Yel'tsin's action as a 'state coup' and voted for dismissal; Rutskoi was formally sworn in as acting President, and an alternative administration began to be formed.[65]

Parliamentary support began to concentrate in the 'White House' in central Moscow in which its meetings took place, and from which the August 1991 coup had earlier been resisted by Yel'tsin himself. Telephone links were cut off, the electricity supply was severed and the water supply was reduced; toilets became unusable, with unpleasant consequences. Demonstrators, meanwhile, began to gather around the building, which was barricaded against a possible assault. On 28 September the White House was sealed off by troops, and the government warned there would be 'serious consequences' for anyone who remained in the building after 4 October.[66] Several possible compromises were suggested, including a 'zero option' put forward by the chairman of the Constitutional Court, Valerii Zor'kin, in which Yel'tsin's decree would be withdrawn; so would the vote to impeach him; and then there would be simultaneous parliamentary and presidential elections (Yel'tsin's supporters claimed it would be dangerous, in a state with nuclear weapons, to hold elections on this basis and risk a 'power vacuum').[67] There were signs that parliamentary support was growing at the level of regional governments throughout the country, though the armed forces remained loyal to the President; there were further calls for a compromise from centrist politicians such as Grigorii Yavlinsky and Nikolai Ryzhkov, many of them supporting Zor'kin's call for simultaneous elections, and direct negotiations began on 1 October, under the auspices of the Orthodox church, in a desperate attempt to reach an accommodation.[68]

The crisis was resolved on the weekend of 3–4 October when a demonstration of about 10,000 parliamentary supporters marched to the White House, raised the blockade and encouraged Rutskoi and Khasbulatov – and many Western journalists – to believe that a popular insurrection had taken place in their support. The demonstrators took control of the Moscow mayor's office, immediately opposite the White House; Rutskoi and Khasbulatov at this point urged the crowd to 'take Ostankino' (the main television centre, which went off the air for some time), and to 'take over the Kremlin'. After a day in which the regime itself had appeared to waver and in which Yel'tsin had shown little clarity of purpose, armed forces were deployed on the morning of 4 October and the White House was subjected to an artillery bombardment. Several floors were taken after a great deal of damage had been inflicted, and by the early evening Rutskoi, Khasbulatov and their remaining supporters had been forced to surrender although sporadic shooting continued into the next day.[69] The parliamentary leaders were arrested and charged with 'organising mass disorder' (they were amnestied, with the conspirators of August 1991, by a parliamentary vote in early 1994);[70] Yel'tsin, in a television broadcast the same evening, accused them of an 'armed rebellion' that had sought to establish a 'bloody communo-fascist dictatorship'.[71] It was reported, meanwhile, that 145 people had lost their lives in what had been the bloodiest street fighting in the Russian capital since the revolution of 1917.[72]

The 'October events' created an unusual and in many respects unhelpful background for the conduct of the elections that Yel'tsin had promised in his September broadcast. There was a brief period of censorship;[73] a number of 'fascist' publications were banned;[74] and some others, including *Pravda*, were ordered to replace their editors and change their names if they wished to resume publication (the paper disappeared for thirty days and changed its editor but in the end retained its distinctive title).[75] A state of emergency in Moscow, incorporating a ban on rallies and demonstrations and a curfew, lasted until 18 October.[76] The Constitutional Court was suspended and its chairman Valerii Zor'kin forced to resign (he remained a member of the Court itself).[77] The Prosecutor General was dismissed and replaced by a Yel'tsin loyalist;[78] regional, district and local soviets were ordered to transfer their powers to presidential representatives pending the election of new and smaller bodies to replace them;[79] and a wide range of opposition groups and their papers were suspended on the grounds that they had been involved in the 'events' of 3–4 October.[80] A number, including the Russian Communist Workers' Party, remained suspended, but several others were eventually legalised including the Communist Party of the Russian Federation and the People's Party of Free Russia, which had been led by Vice-Presient Rutskoi.[81] These were among the parties and movements that were able to contest the elections to an entirely new parliament on Sunday 12 December 1993.

A total of 21 blocs were formed to fight for the 225 seats in the State Duma that had been allocated on a proportional basis to party and electoral alliances, but in the end only 13 raised a sufficient number of signatures to register their candidature.[82] The main reformist grouping was *Vybor Rossii* ('Russia's Choice'), which had begun to form soon after the referendum and which combined 'Democratic Russia', 'Democratic Initiative' and the reform-oriented Peasant Party of Russia. Its list was headed by Yegor Gaidar and other government ministers and it was the most clearly pro-Yel'tsin grouping, although the President did not support it openly; it stood for the rapid continuation of privatisation and market reform, took an early lead in the opinion polls, and enjoyed the greatest exposure on state television.[83] Several other ministers, including deputy premiers Sergei Shakhrai and Alexander Shokhin, headed the list put forward by the Party of Russian Unity and Concord, whose founding congress took place on 17 October. The PRES described itself as the 'party of Russian statehood' and it gave particular prominence to the interests of non-metropolitan Russia; it also favoured a more gradual programme of economic reform. The Yavlinksy-Boldyrev-Lukin or 'Yabloko' bloc was formed at the end of October, led by the radical economist Grigorii Yavlinsky; it was based upon the Republican Party, the Social Democratic Party and the Russian Christian-Democratic Union, and stood for the 'basic values of democracy, freedom and market economy' while avoiding 'explosive measures' of a political or economic kind.

In the centre were a further series of parties and blocs, including

'Women of Russia', formed in October 1993, which was based upon the Union of Russian Women; a feminist grouping, it aimed to increase women's representation as a means of influencing social policy and argued more generally that the market was 'not an end in itself, but a means of improving living standards'. Other broadly centrist blocs included the Civic Union for Stability, Justice and Progress, headed by Arkadii Vol'sky of the Russian Union of Industrialists and Entrepreneurs and representing the interests of factory managers rather more than private investors; Nikolai Travkin's Democratic Party of Russia, which stood for a mixed economy and a more limited presidency; and Mikhail Lapshin's Agrarian Party, which reflected the interests of state and cooperative rather than private agriculture. The other broadly centrist groupings were 'The Future of Russia – New Names' (representing youth), 'Dignity and Charity' (which represented veterans, invalids and Chernobyl victims) and 'Kedr' (an environmentalist grouping). The Democratic Reform Movement, headed by former Moscow mayor Gavriil Popov, placed particular emphasis upon human rights and decentralisation; its list of candidates included St Petersburg mayor Anatolii Sobchak and Alexander Yakovlev, formerly the 'architect of *perestroika*' but now a Yel'tsin adviser.

On the political left was the Communist Party of the Russian Federation, headed by its chairman Gennadii Zyuganov, and the only one of the post-CPSU formations that was able to compete for places in the new Duma. The elections themselves were illegal, in the view of the Communists, but they were prepared to participate so as to 'prevent the dictatorship from being legalised'.[84] The CPRF, together with the Agrarians, stood for the establishment of a 'strong and determined opposition'; more particularly they wanted the restoration of political and economic stability, a stronger parliament, a greater degree of state regulation in the economy, and an end to the 'mass impoverishment of the people'. On the radical right, by contrast, was the Liberal Democratic Party and its controversial leader Vladimir Zhirinovsky. The economy, argued the LDP, could be revived very quickly; its immediate proposals were to end foreign aid, step up arms sales and crack down on organised crime. The LDP stood more generally for a strong state sector with much more limited privatisation, no shift to private ownership of land and no overt unemployment. There should also be a strong and unitary system of government, including the restoration of a Russian state 'within the boundaries of the former USSR' and a strong executive presidency; and the LDP favoured a strongly pro-

Table 8.1 *Elections to the State Duma, December 1993*

Electoral bloc	% vote	party list seats	constituency seats	total seats	seats in %
Russia's Choice	15.4	40	30	70	15.6
Liberal Democrats	22.8	59	5	64	14.2
Communist Party	12.4	32	16	48	10.7
Agrarian Party	7.9	21	12	33	7.3
'Yabloko' bloc	7.8	20	3	23	5.1
Civic Union	1.9	0	1	1	0.2
Democratic Party	5.5	14	0	14	3.1
Dignity and Charity	0.7	0	2	2	0.4
Russian Unity and Accord	6.8	18	1	19	4.2
Women of Russia	8.1	21	2	23	5.1
Dem. Reform Movement	4.1	0	4	4	0.9
Other parties and blocs	—	—	14	14	3.1
Independents	—	—	129	129	28.7

Source: Adapted from *The Economist,* 8 January 1994, p. 30.

Slavic and anti-Western foreign policy, particularly in the former Yugoslavia.[85]

The results took some time to emerge, and the figures that were eventually reported aroused a good deal of controversy.[86] It was nonetheless clear as early as the evening of the poll that the largest share of party-list seats had been taken, sensationally, by the Liberal Democratic Party, with 23.9 per cent of the total. 'Russia's Choice' came second with 14.5 per cent, followed by the Communist Party with 13.6 per cent, the Agrarians with 9 per cent, Women of Russia with 8.5 per cent, the Yavlinsky-Boldyrev-Lukin group with 7.4 per cent, the PRES with 6.7 per cent, and the Democratic Party of Russia with 5.5 per cent. The other groupings, it appeared, would not exceed the 5 per cent threshold and would therefore be unrepresented. The Liberal Democrats had been much less successful in the other half of the State Duma, which was based on single-member constituencies, and in the upper house, the Council of the Federation.[87] The outcome was nonetheless a parliament in which the President had the committed support of about a third of the deputies but faced a communist and nationalist bloc that accounted for another third of the seats, with the remainder made up by minor parties and independents (see Table 8.1). The Russian electorate, clearly, had rejected 'shock therapy', but without giving their support to a set of alternative policies that would be workable; they had made their views apparent much more generally by staying at home (the official turnout was just 54.8 per cent), voting for independents (the largest group in both houses), or voting against all of the candidates on the paper (a record 17 per cent, with a further 7 per cent of the vote invalid).[88]

Responding finally to the results, Yel'tsin laid more emphasis upon the adoption of a new constitution than upon the parliamentary vote.[89] The new constitution was certainly a strongly presidential one, allowing Yel'tsin or his successors to define the 'basic directions of domestic and foreign policy' and to nominate and dismiss the prime minister and other members of government as well as the chairman of the State Bank, members of the Supreme and Constitutional Courts and 'plenipotentiary representatives' in the regions. The President, in addition, could dissolve the Duma, call referenda, initiate legislation, and issue decrees that had the force of law throughout the Federation; in Gorbachev's view these powers were greater than any the Tsar had enjoyed before the revolution, for others they were reminiscent of Napoleon III.[90] Unfortunately for what was supposed to be a 'basic law', there was also some doubt about the legality of its adoption. Yel'tsin had originally called for a 'national vote' on the constitution, which would be valid if more than half of the electorate took part and voted in favour. The turnout that was reported in late December was above this level and the vote in favour was 58.4 per cent, enough to satisfy these requirements.[91] But there was some evidence that the returns had been falsified so as to secure a 50 per cent turnout,[92] and in any case the adoption of a new constitution required a referendum, which in turn required the positive support of more than half of the registered *electorate*. Even on the official figures, only about 31 per cent of those who could have voted had supported the new draft, and eight of the twenty-one republics had voted against. For some, this was a document that should immediately be challenged in the courts; for others it was a first approximation that would require a continuing process of amendment and improvement; for others still it had established a potential dictatorship that could 'take the country back to the GULag'.[93]

These and other ambiguities did not help to resolve a crisis of governability that had begun to place the state itself in question. Chernomyrdin, addressing the Congress of People's Deputies in early 1993, spoke of a 'catastrophic loss of manageability'.[94] Laws were being adopted, but largely ignored. Taxes were being levied, but not paid: Moscow city was collecting only about half of what it was due, and the

Russian budget was itself receiving only two thirds of what it should have collected.[95] At least four republics were making no contribution at all.[96] The authority of the Russian government was called directly into question by the twenty autonomous units that were at that time located within its borders: only 18 of them agreed to sign a federal treaty in March 1992, and at least eight had declared sovereignty over their own territory by the spring of 1993.[97] The Chechen republic, in the North Caucasus, had gone still further and (in its own view) seceded altogether; it refused to take part in the December 1993 elections, or in the constitutional referendum.[98] Who did rule Russia, in the early 1990s? According to surveys in early 1993 it was the mafia (21.8 per cent) or no-one at all (9.3 per cent); 9.7 per cent thought it was President Yel'tsin, but only 3.9 per cent thought the government was in charge, and only 0.2 per cent thought it was the Congress of People's Deputies – the same proportion that thought the country was being run by alcoholics.[99]

From plan to market

The background to these developments, as in the other post-Soviet republics, was a sharply deteriorating economic situation. The report of the State Statistics Committee on economic performance in 1991 was published in February 1992; it described the previous year, for the CIS as a whole, as one of 'intensified decline in the economy and people's standard of living and an exacerbation of the social atmosphere'. Gross national product, which had fallen slightly in 1990, had declined by 17 per cent over the year. Consumption of goods and services more generally had fallen by 15 per cent. Soap, washing powder and many other goods were being rationed. Foreign trade had deteriorated sharply as exports of fuel and raw materials – the main sources of hard currency – had declined. Production levels of oil and coal in 1991 were 10 per cent down on those of the previous year, mainly because of outdated equipment and low investment; a further 15 million tonnes of coal had been lost because of industrial action. Foreign trade turnover was down by 39 per cent, and the CIS's share of world trade had fallen from 3 to 2 per cent. Control over the money supply, meanwhile, had been lost entirely: the volume of cash in circulation had increased nearly five times over 1990, and the consumer price index had nearly doubled. The budgetary deficit, at the same time, was up from 4 per cent in 1990 to 12–14 per cent a year later.[100]

The solution proposed by the Yel'tsin government was what had become known in other countries as 'shock therapy'. It was fore-shadowed in a wide-ranging speech by the Russian President in October 1991, in which he announced a policy of financial stability, privatisation and military conversion. 'We must', Yel'tsin insisted, 'provide economic freedom, lift all barriers to the freedom of enterprise and of entrepreneurship and give people the opportunity to work and to receive as much as they can earn, casting off all bureaucratic constraints'.[101] In the month that followed there were decrees abolishing limits on earnings, liberalising foreign economic relations, and commercialising shops and services.[102] In December a decree on the 'liberalisation of prices' was adopted which abolished controls on all but a 'limited range' of goods and services.[103] Prices were duly 'freed' on 2 January 1992, not only in Russia but in most of the other post-Soviet republics; there was an immediate rise of between three and thirty times, with an average increase of 1200 per cent as compared with the prices that had obtained a year before.[104] A further decree in December 1991 privatised the land that was in state and municipal ownership;[105] later the same month a set of 'basic provisions' on the privatisation of state and municipal enterprises was adopted, which aimed to create conditions for the 'comprehensive development of the process of privatisation in 1993 and 1994'.[106]

A 'memorandum on economic policy' appeared in February 1992 which set out the broader background behind these changes. By the end of March, the memorandum promised, all remaining price controls on consumer goods and services would be removed. Energy prices would be allowed to move to world levels by the end of 1993. The most vulnerable sections of the population would be protected, so far as possible, in the form of cash benefits for those with the lowest income levels. A balanced budget would be achieved by a series of reductions in public expenditure, involving cuts in direct subsidies to enterprises and a fall of up to 15 per cent in public sector employment. Exchange restrictions would be eliminated, and export licences would (in all but a limited number of cases) be abolished as a step towards Russia's full integration into the international economy.[107] A further, more elaborate 'Programme for the deepening of economic reforms in Russia' was approved in July 1992; it dealt with the medium term, up to 1996, and set out the same kinds of goals: deregulation, stabilisation of public finance, privatisation, an 'active social policy', structural change (including demilitarisation) and the creation of a 'competitive market environment'.[108]

The overall picture that was reported in early 1993 and again in 1994

Table 8.2 *The Russian economy in 1989–93 (official data, percentage change on previous year)*

	1989	1990	1991	1992	1993
National income produced	1.9	4.0	− 11.0	− 22.0	− 13.0
Industrial production	1.4	− 0.1	− 8.0	− 18.0	− 16.2
Agricultural production	1.7	− 3.6	− 4.5	− 8.0	− 4.0
Housing construction	− 2.6	− 12.4	− 20.0	− 23.0	1.0
Retail trade turnover	8.4	10.0	− 7.2	− 35.3	− 0.1
Paid services	6.6	10.2	− 20.8	− 41.0	− 30.0

Source: Adapted from *Voprosy ekonomiki*, 1994, no. 2, p. 128.

was still a very gloomy one. Russia, the State Statistics Committee explained, was committing itself irrevocably to the market. The climate of opinion was changing; consumer demand was becoming the regular of production; producers themselves were establishing bilateral relations; and the non-state sector was developing rapidly. But this had to be set against the background of a large and accelerating fall in production, a substantial drop in living standards, and a sharp increase in prices of goods and services. There had certainly been a further sharp decline in all the main indicators of economic activity (see Table 8.2); nor was there any evidence of a shift of resources out of backward into more 'modern' sectors, with consumer goods production (for instance) falling even more than oil, gas and coal.[109] In 1993 there was a further decline in almost all areas, and in early 1994 the year-on-year decline was sharper than ever before; gross domestic product had already fallen by 39.2 per cent since 1989, a fall that was unprecedented in any country in peacetime.[110]

There had been a particularly striking failure to arrest the fall in the value of the ruble, which indeed (according to *Pravda*) had already suffered a 'clinical death'.[111] Enterprise debts had deepened, banks had started to run out of money, and often wages could not be paid because of the absence of currency. From the middle of 1992, to relieve these difficulties, the money supply had been increased to 25 per cent a month, and the banking system, confronted by the possibility of wholesale stoppages of production and by the need to finance the harvest, had extended credits much more generously. Economic activity revived a little, helping to reduce the budgetary deficit, but inflationary processes accelerated. The ruble stood at 161 to the dollar in August 1992; by January 1993 the exchange rate was 468 (and still climbing). The freeing of controls had led to a 2600 per cent increase in the level of consumer prices over the year; incomes increased as well, but they were left far behind. In December 1991, for instance, a refrigerator cost the equivalent of a single monthly salary, and a television set about two; a year later both required six monthly salaries.[112] Rates of inflation showed down in 1993, but the year on year increase was 940 per cent; excluding the jump in prices that had taken place after January 1992, the average monthly rate was higher in 1993 than it had been the previous year, and was expected to remain at about the same level (up to 20 per cent a month) to the end of 1994. The emission of currency was 1.5 trillion rubles in 1992, but 10.9 in 1993; the budget deficit, meanwhile, had widened to a record 15 per cent of gross domestic product.[113]

Official statistics were admittedly more inaccurate than ever before. With the development of the non-state sector, and in particular of more or less unregulated street trading, official measures of the volume of economic activity were likely to understate the real position (by the summer of 1992, for instance, 10 per cent of all goods were being bought from private dealers).[114] There were openly conflicting statistics, such as the increase in export sales that was reported by the Ministry for Foreign Economic Relations at the same time as the State Statistics Committee was reporting a decline.[115] There were at least five different versions of the 1992 Russian budget; even members of the government offered different figures;[116] and the budgetary deficit in 1992 and 1993 was deliberately understated in order to satisfy the requirements of international financiers.[117] The Russian government was itself less than perfectly informed, as Gaidar made clear when he complained in late 1992 of the lack of 'normal financial information' and the absence of a proper system of national accounts; finance minister Boris Fedorov, two months in office, found himself unable to obtain an accurate statement of the money supply.[118] There were different measures of poverty, with some attempt (as with governments elsewhere) to reduce the value of the 'basket of goods' that constituted a subsistence diet.[119] Economic activity across the newly-established borders of the CIS was another weakness: imports and exports between Russia and the Ukraine, for instance, were at best approximations.[120]

For all the inadequacy of the statistics, several trends were reasonable clear. One of them was a deepening crisis of poverty and deprivation. There were cases of elderly men dying in queues,[121] and of students fainting of malnutrition while taking part in demonstrations against their inadequate stipends.[122] In the Pacific fleet, four conscripts died of malnutrition;[123] in south Russia, an elderly pensioner was reduced to living off the pigeons that were caught by his cat.[124] According to authoritative estimates, living standards had fallen by at least half in the course of 1992 and 1993;[125] by early 1994 an estimated 30–40 per cent of the population fell below subsistence levels, with about 7–10 per cent at or below the physiological minimum. The disabled, and pensioners, were unable to buy milk and bread on a daily basis, and despite a great increase in the relative share of spending on foodstuffs the average diet was less nutritious than it had been in the 1970s, with 20 per cent less protein and 50 per cent fewer vitamins.[126] The first night shelters opened in Moscow in 1992;[127] the Salvation Army returned;[128] and the European Community opened the first soup kitchens that had existed since the civil war.[129] There was a 'rapid growth' in the number of homeless, at least in larger cities.[130] Free school meals were phased out;[131] public launderies went out of business as the charges they were forced to make exceeded what ordinary Russians could afford to pay;[132] and kindergartens closed down for the same reason.[133] There were even problems with burials, as fewer and fewer ordinary Russians could meet the costs involved.[134] Many of the 'refuseniks' were elderly people without families, who had to write out a refusal to bury their spouse and then 'live out the rest of their days in unbearable torment because of what they [had] done and because the same fate [would] befall each of them'.[135]

At the other extreme it was clear that some of the skilful, the fortunate or (very often) the openly criminal had prospered. There was Igor Desyatnikov, for instance, a 27 year-old banker, who already owned ten city centre buildings and had $2 million in bank accounts abroad. Three men and a pit bull-terrier guarded his Moscow offices; inside one of the rooms was full of weapons. He had a company in Lichtenstein, but most of his money was in France: 'I just like having lunch in Paris', he told a Western reporter.[136] Many of the new rich could be found in the restaurant of the Moscow Commercial Club on Great Communist Street, just down from Comradely Lane, where lobster was $198 a kilo. One particularly conspicuous diner arrived regularly in his Cadillac, wearing a white sharkskin coat. Other members of the new rich could be found in the increasing number of hard-currency casinos, betting in hundreds and thousands of dollars while their Western counterparts staked tens and twenties. Specialist dealers, meanwhile, were 'doing a roaring trade in secondhand Cadillacs, Lincolns and Oldsmobiles'; and stretch limousines were on hire for $40 an hour (bodyguard extra).[137] This was Moscow, but there was no doubt that, across the society as a whole, the differences between social groups were rapidly widening: in 1992 the richest 10 per cent earned between four and five times as much as the least wealthy 10 per cent; by early 1994 they were earning 11 times as much.[138]

The reform strategy had a number of other direct consequences. One of them was unemployment, as enterprises were forced to close down or at least to shed labour. Only 835,000 were registered as such in early 1994, but the real figure (using the methodology of the International Labour Organization) was much higher, an estimated 3.8 million. Including those who were actively seeking work and those working on a short-time basis the total was still larger, about 7.8 million or 10.4 per cent of the labour force.[139] Another consequence was crime, as social differences widened and the opportunities to dispose of illegal income became greater. The number of crimes that were recorded in 1992, 2.8 million, was a record; there was a further increase in 1993 to a total three times greater than 1990.[140] There were attacks on bankers and businessmen, on deputies and judges, as well as ordinary citizens; there were more murders in Moscow than in New York, and ten times as many per head of population as in the most violent cities of Western Europe.[141] A professional killing could be as easily arranged, in the mid-1990s, as 'say, a restaurant dinner';[142] hitmen could also be hired to conduct 'conversations' with reluctant debtors.[143] Crops began to be seized from the fields, as well as livestock, forcing farmers to organise armed patrols;[144] a collective farm chairman was killed as he tried to defend his holding.[145] Taxi drivers began to arm themselves, as did private detectives.[146] Unfurnished buildings were being occupied, and automatic weapons used in schools;[147] gunfire in central Moscow had become 'quite common', and rocket-propelled grenades were being used in attacks on flats in the city centre.[148] The theft of armaments had meanwhile increased sixteen times between 1987 and 1991, and crimes involving firearms doubled in 1992 and again in 1993.[149]

More worrying still was a deepening demographic crisis, reflected in birth and death rates as well as a steady deterioration in general levels of health. In 1991 the number of deaths exceeded the number of births,[150] and in 1992 there was an absolute fall in the population for the first time since the war; there was a further fall in 1993.[151] By the same year there were one and a half times as many deaths as births; in St Petersburg and Moscow, the two largest cities, deaths were running two or three times ahead of births.[152] There was a fall in average birth weights, and an increase in the number of mothers that died in childbirth (already much higher than in the developed world); levels of infant mortality rose in parallel from 16.8 per thousand in 1991 to 19.1 in 1993.[153] Only about a quarter of school leavers were healthy, and no more than 20 per cent of young men – by international standards – were fit enough for military service.[154] Among adults, rare diseases became more common and common diseases like syphilis became more widespread.[155] There were increases in the incidence of tuberculosis and of diseases connected with malnutrition, particularly among pensioners;[156] there was more diptheria and typhoid.[157] Nor had older problems gone away: half of all marriages were ending in divorce, with all the attendant social costs, and at least 3.5 per cent of the population was estimated to suffer from chronic alcoholism (cases of *delirium tremens* almost doubled in 1991 and 1992, and in 1993 alcohol consumption from all sources became the highest in the world).[158]

This, moreover, was only part of a much wider deterioration in the quality of the Russian physical and cultural environment. Fewer films were being made, and the number of new books published was down to prewar levels.[159] The Academy of Sciences was laying off staff and defaulting on its international subscriptions.[160] Cancer treatment centres were closing and discharging their patients.[161] Nearly half of the men who died in 1991 were of working age, and in some of the most polluted areas average life expectancy was less than retirement age; the minority nationalities of the Far North had a life expectancy of just 46–50.[162] As a report presented to the Russian parliament in October 1992 indicated, about 15 per cent of the country's land area was 'ecologically unsafe', and at least half the population was drinking unhygienic water. Between two and three million were still living in areas affected by radiation from the Chernobyl explosion and the air in most cities was badly polluted, with more than fifty million affected by a 'whole bouquet of harmful substances in concentrations ten times the maximum allowable concentration'. The contamination of major rivers was 'tens or hundreds of times greater than the permissible norms'. Radioactive waste was a particular problem; most of it was in repositories and burial sites that did not satisfy modern safety requirements.[163]

There were two central instruments of government policy that were expected, in due course, to bring Russia out of what was acknowledged to be a deep and many-sided crisis. The first was the scheme, outlined in late 1991, to change the nature of ownership by the distribution of vouchers or 'privatisation cheques' to all members of the population. A scheme for the 'destatification' of industry had in fact been approved by the Soviet parliament in July 1991, based upon a Law on Property adopted the previous year.[164] Yel'tsin's more ambitious proposals, based upon Russian legislation approved in July 1991 and set out more fully in a presidential decree the following December, provided for the privatisation in 1992 alone of half the enterprises in the construction industry, wholesale trade and public catering, together with 60 per cent of enterprises in the food industry, agriculture and retail trade, 70 per cent of enterprises in light industry, construction, motor vehicle transportation and maintenance.[165] In June 1992 the Supreme Soviet approved further legislation under which vouchers worth between 5,000 and 10,000 rubles would be distributed to all citizens to allow them to buy shares in state property. It was estimated that about 25 per cent of state enterprises would be sold off by the end of the year, leaving just a few sectors – including natural resources and defence – in state hands.[166] Privatisation vouchers, as the legislation had provided, began to be distributed on 1 October. 'We need millions of property owners, not just a handful of millionaires', as Yel'tsin put it in a nationwide television address. 'The more property owners there are in Russia ... the sooner prosperity will come to Russia, and the more likely its future will be in safe hands'.[167]

The scheme, however, soon encountered difficulties. Despite an expensive advertising campaign, there was some uncertainty about who could receive the vouchers: they were clearly intended for all citizens, whatever their age, but it was not until January 1993 that the status of refugees and members of the merchant marine was clarified.[168] Many, in spite of the publicity, were rather unclear about what was taking place: in St Petersburg, for instance, as many as 70 per cent had no idea what a voucher actually was.[169] Vouchers, quite improperly, were exchanged for services: in Tyumen' they were being used to cover the cost of dentistry, sold for vodka, or even eau de cologne.[170] In Yaroslavl' vouchers were being accepted from single people as (advance) payment for their funerals.[171] Vouchers were counterfeited and stolen;[172] a quantity of fakes in Rostov on Don was intercepted simply because they had been too skilfully executed.[173] Others were misappropriated. The most spectacular scandal was in St Petersburg, where three companies set up to receive investments simply disappeared – as did the savings of about 400,000 of the local population. The whole incident became known as the 'affair of the century'.[174] By early 1993 a significant shift in property relations had taken place (about 6 per cent of industrial enterprises had been transferred into private ownership, and about 8 per cent of public housing);[175] but it was far from clear what this would contribute to a more general revival of production, and in 1993 the Chernomyrdin government was deliberately slowing down a programme that the prime minister himself compared with the 'collectivisation campaigns' of the 1930s.[176]

The other vital element in the reform strategy was Western economic assistance, including direct investment. Russia became a member of the International Monetary Fund in April 1992 (membership had been agreed in 1944, but never ratified).[177] The following July Russia and the other post-Soviet republics became members of the World Bank.[178] The international community, meanwhile, extended $24 billion towards a ruble stabilisation fund and other purposes in April 1992.[179] At Vancouver, in April 1993, the new American President Bill Clinton announced a $1.6 billion aid package, and he was able to persuade the Group of Seven leading industrial nations to announce a $43 billion package ten days later.[180] The repayment of Soviet foreign debt, an estimated $80 billion, was suspended for ten years as part of these arrangements.[181] And yet the international economy, by itself, was unlikely to achieve the transformation that domestic reforms had not accomplished. Much of the West's humanitarian aid ended up in the hands of the mafia and on street corners (up to 60 per cent, according to Vice-President Rutskoi).[182] Much of it failed to materialise: only about $10 billion of the $24 billion agreed in 1992, for instance, and this was in the form of short-term commercial credits.[183] Russian money and materials, at the same time, was being exported to a value of $17 billion (on some accounts, as much as $40 billion) in 1992 alone.[184] And there was clearly a heavy political cost, in that any Russian government that accepted international assistance was open to the criticism that it had become a client of the IMF.

By the mid 1990s, in the light of these circumstances, it seemed that a new equilibrium was being negotiated. The Gaidar strategy had in fact been harshly criticised by Russian economists since its introduction in early 1992. In March, for instance, Stanislav Shatalin called for a 'major change of course', pointing out the government appeared to have no policies designed to arrest the fall of production and the country's progressive 'deindustrialisation'.[185] Nikolai Petrakov and others attacked the 'cruel and irresponsible' failure of the government in an open letter the same month, noting a 'wave of destruction' in the main productive sectors which might have 'irreversible consequences'. Petrakov was one of the authors of an alternative programme of reform which was made public in the summer of 1992;[186] another alternative programme, this time associated with Leonid Abalkin and the Institute of Economics, was made public in early 1994.[187] The IMF, it began to be pointed out, had 'very rarely achieved the successful implementation of its policies', with positive results only in countries that had retained the regulating role of the state and not relied entirely upon the '"invisible hand of the market"'.[188] The IMF, Georgii Arbatov reminded deputies, had overthrown more governments than military coups had ever managed to accomplish; the policies it had promoted in Russia, as the economist and people's deputy Oleg Bogomolov added in early 1993, had meanwhile led to results that were 'negative for the majority of the people and of benefit only to a clique of *nouveaux riches* and an emerging bourgeoisie'.[189]

The priorities that began to be set out under Chernomyrdin's guidance from late 1992 suggested a change of course that took account of these criticisms, if not a repudiation of market relations as such. The central aims of his programme, as Chernomyrdin explained them in early 1993, involved a strengthening of the currency by reducing the budgetary deficit and the rate of inflation, as well as an attempt to arrest and then reverse the fall in output and to increase the relative share of social security within the total of government spending.[190] The state sector, Chernomyrdin emphasised, would still be vital, even when it was much smaller; equally there would be a need, for some time into the future, to protect Russian industry from the full rigours of international competition, and to hold down the prices of basic commodities.[191] His later speeches called for a 'correction' of the reforms, and even for the resurrection of Gosplan and the allocation agency Gossnab 'in a different form'.[192] Yel'tsin, for his part, accepted that he had placed too much faith in Western aid and that further reforms would have to have a 'strong social orientation'; speaking in December 1993, he urged the government 'not to forget the poor'.[193] It was not yet clear that these somewhat different policies would be more successful; but these were likely at least to be more acceptable, if the elections were any guide, to the Russian public and to those who had previously influenced its economic policymaking.

People and politics in postcommunist Russia

The most important change that had taken place in the transition from a party-dominated to postcommunist system was arguably the emergence of a popular politics. There had, indeed, been no politics in the communist period, if politics was understood as the organised competition of alternatives. For many, the defence of the Russian parliament – the White House – during the attempted coup had been the crucial turning point. For Yel'tsin, speaking just after the coup had collapsed, the Russian people had 'thrown off the fetters of seventy years of slavery'.[194] For *Izvestiya*, speaking editorially, democracy had 'taught the Russian people not to be silent', a reference to Pushkin's *Boris Godunov* in which the population of the time had refused to welcome the False Dmitrii;[195] for the critic Alla Latynina, a 'Russian liberal democratic state' had been born.[196] It was certainly clear, after the end of communist rule, that political parties and all kinds of other associations could be freely formed; that candidates could be rejected at elections; and that open opposition to government policies was legitimate, even commonplace (the first divorces had begun to take place on the grounds of political incompatibility[197]). Political leaders, for their part, had to be able to claim that public opinion was on their side: both Yel'tsin and Khasbulatov attempted to do so during the confrontation between President and Congress in early 1993, both of them maintained a service that processed the letters of ordinary members of the public, and Yel'tsin appointed the head of a survey organisation – the veteran pollster Boris Grushin – to his Presidential Council.[198] What, so far as surveys were able to establish them, were the views of ordinary Russians in the unfamiliar postcommunist world in which they found themselves in the early and mid-1990s?

Boris Yel'tsin, almost invariably, emerged as the people's choice in all investigations of this kind. In November 1992, for instance, he had the support of 24 per cent of Muscovites, followed by Vice-President Alexander Rutskoi with 13 per cent. In the same survey, however, 32 per cent found it difficult to name anybody, and 44 per cent thought there was no politician who reflected their views.[199] In Russia-wide surveys in 1993 Yel'tsin again came out in front, followed by Vice-President Rutskoi, although his support was clearly waning and there were many more who found it difficult to reply or who refused to endorse any of the candidates suggested.[200] To what extent did Muscovites approve of Yel'tsin's activities as Russian President? Only 6 per cent did so 'entirely', 27 per cent did so 'on the whole', while 28 per cent 'on the whole did not' support him, and 25 per cent were entirely opposed. Yel'tsin's supporters, it emerged, were concentrated among the elderly, housewives and managers, and were fewest among the young, workers and students. Muscovites were also asked what impression Yel'tsin created upon them when making a public speech. The largest proportion (28 per cent) found him 'unpredictable', and there was strong support (59 per cent) for his decision not to seek a second term as Russian president.[201] Yel'tsin, nonetheless, was far ahead of all other political leaders in terms of popular support until at least early 1994, and his firm opposition to the Congress of People's Deputies appeared to have strengthened his popular standing although other leaders were sometimes regarded with a greater degree of trust or confidence.[202]

Yel'tsin's support was also much greater than that accorded to the Russian government, or to the Congress of People's Deputies. How much did people trust the government, Russians were asked in the summer of 1992? 'Not much', thought 42 per cent, and 'not at all', thought another 26 per cent.[203] There was little more support for the Congress of People's Deputies (by early 1993 its approval rating had fallen from 28 to 10 per cent), or for the smaller, working Supreme Soviet (by late 1992 its rating was down to 5 per cent).[204] So far as the governmental system as a whole was concerned, 33 per cent of Muscovites thought it had no positive features, and 49 per cent were unable to think of one; those who did mentioned qualities like 'democratism' and 'openness', but far larger numbers thought in terms of 'lack of concern for ordinary people', 'deception', 'betrayal of promises' or 'incompetence' (no wonder, perhaps, that the government had meanwhile engaged a public relations consultant).[205] Across Russia as a whole, in early 1993, 26 per cent trusted the president, but only 7 per cent trusted the government and 6 per cent the Supreme Soviet, and 50 per cent had no trust in any institutions of government whatsoever.[206] The question most Muscovites wanted to ask their deputy was a simple one: 'Do they know how people are living nowadays, and when will we stop living like this?'[207]

Ordinary Russians, reflecting this disappointment, were less and less likely to take part in politics in any form. In 1989, 13 per cent had 'always taken part in sociopolitical life'; by 1992 just 3 per cent did so. And if 11 per cent had no interest in politics in 1988, more than twice as many (25 per cent) had become alienated four years later.[208] Had 1991, in fact, seen the end of communist rule? A year later, 41 per cent thought it had and 41 per cent took the opposite view; two years later opinion was equally divided, with 43 per cent convinced that communist rule had ended and 45 per cent inclined to differ.[209] Was Russia more democratic, two years after the failure of the August coup? Just 18 per cent thought so; 28 per cent thought there was less democracy; and 44 per cent thought little had changed either way.[210] What *had* changed, Muscovites were asked in early 1994? People, for a start: a massive 82 per cent thought ordinary Russians were 'crueller' and 'nastier'. For most of those who replied (54 per cent), it had become more difficult to 'live happily and worthily'. For the same proportion, things were even worse than they had been in the communist period. As for vouchers, 7 per cent thought they had made ordinary Russians into property owners; for 54 per cent, they had made it easier for the 'majority to be robbed by the minority'. And as for the West, 23 per cent it wanted to help; a rather larger proportion, 45 per cent, thought the West wanted to 'weaken Russia in its own interests'.[211] What, in any case, did people call each other, in these postcommunist days? 'Comrades' was still the most popular form of address in late 1993, followed by 'friends', 'citizens' and then 'ladies and gentlement'; older people were particularly likely to address each other as 'comrades', while younger people were more likely to use 'ladies and gentlemen'.[212]

What, then, about the August coup? And had the democrats, installed in government shortly afterwards, justified the hopes that had been invested in them? As many as 9 per cent of Muscovites, a year later, 'remembered' having taken part in the defence of the White House[213] (surveys at the time in fact suggested there had been a 'stable core' of about 15,000, although a wider circle had played some part in the events[214]). Fewer, however, said they would defend the White House a second time, and whatever their personal role in August 1991 there were few that were satisfied with the direction events had taken a year later. More than half (55 per cent) thought their 'hopes and expectations from the victory over the Emergency Committee [had] not been met'; 19 per cent found it 'hard to say', and only 26 per cent were satisfied with subsequent developments.[215] Only 2 per cent were 'completely satisfied', in another survey; 29 per cent were 'largely satisfied'; but 40 per cent were 'largely' and 27 per cent 'entirely dissatisfied'.[216] So far as the coup leaders themselves were concerned, 24 per cent saw them as criminals, but twice as many (46 per cent) thought they were the 'victims of times and circumstances'.[217] Why had things gone wrong since those heady days? For most of those who responded, in a national poll, it was the incompetence of the democrats themselves (23 per cent); many also blamed corruption (20 per cent) or the 'communist legacy' (15 per cent). For 7 per cent it was, on the contrary, the rejection of socialism that was the source of their problems, and for a philosophical 6 per cent it was just the 'age-old backwardness' of their country.[218]

What about government policies, and particularly the rapid move towards market relations with their far-reaching implications? If there was a general response in the early and mid-1990s it was that there was no real alternative to a move in this direction, but that 'some other way' must be found to implement it.[219] Nearly half (47 per cent), in late 1992 and early 1993, accepted that the Russian economy could not develop further without the introduction of private enterprise; but few had personally felt any benefit from the privatisation of state property, and only 7 per cent of those who were asked were private owners or stockholders.[220] Who would actually gain from the form of privatisation the government had chosen? For 42 per cent it was 'black marketeers'; for 23 per cent, members of private cooperatives; and for 22 per cent, the mafia outside Russia altogether (only 13 per cent mentioned the working class).[221] The entire programme of privatisation was seen as 'just' by 11 per cent but as 'unjust' by 48 per cent.[222] Russians generally agreed that 'Marxism is bankrupt' (46 per cent in favour, 11 per cent against); but almost exactly the same proportion took issue with the proposition that 'Only capitalism can save our country' (19 per cent agreed, but 44 per cent took the opposite view). There was little support for the sale of state enterprises (28 per cent were in favour but 40 per cent opposed); and a clear majority preferred a society in which there was greater security for all its members (64 per cent) to a society in which the freedom of the individual was maximised (19 per cent in favour).[223]

What kind of system did they actually have, Russians were asked in 1993? More than half (51.6 per cent) had difficulty in replying; of those who did, 10.5 per cent thought they lived under capitalism, 9.2 per cent thought it was 'chaos, anarchy and rampant lawlessness', 7.9 per cent thought they were living under feudalism, and 4.5 per cent thought they were still living under socialism. An enterprising 0.3 per cent suggested 'slavery'.[224] What kind of society would Russians actually like to live in, they were asked in early 1994? There was strong support for democracy, at least in principle (50 per cent supported it, compared with 27 per cent who favoured a form of dictatorship and 23 per cent who had no particular preference). And there was little support for a return to communist rule (69 per cent were against, with 31 per cent in favour to varying degrees). There was still less support for a return to the monarchy (11 per cent in favour but 87 per cent against). But there was more substantial support for the idea of a strong leader, able to put policies into effect (63 per cent were in favour, 36 per cent against); and there was even more support for the idea of an independent 'government of experts', without party affiliation (71 per cent favoured this option). Only 9 per cent were satisfied with the results that had followed the change of political system; 42 per cent were disappointed and 26 per cent entirely dissatisfied, and the remaining 22 per cent had expected no positive results in the first place. Opinion, more generally, was almost equally divided when people were asked if the new system of government should be persevered with (49 per cent) or replaced by a system that might yield better and quicker results (51 per cent).[225]

Who actually benefitted from the system that had been established in post-communist Russia? For the largest group, in early 1993, it was a system that operated 'for its own benefit, a government of the rich'; 6 per cent thought it was a system that operated 'for the rich and entrepreneurs', and 5 per cent thought it operated 'for the mafia' or 'nobody' (a further 5 per cent). Only 9 per cent thought it was a system that operated 'for the people, for everyone'.[226] And what about the constitutional dispute of early 1993 between President and Congress? The most common reaction was that 'nothing of importance' had taken place (38 per cent); 24 per cent thought the differences between President and Congress had simply been maintained (24 per cent); and 18 per cent found it difficult to answer.[227] So far as the conflict itself was concerned, substantial majorities saw it as a 'struggle for power' or a matter of 'personal ambition' (71 per cent); only 4 per cent saw it as a fundamental disagreement on economic or (5 per cent) political principles.[228] When, in fact, had there been a government in Russia that took account of the needs of ordinary people? For most of those who were asked in late 1992 it was under Brezhnev (21 per cent) or under the tsarist system at the start of the century (14 per cent), but 44 per cent had no idea.[229]

Many Russians, in fact, had little belief that worldly changes of any kind would improve their position. Substantial proportions, certainly, took the view that it would be a long time before Russia emerged from its deep-seated crisis: 20 per cent thought it would take two or three years, but 21 per cent thought it would take at least five years, 23 per cent thought it would take a decade or more, and 7 per cent thought it would 'never' be accomplished.[230] Of much more immediate concern, in the early postcommunist years, were social problems like crime (37 per cent), anarchy or civil war (26 per cent), the death of family members (23 per cent), unemployment (21 per cent) or poverty (17 per cent). More than half of those who were asked, in a Russia-wide poll in early 1992, were seriously concerned about the future of their children in a society of this kind.[231] And a substantial proportion (38 per cent) thought it would be positively irresponsible to give birth to children in such circumstances.[232]

There was, by contrast, a very positive attitude towards religion or spirituality in general. The years of *perestroika*, it was found, had witnessed a 'rapid growth of religious sentiment and a no less rapid decline of atheism', with a particularly strong movement of the 'spiritual pendulum' in the late 1980s.[233] The great majority (64 per cent), in a 1991 Russian survey, thought a greater role for religion would be of benefit to the society, with only 6 per cent opposed; and still greater numbers (83.4 per cent) thought religious literature should be more widely available. What, more particularly, could religion offer to the members of a modern society? For more than half (52 per cent) it was 'moral norms', for 21 per cent it was an 'understanding of the meaning of life', and 9 per cent thought it could save their souls (some of those who described themselves as atheists took the same view).[234] Nearly half of those who were asked, in late 1992, thought there was life after death (31 per cent disagreed); if there was, 21 per cent hoped they would make it to heaven, with a further 20 per cent expecting to go to hell and 59 per cent unsure.[235] The miracles that were reported in the Bible 'definitely' or 'very probably' took place and there was 'certainly' a Devil, according to 62 per cent of those that were asked in the summer of 1993.[236] More generally, nearly three-quarters were strongly or very strongly of the view that they would 'like [their] life to have more of a spiritual content'.[237]

An interest in the spiritual was by no means confined to orthodox religions. Television news, by the early 1990s, had begun to incorporate an 'astrological forecast' for the following day, and several newspapers – including the trade union daily *Trud* – contained a similar column of daily advice. Bookstalls in underground stations reflected the same emphases: there was Nostradamus and Madame Blavatskaya, L. Ron Hubbard and the Bhagavad-Gita, Sigmund Freud and the Tibetan Book of the Dead, as well *Emmanuelle*, the Marquis de Sade and *How to Become a Millionaire in the CIS*. A very substantial proportion (71 per cent) believed astrology had a 'certain scientific basis';[238] it was for their benefit, presumably, that *Argumenty i fakty* reported that Yel'tsin, Karimov, Shevardnadze and Niyazov shared the star sign of Aquarius ('determined people, ambitious, able to get what they want whatever the price').[239] A large majority (64 per cent), according to the polls, were pleased that newspapers and journals had begun to give a greater degree of attention to mysticism, unorthodox medicine, extrasensory perception and matters of this kind. More than half thought those with a special gift could foretell the future (50.4 per cent) and cure the sick by means of hypnosis (62.5 per cent) or television psychotherapy (56.7 per cent). There were many more believers than disbelievers in omens, telepathy, horoscopes, or even flying saucers; and substantial minorities believed in witchcraft (35 per cent) or communication with the dead (11.3 per cent).[240]

Values of this kind left the Russian system in an uncertain state in the early postcommunist years. There were few, as we have seen, who wished to see the Communists return to power; at the same time, most of those who were asked outside the major cities preferred the Soviet system as it existed up to 1991 to the system that had been established under postcommunist auspices,[241] and the unreformed communist system was generally seen as preferable to the political or economic situation that was likely to exist in the near future (East Europeans took a very different and much more optimistic view).[242] So far as the short term was concerned, most Russians thought more order was required (83 per cent) rather than a greater degree of democracy (8 per cent);[243] yet there was a strong and widespread commitment to *glasnost'* and to the diffusion of power that had already occurred in the years of communist rule. This left considerable scope for political leadership, whose support was often crucial for the establishment and consolidation of democratic politics;[244] and yet the political elites were divided, their institutions were discredited, and none of them – including Yel'tsin – could count upon the committed support of a major political party. Other countries had made a successful transition to political democracy; and yet there were few of them that had done so against a background of falling living standards, in the absence of a developed 'civil society' of independent groups and associations, and without an extended experience of democratic rule. Russia, it had been argued in the late 1980s, needed to 'learn democracy';[245] the evidence of the early postcommunist years was that the educational process would be a difficult and extended one with no guarantee of a successful outcome.

Notes

1 From Brezhnev to Gorbachev

1 Calculated from *Narodnoe khozyaistvo SSSR za 70 let*. *Yubileinyi statisticheskii sbornik* (Moscow: Finansy i statistika, 1987), various pages.
2 A. A. Gromyko and B. N. Ponomarev, eds., *Istoriya vneshnei politiki SSSR 1917–1985*, 2 vols. (Moscow: Nauka, 1986), vol. 2, pp. 638–53.
3 *Narodnoe khozyaistvo SSSR za 70 let*, p. 640.
4 A. A. Gromyko and B. N. Ponomarev, eds., *Istoriya vneshnei politiki SSSR 1917–1980*, 2 vols. (Moscow: Nauka, 1981), vol. 2, p. 666. Gromyko expressed very similar views to the 24th Party Congress in 1971: see *XXIV S"ezd KPSS 30 marta – 9 aprelya 1971 goda. Stenograficheskii otchet*, 2 vols. (Moscow: Politizdat, 1971), vol. 1, p. 482.
5 *Vedomosti Verkhovnogo Soveta SSSR*, 1976, no. 19, item 318; *Pravda*, 7 May 1976, p. 1 (other leaders followed suit).
6 *Pravda*, 17 November 1977, p. 1.
7 *Vedomosti Verkhovnogo Soveta SSSR*, 1978, no. 8, art. 117.
8 *Pravda*, 22 April 1979, p. 1; *Pravda*, 26 April 1979, p. 2 (the recipient was Alexander Chakovsky).
9 V. V. Grishin in *Pravda*, 24 February 1981, p. 11; Yu. V. Aksyutin, comp., *L. I. Brezhnev: materialy k biografii* (Moscow: Politizdat, 1991), p. 276.
10 *Pravda*, 20 December 1981, p. 2.
11 *Pravda*, 8 December 1976, p. 2.
12 *Moscow News*, 11 September 1988, p. 8; Zhores Medvedev, *Andropov: His Life and Death*, rev. edn (Oxford: Blackwell, 1985), pp. 103–4.
13 Roy Medvedev in *Moscow News*, 11 September 1988, pp. 8–9. Another well-placed source, Georgii Arbatov, dates Brezhnev's serious illness from December 1974; after that he 'ruled' but did not govern. *Zvezda*, 1990, no. 9, p. 216. The memoirs of Brezhnev's doctor have now appeared: Yevgenii Chazov, *Zdorov'e i vlast'* (Moscow: Novosti, 1992).
14 Medvedev, *Andropov*, pp. 93–6. Tsvigun's obituary appeared in *Pravda*, 21 January 1982, p. 2.
15 Medvedev, *Andropov*, pp. 93–6.
16 *Pravda*, 24 August 1982, p. 2; *The Times*, 15 April 1983, p. 6. A purportedly authentic memoir is now available: Stanley Landau, *Galina Brezhnev and her Gypsy Lover* (London: Quartet, 1989).
17 *Pravda*, 12 November 1982, p. 1.

18 *Pravda*, 23 November 1982, pp. 1–2.
19 *Pravda*, 11 February 1984, p. 1. Andropov's doctor later reported that the General Secretary had read a lot although he had the use of only one eye, and he remained lucid even after his liver, lungs and kidneys had stopped functioning. *Moscow News*, 1991, no. 10, p. 10. On Andropov's career more generally, see Medvedev, *Andropov*, and Jonathan Steele and Eric Abraham, *Andropov in Power* (Oxford: Martin Robertson, 1983).
20 *Pravda*, 14 February 1984, p. 1.
21 *Pravda*, 16 February 1984, p. 1.
22 See for instance *The Observer* (London), 19 February 1984, p. 12; Medvedev, *Andropov*, p. 226.
23 *Pervaya sessiya Verkhovnogo Soveta SSSR (odinnadtsatyi sozyv) 11–12 aprelya 1984g. Stenograficheskii otchet* (Moscow: Izvestiya, 1984), pp. 38–42.
24 See particularly the film, 'Young Years on the Border', which was released in late 1984. *Pravda*, 1 December 1984, p. 4.
25 *Pravda*, 1 March 1985, p. 1.
26 *Trud*, 12 March 1985, p. 2.
27 *Trud*, 12 March 1985, p. 1; *The Times*, 13 March 1985, p. 6.
28 I owe this anecdote to Archie Brown.
29 *Istochnik*, 1993, no. 0, p. 74.
30 See Mark Zlotnik, 'Chernenko's program', *Problems of Communism*, vol. 31, no. 6 (November–December 1982), pp. 70–5. Chernenko's speech to people's controllers of October 1984 and his election address of February 1985 are especially relevant in this connection: *Pravda*, 6 October 1984, pp. 1–2, and 23 February 1985, pp. 1–2.
31 *Spravochnik partiinogo rabotnika*, issue 23 (Moscow: Politizdat, 1983), p. 6.
32 Ibid., p. 99.
33 *Spravochnik partiinogo rabotnika*, issue 24, 2 parts (Moscow: Politizdat, 1984), pt. 1, p. 9. Vorotnikov's subsequent appointment is in *Pravda*, 25 June 1983, p. 1.
34 *Spravochnik partiinogo rabotnika*, issue 24, pt. 1, p. 63.
35 His obituary appeared in *Pravda*, 22 December 1984, p. 1.
36 These biographical details have been drawn from *Sostav tsentral'nykh organov KPSS, izbrannykh XXVI s"ezdom partii* (Moscow: Politizdat, 1982), and *Izvestiya TsK KPSS*, 1989, no. 1, pp. 9–31.
37 *Pravda*, 18 December 1982, p. 2.
38 *Literaturnaya gazeta*, 18 May 1988, p. 11.
39 *Pravda*, 16 June 1983, p. 1. Medunov was expelled from the CPSU in March 1989: *Pravda*, 24 March 1989, p. 2.
40 *Izvestiya*, 9 November 1984, p. 6.
41 *Literaturnaya gazeta*, 18 May 1988, p. 11; *Dokumenty TsK VLKSM 1983* (Moscow: Molodaya gvardiya, 1984), p. 13. See further below, chapter 3.
42 Medvedev, *Andropov*, pp. 97–8. For subsequent developments see below, chapter 3.
43 *Vechernyaya Moskva*, 13 July 1984, p. 2.
44 See Radio Liberty reports RL 254 (28 June 1984), 324 (30 August 1984) and 457 (29 November 1984).

45 *Pravda*, 19 February 1983, p. 6; *Pravda*, 20 March 1983, p. 2.

46 *Vedomosti Verkhovnogo Soveta SSSR*, 1984, no. 36, item 627.

47 Radio Liberty report RL 92 (21 February 1983) and *Pravda*, 28 December 1982, p. 3.

48 *Spravochnik partiinogo rabotnika*, issue 24, pt. 2, pp. 95–9.

49 For instance, *Pravda*, 7 January 1985, p. 1. Gorbachev himself paid tribute in December 1984: *Izbrannye rechi i stat'i*, vol. 2, p. 92.

50 *Trud*, 31 August 1988, pp. 1–2. Stakhanov's obituary appeared in *Pravda*, 6 November 1977, p. 8.

51 *Pravda*, 6 May 1984, pp. 1–2; *Literaturnaya gazeta*, 13 June 1984, p. 2.

52 *The Times*, 4 September 1982, p. 4.

53 The new law on the Soviet frontier was published in *Pravda*, 26 November 1982, pp. 1–3; on postal restrictions see *The Times*, 19 November 1982, p. 8.

54 *The Times*, 22 May 1983, p. 7, and 20 January 1983, p. 5.

55 *The Times*, 5 May 1984, p. 5, and subsequent issues; *Vedomosti Verkhovnogo Soveta SSSR*, 1984, no. 22, item 380.

56 *Vedomosti Verkhovnogo Soveta SSSR*, 1984, no. 29, item 515, and 1983, no. 51, item 797.

57 *Keesing's Contemporary Archives 1984*, p. 33,120; *The Observer*, 10 February 1985, p. 19.

58 The first such report appeared in *Pravda*, 11 December 1982, p. 1. For a detailed analysis of such reports up to 1988, see John Lowenhardt, '*Politburo zasedaet*: reported and secret meetings of the Politburo of the CPSU', *Nordic Journal of Soviet and East European Studies*, vol. 5, no. 2 (1988), pp. 157–74.

59 *Pravda*, 1 February 1983, pp. 1–2, and 30 April 1984, pp. 1–2.

60 *Pravda*, 19 June 1983, pp. 1, 3. For a full study, see Darrell P. Slider, 'Reforming the workplace: the 1983 Soviet Law on Labour Collectives', *Soviet Studies*, vol. 37, no. 2 (1985), pp. 173–83.

61 *Pravda*, 21 October 1984, p. 2.

62 Ibid., 15 November 1983, p. 3, and 20 November 1983, p. 2. A commission on the reform of economic management was mentioned by Chernenko in *Pravda*, 6 October 1984, p. 2. A Council of Ministers commission on the Baikal–Amur railway was reported in *Pravda*, 11 December 1983, p. 3; a Presidium commission on agriculture is mentioned in *The Guardian*, 15 October 1984, p. 8.

63 *Pravda*, 15 June 1983, p. 3, and 16 June 1983, p. 3. (The centre came into existence in 1988.)

64 See *Plenum Tsentral'nogo komiteta KPSS 14–15 iyunya 1983 goda: Stenograficheskii otchet* (Moscow: Politizdat, 1983).

65 *Pravda*, 11 December 1982, p. 1, and 9 January 1983, p. 3.

66 *The Times*, 14 February 1983, p. 10.

67 Yu. V. Andropov, *Izbrannye rechi i stat'i*, 2nd edn (Moscow: Politizdat, 1983), pp. 245–6.

68 Ibid., pp. 286–7, 212 (November 1982).

69 K. U. Chernenko, *Narod i partiya ediny: Izbrannye rechi i stat'i* (Moscow: Politizdat, 1984), p. 246. Chernenko expressed similar sentiments in his 'Na uroven' trebovanii razvitogo sotsializma', *Kommunist*, 1984, no. 18, pp. 3–21.

70 See his articles in *Voprosy filosofii*, 1982, no. 10, pp. 16–29, and 1984, no. 2, pp. 116–23.

71 M. S. Gorbachev, *Izbrannye rechi i stat'i*, 6 vols (Moscow: Politizdat, 1987–9), vol. 3, p. 269. For further discussion of this important debate and related issues see Ernst Kux, 'Contradictions in Soviet socialism', *Problems of Communism*, vol. 33, no. 6 (November–December 1984), pp. 1–27; Rene Ahlberg, 'Konflikttheorie und Konflikterfahrung in der UdSSR', *Osteuropa*, vol. 35, no. 4 (April 1985), pp. 233–55; and Stephen White and Alex Pravda, eds., *Ideology and Soviet Politics* (London: Macmillan, 1988), chs. 1 and 5.

72 *Materialy vneocherednogo Plenuma TsK KPSS 11 marta 1985 goda* (Moscow: Politizdat, 1985), pp. 7–8.

73 Ibid., p. 9.

74 Ibid., pp. 15–16.

75 Zdeněk Mlynář, 'Il mio compagno di studi Mikhail Gorbaciov', *L'Unità*, 9 April 1985, p. 9. On his early dramatic training see Anatolii Sobchak, *Khozhdenie vo vlast'* (Moscow: Novosti, 1991), pp. 198–9.

76 The fullest available biography is Zhores Medvedev, *Gorbachev*, rev. edn (Oxford: Blackwell, 1988). See also Archie Brown, 'Gorbachev: new man in the Kremlin', *Problems of Communism*, vol. 34, no. 3 (May–June 1985), pp. 1–23; Christian Schmidt-Hauer, *Gorbachev: The Road to Power* (London: Tauris, 1986); Michel Tatu, *Gorbatchev. L'URSS va-t-elle changer?* (Paris: Le Centurion, 1987); Dev Murarka, *Gorbachev* (London: Hutchinson, 1988); Strobe Talbott, intr., *Mikhail S. Gorbachev: An Intimate Biography* (New York: Time, 1988); Dusko Doder and Louise Branson, *Gorbachev: Heretic in the Kremlin* (New York: Viking, 1990); Gert Ruge, *Gorbachev* (London: Chatto, 1991); and John Miller, *Mikhail Gorbachev and the End of Soviet Power* (London: Macmillan, 1993).

77 *Gorbachev: An Intimate Biography*, p. 63.

78 Ibid., pp. 198–202. There is now a Western biography: Urda Jürgens, *Raisa* (London: Weidenfeld and Nicolson, 1990).

79 *Izvestiya TsK KPSS*, 1989, no. 5, p. 59.

80 M. S. Gorbachev, *Izbrannye rechi i stat'i*, vol. 5 (Moscow: Politizdat, 1988), p. 486.

81 Gorbachev, *Izbrannye rechi i stat'i*, vol. 5, pp. 58–9.

82 *Izvestiya*, 24 March 1989, p. 3.

83 *Izvestiya TsK KPSS*, 1989, no. 5, pp. 57–60. On his baptism, see ibid., 1989, no. 8, p. 66; on his grandparents, see *Pravda*, 1 December 1990, p. 4. Raisa Gorbachev's experience of Stalinism is in her *Ya nadeyus'* (Moscow: Novosti, 1991), p. 27.

84 *Pravda*, 11 December 1984, pp. 1–2 (full text in Gorbachev, *Izbrannye rechi i stat'i*, vol. 2, pp. 75–108).

85 *Pravda*, 21 February 1985, p. 2 (full text in Gorbachev, *Izbrannye rechi i stat'i*, vol. 2, pp. 117–28).

86 Gorbachev, *Izbrannye rechi i stat'i*, vol. 2, pp. 152–67.

87 *Spravochnik partiinogo rabotnika*, issue 26 (Moscow: Politizdat, 1986), pp. 15–16.

88 Ibid., p. 38.

89 *Tret'ya sessiya Verkhovnogo Soveta SSSR (odinnadtsatyi sozyv) 2–3 iyulya 1985 goda: Stenograficheskii otchet* (Moscow: Izvestiya, 1985), pp. 8, 12.

90 *Vedomosti Verkhovnogo Soveta SSSR*, 1985, no. 48, item 907; *Spravochnik partiinogo rabotnika*, issue 26, p. 39.

91 *Spravochnik partiinogo rabotnika*, issue 27 (Moscow: Politizdat, 1987), p. 121.

92 These and other biographical details are taken from *Izvestiya TsK KPSS*, 1989, no. 1, pp. 9–31.

93 See Evan Mawdsley and Stephen White, 'Renewal and dead souls: the changing Soviet Central Committee', *British Journal of Political Science*, vol. 20, no. 4 (October 1990), p. 539.

94 Roy Medvedev in *Pravda*, 30 May 1989, p. 2.

95 *Spravochnik partiinogo rabotnika*, issue 28 (Moscow: Politizdat, 1988), p. 15; the circumstances of Kunaev's expulsion are set out in *Izvestiya TsK KPSS*, 1989, no. 2, p. 44.

96 *Partiinaya zhizn'*, 1987, no. 13, pp. 3–4.

97 *Kommunist*, 1988, no. 15, p. 3.

98 *Materialy plenuma Tsentral'nogo Komiteta KPSS 19–20 sentabrya 1989 goda* (Moscow: Politizdat, 1989), p. 6.

99 *Pravda*, 26 April 1989, p. 1.

100 *XIX vsesoyuznaya konferentsiya KPSS: Stenograficheskii otchet*, 2 vols. (Moscow: Politizdat, 1988), vol. 2, p. 143; Mawdsley and White, 'Renewal and dead souls', p. 542.

101 *Izvestiya TsK KPSS*, 1990, no. 8, p. 4. For the composition of the Central Committee up to the 28th Congress, see Evan Mawdsley, *The Central Committees of the CPSU since 1917* (Manchester: Lorton Papers, 1990) and the same author's *A Directory of CPSU Central Committee Members, 1917–1990* (Manchester: Lorton Papers, 1990).

102 *Materialy XXVIII s"ezda KPSS* (Moscow: Politizdat, 1990), p. 119, Rule 26.

103 *Materialy*, p. 120, Rule 28. For biographical details of the Politburo and Secretariat appointed in 1990 see *Izvestiya TsK KPSS*, 1990, no. 8, pp. 7–61.

104 *Izvestiya TsK KPSS* 1990, no. 8, p. 5 (where the number of entirely new members is erroneously given as 29).

105 A full listing of these and previous leadership appointments is available in Stephen White, *The Soviet Leadership: The Politburo, Secretariat and Orgburo of the CPSU 1919–1991* (Manchester: Lorton Papers, 1994).

106 *Kommunist*, 1988, no. 13, p. 11.

107 *Pravda*, 8 May 1989, p. 3, and 11 June 1989, p. 4. The Cabinet of Ministers was constituted in early 1991: the list of posts is in *Izvestiya*, 9 April 1991, p. 2.

108 Jyrki Iivonen, personal communication.

109 *Pravda*, 31 March 1989, p. 2.

110 Gorbachev, *Izbrannye rechi i stat'i*, vol. 2, p. 154.

111 Ibid., vol. 3, pp. 181–3.

112 *Pravda*, 26 June 1990, p. 2.

113 Ibid., 9 October 1990, p. 1.

114 Ibid., 16 November 1990, p. 3.

115 For a helpful evaluation of Gorbachev as leader see the discussion in *Soviet*

Economy by George Breslauer, Archie Brown, Jerry Hough, Peter Reddaway and others, conveniently reprinted in Ed Hewett and Victor Winston, eds., *Milestones of Glasnost and Perestroyka*, 2 vols. (Washington DC: Brookings, 1991).

116 See Mikhail Gorbachev, *The August Coup* (London: HarperCollins, 1991), p. 17. The treachery of Valerii Boldin, head of the President's own staff, was particularly hard to bear.

117 *Izvestiya*, 20 December 1990, p. 6.

118 *Komsomol'skaya pravda*, 3 August 1991, p. 3.

119 *Sovetskaya Rossiya*, 23 July 1991, p. 1

120 *Pravda*, 13 August 1991, p. 4 and *Izvestiya*, 16 August 1991, p. 2. Yakovlev expressed similar views in an interview on the same day for *Literaturnaya gazeta*, 28 August 1991, p. 2.

121 Anatolii Sobchak noted his 'complete surprise' in *Khozhdenie*, p. 275. Gorbachev may possibly have given reason to believe that he would support the introduction of a state of emergency (see for instance Amy Knight in *Problems of Communism*, vol. 40. no. 6 (November–December 1991), pp. 39–40); about 6 per cent of the Soviet public, according to opinion polls, saw him as the 'chief instigator' of the coup (*Argumenty i fakty*, 1991, no. 36, p. 1). A detailed chronology and documentation of the coup is available in *Putch. Khronika trevozhnykh dnei* (Moscow: Progress, 1991), and in *Avgust-91* (Moscow: Politizdat, 1991), which is more 'Gorbachevian' in tone; there are also two journalists' accounts, Martin Sixsmith, *Moscow Coup* (London: Simon and Schuster, 1991), and Giulietto Chiesa, *Cronaca del golpe rosso* (Milan: Baldini & Castoldi, 1991). See also Richard Sakwa, 'The revolution of 1991 in Russia: interpretations of the Moscow coup', *Coexistence*, vol. 29, no. 4 (December 1992), pp. 335–75, and Victoria Bonnell et al., *Russia at the Barricades: Eyewitness accounts of the August coup* (Armonk NY: Sharpe, 1993).

122 Gorbachev, *August Coup*, pp. 18–23.

123 *Izvestiya*, 20 August 1991, p. 1.

124 *Pravda*, 20 August 1991, pp. 1–2.

125 *Izvestiya*, 20 August 1991, p. 1.

126 Ibid.

127 *Izvestiya*, 29 August 1991, pp. 4, 8. Pavlov later admitted that he 'probably had a sip': ibid., 10 October 1991, p. 7.

128 *Putch*, pp. 19–20.

129 *Izvestiya*, 21 August 1991, pp. 1–2.

130 *Izvestiya*, 26 August 1991, p. 6 (whether an order was actually given to attack remains unclear: see Knight, p. 40).

131 On Luk'yanov as 'chief ideologist' see *Izvestiya*, 22 August 1991, p. 4; his arrest is reported in ibid., 2 September 1991, p. 1. Bessmertnykh's unconvincing press conference is in *Pravda*, 22 August 1991, p. 5.

132 *Pravda*, 23 August 1991, p. 2.

133 *Izvestiya*, 26 August 1991, p. 2.

134 *Rossiiskaya gazeta*, 27 August 1991, p. 3, and *Izvestiya*, 30 August 1991, p. 2.

135 *Izvestiya*, 25 December 1991, p. 1.

2 Democratising the political system

1 *Materialy XXVII s"ezda KPSS* (Moscow: Politizdat, 1986), p. 22.
2 *Vizit General'nogo Sekretarya TsK KPSS M. S. Gorbacheva v Pol'skuyu narod-nuyu Respubliku 11–14 iyulya 1988 goda* (Moscow: Politizdat, 1988), p. 15.
3 M. S. Gorbachev, *Izbrannye rechi i stat'i*, 6 vols. (Moscow: Politizdat, 1987–89), vol. 4, p. 215.
4 Ibid., p. 428.
5 *Materialy plenuma TsK KPSS 27–28 yanvarya 1987 goda* (Moscow: Politizdat, 1987), pp. 11–15, 24–5.
6 Gorbachev, *Izbrannye rechi i stat'i*, vol. 4, p. 31.
7 *Materialy plenuma TsK KPSS 25–26 iyunya 1987 goda* (Moscow: Politizdat, 1987), pp. 81–2.
8 Gorbachev, *Izbrannye rechi i stat'i*, vol. 5, pp. 410–13.
9 *Materialy XIX Vsesoyuznoi konferentsii Kommunisticheskoi partii Sovetskogo Soyuza 28 iyunya – 1 iyulya 1988 goda* (Moscow: Politizdat, 1988), pp. 35–7.
10 Ibid., p. 149. On the Conference itself, see Michel Tatu, 'The 19th Party Conference', *Problems of Communism*, vol. 38, nos. 3–4 (May–August 1988), pp. 1–15; Boris Meissner, 'Gorbatschow am "Rubikon"', *Osteuropa*, nos. 11 and 12 (1988), pp. 981–1,001 and 1,061–90; and Stephen White, 'Gorbachev, Gorbachevism and the Party Conference', in Walter Joyce *et al.*, eds., *Gorbachev and Gorbachevism* (London: Cass, 1989), pp. 127–60.
11 *Pravda*, 30 November 1988, p. 2.
12 *Materialy XXVII s"ezda KPSS*, pp. 56, 100, 140, 159.
13 *Spravochnik partiinogo rabotnika*, issue 27 (Moscow: Politizdat, 1987), pp. 627–44.
14 See Stephen White, 'Reforming the electoral system', in Joyce *et al.*, eds., *Gorbachev and Gorbachevism*, pp. 3–6, and on the 1977 discussion, G. I. Zlokazov, 'Konstitutsiya 1977 goda: "nesvoevremennye" mysli sovremen-nikov', *Voprosy istorii KPSS*, 1990, no. 10, p. 73.
15 *Materialy plenuma TsK 27–28 yanvarya 1987 goda*, pp. 25–30.
16 See Stephen White, 'Noncompetitive elections and national politics: the USSR Supreme Soviet elections of 1984', *Electoral Studies*, vol. 4, no. 3 (1985), p. 222.
17 *Moscow News*, 1989, no. 3, p. 8; Yu. Burtin, ed., *Pul's reform* (Moscow: Progress, 1989), p. 255.
18 *Izvestiya*, 10 February 1987, p. 1.
19 *Pravda*, 7 March 1984, p. 1.
20 See Rasma Karklins, 'Soviet elections revisited: voter abstention in comparative perspective', *American Political Science Review*, vol. 80, no. 2 (June 1986), p. 451.
21 Victor Zaslavsky and Robert Brym, 'The functions of elections in the USSR', *Soviet Studies*, vol. 30, no. 3 (July 1978), p. 366.
22 *Izvestiya*, 10 February 1987, p. 2.
23 Ibid., 5 July 1986, p. 2.
24 Ibid., 10 February 1987, p. 2.
25 Mark Ya. Azbel, *Refusenik: Trapped in the Soviet Union* (Boston: Houghton Mifflin, 1981), p. 154.

26 *Pravda*, 29 March 1987, p. 2.

27 See, for instance, the response in Karaganda reported in *Izvestiya*, 7 July 1987, p. 2.

28 *Sovetskaya Rossiya*, 11 October 1987, p. 2. For a full account, see Stephen White, 'Reforming the electoral system', in Joyce *et al.*, eds., *Gorbachev and Gorbachevism*, pp. 1–17; and Jeffrey Hahn, 'An experiment in competition: the 1987 elections to the local soviets', *Slavic Review*, vol. 47, no. 2 (Fall 1988), pp. 434–47. For a fuller discussion of electoral reform and of political change more generally, see Stephen White, Graeme Gill and Darrell Slider, *The Politics of Transition: Shaping a post-Soviet future* (Cambridge: Cambridge University Press, 1993).

29 *Materialy XIX Vsesoyuznoi konferentsii*, pp. 47–8.

30 Ibid., p. 120.

31 *Sovetskoe gosudarstvo i pravo*, 1988, no. 6, p. 59; *Izvestiya*, 26 October 1988, p. 3.

32 For the draft, see *Pravda*, 23 October 1988, p. 1–3; for the law as adopted, see *Pravda*, 4 December 1988, pp. 1–3.

33 Boris Strashun in *Izvestiya*, 30 January 1987, p. 3.

34 *Pravda*, 29 November 1988, p. 1.

35 *Materialy XIX Vsesoyuznoi konferentsii*, p. 35.

36 *Izvestiya*, 29 April 1988, p. 3.

37 *Pravda*, 23 November 1988, p. 2.

38 *Sovetskoe gosudarstvo i pravo*, 1988, no. 5, pp. 3–13.

39 Ibid., p. 11.

40 *Kommunist*, 1988, no. 8, pp. 28–36.

41 *Materialy XIX Vsesoyuznoi konferentsii*, pp. 43–55.

42 See *Pravda*, 2 July 1988, p. 10; 30 June 1988, p. 7; 1 July 1988, p. 10; 30 June 1988, p. 4; and 1 July 1988, p. 10.

43 See, for instance, *Pravda*, 1 July 1988, pp. 4, 5, 7, and 2 July 1988, pp. 5, 8.

44 *XIX Vsesoyuznaya konferentsiya Kommunisticheskoi partii Sovetskogo Soyuza 28 iyunya – 1 iyulya 1988 goda. Stenograficheskii otchet*, 2 vols. (Moscow: Politizdat, 1988), vol. 2, p. 71.

45 Ibid., vol. 1, pp. 245–6.

46 Ibid., vol. 1, p. 231.

47 For the draft, see *Izvestiya*, 22 October 1988, pp. 1–2; for the law as adopted, see *Pravda*, 3 December 1988, pp. 1–2.

48 *Kommunist*, 1988, no. 1, p. 6. For a fuller account, see Ronald J. Hill, 'Gorbachev and the CPSU', in Joyce *et al.*, eds, *Gorbachev and Gorbachevism*, pp. 18–34.

49 *Moscow News*, 19 June 1988, p. 2; *Voprosy istorii KPSS*, 1988, no. 6, p. 46.

50 *Voprosy istorii KPSS*, 1988, no. 6, p. 44; *Pravda*, 2 May 1988, pp. 1, 3.

51 See, for instance, *Kommunist*, 1988, no. 3, p. 36.

52 *Pravda*, 2 July 1988, p. 5.

53 *Kommunist*, 1988, no. 3, p. 37; *Partiinaya zhizn'*, 1988, no. 6, p. 28.

54 *Voprosy istorii KPSS*, 1988, no. 6, p. 44.

55 *Partiinaya zhizn'*, 1988, no. 10, p. 38, and no. 5, p. 41.

56 Ibid., 1988, no. 11, pp. 38–9.

57 *Moscow News*, 12 June 1988, p. 8; *Soviet Weekly*, 18 June 1988, p. 10.

58 *Moscow News*, 10 April 1988, p. 8.

59 *Kommunist*, 1988, no. 4, pp. 86–7; *Partiinaya zhizn'*, 1988, no. 9, p. 48.
60 See, for instance, *Kommunist*, 1988, no. 5, pp. 42–5.
61 *Moscow News*, 24 April 1988, p. 7.
62 *Pravda*, 1 July 1988, p. 7.
63 *Kommunist*, 1988, no. 5, p. 45.
64 *Voprosy istorii KPSS*, 1988, no. 6, p. 45; *Kommunist*, 1988, no. 5, p. 45.
65 *Kommunist*, 1988, no. 4, p. 85.
66 *Materialy XIX Vsesoyuznoi konferentsii*, pp. 70–3.
67 *XIX Vsesoyuznaya konferentsiya*, vol. 2, pp. 143–4.
68 *Pravda*, 10 February 1987, p. 2.
69 Ibid., 1 October 1988, p. 1; the membership is listed in *Pravda*, 29 November 1988, pp. 1–2.
70 *Izvestiya TsK KPSS*, 1989, no. 1, pp. 81–91.
71 *Pravda*, 10 February 1989, p. 3.
72 The plenum was reported in full in *Pravda*, 6–8 February 1990; Gorbachev's speech was in *Pravda*, 6 February 1990, pp. 1–2.
73 Ibid., 24 October 1988, p. 2.
74 See *Vedomosti Verkhovnogo Soveta SSSR*, 1987, no. 26, items 388 and 387.
75 Mikhail Gorbachev, *Perestroika* (London: Collins, 1987), pp. 105–9.
76 *Pravda*, 11 May 1988, p. 5; for a more elaborated discussion, see V. Kudryavtsev and E. Lukasheva, 'Sotsialisticheskoe pravovoe gosudarstvo', *Kommunist*, 1988, no. 11, pp. 44–55. The term was also used by V. Savitsky in *Sovetskoe gosudarstvo i pravo*, 1987, no. 9, p. 34; Savitsky had been urging the adoption of this term for about ten years (Nicholas Lampert, personal communication).
77 *Tezisy Tsentral'nogo Komiteta KPSS k XIX Vsesoyuznoi partiinoi konferentsii* (Moscow: Politizdat, 1988).
78 *Materialy XIX Vsesoyuznoi konferentsii*, pp. 145–8.
79 *Pravda*, 30 November 1988, p. 3. On these changes see W. E. Butler, 'Legal Reform in the Soviet Union', *Harrison Institute Forum*, vol. 1, no. 9 (September 1988), and Nicholas Lampert, 'The socialist legal state', in Martin McCauley, ed., *Gorbachev and Perestroika* (London: Macmillan, 1990).
80 *Izvestiya*, 19 July 1991, pp. 1–2; *Pravda*, 16 July 1989, p. 2. For a discussion of these changes, see W. E. Butler and Ian Dennis, eds., 'Criminal law reform: Anglo–Soviet perspectives', a special issue of *Coexistence*, vol. 28, no. 1 (March 1991).
81 *Pravda*, 7 May 1989, p. 3; ibid., 12 September 1990, p. 2 (public relations department); ibid., 15 July 1990, p. 2 (KGB academy); and *Soviet Weekly*, 10 January 1991, p. 4.
82 See, for instance, *Pravda*, 23 January 1988, p. 3.
83 *Literaturnaya gazeta*, 20 January 1988, p. 13.
84 Gorbachev, *Izbrannye rechi i stat'i*, vol. 3, pp. 232–3.
85 *Pravda*, 20 November 1988, p. 3; *Izvestiya*, 28 December 1988, p. 3.
86 *Izvestiya*, 19 August 1988, p. 2, and 6 December 1988, p. 6.
87 *Pravda*, 25 February 1989, p. 2, and 11 January 1989, p. 1.
88 Ibid., 12 June 1990, p. 4, and 17 June 1990, p. 1.
89 See *Izvestiya*, 28 September 1991, p. 2 (League); ibid., 18 January 1992, p. 2

(Insurance Union) and p. 1 (Union of Industrialists). The most important workers' organisations in the early 1990s were the United Workers' Front, the Confederation of Labour and the Union of Labour Collectives: see L. A. Gordon, 'Rabochee dvizhenie v poslesotsialisticheskoi perspektive', *Sotsiologicheskie issledovaniya*, 1991, no. 11, pp. 3–17.

90 For much of what follows I am indebted to the admirable account by Vladimir Brovkin, 'Revolution from below: informal political associations in Russia, 1988–89', *Soviet Studies*, vol. 42, no. 2 (April 1990), pp. 233–57. See also Judith Sedaitis and Jim Butterfield, eds., *Perestroika from Below: Social Movements in the Soviet Union* (Boulder, CO: Westview, 1991), and Geoffrey Hosking, Jonathan Aves and Peter Duncan, *The Road to Post-Communism: New Political Movements in the USSR, 1985–1991* (London: Pinter, 1992).

91 *Moscow News*, 1990, no. 7, p. 9; *Pravda*, 13 September 1990, p. 2. See more generally 'Anatomiya neformal'nogo dvizheniya', *Izvestiya TsK KPSS*, 1990, no. 4, pp. 150–6, V. N. Berezovsky and N. I. Krotov, comps., *Neformal'-naya Rossiya* (Moscow: Molodaya gvardiya, 1990) and its expanded successor, V. N. Berezovsky *et al.*, eds., *Rossiya: partii, assotsiatsii, soyuzy, kluby*, 2 vols. (Moscow: RAU-Press, 1991).

92 *Izvestiya*, 26 August 1988, p. 3; *Moscow News*, 1989, no. 6, p. 4.

93 See *Pravda*, 11 November 1988, p. 3.

94 See chapter 5 below.

95 Jonathan Aves, 'The Democratic Union: a Soviet opposition party?', *Slovo*, vol. 1, no. 2 (November 1988), pp. 92–8; *Pravda*, 14 April 1989, p. 3.

96 See, for instance, *Izvestiya*, 3 June 1987, p. 3 and 27 February 1988, p. 3; *Sovetskaya Rossiya*, 17 July 1987, p. 4.

97 *Pravda*, 10 February 1989, p. 1, and 27 December 1987, p. 1.

98 For a full account of these elections, see Stephen White, 'The Soviet elections of 1989: from acclamation to limited choice', *Coexistence*, vol. 28, no. 4 (December 1991) pp. 513–39, and (for a Soviet view) V. A. Kolosov *et al.*, *Vesna 89. Geografiya i anatomiya parlamentskikh vyborov* (Moscow: Progress, 1990).

99 On this discussion, see Stephen White, '"Democratisation" in the USSR', *Soviet Studies*, vol. 42, no. 1 (January 1990), pp. 3–24.

100 *Izvestiya*, 22 November 1988, p. 2.

101 Ibid., 11 February 1989, p. 1; *Pravda*, 27 February 1989, p. 2. *Sovetskoe gosudarstvo i pravo*, 1989, no. 7, p. 16, also mentions the Tomsk region.

102 *Pravda*, 17 January 1989, p. 1

103 *Sovetskaya Rossiya*, 20 January 1989, p. 2.

104 *Materialy plenuma TsK KPSS 10 yanvarya 1989 goda* (Moscow: Politizdat, 1989), pp. 13–14, 16–29.

105 *Pravda*, 22 January 1989, p. 1.

106 *Literaturnaya gazeta*, 29 March 1989, p. 1.

107 *Izvestiya*, 22 January 1989, p. 5.

108 Ibid., 21 January 1989, p. 2; *Soviet Weekly*, 11 February 1989, p. 4.

109 *Izvestiya*, 27 December 1988, p. 2, and 23 March 1989, p. 1.

110 Ibid., 7 February 1989, p. 1.

111 *Pravda*, 21 March 1989, p. 2.

112 *Izvestiya*, 28 January 1989, p. 3.

113 *Novoe vremya*, 1989, no. 5, p. 25.

114 *Izvestiya*, 19 January 1989, p. 6; *Soviet Weekly*, 18 March 1989, p. 15.

115 *Pravda*, 11 February 1989, p. 2; *Soviet Weekly*, 18 February 1989, p. 6.

116 *Soviet Weekly*, 25 February 1989, p. 6, and 18 March 1989, p. 6.

117 Central TV, 23 March 1989; *Sovetskaya Rossiya*, 26 March 1989, p. 2.

118 *Izvestiya* 19 February 1989, p. 2.

119 *Pravda*, 15 February 1989, p. 1.

120 *Izvestiya*, 3 February 1989, p. 2.

121 *Pravda*, 19 February 1989, p. 1.

122 *Novoe vremya*, 1989, no. 11, p. 25.

123 V. A. Levansky *et al.*, 'Izbiratel'naya kampaniya po vyboram narodnykh deputatov SSSR 1989 g. (Opyt sotsiologicheskogo issledovaniya)', *Sovetskoe gosudarstvo i pravo*, 1989, no. 7, p. 15.

124 *Sovetskaya Estoniya*, 19 February 1989, p. 2.

125 *Izvestiya*, 23 February 1989, p. 2; *Independent*, 13 March 1989, p. 12.

126 *Pravda*, 17 March 1989, p. 1; *Izvestiya TsK KPSS*, 1989, no. 2, pp. 209–87.

127 *Sovetskaya Estoniya*, 19 February 1989, p. 2.

128 *Pravda*, 12 March 1989, p. 1; *Sovetskaya kul'tura*, 14 March 1989, p. 1.

129 *Literaturnaya gazeta*, 29 March 1989, p. 1.

130 Ibid., 29 March 1989, p. 2.

131 *Sovetskaya Rossiya*, 23 March 1989, p. 1, and *Izvestiya*, 23 March 1989, p. 1.

132 *Pravda*, 22 April 1989, p. 3. Sakharov became an active and outspoken parliamentarian but died in December 1989.

133 *Izvestiya*, 16 March 1989, p. 1.

134 The successful candidates were entrusted with a party mandate to guide them in their actions: see *Pravda*, 19 March 1989, pp. 1–2.

135 Ibid., 28 March 1989, p. 1.

136 *Sovetskaya kul'tura*, 28 March 1989, p. 1.

137 *Izvestiya*, 5 April 1989, p. 1.

138 Ibid.

139 *Pravda*, 1 April 1989, p. 1, and *Izvestiya*, 1 April 1989, p. 1; *Izvestiya*, 30 March 1989, p. 1.

140 *Argumenty i fakty*, 1989, no. 21, p. 8; a full list of all the deputies elected appeared in *Izvestiya*, 5 April 1989, pp. 2–12.

141 See *Moskovskaya pravda*, 28 March 1989, p. 2.

142 *Izvestiya*, 6 May 1989, p. 3 (based on 2,044 deputies); 85.3 per cent of all candidates were party members. On the work of the newly established representative institutions see Robert T. Huber and Donald R. Kelley, eds., *Perestroika-Era Politics. The New Soviet Legislature and Gorbachev's Political Reforms* (Boulder CO: Westview, 1991).

143 *Vestnik statistiki*, 1990, no. 1, p. 47.

144 *Moscow News*, 1989, no. 10, p. 14.

145 *Izvestiya*, 6 May 1989, p. 3.

146 *Sovetskaya Rossiya*, 5 April 1989, p. 2 (the offer was declined; ibid., 7 April 1989, p. 3).

147 See, for instance, *Pravda*, 27 April 1989, pp. 4 (Saikin), 6 (Vezirov) and 7 (Mel'nikov).
148 *Izvestiya*, 15 April 1989, p. 1 (re-runs) and 20 May 1989, p. 1 (repeat elections).
149 *Sovetskaya kul'tura*, 8 April 1989, cited in *Izvestiya*, 6 May 1989, p. 3.
150 *Pravda*, 26 May 1989, pp. 1, 4.
151 Ibid., 30 May 1989, p. 1.
152 Ibid., 2 June 1989, p. 2.
153 Ibid.
154 Ibid., 9 June 1989, p. 4.
155 Ibid., 2 June 1989, pp. 3–4.
156 Ibid., 5 June 1989, pp. 2–3; *Guardian*, 10 June 1989, p. 24.
157 Ibid., 5 June 1989, p. 4.
158 Ibid., 11 June 1989, p. 2.
159 Ibid., 3 June 1989, p. 4.
160 *Vedomosti S"ezda narodnykh deputatov SSSR i Verkhovnogo Soveta SSSR*, 1989, no. 1, items 23, 16 and 14.
161 *Pravda*, 30 May 1989, p. 2. The full list of deputies elected to the Supreme Soviet is in *Vedomosti*, 1989, no. 1, item 12.
162 *Pravda*, 28 May 1989, p. 1.
163 *Vedomosti*, 1989, no. 1, items 33, 36 and 40.
164 *Pravda*, 1 December 1989, p. 3, and 20 July 1989, p. 2.
165 Ibid., 27 June 1989, p. 1; *Soviet Weekly*, 12 August 1989, p. 4.
166 *Pravda*, 20 July 1989, p. 2, and 31 July 1989, p. 2.
167 Ibid., 11 June 1989, p. 4.
168 Anatolii Sobchak, *Khozhdenie vo vlast'* (Moscow: Novosti, 1991), p. 66.
169 *Pravda*, 18 July 1989, p. 2. The full list of ministerial posts was published in ibid., 6 July 1989, p. 1.
170 Sobchak, *Khozhdenie*, pp. 41, 68.
171 *Sovety narodnykh deputatov*, 1989, no. 5, pp. 11–13. The representation of social organisations was also defended by V. E. Guliev: *Kommunist*, 1989, no. 18, pp. 43–4.
172 See for instance *Sovety narodnykh deputatov*, 1989, no. 11, p. 62. S. Avak'yan took the same view in *Vestnik MGU: Pravo*, 1989, no. 6, p. 9.
173 *Obshchestvennoe mnenie v tsifrakh*, no. 2 (September 1989), pp. 4–8. In a separate poll sponsored by *Sovetskaya Rossiya* and the Institute of Sociology of the USSR Academy of Sciences, 45 per cent were opposed to selection conferences: *Sovetskoe gosudarstvo i pravo*, 1990, no. 6, p. 34. A Moscow poll reported in *Sotsiologicheskie issledovaniya*, 1989, no. 5, p. 34, found 46 per cent opposed and 20 per cent in favour; 39 per cent were opposed to the allocation of seats to social organisations and only 19 per cent were in favour.
174 *Izvestiya*, 24 October 1989, p. 2.
175 Ibid., 17 December 1989, pp. 2–3; the text of the legislation is in ibid., 23 December 1989, pp. 1, 4.
176 Ibid., 7 March 1990, p. 2 (Kazakhstan); ibid., 15 February 1990, p. 1 (Belorussia); *Moscow News*, 1989, no. 45, p. 10 (Ukraine).
177 *Izvestiya*, 17 December 1989, p. 2.

178 An 'elector's calendar' appeared in *Pravda*, 4 December 1989, p. 3. Other variations in republican provision included multimember as well as single member constituencies, different definitions of the franchise, and the representation of military servicemen. For a general review, see *Narodnyi deputat*, 1990, no. 1, pp. 61–7, *Sovetskoe gosudarstvo i pravo*, 1990, no. 6, pp. 29–39, Darrell Slider, 'The Soviet Union', *Electoral Studies*, vol. 9, no. 4 (December 1990), pp. 295–302, and Commission on Security and Cooperation in Europe, *Elections in the Baltic States and Soviet Republics* (Washington DC: US Government Printing Office, 1990).

179 *Pravda*, 30 March 1990, p. 2; *Soviet Weekly*, 7 June 1990, p. 14. For a general discussion of the republican elections in the Baltic see Rein Taagepera, 'Baltic elections, February–April 1990', *Electoral Studies*, vol. 9, no. 4 (December 1990), pp. 303–11.

180 *Izvestiya*, 26 February 1990, p. 1; *Pravda*, 25 February 1990, p. 3; *Soviet Weekly*, 7 June 1990, p. 14.

181 *Pravda*, 20 March 1990, p. 4; *Moscow News*, 1990, no. 12, p. 4. On the controversial question of residence requirements in the Baltic republics see *Narodnyi deputat*, 1990, no. 1, pp. 63–4, and *Sovetskoe gosudarstvo i pravo*, 1990, no. 6, p. 30.

182 *Pravda*, 4 March 1990, p. 2; ibid., 23 January 1990, p. 1.

183 *Izvestiya*, 5 March 1990, p. 1, and 6 March 1990, p. 4.

184 *Pravda*, 14 March 1990, p. 2; *Izvestiya*, 5 March 1990, p. 2.

185 *Pravda*, 26 March 1990, p. 2; *Izvestiya*, 19 March 1990, p. 1.

186 *Pravda*, 26 March 1990, p. 2.

187 *Izvestiya*, 29 May 1990, p. 1.

188 Ibid., 21 April 1990, p. 4; *Moskovskie novosti*, 1990, no. 22, p. 5.

189 Yel'tsin announced his resignation at the 28th Party Congress: *Pravda*, 13 July 1990, p. 3. Popov and Sobchak communicated their decision to a press conference: ibid., 14 July 1990, p. 4.

190 Ibid., 14 March 1990, p. 2.

191 *Izvestiya*, 19 March 1990, p. 1.

192 Ibid.

193 *Moscow News*, 1990, no. 12, p. 4, and no. 10, p. 5.

194 *Pravda*, 4 March 1990, p. 2.

195 Ibid., 14 March 1990, p. 2.

196 Ibid., 22 March 1990, p. 3.

197 *Izvestiya*, 4 June 1990, p. 2.

198 *Pravda*, 14 November 1990, p. 2 (results); ibid., 15 November 1990, p. 2.

199 Ibid., 16 February 1990, p. 1.

200 Ibid., 26 February 1990, p. 1; *Izvestiya*, 1 March 1990, p. 2.

201 *Pravda*, 26 February 1990, p. 1; *Narodnyi deputat*, 1990, no. 2, p. 33

202 *Pravda*, 26 March 1990, p. 2.

203 *Glasnost'*, 1991, no. 12, p. 2; *Pravda*, 28 February 1991, p. 2 (republican level).

204 This distinction is made in *Pravda*, 16 January 1991, p. 5.

205 For the law see *Izvestiya*, 16 October 1990, pp. 1–2. See also more generally Vera Tolz, *The USSR's Emerging Multiparty System* (London: Praeger, 1991); Stephen White with Peter Lentini, 'The USSR', in Bogdan Szajkowski, ed.,

New Political Parties of Eastern Europe and the Soviet Union (London: Longman, 1991); M. A. Babkina, ed., *New Political Parties and Movements in the Soviet Union* (Commack NY: Nova, 1991); V. Pribylovskii, comp., *Dictionary of Political Parties and Organizations in Russia* (Moscow: Postfactum, 1992); and V. N. Berezovsky et al., eds., *Rossiya: partii, assotsiatsii, soyuzy, kluby*, 10 vols (Moscow: RAU Press, 1992–3). Two useful short discussions are B. Slavin, 'U istokov mnogopartiinosti', *Sotsial'no-politicheskie nauki*, 1990, no. 8, pp. 33–44, and Slavin and V. Davydov, 'Stanovlenie mnogopartiinosti', *Partiinaya zhizn'*, 1991, no. 18, pp. 6–16.

206 See Berezovsky *et al.*, eds., *Rossiya*.
207 Ibid., 30 March 1991, p. 1, and 14 October 1991, p. 1.
208 *Izvestiya*, 13 August 1991, p. 4.
209 *Delovaya zhizn'*, 1991, no. 24, p. 52.
210 Radio Free Europe/Radio Liberty *Report on the USSR*, vol. 3, no. 46 (15 November 1991), p. 46.
211 *Izvestiya*, 12 February 1992, p. 3.
212 *Delovaya zhizn'*, 1991, no. 24, pp. 42–4. On the Liberal Democratic Party see *Sotsial'no-politicheskie nauki*, 1991, no. 1, pp. 97–9, and for its documents *Liberal'no-demokraticheskaya partiya. Dokumenty i materialy* (Moscow: Politizdat, 1991).
213 *Izvestiya TsK KPSS*, 1990, no. 12, pp. 104–5; see also the reports in *Pravda*, 22 October 1990, p. 2, and 23 October 1990, p. 2.
214 *Kuranty*, 12 November 1991, p. 1; similarly *Pravda*, 11 November 1991, p. 2, and 12 December 1991, p. 1.
215 For a general discussion see *Sotsial'no-politicheskie nauki*, 1990, no. 11, pp. 66–74.
216 *Moscow News*, 1991, no. 50, p. 9.
217 *Izvestiya TsK KPSS*, 1990, no. 8, pp. 153–4. Reports of the founding congress appeared in *Sovetskaya kul'tura*, 2 June 1990, p. 2, and *Izvestiya*, 26 May 1990, p. 2. The Party's 'Declaration' is in *Voprosy ekonomiki*, 1990, no. 8, pp. 152–4.
218 *Izvestiya*, 26 April 1991, p. 4.
219 *Izvestiya* 17 December 1991, p. 1; *Kuranty*, 17 December 1991, pp. 1, 4.
220 On the Socialists and Social Democrats see *Sotsial'no-politicheskie nauki*, 1990, no. 12, pp. 88–95, and 1991, no. 5, pp. 97–105. On the Greens see ibid., 1991, no. 8, pp. 94–7, and on the anarchists, ibid., 1991, no. 10, pp. 84–91.
221 *Izvestiya TsK KPSS*, 1990, no. 12, p. 101.
222 *Glasnost'*, 1991, no. 12, p. 2.
223 See respectively *Soviet Weekly*, 21 November 1991, p. 2, and *Izvestiya*, 5 September 1991, p. 1; *Pravda*, 25 November 1991, p. 2; ibid., 17 December 1991, p. 2; ibid., 5 December 1991, p. 2; and *Izvestiya*, 5 February 1992, p. 2.
224 *Pravda*, 28 October 1991, p. 2, and (for its membership) *Moskovskie novosti*, 1992, no. 4, p. 8.
225 *Pravda*, 13 April 1990, p. 1.
226 Radio Free Europe/Radio Liberty *Research Report*, vol. 1, no. 4 (26 January 1992), p. 3.
227 *Izvestiya*, 3 February 1992, p. 2; on *Pamyat'*, see the special issue of *Nationalities Papers*, vol. 19, no. 2 (Fall 1991).

228 Sobchak, *Khozhdenie*, p. 163.
229 Fedor Burlatsky quoted in Dusko Doder and Louise Branson, *Gorbachev: Heretic in the Kremlin* (New York: Viking, 1990), pp. 279–80.
230 *Sovetskoe gosudarstvo i pravo*, 1990, no. 7, pp. 3–4.
231 A. A. Protashchik, ed., *Cherez ternii* (Moscow: Progress, 1989), p. 702; A. D. Sakharov, *Trevoga i nadezhda* (Moscow: Interverso, 1990), pp. 272, 274. Proposals for a 'firm hand' at the top in any transition from totalitarian to democratic rule had a similar logic: A. Migranyan in *Novyi mir*, 1990, no. 7, pp. 166–84, and Migranyan and I. Klyamkin in *Literaturnaya gazeta*, 16 August 1989, p. 10.
232 *Materialy plenuma Tsentral'nogo Komiteta KPSS 5–7 fevralya 1990 g.* (Moscow: Politizdat, 1990), p. 19.
233 *Vneocherednoi tretii s"ezd narodnykh deputatov SSSR 12–15 marta 1990 g. Stenograficheskii otchet*, 3 vols. (Moscow: Izvestiya 1990), vol. 1, pp. 17–18.
234 Ibid., pp. 45–6 (Afanas'ev), 126 (N. T. Dabizha), 58–61 (Gumbaridze, one of those who advanced republican arguments), and 395–6 (vote).
235 Ibid., p. 193.
236 Ibid., vol. 3, p. 55.
237 Ibid., p. 178.
238 Ibid., vol. 2, pp. 385–6.
239 For the text of the law see ibid., vol. 3, pp. 192–207.
240 *Izvestiya*, 26 September 1990, p. 1.
241 *Pravda*, 28 December 1990, p. 2.
242 For the text of the constitutional changes see *Sovetskaya Rossiya*, 27 December 1990, pp. 1, 3.
243 *Pravda*, 16 December 1990, p. 2.
244 Ibid., 1 December 1990, p. 4.
245 *Izvestiya*, 6 April 1991, p. 1.
246 For the decree, see *Pravda*, 26 July 1990, p. 1; for the rejection, see ibid., 3 August 1990, p. 2.
247 Ibid., 2 February 1991, p. 4.
248 Ibid., 2 February 1991, p. 4, 1 February 1991, p. 2, and 2 February 1991, p. 4.
249 *Izvestiya*, 29 May 1989, p. 8.
250 Ibid., 31 May 1989, p. 7, and 29 May 1989, p. 8.
251 *Pravda*, 20 July 1989, p. 2.
252 *Izvestiya*, 22 April 1989, p. 6.
253 Levansky, 'Izbiratel'naya kampaniya', p. 25. In a related poll in Moscow, 34 per cent were doubtful at the time of its adoption if the new electoral law would introduce significant changes; by the time of the campaign, however, the proportion of sceptics had fallen to 10–14 per cent, and after the vote itself only 8 per cent of respondents claimed to see no improvement in the new arrangements. See *Sotsiologicheskie issledovaniya*, 1989, no. 5, p. 33.
254 *Izvestiya*, 12 May 1989, p. 3.
255 Ibid., 15 April 1989, p. 1, and 20 May 1989, p. 1.
256 *Sovetskaya kul'tura*, 28 March 1989, p. 1.
257 *Izvestiya*, 27 March 1989, p. 2, and 12 May 1989, p. 7.

258 Levansky, 'Izbiratel'naya kampaniya', p. 16.
259 *Izvestiya*, 28 March 1989, p. 1; *Leningradskaya pravda*, 27 March 1989, p. 1; *Izvestiya*, 27 March 1989, p. 2.
260 *Pravda*, 27 March 1989, p. 1; *Sovetskaya Rossiya*, 27 March 1989, p. 2 (similarly *Argumenty i fakty*, 1989, no. 13, p. 1). For the text of the union treaty, see *Pravda*, 9 March 1991, p. 3.
261 *Izvestiya*, 23 March 1992, p. 3.
262 *Pravda*, 4 February 1991, p. 4.
263 Protashchik, ed., *Cherez ternii*, p. 777, and V. Yadov in *Kommunist*, 1991, no. 6, p. 69 ('general distrust'). For other comparable findings, see B. E. Boikov et al., *Obshchestvennoe soznanie i perestroika* (Moscow: Politizdat, 1990), pp. 154, 268–9.
264 *Pravda*, 31 March 1989, p. 1.
265 *Sotsiologicheskie issledovaniya*, 1988, no. 5, p. 11; *Pravda*, 2 August 1988, p. 1. The term 'learning democracy' comes from Burlatsky, *Pravda*, 18 July 1987, p. 3.
266 *Moskovskaya pravda*, 21 March 1989, p. 1; *Argumenty i fakty*, 1989, no. 27, p. 4.
267 See *Pravda*, 15 January 1990, p. 2, and 6 February 1990, pp. 1–2.

3   *Glasnost'* and public life

1 The historical background is provided in Raymond Hutchings, *Soviet Secrecy and Non-Secrecy* (London: Macmillan, 1987).
2 Zdeněk Mlynář, *Night Frost in Prague* (London: Hurst, 1980), p. 239.
3 M. S. Gorbachev, *Izbrannye rechi i stat'i*, 6 vols. (Moscow: Politizdat, 1987–89), vol. 2, p. 95.
4 Ibid., p. 131.
5 Mikhail Gorbachev, *Perestroika* (London: Collins, 1987), p. 75. Very similar sentiments were expressed to a congress of shockworkers in September 1985: Gorbachev, *Izbrannye rechi i stat'i*, vol. 2, p. 433.
6 *Sovetskaya Rossiya*, 24 November 1985, p. 1.
7 Ibid.
8 Ibid., 5 January 1986, p. 3.
9 *Sovetskaya kul'tura*, 21 May 1987, p. 6.
10 *Izvestiya*, 22 December 1988, p. 5.
11 *Sovetskaya Rossiya*, 24 November 1985, p. 1.
12 Ithiel de Sola Pool *et al.*, eds., *Handbook of Communication* (Chicago: Rand McNally, 1973), p. 479; *Independent*, 23 January 1987, p. 8 (BBC); David Wedgwood Benn, *Persuasion and Soviet Politics* (Oxford: Blackwell, 1989), p. 198.
13 *Sovetskaya Rossiya*, 5 January 1986, p. 3.
14 *Izvestiya*, 19 June 1989, p. 5.
15 *Pravda*, 6 February 1987, pp. 2–3. Zaslavskaya expressed very similar views in *Sotsiologicheskie issledovaniya*, 1987, no. 2, pp. 3–15.
16 Gorbachev, *Izbrannye rechi i stat'i*, vol. 3, p. 181.
17 *Pravda*, 19 December 1986, p. 3.
18 Gorbachev, *Izbrannye rechi i stat'i*, vol. 5, p. 408.

19 *Pravda*, 3 April 1988, p. 6; Medvedev in *Rabochii klass i sovremennyi mir*, 1988, no. 6, p. 155.

20 K. T. Mazurov as reported in *Voprosy istorii KPSS*, 1989, no. 10, p. 18.

21 *Nedelya*, 1988, no. 29, pp. 14–15.

22 *Literaturnaya gazeta*, 18 May 1988, p. 13.

23 *Pravda*, 31 December 1988, p. 3. Churbanov was subsequently stripped of his state honours: see *Izvestiya*, 25 July 1989, p. 8.

24 *Pravda*, 21 July 1988, p. 6; *Izvestiya*, 25 July 1989, p. 8.

25 *Pravda*, 7 January 1988, p. 1.

26 Ibid., 30 December 1988, p. 2 (Chernenko was similarly treated); *Izvestiya*, 29 September 1989, p. 3 (Order of Victory); ibid., 7 February 1991, p. 1 (paint attack).

27 *Izvestiya*, 16 January 1988, p. 3.

28 *Time*, 10 April 1989, p. 29 (Brezhnev was assessed 'negatively' or 'very negatively' by 69 per cent of respondents, Stalin by 52 per cent); similar results were reported in *Soviet Weekly*, 18 February 1989, p. 6, and in *Dialog*, 1990, no. 2, p. 5.

29 *Moscow News*, 1988, no. 38, p. 10.

30 *Soviet Weekly*, 18 February 1989, p. 6.

31 See Gorbachev, *Izbrannye rechi i stat'i*, vol. 5, p. 407.

32 *Literaturnaya gazeta*, 24 February 1988, p. 14.

33 *Izvestiya TsK KPSS*, 1989, no. 3, pp. 128–70; *Argumenty i fakty*, 1989, nos. 13 and 14 (later versions of the memoirs appeared in *Ogonek*, *Znamya* and *Voprosy istorii*); *Novoe vremya*, 1988, no. 2, p. 2; and *Pravda*, 19 March 1991, p. 6 (Grozny). The memoirs of Khrushchev's son-in-law, Alexei Adzhubei, appeared in *Znamya* in 1988; his son's recollections appeared the same year in *Ogonek*.

34 See Stephen F. Cohen, *Rethinking the Soviet Experience* (New York: Oxford University Press, 1985), ch. 4, and Alec Nove, *Glasnost' in Action* (Boston: Unwin Hyman, 1989), ch. 2.

35 Gorbachev, *Izbrannye rechi i stat'i*, vol. 3, p. 162.

36 Ibid., vol. 4, p. 373, and vol. 5, p. 217.

37 Ibid., vol. 5, pp. 397–402.

38 *Pravda*, 18 August 1988, p. 3.

39 Ibid., 6 February 1988, p. 1 (a copy of the Court's decision appeared in *Izvestiya TsK KPSS*, 1989, no. 1, p. 121).

40 *Pravda*, 10 July 1988, p. 1, and 21 October 1988, p. 2.

41 *Kommunist*, 1988, no. 2, pp. 93–102; N. I. Bukharin, *Izbrannye proizvedeniya* (Moscow: Politizdat, 1988). Bukharin's oration on the first anniversary of Lenin's death appeared in *Pravda*, 12 February 1988, p. 3; his 'Notes of an economist' appeared in *EKO*, 1988, no. 8; and his writings were included together with those of Preobrazhensky in *Voprosy ekonomiki*, 1988, no. 9. A volume of Bukharin's scientific writings appeared in 1988 (*Izbrannye trudy. Istoriya i organizatsiya nauki i tekhniki* (Leningrad: Nauka)), and his *Etyudy* (Moscow: Kniga) and *Politicheskaya ekonomiya rant'e* (Moscow: Orbita) were reissued. Bukharin's widow, Anna Larina, published her memoirs in *Znamya* in 1988.

42 *Izvestiya TsK KPSS*, 1989, no. 2, pp. 124–5, and no. 1, p. 109.
43 *Pravda*, 2 November 1988, p. 1, 27 January 1989, p. 2, and 3 December 1990, p. 2.
44 *Izvestiya*, 22 November 1988, p. 3 (sentenced to five years' imprisonment in 1935, he was shot in 1937).
45 An early reassessment by V. Ivanov in *Sovetskaya Rossiya*, 27 September 1987, p. 4, noted Trotsky's willpower and personal courage but also emphasised his arrogance, ambition and lack of firm principle. A fuller account by N. A. Vasetsky, 'L. D. Trotsky: politicheskii portret', *Novaya i noveishaya istoriya*, 1989, no. 3, emphasised Trotsky's 'contradictory' character, valuable where he had acted as a party and state leader, but not where his 'personal ambitions' had led him into conflict with the party line (p. 165). Trotsky's 'New course' and other writings of 1923 were reprinted in *Molodoi kommunist*, 1989, no. 8; his 'Stalinist School of Falsification' appeared in *Voprosy istorii*, 1989, no. 7, with other works to follow. For a survey, see Ian D. Thatcher, 'Recent Soviet writings on Leon Trotsky', *Coexistence*, vol. 27, no. 3 (September 1990), and Thatcher, 'Recent Soviet writings on Leon Trotsky: an update', *Coexistence*, vol. 29, no. 1 (March 1992).
46 *Pravda*, 5 July 1988, p. 1, and 31 October 1990, p. 6. The monument was constructed of stone taken from the Solovki islands prison camp.
47 Ibid., 14 August 1990, p. 1, and 6 June 1990, p. 2 (totals). On the larger question of historical reassessment, see R. W. Davies, *Soviet History in the Gorbachev Revolution* (London: Macmillan, 1989). About 70,000 were rehabilitated by the CPSU after 1953, 20,000 of them between 1988 and 1990: see *Voprosy istorii KPSS*, 1991, no. 4, p. 24. The party status of Zinoviev and Kamenev still remained unresolved: *Pravda*, 13 April 1991, p. 2.
48 *Yunost'*, 1988, no. 3, p. 53. The Pavlik Morozov case excited a considerable discussion: see for instance *Izvestiya*, 15 July 1989, p. 3.
49 Vaksberg in *Literaturnaya gazeta*, 21 January 1988, p. 13. For a fuller discussion see the same author's 'Stranitsy odnoi zhizni', *Znamya*, 1990, no. 5, pp. 152–77, and no. 6, pp. 122–43.
50 *Pravda*, 18 January 1989, p. 3.
51 *Nedelya*, 1988, no. 8, pp. 11–12; *Izvestiya*, 19 October 1988, p. 3.
52 Alexander Yakovlev in *Pravda*, 18 August 1989, pp. 1–2. The original of the Nazi-Soviet Pact was finally discovered in the CPSU archives: *Izvestiya*, 30 October 1992, pp. 1–2; the secret protocols were published in *Vosprosy istorii*, 1993, no. 1, pp. 3–16.
53 Yuri Polyakov as quoted in the *Guardian*, 10 October 1987, p. 7; *Moscow News*, 1988, no. 48, pp. 8–9 (Medvedev gave a total of 40 million 'victims of Stalinism' in an interview in *Argumenty i fakty*, 1989, no. 5); and for the KGB figure, *Pravitel'stvennyi vestnik*, 1990, no. 7, p. 11. More rigorous investigations are available in *Voprosy istorii*, 1989, no. 4, pp. 175–81 and *Sotsial'no-politicheskie nauki*, 1990, no. 7, pp. 90–100, which suggests a total of 3.4–3.7 million for the 'politically repressed' of the Stalin era. On the numbers in detention see V. N. Zemskov in *Sotsiologicheskie issledovaniya*, 1990, no. 11, and 1991, nos. 1, 6 and 7, and 1992, no. 2, and in *Istoriya SSSR*, 1991, no. 5; see

also E. V. Tsaplin in *Voprosy istorii*, 1991, nos. 4–5. The current state of research is considered in J. Arch Getty and Roberta T. Manning, eds., *Stalinist Terror: New perspectives* (Cambridge: Cambridge University Press, 1993).

54 *Izvestiya*, 12 September 1988, p. 4, 27 November 1988, p. 3, and 25 January 1989, p. 1 (number of victims).

55 *Literaturnaya gazeta*, 26 April 1989, p. 2 (there had been up to 240,000 deaths, originally ascribed to the Nazis); *Pravda*, 4 July 1989, p. 6; *Komsomol'skaya pravda*, 30 June 1989, p. 1 (the 'Leningrad Kuropaty' was believed to contain over 46,000 bodies). A mass grave in Irkutsk was reported in *Izvestiya*, 22 October 1989, p. 4.

56 *Sovetskaya Rossiya*, 4 February 1989, p. 6; *Pravda*, 11 May 1989, p. 6; *Independent*, 6 September 1989, pp. 9–10; Yuri Vlasov in *Pravda*, 2 June 1989, p. 4. KGB investigations confirmed the existence of several secret mass burial sites in Moscow and elsewhere in late 1990: *Pravda*, 6 December 1990, p. 1. Many other sites of mass killings were identified including Drogobych, in the Ukraine, where about 500 had died (*Pravda*, 2 July 1991, p. 1); near Bishkek, in Kirgizia, where the dead included the first Kirgiz professor and the father of the writer Chingiz Aitmatov (*Izvestiya*, 2 August 1991, p. 2); in a village near Chita (*Pravda*, 1 August 1991, p. 1); and in the Don crematorium, Moscow (*Izvestiya*, 17 August 1991, p. 1).

57 *Pravda*, 9 August 1987, p. 3; the new head, M. A. Korolev, was interviewed in *Pravda*, 11 August 1987, p. 2 (he had headed the Central Statistical Administration since 1985). Korolev's successor, Vadim Kirichenko, committed the service to a 'true and objective picture of the state of our society': *Pravitel'stvennyi vestnik*, 1989, nos. 14–15, p. 20.

58 *Narodnoe khozyaistvo SSSR v 1985 godu* (Moscow: Finansy i statistika, 1986), p. 547 (the Soviet definition of infant mortality was a much more restrictive one than that employed by the World Health Organisation: *Pravda*, 16 December 1988, p. 3).

59 Vladimir Treml in *AASASS Newsletter*, May 1989, pp. 5–6. See also Treml, 'Perestroika and Soviet statistics', *Soviet Economy*, vol. 4, no. 1 (1988), pp. 65–94, and Tim Heleniak and Albert Motivans, 'A note on *glasnost'* and the Soviet statistical system', *Soviet Studies*, vol. 43, no. 3 (1991), pp. 473–90. For a comprehensive bibliography of these sources see Timothy E. Heleniak, *Biography of Soviet Statistical Handbooks*, rev. edn (Newtonville MA: Oriental Research Partners, 1992).

60 *Naselenie SSSR 1987. Statisticheskii sbornik* (Moscow: Finansy i statistika, 1988), pp. 318–19.

61 *Nedelya*, 1987, no. 38, p. 12; *Pravda*, 16 December 1988, p. 3.

62 *Izvestiya*, 13 October 1988, p. 3 (deaths from illegal abortions); *Nedelya*, 1987, no. 38, p. 12.

63 *Pravda*, 30 June 1988, p. 4. A comprehensive health programme for the period up to 2000 was approved in 1988: text in *Izvestiya*, 27 June 1988, p. 1.

64 *Ogonek*, 1989, no. 3, pp. 14–17; also *Komsomol'skaya pravda*, 18 January 1989, p. 1.

65 *Izvestiya*, 14 February 1989, p. 6.

66 *Pravda*, 12 August 1989, pp. 1, 3; *Sovetskoe gosudarstvo i pravo*, 1991, no. 2, p. 20; and (for the 1991 data and the long-term doubling) *Izvestiya*, 11 January 1992, p. 6, and 29 January 1992, p. 1. The annual rate of increased over the previous twenty years had been about 4 per cent: M. P. Vyshinsky, ed., *Pravo i vlast'* (Moscow: Progress, 1990), p. 172.

67 *Izvestiya*, 8 February 1989, p. 6; *Pravda*, 5 October 1990, p. 2 (Ryzhkov).

68 *Izvestiya*, 30 August 1988, p. 6. For a survey of the Soviet press treatment of prostitution, see Elizabeth Waters, 'Restructuring and the "woman question": *perestroika* and prostitution', *Feminist Review*, no. 33 (autumn 1989), pp. 3–19.

69 *Sovetskaya Rossiya*, 13 March 1987, p. 4.

70 *Sotsiologicheskie issledovaniya*, 1987, no. 6, pp. 61–8.

71 *Trud*, 31 July 1987, p. 4; and on the question of legalisation, *Sovetskoe gosudarstvo i pravo*, 1991, no. 2, p. 71.

72 *Pravda*, 6 January 1987, p. 2. For a fuller treatment of this subject, see John M. Kramer, 'Drug abuse in the Soviet Union', *Problems of Communism*, vol. 37, no. 2 (March–April 1988), pp. 28–40. For a further discussion of drugs and related social issues see Andrew Wilson and Nina Bachkatov, *Living with Glasnost. Youth and Society in a Changing Russia* (Harmondsworth: Penguin, 1988); T. Anthony Jones et al., eds., *Soviet Social Problems* (Boulder CO: Westview, 1991); and Walter Joyce, ed., *Social Change and Social Issues in the Former USSR* (London: Macmillan, 1992).

73 *Izvestiya*, 13 May 1987, p. 6.

74 Ibid., 30 June 1986, p. 2.

75 *Argumenty i fakty*, 1990, no. 29, p. 5; the law is in *Izvestiya*, 10 May 1990, p. 2.

76 *Pravda*, 2 July 1988, p. 11. Pukhova was replaced by A. V. Fedulova in 1991: *Pravda*, 22 February 1991, p. 2.

77 *Pravda*, 9 March 1989, p. 2; see also *Pravda*, 5 March 1988, p. 1.

78 For a good review of these studies, see Mary Buckley, *Women and Ideology in the Soviet Union* (Hemel Hempstead: Wheatsheaf, 1989).

79 Gorbachev, *Izbrannye rechi i stat'i*, vol. 3, p. 232.

80 Gorbachev, *Perestroika*, pp. 116–17.

81 *Pravda*, 2 July 1988, p. 7.

82 *Soviet Weekly*, 29 July 1989, p. 5, and 25 November 1988, p. 15.

83 N. Zakharova, A. Posadskaya and N. Rimashevskaya, 'Kak my reshaem zhenskii vopros', *Kommunist*, 1989, no. 4, pp. 56–65. See the related discussion in *Marxism Today*, July 1989, pp 30–3.

84 On female representation in the USSR Congress of People's Deputies, see above, p. 49; on representation at other levels, see *Izvestiya*, 13 May 1990, p. 1. The letters to the Central Committee are in *Izvestiya TsK KPSS*, 1990, no. 12, pp. 133–8, at p. 134. Support for quota-based representation appeared in *Pravda*, 25 June 1990, p. 5, *Izvestiya*, 25 November 1990, p. 2, and *Izvestiya TsK KPSS*, 1990, no. 12, p. 134. A women's party was mooted in *Pravda*, 15 August 1990, p. 4, and *Izvestiya*, 13 May 1990, p. 1, and 21 October 1990, p. 2. For the nomination of a woman presidential candidate, see *Pravda*, 9 December 1990, p. 3, and 11 February 1991, p. 4, and *Izvestiya*, 22 March 1991, p. 7. The 'politological courses' were reported in *Pravda*, 9 April 1991, p. 1,

and supported in a party resolution on women, the first of its kind since the 1920s: *Izvestiya TsK KPSS*, 1991, no. 6, pp. 26–31. For a recent review of such issues see Mary Buckley, ed., *Perestroika and Soviet Women* (Cambridge: Cambridge University Press, 1992).

85 *Komsomol'skaya pravda*, 11 November 1987, p. 4 (similar cases were reported in *Izvestiya*, 11 July 1987, p. 3). Regulations designed to eliminate these abuses came into force in March 1988: see *Izvestiya*, 15 January 1988, p. 6. Amnesty International and US psychiatrists were able to visit Soviet institutions in 1989: see the *Guardian*, 4 February 1989, p. 5, and 13 March 1989, p. 8.

86 *Smena*, 1989, no. 12, p. 20; *Pravda*, 16 November 1988, p. 6.

87 *Literaturnaya gazeta*, 2 March 1988, p. 12.

88 Cited in the *Guardian*, 6 July 1985, p. 15.

89 *Pravda*, 30 January 1989, p. 5, and 19 April 1989, p. 4.

90 Ibid., 30 May 1989, p. 2, 7 June 1989, p. 3, and 10 June 1989, p. 3.

91 *Ogonek*, 1989, no. 16, pp. 10–14; *Tass* in English, 16 June 1989.

92 *Komsomol'skaya pravda*, 2 June 1989, p. 4; *Sotsiologicheskie issledovaniya*, 1990, no. 6, pp. 3–25, and no. 7, pp. 50–70 (there was a related publication in *Vestnik statistiki*, 1990, no. 7, pp. 65–79); and *Izvestiya*, 8 February 1990, p. 3 (Ukrainian famine; for a fuller discussion see *Istoriya SSSR*, 1991, no. 5, pp. 18–26).

93 *Izvestiya*, 6 April 1991, p. 6 (death penalty); *Pravda*, 24 September 1991, p. 2, and *Izvestiya*, 10 January 1992, pp. 1, 8 (among other reports of formerly secret cities).

94 *Izvestiya*, 24 March 1989, p. 3; *Pravda*, 29 July 1990, pp. 1–2.

95 VTsIOM was headed by Tat'yana Zaslavskaya, who was interviewed about its activities in *Pravda*, 18 March 1988, p. 2. Its first poll was reported in *Moscow News*, 1988, no. 35, p. 10.

96 *Literaturnaya gazeta*, 25 February 1987, p. 6; *Moscow News*, 1988, no. 23, p. 14.

97 Developments in Soviet literature in the Gorbachev period are surveyed in Julian Graffy and Geoffrey A. Hosking, eds., *Culture and the Media in the USSR Today* (London: Macmillan, 1989), ch. 7; Nove, *Glasnost' in Action*, ch. 6; and Riitta Pittman, '*Perestroika* and Soviet cultural politics: the case of the major literary journals', *Soviet Studies*, vol. 42, no. 1 (January 1990), pp. 111–32.

98 *Izvestiya*, 18 September 1991, p. 3.

99 *Druzhba narodov*, 1987, nos. 4–6. See the discussion in John Barber, 'Children of the Arbat', *Detente*, no. 11 (1988), pp. 8–11, 38.

100 *Literaturnaya gazeta*, 5 August 1987, p. 16 (I am grateful to Nick Lampert for drawing my attention to this item).

101 Ibid., 25 February 1987, p. 8.

102 Developments in film in the Gorbachev period are considered in Anna Lawton, *Kinoglasnost: Soviet Cinema in Our Time* (Cambridge: Cambridge University Press, 1992).

103 *Pravda*, 20 April 1989, p. 3.

104 *Izvestiya*, 21 April 1989, p. 2; *Pravda*, 5 May 1991, p. 6.

105 Ibid., 27 November 1988, p. 6; *Sovetskie arkhivy*, 1990, no. 6, pp. 10–12 (30-year rule) and no. 4, pp. 29–31 (party archives).

106 *Pravda*, 21 December 1987, p. 2.

107 *Sotsiologicheskie issledovaniya*, 1987, no. 4, pp. 35–43.

108 *Moscow News*, 1987, no. 13, p. 10, and no. 15, pp. 8–9.

109 *Pravda*, 3 February 1987, p. 4.

110 *Guardian*, 27 December 1988, p. 8; *Izvestiya*, 13 February 1992, p. 1.

111 *Izvestiya*, 11 April 1987, p. 7.

112 Ellen Mickiewicz, 'Changes in the media under Gorbachev: the case of television', in Walter Joyce *et al.*, eds., *Gorbachev and Gorbachevism* (London: Cass, 1989), pp. 38–9. See also *Vestnik MGU: zhurnalistika*, 1988, no. 3, pp. 32–8.

113 On these and other matters, see Ellen Mickiewicz, *Split Signals* (New York: Oxford University Press, 1988), and James Dingley, 'Soviet television and glasnost'', in Graffy and Hosking, eds., *Culture and the Media*, pp. 6–25.

114 *Izvestiya*, 22 April 1989, p. 6.

115 Subscriptions to Soviet periodicals rose by 14 million in 1987, and by 18 million in 1988: see *Pravda*, 21 February 1989, p. 1, and *Sovetskaya kul'tura*, 9 July 1988, p. 2. Many periodicals, however, experienced a fall in circulation in 1990: see *Moscow News*, 1989, no. 47, p. 4. For the fall in Western radio listening see *Izvestiya*, 1 June 1991, p. 1.

116 *Izvestiya*, 3 November 1988, p. 3, and 9 October 1990, p. 8 (a new body, the Chief Administration for the Protection of State Secrets in the Press and Other News Media, took the place of the body known as Glavlit).

117 *Pravda*, 29 December 1986, p. 3.

118 Gorbachev took particular exception to a poll of the popularity of deputies which placed Sakharov first: see *Argumenty i fakty*, 1989, no. 40, p. 1 (and below, p. 258).

119 *Pravda*, 15 March 1987, p. 3.

120 *Moskovskaya pravda*, 10 February 1987, pp. 2–3; *Pravda*, 9 February 1987, p. 3.

121 *Pravda*, 13 February 1986, p. 3.

122 *XXVII s"ezd Kommunisticheskoi partii Sovetskogo Soyuza 25 fevralya – 6 marta 1986 goda. Stenograficheskii otchet*, 3 vols. (Moscow: Politizdat, 1986), vol. 1, pp. 143–4, 236.

123 *Pravda*, 30 June 1988, p. 2.

124 *Pravda*, 1 July 1988, p. 7. An opinion poll on the question of privileges was conducted in Moscow by *Moscow News* (1988, no. 27, pp. 10–11). It found that chauffered cars were acceptable to 42 per cent of those polled, but food packages and special shops only to 9 per cent; leaders of the country were seen as the most deserving group in this connection, and Komsomol executives the least deserving of the ten groups considered.

125 Gorbachev, *Izbrannye rechi i stat'i*, vol. 4, p. 100.

126 *Pravda*, 13 June 1986, p. 2.

127 *Guardian*, 23 May 1989, p. 10. Soviet reporting of the Chernobyl incident is considered in Ellen Jones and Benjamin L. Woodbury II, 'Chernobyl' and glasnost'', *Problems of Communism*, vol. 35, no. 6 (November–December 1986), pp. 28–38; Ottorino Cappelli, 'Soviet crisis behaviour and information management: the case of Chernobyl'', *Journal of Communist Studies*, vol. 2, no. 4 (December 1986), pp. 404–31; Mickiewicz, *Split Signals*, pp. 60–8; and Thomas F. Remington, *The Truth of Authority. Ideology and*

Communication in the Soviet Union (Pittsburgh: University of Pittsburgh Press, 1989), pp. 118–20. Astonishingly, the third anniversary of the disaster was marked by the imposition of stricter controls on the reporting of accidents and breakdowns at nuclear and conventional power stations: see *Izvestiya*, 26 April 1989, p. 6. Politburo minutes, published subsequently, appeared to show a deliberate cover-up: *Izvestiya*, 24 April 1992, p. 3.

128 *Moscow News*, 1989, no. 17, p. 5.
129 For this term see *Sovetskaya Rossiya*, 26 April 1989, p. 1.
130 See, for instance, *Pravda*, 2 July 1988, pp. 3, 6, 10.
131 Ibid., 9 October 1990, p. 1, and 17 January 1991, p. 2.
132 *Izvestiya*, 20 June 1990, p. 3.
133 *Komsomol'skaya pravda*, 7 October 1990, p. 2, and *Izvestiya*, 14 March 1991, p. 1.
134 *Pravda*, 5 April 1991, p. 1, and 18 November 1991, pp. 1, 3.
135 Radio Free Europe/Radio Liberty *Research Report*, 28 February 1992, p. 55; circulation data for 1988 are taken from *Moscow News*, 1988, no. 8.
136 *Moscow News*, 1991, no. 47, p. 4; and for publishing, *Pravda*, 18 November 1991, p. 3.
137 *Pravda*, 5 April 1991, p. 3; Nenashev expressed similar concerns in ibid., 18 November 1991, pp. 1, 3.
138 Ibid., 12 February 1991, p. 2, and 15 November 1990, p. 2 (Kravchenko appointment).
139 *Izvestiya*, 8 January 1991, p. 8.
140 *Nezavisimaya gazeta*, 19 March 1991, p. 1.
141 For the law see *Izvestiya*, 20 December 1991, p. 1; a letter of concern appeared in ibid., 23 December 1991, p. 3. The law, as amended, dropped the requirement that journalists disclose their sources but made them answerable for unwittingly disclosing state secrets: *Rossiiskaya gazeta*, 31 December 1991, p. 2. For the subsidy to (among others) *Rossiiskaya gazeta* see *Izvestiya*, 10 March 1992, p. 1. These and other issues are considered in David Wedgwood Benn, *From Glasnost to Freedom of Speech: Soviet Openness and International Relations* (London: Pinter, 1992). On Bragin's appointment see *Izvestiya*, 12 January 1993, p. 1, and *Nezavisimaya gazeta*, 23 February 1993, p. 1.

4 Reforming the planned economy

1 S. N. Prokopovich, *Opyt ischisleniya narodnogo dokhoda 50 gubernii Evropeiskoi Rossii* (1918), as cited in Peter Gatrell, *The Tsarist Economy 1850–1917* (London: Batsford, 1986), p. 31.
2 See Paul R. Gregory, *Russian National Income 1885–1913* (Cambridge: Cambridge University Press, 1982), pp. 4–8, 11, 154, 159. On comparisons of Soviet–American labour productivity, see N. Shmelev and V. Popov, *Na perelome. Ekonomicheskaya perestroika v SSSR* (Moscow: Novosti, 1989), p. 51.
3 These data are taken from *Narodnoe khozyaistvo SSSR v 1987 godu* (Moscow: Finansy i statistika, 1988), pp. 5, 8, 13, 14. On comparisons with tsarist

growth rates, see *Kommunist*, 1991, no. 1, p. 74; on international comparisons see *Narodnoe khozyaistvo SSSR v 1987 g.*, p. 666, and the *World Developmentment Report* and *UNESCO Yearbook*, various issues.

4 M. S. Gorbachev, *Izbrannye rechi i stat'i*, 6 vols. (Moscow: Politizdat, 1987–89), vol. 2, pp. 352–3 (the version in *Time* itself was slightly different). Gorbachev's trips in the 1940s are mentioned in his *Perestroika* (London: Collins, 1987), p. 41.

5 See Anders Aslund, *Gorbachev's Struggle for Economic Reform* (London: Pinter, 1989), p. 15. Shmelev and Popov, *Na perelome*, p. 356, take a similar view.

6 Shmelev and Popov, *Na perelome*, p. 131.

7 *EKO*, 1987, no. 11, pp. 50–2; Shmelev and Popov, *Na perelome*, pp. 169–71, 181–204. The steady fall in relative plan fulfilment is noted in *Na perelome*, p. 131.

8 Shmelev and Popov, *Na perelome*, p. 44. Grigorii Khanin argued that plan fulfilment in road transport was in fact no more than 20 per cent of the reported level (in T. I. Zaslavskaya and R. V. Ryvkinaya, eds., *Sotsiologiya i perestroika* (Moscow: Progress, 1989), p. 51).

9 *Novyi mir*, 1987, no. 2, pp. 181–201. Khanin published slightly different figures in *Kommunist* in 1988 and in his book *Dinamika ekonomicheskogo razvitiya SSSR* (Novosibirsk: Nauka, 1991). Similar although less pessimistic calculations were published by B. Bolotin in *Mirovaya ekonomika i mezhdunarodne otnosheniya*, 1987, nos. 11 and 12, pp. 145–57 and 141–8. A series of articles in *Voprosy ekonomiki*, 1992, nos. 4–6, identified several causes of the economic slowdown including overconcentration, failure to absorb technological advance, a lack of reinvestment in existing plant, and militarisation.

10 S. S. Shatalin and E. T. Gaidar, *Ekonomicheskaya reforma: prichiny, napravleniya, problemy* (Moscow: Ekonomika, 1989), p. 16; Gorbachev in *Pravda*, 16 March 1989, p. 3.

11 Abel Aganbegyan in *Literaturnaya gazeta*, 18 February 1987, p. 13, and in *Izvestiya*, 25 August 1987, p. 2.

12 Shmelev and Popov, *Na perelome*, p. 50; *Narkhoz 1988*, p. 680. Authoritative estimates suggested that Soviet national income by the late 1980s may have been no more than 35 per cent of the US figure: see *Svobodnaya mysl'*, 1991, no. 17, p. 96; or even 16.6 per cent of the US figure: see *Mirovaya ekonomika i mezhdunarodnye otnosheniya*, 1992, no. 1, p. 146.

13 V. Perevedentsev in *Rabochii klass i sovremennyi mir*, 1988, no. 4, pp. 57–67.

14 Abel Aganbegyan in *The Challenge: Economics of Perestroika* (London: Hutchinson, 1988), pp. 68–9, and in G. M. Sorokin, ed., *Intensifikatsiya i effektivnost' sotsialisticheskogo proizvodstva* (Moscow: Nauka, 1988), p. 10. Goskomstat predicted a fall in the working age population in the Ukraine in 1991–95, and in the Russian Republic, Ukraine and some regions of Belorussia, Latvia and Estonia in 2006–15: *Vestnik statistiki*, 1990, no. 10, p. 41.

15 Aganbegyan, *The Challenge*, p. 72, and on the Noyabr'skoe field, in Sorokin, ed., *Intensifikatsiya*, p. 11.

16 See Peter Hauslohner, 'Gorbachev's social contract', *Soviet Economy*, vol. 3,

no. 1 (1987), pp. 54–89. For an earlier use of this term, see Alex Pravda in Rudolf L. Tokes, ed., *Opposition in Eastern Europe* (London: Macmillan, 1979).

17 As noted by Peter Frank, 'Gorbachev's dilemma: social justice or political instability?', *World Today*, vol. 42, no. 6 (June 1986), pp. 93–5.

18 Gorbachev, *Izbrannye rechi i stat'i*, vol. 2, pp. 86 and 154–5 (April 1985); Abalkin on Moscow radio in BBC Summary of World Broadcasts, 10 February 1989, SU/0386 B/6; Nikolai Shmelev in *Znamya*, 1988, no. 7, p. 179. On the term 'Administrative System', see Gavriil Popov, *Puti perestroiki. Zametki ekonomista* (Moscow: Ekonomika, 1989), and Popov, *Blesk i nishcheta administrativnoi sistemy* (Moscow: Pik, 1990).

19 Gorbachev, *Izbrannye rechi i stat'i*, vol. 3, p. 182.

20 Ibid., pp. 199–202.

21 Ibid., pp. 202–23.

22 *Pravda*, 25 May 1985, p. 1, and Gorbachev in *Pravda*, 12 June 1985, pp. 1–2.

23 The Directives appeared in *Pravda*, 9 March 1986, pp. 1–6; the Five Year Plan, as adopted, is in *Pyataya sessiya Verkhovnogo Soveta SSSR (odinnadtsatyi sozyv) 18–19 iyunya 1986g. Stenograficheskii otchet* (Moscow: Izvestiya, 1986), pp. 314–20.

24 Gorbachev, *Izbrannye rechi i stat'i*, vol. 5, pp. 157–9.

25 Ibid., p. 143.

26 Ibid., p. 148.

27 Ibid., pp. 151, 136, 138–9.

28 P. Bunich in *Pravda*, 2 June 1989, p. 4. Shmelev and Popov point out that one-fifth of nuclear power stations and all Soviet coal mines worked at a loss: *Na perelome*, p. 223.

29 Gorbachev, *Izbrannye rechi i stat'i*, vol. 5, p. 185.

30 The Basic Directives appeared in *Materialy plenuma Tsentral'nogo komiteta KPSS 25–26 iyunya 1987 goda* (Moscow: Politizdat, 1987), pp. 83–111; the Law on the State Enterprise is conveniently available in *O korennoi perestroike upravleniya ekonomikoi* (Moscow: Politizdat, 1988).

31 M. S. Gorbachev, *Revolyutsionnoi perestroike – ideologiyu obnovleniya* (Moscow: Politizdat, 1988), pp. 24–7.

32 For the text of the Law see *Pravda*, 1 July 1987, pp. 1–4, and *O korennoi perestroike*, pp. 3–52. My discussion of the Law is indebted to Walter Joyce, 'The Law of the State Enterprise', in Joyce *et al.*, eds., *Gorbachev and Gorbachevism* (London: Cass, 1989), pp. 71–82, and Richard E. Ericson, 'The New Enterprise Law', *Harriman Institute Forum*, vol. 1, no. 2 (February 1988).

33 *Materialy plenuma 25–26 iyunya 1987 goda*, pp. 53–4.

34 Gorbachev, *Izbrannye rechi i stat'i*, vol. 5, p. 183. The texts of these related decrees are in *O korennoi perestroike*, pp. 55ff.

35 Gorbachev's speech appeared in *Pravda*, 16 March 1989, pp. 1–4. The Central Committee resolution on leaseholding was in *Pravda*, 1 April 1989, pp. 1–2.

36 On these earlier developments see particularly V. P. Gagnon, Jr., 'Gorbachev and the collective contract brigade', *Soviet Studies*, vol. 39, no. 1 (January 1987), pp. 1–23, and John Channon, 'The rise and fall of the Soviet peasantry', *Slovo*, vol. 2, no. 1 (May 1989), pp. 14–32.

37 Shmclev and Popov, *Na perelome*, p. 223.
38 *Pravda*, 31 July 1989, p. 8.
39 Ibid., 20 November 1986, p. 3. The Law itself appeared in *Shestaya sessiya Verkhovnogo Soveta SSSR (odinnadtsatyi sozyv) 17–19 noyabrya 1986g. Stenograficheskii otchet* (Moscow: Izvestiya, 1986), pp. 374–83.
40 Ibid., p. 344.
41 See Aslund, *Gorbachev's Struggle*, p. 163. The Law itself, as adopted, is in *Devyataya sessiya Verkhovnogo Soveta SSSR (odinnadtsatyi sozyv) 24–26 maya 1988g. Stenograficheskii otchet* (Moscow: Izvestiya, 1988), pp. 387–441.
42 Ibid., pp. 8–52.
43 For the original proposals, see *Izvestiya*, 20 March 1988, p. 2. The revised arrangements appeared in *Vedomosti Verkhovnogo Soveta SSSR*, 1989, no. 9, item 62.
44 As noted by Michael Ellman, *The USSR in the 1990s: Struggling out of Stagnation* (London: Economist Intelligence Unit, 1989), p. 44.
45 *Vestnik statistiki*, 1991, no. 9, pp. 3–11. Earlier figures are in *Narodnoe khozyaistvo SSSR v 1989 g.* (Moscow: Finansy i statistika, 1990), pp. 268–9.
46 V. F. Yakovlev, ed., *Kooperativy segodnya i v budushchem* (Moscow: Yuridicheskaya literatura, 1989), pp. 46–7; *Izvestiya*, 26 August 1988, p. 1.
47 *Izvestiya*, 1 May 1987, p. 3.
48 Yakovlev, ed., *Kooperativy*, p. 62; Abalkin in *Sovetskaya Rossiya*, 27 July 1988, p. 3.
49 *XXVII s"ezd Kommunisticheskoi partii Sovetskogo Soyuza 25 fevralya – 6 marta 1986 goda. Stenograficheskii otchet*, 3 vols. (Moscow: Politizdat, 1986), vol. 2, p. 41.
50 *Spravochnik partiinogo rabotnika*, issue 27 (Moscow: Politizdat, 1987), pp. 488–92.
51 *Vneshnyaya torgovlya*, 1989, no. 2, Appendix; for the formation of the ministry, *Pravda*, 17 January 1988, p. 3; and for the presidential decree, *Izvestiya*, 26 October 1990, p. 1.
52 *Narodnoe khozyaistvo SSSR v 1989 g.*, pp. 670, 641.
53 Cited in Aslund, *Gorbachev's Struggle*, p. 138; see more generally ibid., pp. 136–41.
54 Shatalin and Gaidar, *Ekonomicheskaya reforma*, p. 64.
55 *Narkhoz 1987*, p. 55; Aganbegyan in *Literaturnaya gazeta*, 18 February 1987, p. 13.
56 *Narodnoe khozyaistvo SSSR v 1989 g.*, p. 9.
57 *Pravda*, 15 January 1989, p. 3.
58 *XIX Vsesoyuznaya konferentsiya Kommunisticheskoi partii Sovetskogo Soyuza 28 iyunya – 1 iyulya 1988 goda. Stenograficheskii otchet*, 2 vols. (Moscow: Politizdat, 1988), vol. 1, p. 116.
59 *Pravda*, 22 January 1989, pp. 3, 4. The 1985–88 comparison is in *Kommunist*, 1989, no. 2, p. 22.
60 *Pravda*, 28 January 1990, pp. 1–3.
61 *Soviet Weekly*, 1 July 1989, p. 15; *Independent*, 30 January 1990, p. 10.
62 *Pravda*, 22 January 1989, p. 5.
63 *Kommunist*, 1989, no. 2, p. 31. Ryzhkov revealed to the Congress of People's Deputies in 1989 that the Soviet hard currency debt was 34bn rubles, the servicing of which alone cost 12bn rubles: *Pravda*, 10 June 1989, p. 3.

64 *Pravda*, 15 January 1988, p. 1. By 1990 expenditure had already reached 9.2 billion, and further measures had been required: ibid., 26 April 1990, p. 2, and 28 April 1990, pp. 1, 5.
65 Ibid., 29 December 1988, p. 1.
66 Ibid., 25 May 1989, p. 1.
67 *Voprosy ekonomiki*, 1991, no. 3, p. 36. The whole question of monopoly is discussed further in several articles in ibid., 1990, no. 6.
68 *XIX Vsesoyuznaya konferentsiya*, vol. 1, p. 116.
69 *Sotsialisticheskaya industriya*, 5 January 1988, p. 2.
70 Shmelev in *Novyi mir*, 1988, no. 4, p. 167.
71 Gorbachev, *Izbrannye rechi i stat'i*, vol. 6, pp. 332, 339.
72 The title of an article by V. Radaev, *Voprosy ekonomiki*, 1989, no. 7, pp. 48–59; the quotation is on p. 49.
73 *Pravda*, 12 January 1987, p. 1.
74 *Izvestiya*, 1 March 1988, p. 2.
75 Vorotnikov in *Pravda*, 21 July 1989, p. 4. Similarly Solov'ev in *Pravda*, 22 April 1989, p. 4.
76 Ibid., 24 May 1989, p. 3.
77 Ibid., 27 April 1989, pp. 4, 5.
78 Ibid., 22 January 1989, p. 5; *Izvestiya*, 1 August 1987, p. 3.
79 *Pravda*, 31 May 1989, p. 2.
80 Ibid., 9 April 1989, p. 2. *Izvestiya*, reported official statistics which indicated that ministerial personnel had fallen by 23 per cent (the number of republican ministries, for instance, had fallen from 800 to 600), but managerial personnel in all enterprises and organisations increased from 12.5 to 13.1 million despite a fall of a million in the total number of workers and white-collar staff (7 March 1989, p. 1).
81 Afanas'ev in *Leningradskaya pravda*, 11 May 1988, p. 2 (similarly a *Pravda*, editorial, 28 July 1989, p. 1); *Izvestiya*, 14 December 1988, p. 6; *Pravda*, 8 August 1988, p. 2.
82 See Vladimir G. Treml, 'A noble experiment: Gorbachev's antidrinking campaign', in Maurice Friedberg and Hayward Isham, eds., *Soviet Society under Gorbachev* (Armonk, NY: Sharpe, 1987), pp. 52–75; Walter Joyce, 'The battle continues: Gorbachev's anti-alcohol policies', in Joyce, ed., *Social Change and Social Issues in the Former USSR* (London: Macmillan, 1992); and Daniel Tarschys, 'The success of a failure: Gorbachev's alcohol policy, 1985–88', *Europe-Asia Studies*, vol. 45, no. 1 (1993), pp. 7–25.
83 *Pravda*, 15 November 1987, p. 3.
84 Text in *Pravda*, 17 May 1985, p. 1.
85 *Izvestiya*, 2 June 1987, pp. 1–2.
86 Shmelev and Popov, *Na perelome*, p. 382.
87 Ibid., p. 383; and Shmelev to the Congress of People's Deputies, *Pravda*, 9 June 1989, p. 2.
88 *Pravda*, 2 April 1989, p. 1.
89 Ibid., 8 May 1989, p. 1.
90 Ibid., 16 January 1989, p. 1.
91 Ibid., 30 October 1989, p. 3.

92 Ibid., 3 June 1989, p. 6.

93 Ibid., 25 May 1989, p. 1.

94 Ibid., 27 April 1989, p. 3.

95 Ibid., 11 July 1989, p. 2.

96 Ibid., 1 June 1989, p. 1, and 11 July 1989, p. 2.

97 *Literaturnaya gazeta*, 5 January 1989, p. 13.

98 *Obshchestvennoe mnenie v tsifrakh*, issue 3 (Moscow: VTsIOM, 1989), p. 5.

99 *Izvestiya TsK KPSS*, 1989, no. 10, p. 16.

100 *Pravda*, 21 September 1987, p. 3, and 23 November 1987, p. 1.

101 Ibid., 11 July 1988, p. 3.

102 *Izvestiya*, 2 February 1989, p. 1.

103 *Pravda*, 22 January 1989, p. 5.

104 *Trud*, 12 August 1988, p. 2; Shmelev and Popov, *Na perelome*, p. 266. For
     a further discussion of the black economy see *Voprosy ekonomiki*, 1990,
     no. 3.

105 *Pravda*, 26 May 1989, p. 4.

106 Ibid., 1 September 1988, p. 3.

107 Ibid., 6 January 1988, p. 3.

108 Ibid., 18 July 1988, p. 1.

109 Ibid., 3 August 1988, p. 2.

110 *Voprosy ekonomiki*, 1989, no. 8, p. 28; *Izvestiya*, 19 January 1989, p. 1.

111 *Pravda*, 21 November 1988, p. 4.

112 *Sotsialisticheskaya industriya*, 3 March 1988, p. 2.

113 Yakovlev, ed., *Kooperativy*, pp. 201, 212.

114 Ibid., p. 215.

115 *Pravda*, 3 June 1989, p. 5.

116 Shmelev and Popov, *Na perelome*, p. 365; Yakovlev, ed., *Kooperativy*, notes
     the connection between the cooperatives and organised crime and the
     prevalence of double bookkeeping and other practices (p. 222). In 1989 an
     estimated 3 billion rubles was taken out of retail trade and resold at higher
     prices: *Sovetskoe gosudarstvo i pravo*, 1990, no. 5, p. 26. For a more general
     discussion see B. Ya. Shetelin, 'Prestupnost' v sfere kooperativnoi deyatel'-
     nosti', *Sotsiologicheskie issledovaniya*, 1991, no. 12, pp. 70–5.

117 *Izvestiya*, 31 December 1988, p. 2; *Pravda*, 19 July 1989, p. 2 (miners'
     demands); *Izvestiya*, 3 February 1989, pp. 1–2 and *Vedomosti*, 1989, no. 18,
     item 345 (further restrictions); and *Izvestiya*, 3 November 1990, p. 2 (law on
     speculation). For a survey of public attitudes see E. G. Antosenkov, 'Obsh-
     chestvennoe mnenie o kooperatsii', *Sotsiologicheskie issledovaniya*, 1988, no.
     6, pp. 3–11; and *Obshchestvennoe mnenie v tsifrakh*, issue 14 (Moscow:
     VTsIOM, 1990).

118 See *Izvestiya TsK KPSS*, 1989, no. 33, pp. 86–92.

119 Ibid., no. 8, pp. 149–50.

120 *Pravda*, 24 March 1989, p. 4.

121 Ibid., 3 June 1989, p. 5.

122 Ibid.

123 See, for instance, *Pravda*, 20 September 1988, p. 3 (large families); *Izvestiya
     TsK KPSS*, 1989, no. 8, p. 150, and *Pravda*, 3 June 1989, p. 6 (pensioners).

124 See, for instance, *Izvestiya*, 16 January 1989, p. 2 (a proper cost of living index was being developed, according to the chairman of the State Statistics Committee: *Izvestiya*, 16 January 1989, p. 2).

125 *Pravda*, 1 September 1988, p. 3. A full range of data on income distribution appeared in *Pravitel'stvennyi vestnik*, 1989, no. 17, p. 12: it indicated that in 1988 41 million people (14.5 per cent of the population) had an income of less than the official poverty level of 78 rubles a month.

126 *Pravda*, 22 January 1989, p. 3.

127 Ibid., 28 January 1990, p. 1.

128 Ibid., 27 April 1989, p. 6.

129 Ibid., 9 May 1989, p. 4.

130 *Moscow News*, 7 May 1989, p. 4.

131 See Shmelev and Popov, *Na perelome*, p. 224.

132 *Pravda*, 24 October 1988, p. 4.

133 Ibid.

134 Yu. Maslyukov in ibid., 5 August 1989, p. 1.

135 Ibid., 28 January 1990, pp. 1–3; *Narodnoe khozyaistvo SSSR v 1989 g.*, pp. 8–10.

136 *Ekonomika i zhizn'*, 1991, no. 5, pp. 9–13. For the fall in oil production see *Izvestiya*, 6 August 1991, p. 1.

137 The programme and related documents are printed in *O merakh po ozdorovleniyu ekonomiki, etapakh ekonomicheskoi reformy i printsipial'nykh podkhodakh k razrabotke trinadtsatogo pyatiletnego plana* (Moscow: Izdatel'stvo politicheskoi literatury, 1990).

138 *Izvestiya*, 19 October 1990, p. 1. The Supreme Soviet's resolution is in *Pravda*, 21 October 1990, pp. 1, 3.

139 *Pravda*, 14 June 1990, p. 1, and 16 June 1990, pp. 1–2.

140 For Shatalin's presentation of his proposals, see *Pravda*, 18 September 1990, p. 2, and for the proposals themselves, *Perekhod k rynku* (Moscow: Arkhangel'skoe, 1990). The Russian Republican decision is in *Pravda*, 12 September 1990, p. 2.

141 See for instance his speech to the Supreme Soviet, *Pravda*, 12 September 1990, p. 1.

142 For Aganbegyan's presentation of his proposals, see ibid., 18 September 1990, p. 2; for his report see *Voprosy ekonomiki*, 1990, no. 10, pp. 109–48.

143 *Pravda*, 18 September 1990, pp. 1–2.

144 The vote was 356 in favour, 12 against, with 26 abstentions: *Izvestiya*, 19 October 1990, p. 1. The Supreme Soviet's resolution is in *Pravda*, 21 October 1990, pp. 1, 3.

145 Gorbachev's speech is in *Pravda*, 20 October 1990, pp. 1–2; the Guidelines are in ibid., 18 October 1990, pp. 1–4. On the debates more generally, see Anders Aslund, 'The making of economic policy in 1989 and 1990', *Soviet Economy*, vol. 6, no. 1 (January–March 1990), pp. 65–93, and Ed. A. Hewett, 'The new Soviet plan', *Foreign Affairs*, vol. 69, no. 5 (Winter 1990/1), pp. 146–67. Leonid Abalkin's own account of these debates is in his *Neispol'zovannyi shans. Poltora goda v pravitel'stve* (Moscow: Politizdat, 1991).

146 *Pravda*, 26 October 1990, p. 1; ibid., 28 February 1991, p. 2.

147 Ibid., 19 August 1990, pp. 1–2.

148 *Materialy XXVIII s"ezda KPSS* (Moscow: Politizdat, 1990), pp. 9–15.
149 *Pravda*, 12 September 1990, p. 1.
150 Ibid., 19 October 1990, p. 1.
151 *Komsomol'skaya pravda*, 4 November 1990, p. 2.
152 *Izvestiya*, 21 October 1990, p. 2.
153 See for instance the Politburo's conclusions on this subject, *Pravda*, 15 September 1990, p. 1.
154 Ibid., 28 February 1991, p. 2.
155 Ibid., 5 July 1990, pp. 2–3.
156 Ibid., 5 July 1990, p. 3.
157 See for instance Ligachev, ibid., 11 July 1990, pp. 5–6; Baklanov, ibid., 7 July 1990, p. 6; and Ivashko, ibid., 12 July 1990, p. 2.
158 Ibid., 11 December 1990, p. 2.
159 *Moscow News*, 1990, no. 10, p. 10.
160 See for instance *Narodnyi deputat*, 1990, no. 12, p. 50: 54 per cent found unemployment 'unacceptable'.
161 See respectively *Pravda*, 17 September 1990, p. 2; ibid., 9 September 1990, p. 2; ibid., 15 October 1990, p. 2; and ibid., 1 December 1990, pp. 1–3.
162 *Kommunist*, 1991, no. 2, p. 40.
163 See for instance *Voprosy ekonomiki*, 1990, no. 1, p. 138; *Narodnyi deputat*, 1990, no. 8, p. 53.
164 See for instance *Izvestiya*, 10 October 1990, p. 3, and *Argumenty i fakty*, 1990, no. 48, pp. 5–6.
165 *Izvestiya*, 24 May 1990, p. 1; slightly different figures are given in *Voprosy ekonomiki*, 1990, no. 7, p. 58.
166 *Sotsial'no-politicheskie nauki*, 1990, no. 8, pp. 17–18.
167 *Moskovskie novosti*, 1990, no. 50, p. 10.
168 Ibid., 1990, no. 49, p. 9; *Izvestiya*, 6 December 1991, p. 6.
169 *Izvestiya*, 22 October 1990, p. 2.
170 *Pravda*, 16 November 1990, pp. 1–2, and 25 March 1991, p. 3 (milk); *Izvestiya TsK KPSS*, 1990, no. 12, pp. 140–3 and (on Karelia) *Pravda*, 8 September 1990, p. 1.
171 *Pravitel'stvennyi vestnik*, 1990, no. 18, p. 2 (tea); *Pravda*, 13 April 1990, p. 3 (children's books).
172 *Pravda*, 1 April 1991, p. 1.
173 See *Izvestiya*, 8 August 1991, p. 2 and 22 January 1992, p. 1 (typhoid); *Pravda*, 26 June 1991, p. 1 and 20 July 1991, p. 1 (cholera); and *Izvestiya*, 3 October 1991, p. 8 (diptheria).
174 *Argumenty i fakty*, 1991, no. 43, p. 5.
175 *Komsomol'skaya pravda*, 21 March 1991, p. 2.
176 *Daily Record*, 6 January 1992, p. 2; *Izvestiya*, 30 October 1991, p. 2.
177 Ibid., 24 December 1990, p. 1.
178 Ibid., 12 October 1990, p. 1.
179 *Izvestiya TsK KPSS*, 1991, no. 2, p. 92.
180 *Izvestiya*, 31 January 1991, p. 2.
181 *Dialog*, 1991, no. 2, p. 3. An emigration law was adopted in 1991: *Pravda*, 22 May 1991, p. 2.
182 *Pravda*, 29 October 1990, p. 2; *Izvestiya*, 1 August 1991, p. 1.

183 *Izvestiya TsK KPSS*, 1991, no. 2, p. 92.

184 *Pravda*, 14 September 1990, p. 1.

185 Ibid., 25 October 1990, p. 1 (sugar).

186 *Izvestiya*, 4 November 1991, p. 1.

187 *Pravda*, 22 October 1990, p. 1.

188 Ibid., 20 October 1990, p. 4.

189 *Ekonomika i zhizn'*, 1991, no. 10, p. 13.

190 *Kommunist*, 1990, no. 1, p. 51. Other official estimates were 70–80 bn (*Izvestiya*, 15 May 1991, p. 1), 110–130 bn (*Pravda*, 25 October 1991, p. 1) or as high as 200 bn rubles (ibid., 3 February 1992, p. 3).

191 *Sovetskoe gosudarstvo i pravo*, 1990, no. 6, p. 22. On Tarasov see for instance *Pravda*, 5 February 1991, p. 2.

192 *Izvestiya*, 17 October 1990, p. 2. Another estimate was 80 million: *Ekonomika i zhizn'*, 1990, no. 23, p. 9.

193 *Kommunist*, 1990, no. 3, p. 29.

194 *Pravda*, 30 October 1990, p. 2.

195 Ibid., 25 January 1991, p. 1.

196 *Sovetskaya Rossiya*, 22 March 1991, p. 2.

197 *Izvestiya*, 21 March 1991, p. 1, and 22 March 1991, pp. 1–2.

198 *Pravda*, 19 February 1991, pp. 1–2.

199 For the legislation see respectively *Pravda*, 11 April 1991, p. 2; *Izvestiya*, 8 August 1991, p. 3; and ibid., 24 July 1991, p. 4. On medical insurance see ibid., 1 February 1992, p. 3; and on the reopening of labour exchanges, *Pravda*, 4 July 1991, p. 3.

200 For the detailed regulations, see *Ekonomicheskaya gazeta*, 1987, no. 1, pp. 1–2.

201 Shmelev and Popov, *Na perelome*, p. 224; similarly A. N. Komin, *Radikal'-naya reforma tsen* (Moscow: Ekonomika, 1989).

202 *Pravda*, 2 June 1989, p. 4.

203 Popov, *Puti perestroiki*, pp. 285–9 (on housing), 311–12, 349, 373–4 (milk and meat would however continue to be subsidised, p. 373), and his speech to the Congress of People's Deputies, *Pravda*, 11 June 1989, p. 2. Popov was accused of identifying Lenin as the founder of the 'Administrative system': ibid., 2 June 1989, p. 3.

204 *Izvestiya*, 22 April 1988, p. 3.

205 Shmelev in *Novyi mir*, 1987, no. 6, pp. 142–58, and in *Znamya*, 1988, no. 7, pp. 179–84 (where he argued that 20–25 per cent of the labour force were surplus to requirements). I. E. Zaslavsky, in a more detailed study, similarly emphasised the existence of considerable de facto unemployment and the costs of maintaining nominally full employment: *Rabochii klass i sovremennyi mir*, 1988, no. 5, pp. 27–37.

206 *Pravda*, 9 June 1989, p. 2; *Sovetskoe gosudarstvo i pravo*, 1990, no. 7, p. 42.

207 *Vestnik statistiki*, 1990, no. 4, p. 14 (the same point is made, with some reservations, in *Kommunist*, 1990, no. 11, p. 72).

208 *Pravda*, 9 June 1989, p. 3; similarly *Voprosy ekonomiki*, 1990, no. 11, p. 14.

209 *Pravda*, 28 August 1990, p. 3, and 25 May 1989, p. 2.

210 *Kommunist*, 1990, no. 14, p. 15 (using ILO data).

211 Ibid., p. 18.

212 See F. M. Borodkin et al., eds., *Postizhenie: Sotsiologiya. Sotsial'naya politika. Ekonomicheskaya reforma* (Moscow: Progress, 1989), p. 453, and A. Zaichenko as quoted in *Voprosy ekonomiki*, 1992, no. 1, p. 135.

213 Shatalin and Gaidar, *Ekonomicheskaya reforma*, pp. 99–100; S. M. Nikitin et al. in *Rabochii klass i sovremennyi mir*, 1988, no. 6, pp. 133–41.

214 *Izvestiya*, 24 December 1988, p. 3; *Sotsiologicheskie issledovaniya*, 1991, no. 8, p. 6.

215 *Pravda*, 2 June 1989, p. 2.

216 Ibid., 9 June 1989, p. 4.

217 See particularly Sergei Andreev, 'Struktura vlasti i zadachi obshchestva', *Neva*, 1989, no. 1, pp. 144–73; a similar argument is presented in Borodkin et al., *Postizhenie*, pp. 481–588. See also V. Kholodkov, 'Gosudarstvennyi sotsializm i obrazovanie novogo klassa v SSSR', *Voprosy ekonomiki*, 1992, no. 1, pp. 126–35.

218 *Izvestiya TsK KPSS*, 1989, no. 8, p. 64.

219 Ibid., no. 8, p. 27 (a contribution of 500 million rubles).

5   The Soviet multinational state

1 *Pravda*, 29 June 1989, p. 4.

2 *Voprosy istorii*, 1989, no. 6, p. 134. A figure of 400 is cited in *Soviet Weekly*, 15 July 1989, p. 7.

3 There is a large literature on the national question in the USSR: see, for instance, Zev Katz, ed., *A Handbook of Major Soviet Nationalities* (New York: Free Press, 1975); Hélène Carrère d'Encausse, *An Empire in Decline* (New York: Newsweek, 1979); Walker Connor, *The National Question in Marxist–Leninist Theory and Practice* (Princeton, NJ: Princeton University Press, 1984); Ronald Wixman, *The Peoples of the USSR: An Ethnographic Handbook* (Armonk NY: Sharpe, 1984); Rasma Karklins, *Ethic Relations in the USSR: The Perspective from Below* (Boston: Allen and Unwin, 1986); Alexander J. Motyl, *Will the Non-Russians Rebel?* (Ithaca: Cornell University Press, 1987); V. I. Kozlov, *The Peoples of the Soviet Union* (London: Hutchinson, 1988); Bohdan Nahajlo and Victor Swoboda, *Soviet Disunion: A History of the Nationalities Problem in the USSR* (London: Hamish Hamilton, 1990); Graham Smith, ed., *The Nationalities Question in the Soviet Union* (London: Longmans, 1990); Gail Lapidus et al., *From Union to Commonwealth* (Cambridge: Cambridge University Press, 1992); and Ian Bremmer and Ray Taras, eds., *Nations and Politics in the Soviet Successor States* (Cambridge: Cambridge University Press, 1993).

4 Comparisons between Russian and non-Russian urban areas, for instance, were noted in *Istoriya SSSR*, 1987, no. 6, p. 63.

5 On these developments see John B. Dunlop, *The Faces of Contemporary Russian Nationalism* (Princeton NJ: Princeton University Press, 1983), and *The New Russian Nationalism* (New York: Praeger, 1985).

6 *Pravda*, 7 June 1989, p. 5.

7 Ibid., 3 June 1989, p. 3.

8 The decision, by a city referendum, was approved by the Russian parliament in September: *Izvestiya*, 9 September 1991, p. 1.

9 See Bogdan Krawchenko, *Social Change and National Consciousness in Twentieth Century Ukraine* (London: Macmillan, 1985), and Orest Subtelny, *Ukraine: A History* (Toronto: University of Toronto Press, 1988).

10 On the famine, see particularly James E. Mace. *Communism and National Liberation: National Communism in Soviet Ukraine 1918–1933* (Cambridge MA: Harvard University Press, 1983), and Robert Conquest, *Harvest of Sorrow* (London: Hutchinson, 1986).

11 On earlier developments, see Ivan Dzyuba, *Internationalism or Russification?* (London: Weidenfeld and Nicolson, 1968) and Michael Brown, ed., *Ferment in the Ukraine* (London: Macmillan, 1971). On environmental concerns, see, for instance, the petition with 6,000 signatures calling for the review of nuclear power policy in the Ukraine presented to the 19th Party Conference: *Pravda*, 2 July 1988, p. 8.

12 For a good general account, see Steven L. Guthier, 'The Belorussians: national identification and assimilation, 1897–1970', 2 parts, *Soviet Studies*, vol. 39, no. 1 (January 1977), pp. 37–61, and no. 2 (April 1977), pp. 270–83.

13 On the historical background, see Romuald J. Misiunas and Rein Taagepera, *The Baltic States: Years of Dependence, 1940–1980* (Berkeley CA: University of California Press, 1983); and on Estonia in particular, Toivo U. Raun, *Estonia and the Estonians*, 2nd edn. (Stanford: Hoover Institution Press, 1991).

14 *Itogi Vsesoyuznoi perepisi naseleniya 1970 goda*, 7 vols. (Moscow: Statistika 1972–74), vol. 3, p. 570.

15 Calculated from *Narodnoe khozyaistvo SSSR v 1987 godu* (Moscow: Finansy i Statistika, 1988), pp. 536, 523–4.

16 On car ownership, see *Izvestiya*, 14 August 1988, p. 3; on housing, see ibid., 4 September 1988, p. 2.

17 Monika Zile, *Latvia* (Moscow: Novosti, 1987), p. 17.

18 Carrère d'Encausse, *Empire*, pp. 212–13. See also more generally Ronald G. Suny, *The Making of the Georgian Nation* (London: Tauris, 1988), and on Armenia, David Marshall Lang, *The Armenians: A People in Exile*, rev. edn (London: Unwin, 1988). All three Caucasian republics have had official status for their national languages since 1978: see *Izvestiya*, 7 January 1989, p. 3.

19 The literature on the Soviet Islamic peoples includes Shirin Akiner, ed., *The Islamic Peoples of the Soviet Union*, 2nd edn (London: Kegan Paul International, 1986); Alexandre Bennigsen and S. Enders Wimbush, eds., *Muslims of the Soviet Empire: A Guide* (Bloomington: Indiana University Press, 1986); Martha Olcott, *The Kazakhs* (Stanford: Hoover Institution Press, 1987); Edward Allworth, *The Modern Uzbeks* (Stanford: Hoover Institution Press, 1989); and Edward Allworth, ed., *Central Asia: 120 Years of Russian Rule* (Durham NC: Duke University Press, 1989).

20 See, for instance, *Pravda*, 12 October 1985, p. 3.

21 For this appointment, see *Pravda*, 31 October 1988, pp. 1, 3.

22 No less than 270 cases of self-immolation over two years were reported in Uzbekistan alone: *Pravda*, 5 February 1988, p. 2.

23 On intermarriage see below, pp. 124–6. Data on knowledge of Russians are in *Chislennost' i sostav naseleniya SSSR* (Moscow: Finansy i statistika, 1984), p. 71. The figures for knowledge of Russian in Central Asia, it was subsequently acknowledged, were artificially inflated (*Istoriya SSSR*, 1987, no. 6, p. 62).

24 See, for instance, Murray Feshbach, *The Soviet Union: Population Trends and Dilemmas* (Washington DC: Population Reference Bureau, 1982).

25 Calculated from *Vestnik statistiki*, 1990, no. 10, pp. 69–71.

26 *Narkhoz 1987*, pp. 536–9.

27 See Ellen Jones and Fred W. Grupp, 'Modernization and ethnic equalization in the USSR', *Soviet Studies*, vol. 36, no. 2 (April 1984), pp. 172–5.

28 *Spravochnik partiinogo rabotnika*, issue 12 (Moscow: Politizdat, 1972), p. 43.

29 *Programma Kommunisticheskoi partii Sovetskogo Soyuza* (Moscow: Politizdat, 1971), p. 113 ('*polnoe edinstvo*'). The term *sliyanie* ('fusion') was not contained in the Programme, although it was used at the 1961 Congress. On the place of these terms in party discourse see Peter Duncan, 'Ideology and the national question', in Stephen White and Alex Pravda, eds., *Ideology and Soviet Politics* (London: Macmillan, 1988).

30 Alex Inkeles and Raymond A. Bauer, *The Soviet Citizen. Daily Life in a Totalitarian Society* (Cambridge MA: Harvard University Press, 1961), pp. 338–73.

31 See Rasma Karklins, 'Nationality policy and ethnic relations in the USSR', in James R. Millar, ed., *Politics, Work, and Daily Life in the USSR* (Cambridge: Cambridge University Press, 1987), pp. 301–31.

32 See V. N. Pimenova, *Svobodnoe vremya v sotsialisticheskom obshchestve* (Moscow: Nauka, 1974), p. 298; *Sovetskaya etnografiya*, 1973, no. 4, pp. 7–12.

33 Yu. V. Arutyunyan, ed., *Sotsial'noe i natsional'noe* (Moscow: Nauka, 1973), pp. 26–8, 52–3.

34 Yu. V. Arutyunyan in *Istoriya SSSR*, 1978, no. 4, pp. 94–104.

35 Yu. V. Arutyunyan and L. M. Drobizheva in *Voprosy istorii*, 1982, no. 7, pp. 3–14.

36 *Pravda*, 29 March 1991, p. 3.

37 A. T. Kholmogorov, *Internatsional'ne cherty sovetskikh natsn* (Moscow: Nauka, 1974), p. 37; *Itogi Vsesoyuznoi perepisi*, vol. 4, p. 5.

38 Alexandre Bennigsen, 'Islam in the Soviet Union', in Bohdan R. Bociurkiw and John W. Strong, eds., *Religion and Atheism in the USSR and Eastern Europe* (London: Macmillan, 1975), p. 97.

39 Yu. V. Arutyunyan and Yu. V. Bromlei, eds., *Sotsial'no-kul'turnyi oblik sovetskikh natsii* (Moscow: Nauka, 1986), p. 153.

40 Ibid., p. 332; and (for the 1989 results) Radio Liberty, *Report on the USSR*, vol. 1, no. 42 (20 October 1989), p. 3.

41 *Chislennost' i sostav*, p. 71.

42 Brian Silver, 'Bilingualism and maintenance of the mothertongue in Soviet Central Asia', *Slavic Review*, vol. 35, no. 3 (Sept. 1976), pp. 409–10.

43 *Sotsial'no-kul'turnyi oblik*, p. 32.

44 Ibid., pp. 34–5, 32.

45 On the circulation of newspapers, see *Narkhoz 1987*, pp. 538–9. On loan words, see Allworth, ed., *Central Asia*, p. 546.

46 Teresa Rakowska-Harmstone, 'The dialectics of nationalism in the USSR', *Problems of Communism*, vol. 23, no. 3 (May–June 1974), pp. 1–22.

47 *Kommunist*, 1977, no. 15, pp. 10–11.

48 See, for example, *Izvestiya*, 7 June 1988, p. 2. For a more general account see Eli Weinerman, 'The elite and common people of Kazakhstan under Kunaev', *Soviet Studies* (forthcoming).

49 *Literaturnaya gazeta*, 1987, no. 1, p. 10.

50 *Guardian*, 19 February 1987, p. 6; *Independent*, 8 May 1987, p. 9. In the summer of 1989 there were further conflicts in the new town of Novy Uzen, in western Kazakhstan; *Izvestiya* reported 'disorders' caused by 'groups of hooligans' and at least three deaths (20 June 1989, p. 6).

51 *Guardian*, 10 June 1988, p. 8. On the Tatars, see Edward Allworth, ed., *The Tatars of the Crimea* (Durham NC: Duke University Press, 1988).

52 On the deported nationalities, see Robert Conquest, *The Nation Killers* (London: Macmillan, 1970), and Alexander M. Nekrich, *The Punished Peoples* (New York: Norton, 1978).

53 *Pravda*, 24 July 1987, p. 2.

54 Ibid., 9 June 1988, p. 6.

55 Ibid., 8 December 1990, p. 2, and 13 February 1991, p. 2 (the referendum produced an affirmative vote of 93.3 per cent: ibid., 28 January 1991, p. 1).

56 *The Times*, 24 August 1987, p. 1, and 27 August 1987, p. 7. There were disparaging reports in *Pravda*, 24 August 1987, p. 8, and *Izvestiya*, 25 August 1987, p. 3.

57 A Lithuanian parliamentary commission in August 1989 declared illegal not simply the 1939 Soviet–German treaties but also Lithuania's decision to join the USSR in July 1940 and the Soviet acceptance of that application in August 1940. See *Pravda*, 25 August 1989, p. 8. The Latvian Popular Front called for the parliamentary vote of July 1940 which led to Latvia's 'annexation by the Soviet Union' to be annulled: *Guardian*, 5 September 1989, p. 20. The Estonian parliament similarly described the incorporation of the republic into the USSR in 1940 as an act of 'annexation': *Sovetskaya Estoniya*, 14 November 1989, p. 1.

58 *Izvestiya*, 12 February 1988, p. 3; *Sotsial'no-kul'turnyi oblik*, p. 38 (towns); *Voprosy istorii*, 1989, no. 5, p. 18 (Latvia).

59 *Guardian*, 26 August 1988, p. 6; Peter Ferdinand, 'The rise of ethnic nationalism in communist regimes in the 1980s', *Journal of Communist Studies* (forthcoming).

60 *XIX Vsesoyuznaya konferentsiya KPSS 28 iyunya – 1 iyulya 1988 goda. Stenograficheskii otchet*, 2 vols. (Moscow: Politizdat, 1988), vol. 1, p. 341.

61 Ibid., vol. 2, p. 71.

62 Ibid., vol. 1, p. 245.

63 Ibid., vol. 1, pp. 340–1.

64 Ibid., vol. 2, p. 157.

65 *Atgimimas*, no. 3, 15 October 1988, pp. 6–7. Brief reports appeared in *Sovetskaya Litva*, 23 and 25 October 1988.

66 *Padomju Jaunatne*, 19 October 1988, p. 3. See also *Sovetskaya Latviya*, 9 and 11 October 1988.

67 On the flags, see *Independent*, 23 August 1988, p. 10 (Estonia), *Guardian*, 21 October 1988, p. 12 (Latvia), *Pravda*, 8 October 1988, p. 3 (Lithuania). On the Lithuanian national anthem, *Pravda*, 8 October 1988, p. 3. On the Lithuanian and Estonian languages, *Sovetskaya Litva*, 19 November 1988, p. 1, and *Guardian*, 21 October 1988, p. 12. Latvian became an official state language somewhat later: *Pravda*, 6 May 1989, p. 3.

68 *Tiesa*, 22 October 1988, pp. 1, 3.

69 *Independent*, 23 August 1988, p. 10.

70 See, for instance, *Pravda*, 26 October 1988, p. 3, 30 October 1988, p. 3, and *Izvestiya*, 19 November 1988, p. 2. On this discussion, see more generally Stephen White, '"Democratisation" in the USSR', *Soviet Studies*, vol. 42, no. 1 (January 1990), pp. 15–16.

71 Gorbachev in *Pravda*, 30 November 1988, p. 2. The Lithuanian Supreme Soviet none the less adopted a constitutional amendment in May 1989 providing that laws of the USSR should be effective in Lithuania only after they had been ratified by its legislature: *Sovetskaya Litva*, 19 May 1989, p. 1. A similar decision was adopted in Latvia: *Sovetskaya Latviya*, 29 July 1989, p. 1.

72 *Vedomosti S"ezda narodnykh deputatov SSSR i Verkhovnogo Soveta SSSR*, 1989, no. 8, item 187; *Izvestiya*, 3 December 1989, p. 1. On Belorussia see ibid., 15 September 1989, pp. 1–2.

73 *Pravda*, 7 January 1989, p. 3.

74 *Sovetskaya Litva*, 19 May 1989, p. 1. For the Latvian draft law on citizenship see *Sovetskaya Latviya*, 27 July 1989, p. 2.

75 *Zakon ESSR o vyborakh v mestnye sovety Estonskoi SSR* (Tallinn: Eesti raamat, 1989), p. 3 (similar legislation was adopted in Latvia: *Sovetskaya Latviya*, 29 July 1989, p. 1). The operation of the law was suspended by the Estonian Supreme Soviet in October (*Sovetskaya Estoniya*, 6 October 1989, p. 1); a new law dropped the restrictions on voting but retained those that related to the deputies themselves (ibid., 23 November 1989, pp. 2–3). Latvia also retained a residence requirement for deputies if not voters: *Sovetskaya Latviya*, 11 November 1989, p. 1.

76 *Vedomosti S"ezda*, 1989, no. 11, item 256. The figure of 80,000 is quoted in *Pravda*, 17 August 1989, p. 3.

77 *Pravda*, 10 January 1989, p. 3 (the Estonian body, 'Intermovement', held its founding congress in March: ibid., 5 March 1989, p. 3). Anxious letters appeared, for instance, in ibid., 21 October 1988, p. 1, 5 November 1988, p. 1, and 15 August 1989, p. 2. Leadership responses were apparent, among others, in Chebrikov's speech in Tallinn: ibid., 15 November 1988, p. 5.

78 *Pravda*, 27 August 1989, p. 1.

79 Some 98 per cent of Estonians, for instance, approved of the republic's constitutional amendments of November 1988: *Voprosy istorii*, 1989, no. 6, p. 140. Sajudis collected 1.8 million signatures to a petition calling for the constitutional amendments not to be discussed: *Vneocherednaya dvenadtsataya sessiya Verkhovnogo Soveta SSSR. 29 noyabrya – 1 dekabrya 1988g. Stenograficheskii otchet* (Moscow: Izvestiya, 1988), p. 63.

80 *The Times*, 24 August 1989, p. 1; *Pravda*, 24 August 1989, p. 3, reported only 'hundreds of thousands'.

81 *Pravda*, 26 June 1989, p. 2, and the *Independent*, 24 August 1989, p. 10. On the Baltic Assembly see *Pravda*, 22 May 1989, p. 2; the full text of the resolutions that were adopted is in *Atmoda*, 19 May 1989, pp. 2–3.

82 The Lithuanian party, in its draft programme, claimed to be 'seeking independence' while still united to the CPSU by a 'common ideological platform': *Sovetskaya Litva*, 22 September 1989, pp. 1, 4. Its direct links with the PUWP are noted in *Pravda*, 27 June 1989, p. 1. Discussions in the Latvian party including the option of full organisational independence are noted in *Pravda*, 31 August 1989, p. 2; the party's draft 'Action programme' sought a 'new status' within the CPSU: *Sovetskaya Latviya*, 5 September 1989, pp. 1–2. An Estonian draft party programme was published in *Rahva Haal*, 11 September 1989, pp. 1–2. For the Lithuanian party's decision in December 1989 to secede from the CPSU, see below, p. 253.

83 *Pravda*, 13 March 1990, p. 3.

84 The Congress of People's Deputies resolved to this effect: *Izvestiya*, 17 March 1990, p. 1.

85 *Pravda*, 14 April 1990, p. 1, and 20 April 1990, p. 1.

86 Ibid., 31 March 1990, p. 2 (Estonia) and *Izvestiya*, 6 May 1990, p. 1 (Latvia). Both decisions were declared invalid by Gorbachev: *Pravda*, 15 May 1990, p. 2.

87 *Pravda*, 30 June 1990, p. 1.

88 Ibid., 7 April 1990, p. 2.

89 Yazov in ibid., 15 January 1991, p. 1.

90 Ibid., 14 January 1991, p. 2, and 26 January 1991, p. 2.

91 Ibid., 15 January 1991, pp. 1 (Yazov) and 2.

92 See its declaration of intent: ibid., 17 January 1991, p. 2.

93 Ibid., 11 February 1991, p. 2.

94 *Sovetskaya Latviya*, 5 March 1991, p. 1 (Latvian result, 87.6 per cent turnout), and *Pravda*, 5 March 1991, p. 2 (Estonian result, 83 per cent turnout).

95 *Pravda*, 13 February 1991, p. 2.

96 Estonia was the last to do so: ibid., 24 February 1990, p. 2.

97 The Estonian suspension of contributions, for instance, was reported in ibid., 17 January 1990, p. 1.

98 On customs services see ibid., 30 November 1990, p. 2 (Lithuania), 4 September 1990, p. 2 (Estonia) and 6 October 1990, p. 2 (Latvia); on stamps and passports see ibid., 8 October 1990, p. 2, and *Izvestiya*, 10 November 1990, p. 1.

99 *Ekho Litvy*, 17 April 1991, p. 1 (Lithuanian budget); *Komsomol'skaya pravda*, 29 March 1991, p. 2 (Latvian currency).

100 *Pravda*, 7 September 1991, p. 1.

101 A good background account is available in Elizabeth Fuller and Kevin Devlin, 'The Armenian imbroglio', in Vojtech Mastny, ed., *Soviet/East European Survey, 1987–1988* (Boulder, CO: Westview Press, 1989), pp. 161–74; for more recent developments see Christopher J. Walker, ed., *Armenia and the Karabagh: the struggle for unity* (London: Minority Rights Group, 1991).

102 The 1979 census data are in *Chislennost' i sostav*, p. 126.
103 Fuller and Devlin, 'Armenian imbroglio', p. 161.
104 *Yezhegodnik Bol'shoi Sovetskoi entsiklopedii 1989 g.* (Moscow: Sovetskaya entsiklopediya, 1989), p. 107. There have been suggestions that the KGB encouraged or at least permitted this remarkable vote: see *Izvestiya*, 24 February 1992, p. 2.
105 *Guardian*, 1 June 1988, p. 6.
106 *Sovetskaya Rossiya*, 22 March 1988, p. 4, citing USSR Procuracy figures.
107 *Pravda*, 24 March 1988, p. 5.
108 Ibid., 24 March 1988, p. 5, and 28 March 1988, p. 3.
109 *Izvestiya*, 17 June 1988, p. 2, and 19 June 1988, p. 2.
110 *Vedomosti Verkhovnogo Soveta SSSR*, 1988, no. 30, p. 547.
111 *Guardian*, 7 December 1988, p. 24 (an official figure of 43 deaths was later reported: *Pravda*, 7 January 1989, p. 6). On refugee numbers, see *Pravda*, 27 April 1989, p. 6, and 2 June 1989, p. 2, respectively.
112 *Vedomosti Verkhovnogo Soveta SSSR*, 1989, no. 3, item 14.
113 *Pravda*, 10 May 1989, p. 2.
114 Ibid., 5 June 1989, p. 8.
115 *Pravda*, 29 November 1989, p. 1.
116 Ibid., 11 January 1990, p. 1.
117 *Pravda*, 24 January 1990, p. 5.
118 *Argumenty i fakty*, 1989, no. 39, p 1.
119 *Guardian*, 13 June 1989, p. 8. Unofficial Muslim sources put the death toll at several hundred and the number of injured at about 3,000 (ibid.).
120 *Independent*, 7 June 1989, p. 15. The casualty figures were in *Pravda*, 7 June 1989, p. 8.
121 *Independent*, 7 June 1989, p. 15.
122 *Pravda*, 7 June 1989, p. 8.
123 For the historical background, see Conquest, *Nation Killers*, pp. 48–9, 188–9. Present numbers as cited in *Pravda*, 7 June 1989, p. 6.
124 *Guardian*, 9 June 1989, p. 8; *Independent*, 7 June 1989, p. 15.
125 *Guardian*, 9 June 1989, p. 8; *Izvestiya*, 15 June 1989, p. 6.
126 *Pravda*, 10 June 1989, p. 8, and 15 June 1989, p. 6.
127 *Izvestiya*, 15 June 1989, p. 6, and *Pravda*, 15 June 1989, p. 6.
128 *Izvestiya*, 18 June 1989, p. 6.
129 *Guardian*, 14 June 1989, p. 10.
130 *Pravda*, 16 June 1989, pp. 2, 5, and 15 June 1989, p. 2.
131 Ibid., 26 July 1990, p. 3.
132 Ibid., 15 June 1989, p. 6
133 Ibid., 26 July 1990, p. 3.
134 According to the 1979 census, 96.1 per cent of Georgians lived in the Georgian SSR and 68.8 per cent of its population was Georgian (only 7.4 per cent, a steadily declining share, was Russian): *Sotsial'no-kul'turnyi oblik*, pp. 32, 34.
135 On these events see Suny, *Making*, pp. 303, 309.
136 *Pravda*, 3 January 1989, p. 2.
137 *Guardian*, 27 February 1989, p. 8.

138 Ibid., 8 April 1989, p. 6; *Pravda*, 4 June 1989, p. 6.
139 *Guardian*, 8 April 1989, p. 6 (the dismissal was reported in *Pravda*, 7 April 1989, p. 5).
140 *Pravda*, 4 June 1989, p. 6.
141 *Guardian*, 8 April 1989, p. 6. According to the 1979 census Georgians accounted for 43.8 per cent of the Abkhaz ASSR population, and Abkhazians themselves for just 17.1 per cent (*Chislennost' i sostav*, p. 124).
142 *Pravda*, 10 April 1989, p. 1, and 12 April 1989, p. 6.
143 *Guardian*, 10 April 1989, p. 1; Tass in *Pravda*, 10 April 1989, p. 8; and on the use of gas, *Guardian*, 26 April 1989, p. 10.
144 Shevardnadze's hints to this effect were reported in the *Guardian*, 15 April 1989, p. 24.
145 *Pravda*, 14 April 1989, p. 1.
146 Ibid., 15 April 1989, p. 3.
147 *Guardian*, 29 May 1989, p. 7.
148 *Pravda*, 17 July 1989, p. 8. Ten days later the death toll was 18 and 294 had been wounded: *Pravda*, 27 July 1989, p. 6.
149 Ibid., 25 November 1990, p. 2.
150 *Izvestiya*, 2 April 1991, p. 1 (vote) and 9 April 1991, p. 1.
151 Gamsakhurdia's election is in ibid., 27 May 1991, p. 1, and his flight is in ibid., 6 January 1992, p. 1. For Shevardnadze's appointment see *Pravda*, 10 March 1991, p. 1.
152 *Izvestiya*, 11 September 1989, p. 3. Rukh's programme appeared in *Literarna Ukraina*, 28 September 1989, pp. 4–5, and its statute in ibid., p. 6. According to *Pravda* (15 September 1989, p. 1) Rukh already had a 280,000 membership. The declaration of sovereignty is in ibid., 17 July 1990, p. 2.
153 *Pravda*, 28 June 1989, p. 6.
154 Ibid., 2 April 1989, p. 1. The first Congress of Germans of the USSR took place in October 1991: see *Izvestiya*, 28 October 1991, p. 3; the demand for an autonomous republic was reiterated.
155 Ibid., 28 Aug. 1989 and ff. (riots), and 1 September 1989, p. 4 (law).
156 *Pravda*, 3 June 1989, pp. 3, 4, 1 September 1990, p. 3, and 13 October 1990, p. 1.
157 *Sovetskaya Rossiya*, 11 September 1989, p. 2, and similarly 18 June 1989, p. 3; *Izvestiya*, 7 April 1989, p. 3, and 15 June 1989, p. 4; and *Kommunist*, 1988, no. 16, pp. 76–83.
158 *Izvestiya*, 26 May 1990, pp. 1–2.
159 Ibid., 12 June 1990, p. 1.
160 *Pravda*, 21 June 1990, p. 1, reported the decision to form such a party; Polozkov's election is in ibid., 24 June 1990, p. 1.
161 See ibid., 19 February 1990, p. 2, 24 November 1990, p. 2, *Izvestiya*, 10 April 1991, p. 1 (Academy of Sciences), ibid., 6 May 1991, p. 1 (KGB) and ibid., 12 May 1991, p. 1 (television and radio service).
162 *Pravda*, 17 June 1990, p. 1.
163 Ibid., 2 September 1990, p. 2.
164 Ibid., 18 October 1990, p. 4.
165 Ibid., 6 June 1990, p. 3; an attack on the 'myth of the 70 billion' appeared in *Soyuz*, 1991, no. 2, p. 9.

166 *Narodnoe khozyaistvo SSSR v 1989 g.* (Moscow: Finansy i statistika, 1990), pp. 639–40.

167 *Pravda*, 18 October 1990, p. 5, and ibid., 28 February 1991, p. 2.

168 *Moscow News*, 1991, no. 1, p. 6 (event of year and man of year); the *Financial Times*, 4 September 1990, p. 6, noted that he had overtaken Gorbachev in popularity.

169 *Sem's plyusom*, 1991, no. 12, p. 4.

170 For criticism of Yel'tsin see *Pravda*, 1 April 1991, p. 2, and 2 April 1991, p. 2. His call for the resignation of the President (ibid., 20 February 1991, pp. 1–2) was deemed unconstitutional by the Supreme Soviet (ibid., 22 February 1991, p. 1).

171 *Izvestiya*, 24 April 1991, p. 1.

172 M. S. Gorbachev, *Izbrannye rechi i stat'i*, 6 vols. (Moscow: Politizdat, 1987–89), vol. 1, pp. 50–3, 69–78.

173 Ibid., pp. 225–36.

174 Ibid., vol. 2, p. 96.

175 *Materialy vneochernogo plenuma TsK KPSS 11 marta 1985 goda* (Moscow: Politizdat, 1985), p. 13; Gorbachev, *Izbrannye rechi i stat'i*, vol. 2, p. 196.

176 Gorbachev, *Izbrannye rechi i stat'i*, vol. 3, p. 233.

177 Mikhail Gorbachev, *Perestroika: New Thinking for Our Country and the World* (London: Collins, 1987), pp. 118–22.

178 Gorbachev, *Izbrannye rechi i stat'i*, vol. 4, pp. 329–31.

179 Ibid., vol. 4, p. 374.

180 Ibid., vol. 5, p. 415, and vol. 6, p. 73.

181 *XIX Vsesoyuznaya konferentsiya*, vol. 1, pp. 65–7.

182 Ibid., vol. 2, pp. 156–60.

183 *Pravda*, 3 December 1988, pp. 1–2.

184 Ibid., 12 November 1988, p. 1.

185 Ibid., 14 March 1989, pp. 2–3.

186 See for example Slyun'kov to a CC conference, *Pravda*, 1 February 1989, p. 2, and an article by Maslyukov with this title, *Pravda*, 23 March 1989, p. 2.

187 See for instance *Pravda*, 16 February 1989, p. 3.

188 Ibid., 17 August 1989, pp. 1–2.

189 Ibid., 20 September 1989, pp. 2–3.

190 *Pravda*, 16 March 1990, p. 2.

191 Ibid., 13 March 1990, p. 1.

192 *Materialy XXVIII s"ezda KPSS* (Moscow: Politizdat, 1990), pp. 22–4.

193 *Pravda*, 4 July 1990, p. 2.

194 Ibid., 8 July 1990, p. 7.

195 Ibid., p. 3.

196 Ibid., p. 4.

197 Ibid., 12 July 1990, p. 2.

198 Ibid., 3 May 1990, pp. 1–2.

199 Ibid., 7 May 1990, p. 5.

200 Ibid., 17 April 1990, pp. 1–2.

201 The Gorno-Altai autonomous region, for example, declared itself an autonomous republic: *Izvestiya*, 26 October 1990, p. 3.

202 Ibid., 24 November 1990, pp. 1–2.

203 *Pravda*, 19 August 1990, pp. 1–2.

204 *Materialy plenuma Tsentral'nogo komiteta KPSS 8–9 oktyabrya 1990 g.* (Moscow: Politizdat, 1990), pp. 11–12.

205 *Pravda*, 13 December 1990, p. 1.

206 Ibid., 12 December 1990, p. 3.

207 Gorbachev's speech is in ibid., 18 December 1990, p.. 2; the resolution is in ibid., 26 December 1990, p. 1.

208 *Izvestiya*, 9 March 1991, p. 2.

209 *Materialy plenuma Tsentral'nogo komiteta KPSS 10–11 dekabrya 1990 g.* (Moscow: Politizdat, 1991), p. 45.

210 For an overview of the referendum see *Report on the USSR*, vol. 3, no. 13 (29 March 1991) and Commission on Security and Cooperation in Europe, *Referendum in the Soviet Union* (Washington DC: US Government Printing Office, 1991).

211 *Pravda*, 20 March 1991, pp. 1–2.

212 The Supreme Soviet resolution on the results is in ibid., 22 March 1991, pp. 1; the full results are in *Izvestiya*, 28 March 1991, pp. 1, 3. For the vote in (for instance) Lithuania see *Pravda*, 21 March 1991 p. 3 (98.98 per cent of those who voted supported the proposition).

213 *Izvestiya*, 27 March 1991, p. 3.

214 *Nezavisimaya gazeta*, 21 March 1991, p. 1.

215 *Leninskoe znamya*, 21 March 1991, p. 1.

216 *Nezavisimaya gazeta*, 21 March 1991, p. 1.

217 *Izvestiya*, 10 April 1991, p. 1.

218 Ibid., 24 July 1991, p. 1.

219 *Pravda*, 15 August 1991, p. 2.

220 *Izvestiya*, 20 December 1991, p. 2.

221 *Pravda*, 3 September 1991, p. 1.

222 See *Vedomosti S"ezda narodnykh deputatov SSSR i Verkhovnogo Soveta SSSR*, 1991, no. 37, item 1082.

223 *Izvestiya*, 15 November 1991, p. 1; the text was printed in *Pravda*, 27 November 1991, pp. 1–2.

224 *Pravda*, 6 December 1991, p. 1.

225 *Izvestiya*, 10 December 1991, p. 1.

226 Ibid., 23 December 1991, p. 1.

227 Ibid., 26 December 1991, p. 1.

228 *Voprosy ekonomiki*, 1991, no. 12, p. 6.

229 *Izvestiya*, 7 February 1992, p. 1.

230 Ibid., 10 April 1991, p. 2.

231 Makhkamov in *Pravda*, 2 June 1989, p. 5.

232 Ibid., 3 January 1989, p. 2.

233 *Izvestiya*, 7 January 1989, p. 3; similarly *Pravda*, 12 July 1989, p. 3.

234 For the figure of 75 million see Gorbachev in *Pravda*, 7 February 1991, p. 2 (in ibid., 25 March 1991, he gave the figure of 70 million). According to the 1989 census only 3.5 per cent of Russians had a fluent knowledge of another Soviet language (*Chislennost' i sostav*, p. 71).

235 *Kommunist*, 1987, no. 13, p. 12. In Kirgizia the introduction of Kirgiz as a state language had to be postponed because of such shortages: *Izvestiya*, 29 April 1993, p. 1.

236 *Izvestiya*, 20 December 1991, p. 1.

237 Ibid., 19 November 1991, p. 1. The Dnestr republic was declared on 25 August 1991; the declaration was confirmed in a referendum on 1 December 1991 (*Pravda*, 4 June 1992, p. 2).

238 *Pravda*, 29 November 1991, p. 1.

239 *Izvestiya*, 5 June 1992, p. 1; *Rossiiskaya gazeta*, 8 April 1992, p. 4 (Rutskoi). The Dnestr area, it was later agreed, should be given a special status with extensive autonomy: *Izvestiya*, 5 March 1993, p. 2. Foreign ministry spokesmen pointed out that, with their families, up to 50 million people of Russian descent lived elsewhere in the former USSR (*Izvestiya*, 26 June 1992, p. 6), and their exclusion from the franchise was vigorously contested (see ibid., 2 April 1992, p. 5, 14 April 1992, p. 5, and 8 May 1992, p. 1).

240 Ibid., 25 October 1991, p. 2, and 27 December 1991, p. 1. For the referendum result see ibid., 23 March 1992, p. 1 (61.4 per cent voted in favour on an 81.6 per cent turnout). The Russian Constitutional Court's ruling on the referendum is in *Izvestiya*, 18 March 1992, p. 2.

241 Ibid., 15 February 1992, p. 1.

242 *Pravda*, 30 November 1991, p. 1.

243 Ibid., 16 December 1991, p. 1 (referendum; the declaration of independence was originally made in September: ibid., 4 September 1991, p. 1); *Izvestiya*, 13 December 1991, p. 1 (Commonwealth application); ibid., 28 November 1991, p. 1 (Azerbaijani resolution).

244 *Pravda*, 25 March 1991, p. 5.

245 *Rossiiskaya gazeta*, 27 August 1991, p. 2.

246 *Izvestiya*, 1 February 1991, p. 1, and (for Meshkov's election), ibid., 1 February 1994, p. 1.

247 *International Herald Tribune*, 25 February 1992, p. 1.

248 *Izvestiya*, 17 February 1992, p. 1.

249 Ibid., 11 February 1992, p. 1.

250 Ibid., 14 September 1991, p. 1. On the Russian-Estonian border dispute more particularly see *Nezavisimaya gazeta*, 18 March 1992, p. 2.

251 *Izvestiya*, 14 February 1992, p. 2, and 20 March 1992, p. 3.

252 Ibid., 3 December 1991, p. 2.

253 See *Radio Liberty Research Bulletin* RL 221/85, 3 July 1985.

254 E. Bagramov in *Pravda*, 14 August 1987, p. 2.

6 The Soviet Union and the wider world

1 For the historical background on Soviet–Western dealings see Paul Dukes, *October and the World* (London: Macmillan, 1979), chs. 1–3.

2 Isaiah Berlin, *Russian Thinkers* (Harmondsworth: Penguin, 1979), p. 181.

3 On Russian messianism, see, for instance, Alexander Yanov, *The Russian Challenge and the Year 2000* (Oxford: Blackwell, 1987), and Mikhail S. Agursky, *The Third Rome: National Bolshevism in the USSR* (Boulder, CO: Westview, 1987).

4 On Tsarist–Soviet continuities, see Ivo J. Lederer, *Russian Foreign Policy: Essays in Perspective* (New Haven: Yale University Press, 1962).

5 See David R. Jones, 'The Soviet defence burden through the prism of history', in Carl G. Jacobsen, ed., *The Soviet Defence Enigma* (Oxford University Press, 1987), pp. 151–74.

6 A. A. Gromyko *et al.*, eds., *Diplomaticheskii slovar'*, 4th edn, 3 vols. (Moscow: Nauka, 1984–86), vol. 1, pp. 312–24; and (for the late 1980s figure) *Mezhdunarodnaya zhizn'*, 1991, no. 2, p. 160.

7 *Pervyi kongress Kominterna* (Moscow: Partiinoe izdatel'stvo, 1933), p. 199.

8 *Narodnoe khozyaistvo SSSR v 1987 godu* (Moscow: Finansy i statistika, 1988), p. 611.

9 *Vneshnyaya torgovlya SSSR v 1987 g. Statisticheskii sbornik* (Moscow: Finansy i statistika, 1988), p. 4.

10 *Narkhoz 1988*, p. 654.

11 Ibid., p. 574.

12 *United Nations Statistical Yearbook* (New York: United Nations, various dates) and *Pravda*, 24 September 1988, p. 3.

13 *UNESCO Statistical Yearbook 1988* (Paris: UNESCO, 1988), tables 7.12 and 3.11.

14 V. I. Lenin, *Polnoe sobranie sochinenii*, 5th edn, 55 vols. (Moscow: Politizdat, 1958–65), vol. 39, p. 89. For similar sentiments, see ibid., vol. 37, pp. 511, 520.

15 *Kommunisticheskii internatsional*, 1924, no. 1, cols. 142–7.

16 The figure of 26.6 million deaths is given in *Vestnik statistiki*, 1990, no. 10, p. 27; for earlier assessments see *Voprosy istorii*, 1989, no. 2, pp. 132–9, and *Sotsiologicheskie issledovaniya*, 1989, no. 1, pp. 60–6.

17 A. A. Gromyko *et al.*, eds., *Istoriya diplomatii*, 2nd edn, 5 vols. (Moscow: Nauka, 1959–79) vol. 5, part 1, pp. 120, 133.

18 On these developments, see, for instance, Hugh Seton-Watson, *The East European Revolution* (London: Methuen, 1961), and Martin McCauley, ed., *Communist Power in Europe, 1944–1949* (London: Macmillan, 1977). More general works on Soviet foreign policy include Adam Ulam, *Expansion and Coexistence: Soviet Foreign Policy 1917–1973*, 2nd edn (New York: Praeger, 1974), and Adam Ulam, *Dangerous Relations: The Soviet Union in World Politics 1970–1982* (New York: Oxford University Press, 1983). On the Brezhnev years, Robin Edmonds, *Soviet Foreign Policy: The Brezhnev Years* (Oxford University Press, 1983), and Jonathan Steele, *The Limits of Soviet Power* (Harmondsworth: Penguin, 1985) are particularly valuable. On changes in doctrine, see Margot Light, *The Soviet Theory of International Relations* (Brighton: Wheatsheaf, 1988).

19 Leonid Brezhnev, *Leninskim kursom*, 9 vols. (Moscow: Politizdat, 1970–83), vol. 6, p. 100.

20 For these developments, see, for instance, Hugh Seton-Watson, *The Imperialist Revolutionaries: World Communism in the 1960s and 1970s* (London: Hutchinson, 1980), and Adam Westoby, *Communism since World War II* (Brighton: Harvester, 1981). Current events are well covered in the *Yearbook of International Communist Affairs* (Stanford: Hoover Institution, annually since 1966).

21 The renewal of the WTO for twenty years was reported in *Pravda*, 27 April 1985, p. 1; for a more extensive documentation, see *Organizatsiya Varshavskogo dogovora 1955–1985: Dokumenty i materialy* (Moscow: Politizdat, 1986). The CMEA was founded in 1949; Mongolia became a member in 1962, Cuba in 1972, and Vietnam in 1978. For a comprehensive documentation, see *Osnovnye dokumenty SEV*, 4th edn, 2 vols. (Moscow: SEV, 1981–83).

22 On the question of classification, see, for instance, Stephen White, 'What is a communist system?', *Studies in Comparative Communism*, vol. 16, no. 4 (winter 1983), pp. 247–63.

23 V. P. Agafonov and V. F. Khalipov, *Sovremennaya epokha i mirovoi revolyutsionnyi protsess* (Moscow: Vysshaya shkola, 1988), p. 20.

24 On the earlier history of the world communist movement, see, for instance, Hugh Seton-Watson, *The Pattern of Communist Revolution: A Historical Analysis* (London: Methuen, 1960). The Soviet interpretation is recorded in B. N. Ponomarev *et al.*, eds., *Mezhdunarodnoe rabochee dvizhenie*, 8 vols. (Moscow: Mysl', 1976–85).

25 For the full record see *Mezhdunarodnoe soveshchanie kommunisticheskikh i rabochikh partii. Dokumenty i materialy* (Moscow: Politizdat, 1969).

26 M. S. Gorbachev, *Izbrannye rechi i stat'i*, 6 vols. (Moscow: Politizdat, 1987–89), vol. 3, p. 255.

27 Ibid., vol. 2, pp. 99–103. For helpful background discussions see Margot Light, '"New thinking" in Soviet foreign policy?', *Coexistence*, vol. 24, no. 3 (1987), pp. 233–43; Boris Meissner, '"New thinking" and Soviet foreign policy', *Aussenpolitik*, vol. 40, no. 2 (1989), pp. 101–18; and David Holloway, 'Gorbachev's new thinking', *Foreign Affairs*, vol. 68, no. 1 (1989), pp. 66–81.

28 Gorbachev, *Izbrannye rechi i stat'i*, vol. 2, pp. 109–16.

29 Ibid., pp. 125–6. Gorbachev's policy towards Europe was fully set out in his *Perestroika: New Thinking for Our Country and the World* (London: Collins, 1987), ch. 6; for a critical discussion, see Neil Malcolm, *Soviet Policy Perspectives on Western Europe* (London: Routledge, 1989). Alexander Yakovlev, speaking to the Italian Communist Party, took the view that 'objectively only one Europe exists' (*Pravda*, 21 March 1989, p. 4).

30 Gorbachev, *Izbrannye rechi i stat'i*, vol. 2, p. 131.

31 Ibid., pp. 167–72.

32 Ibid., pp. 460, 466–7.

33 Ibid., vol. 3, p. 9.

34 Ibid., pp. 183–96.

35 For the text, see *Spravochnik partiinogo rabotnika*, issue 27 (Moscow: Politizdat, 1987), pp. 342–4.

36 Gorbachev, *Izbrannye rechi i stat'i*, vol. 4, pp. 376–91.

37 Ibid., vol. 2, p. 178; *Pravda*, 30 July 1985, p. 1 and 27 February 1987, p. 4 (resumption); *Pravda*, 16 January 1986, pp. 1–2.

38 Gorbachev, *Izbrannye rechi i stat'i*, vol. 3, p. 248; WTO communiqué in *Pravda*, 12 June 1986, pp. 1–2 (the meaning of 'reasonable sufficiency' remained somewhat opaque).

39 A cut of 500,000 men and a 'substantial' reduction in military spending were formally approved by the USSR Supreme Soviet Presidium in March

1989 (*Pravda*, 22 March 1989, p. 1). WTO figures for the East–West balance in Europe were made public in *Pravda*, 30 January 1989, p. 5, and for tactical nuclear weapons in *Pravda*, 19 April 1989, p. 4.

40 *Tezisy Tsentral'nogo komiteta KPSS k XIX Vsesoyuznoi partiinoi konferentsii* (Moscow: Politizdat, 1988), pp. 27–30.

41 The first open attack on the Brezhnev-Gromyko legacy in foreign policy appeared in *Literaturnaya gazeta*, 18 May 1988, p. 14. On the importance of democratic control see for example Shevardnadze's interview in *Izvestiya*, 22 March 1989, p. 5. He and Gorbachev, he explained later, although Politburo members at the time, had learned of the intervention in Afghanistan only from newspapers and the radio (*Pravda*, 24 October 1989, p. 3).

42 *Pravda*, 8 December 1988, pp. 1.2.

43 For the Soviet text see *Vneshnyaya politika Sovetskogo Soyuza 1963 god* (Moscow: Mezhdunarodnye otnosheniya, 1964), pp. 172–5. For a good general guide to arms control issues, see Morris McCain, *Understanding Arms Control: The Options* (New York: Norton, 1989). On Soviet doctrine more particularly, see Michael MccGwire, *Military Objectives in Soviet Foreign Policy* (Washington: Brookings, 1987), and Stephen Shenfield, *The Nuclear Predicament, Explorations in Soviet Ideology* (London: Routledge, 1987). On Soviet policy, see David Holloway, *The Soviet Union and the Arms Race* (New Haven: Yale University Press, 1983).

44 McCain, *Understanding Arms Control*, pp. 129–31.

45 Text in *Vneshnyaya politika 1968 god*, pp. 154–62.

46 Text in ibid., *1971 god*, pp. 11–16.

47 For the Soviet texts of the SALT I and ABM treaties see *Sbornik deistvuyushchikh dogovorov, soglashenii i konventsii, zaklyuchennykh SSSR s inostrannymi gosudarstvami*, issue 28 (1973), pp. 35–7 and 31–5. For the Basic Principles, see *Vneshnyaya politika 1972 god*, pp. 84–6.

48 *Vneshnyaya politika 1973 god*, pp. 67–70; *1974 god* pp. 168–72.

49 Text in ibid., *1979 god*, pp. 93–102. For the background to the negotiations, see Strobe Talbott, *Endgame* (New York: Harper and Row, 1979) and *Deadly Gambits* (New York: Knopf, 1984). A fuller account, generally less favourable to the American than the Soviet side, is in Raymond L. Garthoff, *Detente and Confrontation: American–Soviet Relations from Nixon to Reagan* (Washington: Brookings, 1985). For current perspectives, see Arnold L. Horelick, ed., *US–Soviet Relations: The Next Phase* (Ithaca: Cornell University Press, 1986), and Daniel N. Nelson and Roger B. Anderson, eds., *Soviet–American Relations: Understanding Differences, Avoiding Conflicts* (Wilmington: Scholarly Resources, 1988).

50 Quoted in *Sovetskaya-amerikanskaya vstrecha na vysshem urovne. Moskva 29 maya – 2 iyunya 1988 goda. Dokumenty i materialy* (Moscow: Politizdat, 1988), pp. 58, 165.

51 For the Soviet text of the Final Act, see *Vo imya mira, bezopasnosti i sotrudnichestva* (Moscow: Politizdat, 1975).

52 *Sovetskaya-amerikanskaya vstrecha na vysshem urovne. Zheneva 19–21 noyabrya 1985 goda. Dokumenty i materialy* (Moscow: Politizdat, 1985, p. 13).

53 Ibid., pp. 18–20.

54 Ibid., p. 48.

55 Ibid., p. 14.

56 Ibid., pp. 39, 59, 30, 66, 31, 39.

57 *Izvestiya*, 21 August 1986, p. 4; *Pravda*, 23 September 1986, p. 5.

58 *Sovetskaya-amerikanskaya vstrecha na vysshem urovne. Rei'kyavik, 11–12 noya-brya 1986 goda* (Moscow: Politizdat, 1986), p. 36.

59 Ibid., pp. 12–15.

60 Ibid., pp. 32–3.

61 *Vizit General'nogo sekretarya TsK KPSS M. S. Gorbacheva v Soedinennye Shtaty Ameriki 7–10 dekabrya 1987 goda. Dokumenty i materialy* (Moscow: Politizdat, 1987). For the treaty text, see pp. 36–56; for the final communiqué see pp. 141–53.

62 Ibid., pp. 164–9.

63 Ibid., p. 170.

64 *Pravda*, 17 December 1988, p. 4 (poll); *Pravda*, 11 February 1988, p. 4; and *Izvestiya*, 4 May 1988, p. 5 (letters).

65 *Sovetskaya-amerikanskaya vstrecha na vysshem urovne. Moskva, 29 maya–2 iyunya 1988 goda*, p. 186.

66 Ibid., pp. 185–202, 140–5 (press conference), 216 (Politburo).

67 A full record of the summit is available in *Gosudarstvennyi vizit Presidenta SSSR M. S. Gorbacheva v Soedinennye Shtaty Ameriki 30 maya – 4 iyunya 1990 goda* (Moscow: Politizdat, 1990).

68 The results of the summit were summed up at the two leaders' final press conference: *Izvestiya*, 1 August 1991, p. 6.

69 For good background accounts, see, for instance, Sarah M. Terry, *Soviet Policy in Eastern Europe* (New Haven: Yale University Press, 1984); Robert L. Hutchings, *Soviet–East European Relations: Consolidation and Conflict, 1968–80* (Madison: University of Wisconsin Press, 1983); Hélène Carrère d'Encausse, *Big Brother. The Soviet Union and Soviet Europe* (New York: Holmes and Meier, 1987); J. F. Brown, *Eastern Europe and Communist Rule* (Durham: Duke University Press, 1988); Karen L. Dawisha, *Eastern Europe, Gorbachev and Reform*, 2nd edn. (Cambridge: Cambridge University Press, 1990); and Charles Gati, *The Bloc that Failed. Soviet–East European Relations in Transition* (London: Tauris, 1990).

70 *Pravda*, 22 August 1968, p. 1; Brezhnev, *Leninskim kursom*, vol. 2, p. 329.

71 A full and judicious account of the historical background is available in Norman Davies, *God's Playground. A History of Poland*, 2 vols. (New York: Columbia University Press, 1982).

72 *Pravda*, 12 June 1981, p. 2.

73 *Pravda*, 14 December 1981, p. 4.

74 *Izvestiya*, 20 August 1989, p. 3, praised the new prime minister's 'prudence'; the Council of Ministers' official congratulations appeared in *Pravda*, 26 August 1989, p. 4.

75 See Light, *Soviet Theory*, pp. 306–7.

76 For a background account with documentation, see John Gittings, *Survey of the Sino-Soviet Dispute* (London: Oxford University Press, 1968). The origins of the dispute and bloc relations in general are considered in Zbigniew K.

Brzezinski, *The Soviet Bloc: Unity and Conflict*, rev. edn (Cambridge MA: Harvard University Press, 1967).

77 *Pravda*, 22 November 1957, p. 3.

78 Brezhnev, *Leninskim kursom*, vol. 5, p. 459, and vol. 8, pp. 642–3.

79 Gorbachev, *Izbrannye rechi i stat'i*, vol. 2, p. 131.

80 *Pravda*, 18 March 1985, p. 4.

81 *Izvestiya*, 6 April 1985, p. 4; *Pravda*, 11 July 1985, p. 4.

82 Gorbachev, *Izbrannye rechi i stat'i*, vol. 3, p. 254.

83 Ibid., vol. 4, pp. 25–34.

84 *Pravda*, 6 December 1988, p. 5; ibid., 6 February 1989, p. 1.

85 Ibid., 16 May 1989, p. 2, 18 May 1989, p. 1, and 19 May 1989, p. 1 (final communiqué).

86 Soviet policy towards the developing world has been very fully investigated: see, for instance, Elizabeth K. Valkenier, *The Soviet Union and the Third World: An Economic Bind* (New York: Praeger, 1983); Jerry F. Hough, *The Struggle for the Third World* (Washington: Brookings, 1986); and Galia Golan, *The Soviet Union and National Liberation Movements in the Third World* (Boston: Unwin Hyman, 1988).

87 See, for instance, R. A. Ul'yanovsky, 'O stranakh sotsialisticheskoi orientatsii', *Kommunist*, 1979, no. 11, pp. 119–29.

88 For the background, see, for instance, Henry S. Bradsher, *Afghanistan and the Soviet Union* (Durham: Duke University Press, 1983); Thomas T. Hammond, *Red Flag over Afghanistan* (Boulder: Westview, 1984); and Amin Saikal and William Maley, eds., *The Soviet Withdrawal from Afghanistan* (Cambridge: Cambridge University Press, 1989).

89 *Pravda*, 29 December 1979, p. 4. According to sources made available in 1989, Soviet diplomats had warned Moscow of an increasing US military presence in the Afghan capital: *Krasnaya zvezda*, 18 November 1989, pp. 3–4

90 *Pravda*, 28 December 1979, p. 4, and 29 December 1979, p. 4.

91 Brezhnev, *Leninskim kursom*, vol. 8, p. 645.

92 *Pravda*, 5 May 1986, p. 4.

93 Ibid., 2 January 1987, p. 4 (Najibullah to the PDPA Central Committee).

94 *Pravda*, 8 June 1986, p. 3.

95 Ibid., 17 August 1989, p. 6.

96 See Jim Riordan, 'Return of the Afgantsy', *Detente*, no. 12 (1988), pp. 13–15, 37.

97 *Pravda*, 25 November 1987, p. 6.

98 Brezhnev, *Leninskim kursom*, vol. 8, p. 665.

99 For the texts of the agreements, see *Izvestiya*, 16 April 1988, p. 5.

100 *Pravda*, 15 April 1988, p. 1.

101 Ibid., 24 October 1989, p. 3.

102 See, for instance, Fred Halliday, *Threat from the East?* (Harmondsworth: Penguin, 1982).

103 See Karen L. Dawisha, *Soviet Policy towards Egypt* (London: Macmillan, 1979).

104 Brezhnev, *Leninskim kursom*, vol. 8, p. 646.

105 *Pravda*, 22 August 1988, p. 1.
106 See Peter Duncan, *The Soviet Union and India* (London: Routledge, 1989).
107 *Pravda*, 28 November 1986, p. 1; see also above, p. 197.
108 *Pravda*, 21 November 1988, pp. 1–2.
109 Brezhnev, *Leninskim kursom*, vol. 8, p. 645.
110 *Pravda*, 6 March 1985, p. 4, and 7 March 1988, p. 5.
111 Gorbachev, *Izbrannye rechi i stat'i*, vol. 3, pp. 256–7.
112 See Stephen White, *Soviet Communism: Programme and Rules* (London: Routledge, 1989), p. 99, and for commentaries, *Pravda*, 14 November 1986, pp. 2–3 (Ye. Plimak) and 10 July 1987, p. 4 (Ye. Primakov).
113 Gorbachev, speaking in Minsk, asked why Iraq was seen as an aggressor but not Israel, which had also violated UN resolutions. And why had the United States, which had invaded Grenada and Panama, been allowed to expatiate about the rights of man? (*Pravda*, 28 February 1991, p. 2). Gorbachev's statement on the outbreak of the war, however, emphasised that everything must be done to bring it to an end in cooperation with other countries and the UN (ibid., 18 January 1991, p. 1), and foreign ministry statements took the same line (for instance ibid., 13 December 1990, p. 5).
114 Brezhnev, *Leninskim kursom*, vol. 9, p. 304.
115 Holloway, 'Gorbachev's new thinking', p. 80.
116 In January 1990 the Soviet Union and Israel concluded a trading agreement signifying the resumption of official relations after a gap of more than twenty years (see *Izvestiya*, 24 January 1990, p. 4); full diplomatic relations were restored the following year (*Izvestiya*, 19 October 1991, p. 1). Consular relations with South Africa were restored at the same time: ibid., 11 November 1991, p. 1.
117 Results for several West European countries were reported in *Izvestiya*, 14 June 1987, pp. 4–5, and in the *Guardian*, 27 May 1989, p. 24. West Germans were generally the most favourably inclined (*Guardian*, 19 October 1988, p. 5), the French the most sceptical (*Guardian*, 4 July 1989, p. 10).
118 Cited in *Pravda*, 8 January 1988, p. 4, and 4 October 1987, p. 4.
119 To quote the title of Stephen Sestanovich, 'Gorbachev's foreign policy: a diplomacy of decline', *Problems of Communism*, vol. 37, no. 1 (January–February 1988), pp. 1–15.
120 *Pravda*, 10 December 1989, p. 2.
121 By 1989 the CPSU was compelled to recognise more than one communist party in Australia, Costa Rica, Finland, Greece, India, New Zealand, Spain and Sweden (*Problems of Communism*, vol. 38, no. 1 (January–February 1989), p. 48).
122 See Center for Defense Information, 'Soviet geopolitical momentum: myth or menace?', in Robbin F. Laird and Erik P. Hoffmann, eds., *Soviet Foreign Policy in a Changing World* (New York: Aldine, 1986), pp. 701–12.
123 *Vestnik Ministerstva inostrannykh del*, 26 August 1987, p. 31.
124 *Pravda*, 13 April 1988, p. 4; *Izvestiya*, 1 January 1990, p. 5.
125 Gorbachev, for instance, remarked in his visit to Paris in 1989 that communism and social democracy were two branches of the same tree (*Pravda*, 7 July 1989, p. 5). His remarks about social democracy in his theoretical

statement, 'The socialist idea and revolutionary *perestroika*', were especially warm (*Pravda*, 26 November 1989, p. 1). For the Soviet reconsideration of social democracy more generally, see Heinz Timmerman, 'The Communist Party of the Soviet Union's reassessment of international social democracy', *Journal of Communist Studies*, vol. 5, no. 2 (June 1989), pp. 173–84.

7 Gorbachev and the politics of *perestroika*

1 M. S. Gorbachev, *Izbrannye rechi i stat'i*, 6 vols. (Moscow: Politizdat, 1987–89), vol. 2, p. 154.

2 Ibid., vol. 4, p. 110. The notion of 'humane, democratic socialism' was endorsed by the 28th Party Congress in 1990: *Materialy XXVIII s"ezda KPSS* (Moscow: Politizdat, 1990), pp. 77–98.

3 For some recent and representative discussions, see, for instance, Alec Nove, *The Economics of Feasible Socialism* (London: George Allen and Unwin, 1982); Anthony Wright, *Socialisms: Theories and Practices* (Oxford: Oxford University Press, 1986); Ellen Frankel Paul *et al.*, eds., *Socialism* (Oxford: Blackwell, 1989); Michael Harrington, *Socialism: Past and Future* (New York: Arcade, 1989); Jon Elster and Karl O. Moeve, eds., *Alternatives to Capitalism* (Cambridge: Cambridge University Press, 1989); Eric Hobsbawm, *Politics for a Rational Left* (London and New York: Verso, 1989); and David Miller, *Market, State, and Community* (Oxford: Clarendon Press, 1989).

4 Gorbachev, *Izbrannye rechi i stat'i*, vol. 2, p. 129.

5 Ibid., pp. 152–73, esp. pp. 153–67.

6 Texts of all of these editions are conveniently available in *Programmy i ustavy KPSS* (Moscow: Politizdat, 1969). For a discussion of these earlier documents and a text of the 1986 Programme see Stephen White, *Soviet Communism: Programme and Rules* (London: Routledge, 1989).

7 White, *Soviet Communism*, p. 10.

8 For a discussion, see Alfred B. Evans, 'Developed socialism and the new Programme of the CPSU', in Stephen White and Alex Pravda, eds., *Ideology and Soviet Politics* (London: Macmillan, 1988), pp. 83–113.

9 *XXVI s"ezd Kommunisticheskoi partii Sovetskogo Soyuza 23 fevralya–3 marta 1981 goda. Stenograficheskii otchet*, 3 vols. (Moscow: Politizdat, 1981), vol. 1, pp. 97–8.

10 Yu. V. Andropov, *Izbrannye rechi i stat'i*, 2nd edn (Moscow: Politizdat, 1983), pp. 245–6.

11 *Pravda*, 16 June 1983, pp. 1–2.

12 Ibid., 26 April 1984, p. 1.

13 Gorbachev, *Izbrannye rechi i stat'i*, vol. 3, pp. 6–8.

14 Ibid., p. 275. On the discussion, see White, *Soviet Communism*, pp. 14–17.

15 Gorbachev, *Izbrannye rechi i stat'i*, vol. 3, p. 275.

16 White, *Soviet Communism*, pp. 18–19.

17 Ibid., p. 42 (and in the Rules, p. 117).

18 Gorbachev, *Izbrannye rechi i stat'i*, vol. 3, p. 276, and vol. 4, p. 110 ('developing socialism').

19 Ibid., vol. 6, pp. 395–7.
20 *Perestroika raboty partii – vazhneishaya klyuchevaya zadacha dnya* (Moscow: Politizdat, 1989), pp. 30–1.
21 *Pravda*, 26 November 1989, pp. 1–3.
22 *Izvestiya TsK KPSS*, 1991, no. 2, pp. 17–22. The 'Programmatic Declaration' is in *Materialy XXVIII s"ezda*, pp. 77–98.
23 *Literaturnaya gazeta*, 20 April 1988, p. 2.
24 On Kurashvili, see Ronald Amann, 'Towards a new economic order: the writings of B. P. Kurashvili', *Detente*, no. 8 (winter 1987), pp. 8–10.
25 *Moscow News*, 5 June 1988, p. 13.
26 *Sovetskoe gosudarstvo i pravo*, 1989, no. 8, pp. 99–110.
27 A. P. Butenko, *Vlast' naroda posredstvom samogo naroda* (Moscow: Mysl' 1988), pp. 168, 144, 173. For the discussion on contradictions see White and Pravda, eds., *Ideology and Soviet Politics*, pp. 14–16.
28 *Pravda*, 8 August 1989, p. 3.
29 See 'Problemy razrabotki kontseptsii sovremennogo sotsializma', *Voprosy filosofii*, 1988, no. 11, pp. 31–71.
30 *Pravda*, 14 July 1989, p. 2, and 16 July 1989, p. 3. An article in *Kommunist*, 'K novomu obliku sotsializma', was also influential; it called for the rebirth of civil society, obtainable only through economic pluralism (*Kommunist*, 1989, no. 13, pp. 3–24). Hayek's *Road to Serfdom* was published in *Voprosy filosofii*, 1990, nos. 10 and 11, and in *Novy mir*, 1991, nos. 7–8; he was described as the 'idol' of economic oppositionists in *Pravda*, 6 June 1990, p. 4.
31 *Kommunist*, 1991, no. 1, p. 29 (Krasin); *Dialog*, 1990, no. 9, pp. 56–64 (Alekseev); *Kommunist*, 1991, nos. 4 and 5 (Shakhnazarov); and on capitalist private property, V. E. Guliev, ed., *Politicheskaya reforma: tseli, protivorechiya, etapy* (Moscow: Institute of State and Law, 1990), p. 30.
32 The text of the draft Programme appeared in *Pravda*, 8 August 1991, pp. 3–4, and *Kommunist*, 1991, no. 12, pp. 3–15. For 'Bad Godesberg' see Alla Nazimova and Viktor Sheinis in V. I. Mukomel', ed., *SSSR: Demograficheskii diagnoz* (Moscow: Progress, 1989), p. 675, and Volkov and Krasin in *Kommunist*, 1990, no. 7, p. 15. Gidaspov's comment is in *Pravda*, 27 July 1991, p. 4; V. Tiskov later explained that the 'communist perspective' had originally been omitted and was included for the sake of compromise: *Izvestiya*, 8 August 1991, p. 4. For a further discussion of the background to the draft Programme see *Report on the USSR*, vol. 3, no. 32 (9 August 1991), pp. 1–5.
33 *Pravda*, 26 July 1991, pp. 1, 2.
34 See, for instance, G. N. Yenukidze in *Sotsiologicheskie issledovaniya*, 1984, no. 3, pp. 11–20.
35 *Pravda*, 23 April 1986, pp. 1–2.
36 See, for instance, his interview in *Izvestiya*, 22 March 1989, p. 5.
37 *Pravda*, 5 October 1988, p. 4.
38 Ibid., 2 March 1989, p. 2, and 22 April 1989, pp. 1–3.
39 *Perestroika raboty partii*, pp. 85–88.
40 *Pravda*, 10 April 1987, p. 3.
41 *Sovetskaya kul'tura*, 21 July 1987, p. 2.

42 *Pravda*, 2 April 1987, p. 2.

43 Ibid., 13 August 1988, p. 2.

44 Ibid., 17 December 1988, p. 2.

45 Ibid., 23 June 1989, p. 2.

46 Ibid., 28 February 1989, p. 2. Yakovlev's lecture with discussion at Moscow University in 1990 was particularly searching: see *Kommunist*, 1990, no. 4, pp. 8–22. A more extended statement of his views is available in *Muki prochteniya bytiya* (Moscow: Novosti, 1991).

47 Ibid., 4 June 1987, p. 2.

48 E. K. Ligachev, *Izbrannye rechi i stat'i* (Moscow: Politizdat, 1989), pp. 207–10.

49 *Pravda*, 6 August 1988, p. 2.

50 Ibid., 21 July 1989, p. 3, and 3 March 1989, p. 2.

51 Yegor Ligachev, *Gdlyan i drugie* (Moscow: Veteran, 1991) pp. 4–5, and for instance in Ligachev, *Izbrannye rechi*, pp. 246–7, 262, 212.

52 *Komsomol'skoe znamya*, 5 February 1991, pp. 4–5. Ligachev's memoirs began to appear in 1991 in *Argumenty i fakty*.

53 *Pravda*, 30 September 1987, pp. 1–2.

54 Ibid., 11 September 1987, p. 3.

55 Ibid., 13 December 1990, p. 1.

56 *Kommunist*, 1991, no. 2, pp. 22–3.

57 *Pravda*, 6 August 1990, pp. 1–2.

58 Ibid., 4 February 1991 p. 3.

59 *Sovetskaya Rossiya*, 23 November 1989, p. 2, *Pravda*, 28 November 1989, p. 2, and 12 April 1991, p. 2.

60 *Sovetskaya Rossiya*, 13 March 1988, p. 3. Another letter appeared in *Molodaya gvardiya*, 1989, no. 7, pp. 272–7.

61 *Pravda*, 5 April 1988, p. 2.

62 *Sovetskaya Rossiya*, 15 April 1988, p. 3.

63 For the background to these surveys, see Elizabeth Weinberg, *The Development of Sociology in the Soviet Union* (London: Routledge, 1974), chapter 6.

64 See, for instance, Walter D. Connor and Zvi Gitelman, *Public Opinion in European Socialist Systems* (New York: Praeger, 1977), and William A. Welsh, ed., *Survey Research and Public Attitudes in Eastern Europe and the Soviet Union* (New York: Pergamon, 1981).

65 *Pravda*, 15 June 1983, p. 3, and 16 June 1983, p. 3.

66 Ibid., 18 March 1988, p. 2.

67 A joint Soviet–French poll, for instance, was reported in *Izvestiya*, 7 November 1987, p. 5; the 'most extensive Soviet poll on *perestroika* ever conducted for a foreign publication' appeared in *Time*, 10 April 1989, pp. 28–9.

68 *Izvestiya*, 5 May 1987, p. 2.

69 Ibid., 16 June 1987, p. 2.

70 *Pravda*, 5 April 1989, p. 3; the VTsIOM poll is reported in *Soviet Weekly*, 15 July 1989, p. 12.

71 *Literaturnaya gazeta*, 29 March 1989, p. 12.

72 On letters, see Stephen White, 'Political communications in the USSR: letters to party, state and press', *Political Studies*, vol. 31, no. 1 (January 1983), pp. 43–60; see also Jan S. Adams, 'Critical letters to the Soviet press' in Donald E. Shulz and Adams, eds., *Political Participation in Communist*

Systems (New York: Praeger, 1981), and Jim Riordan and Sue Bridger, eds., *Dear Comrade Editor. Readers' Letters to the Soviet Press under Perestroika* (Bloomington, IN: Indiana University Press, 1992). A broader survey of popular pressures of this kind is available in Nicholas Lampert, *Whistle-blowing in the Soviet Union* (London: Macmillan, 1985). For some of what follows I have drawn upon Stephen White, 'Dear comrade, sir', *Detente*, no. 11 (1988), pp. 14–16.

73 *Izvestiya TsK KPSS*, 1989, no. 1, pp. 156–99.

74 *Pravda*, 19 October 1987, p. 1.

75 Mikhail Gorbachev, *Perestroika: New Thinking for Our Country and the World* (London: Collins, 1987), pp. 77, 68, 72.

76 He had already received about 80,000 letters from Americans, Gorbachev told NBC in December 1987; this was about a third of all his foreign mail (*Vizit General'nogo sekretarya TsK KPSS M. S. Gorbacheva v SShA 7–10 dekabrya 1987 goda. Dokumenty i materialy* (Moscow: Politizdat, 1987), p. 3).

77 *Pravda*, 6 January 1990, p. 3.

78 *Observer*, 14 December 1986, p. 37.

79 *XXVII s"ezd Kommunisticheskoi partii Sovetskogo Soyuza 25 fevralyu – 6 marta 1986 goda. Stenograficheskii otchet*, 3 vols. (Moscow: Politizdat, 1986), vol. 1, p. 236.

80 *Pravda*, 21 September 1987, p. 1.

81 Ibid., 20 July 1987, p. 1.

82 Ibid., 13 July 1987, p. 1.

83 Ibid., 12 October 1987, p. 1, and 5 October 1987, p. 2.

84 Ibid., 28 September 1987, p. 1.

85 Ibid., 29 November 1987, p. 1.

86 Ibid., 17 August 1987, p. 1.

87 Ibid., 21 September 1987, p. 3.

88 Ibid., 28 September 1987, p. 1.

89 Ibid., 5 October 1987, p. 2.

90 Ibid., 21 September 1987, p. 3.

91 Ibid., 16 November 1987, p. 1.

92 Ibid., 3 August 1987, p. 1.

93 Ibid., 17 August 1987, p. 1; 16 August 1987, p. 3; 24 August 1987, p. 1; and 23 November 1987, p. 1.

94 Ibid., 6 July 1987, p. 1.

95 Ibid., 5 February 1987, p. 2.

96 Ibid., 6 July 1987, p. 1.

97 Ibid., 12 October 1987, p. 1; 20 April 1987, p. 2; and 11 May 1987, p. 2.

98 Ibid., 25 May 1987, p. 2.

99 Ibid., 18 January 1988, p. 2.

100 *Komsomol'skaya pravda*, 21 February 1988, p. 2.

101 *Pravda*, 9 October 1982, p. 2.

102. Ibid., 13 January 1989, p. 3.

103. *Kommunist*, 1989, no. 7, pp. 68–9.

104 *Soviet Weekly*, 24 June 1989, p. 10.

105 *Obshchestvennoe mnenie v tsifrakh*, issue 1 (Moscow: VTsIOM, 1989), p. 4.

106 Ibid., issue 4, p. 3, and issue 3, p. 9. For the other polls, see *Pravda*, 14 November 1989, p. 2, and *Moscow News*, 18 March 1990, p. 11).

107 *Moskovskie novosti*, 1990, no. 49, p. 9.

108 Ibid., 1991, no. 1, p. 6, and no. 12, p. 7.

109 *Argumenty i fakty* 1991, no. 11, p. 6.

110 *Moskovskie novosti*, 1991, no. 12, p. 7.

111 Ibid., 1990, no. 44, pp. 8–9.

112 *Izvestiya*, 24 April 1991, p. 1.

113 *Pravda*, 3 January 1991, p. 3 (and similarly in *Izvestiya TsK KPSS*, 1991, no. 2, pp. 6–7).

114 *Izvestiya TsK KPSS*, 1990, no. 4, pp. 191–3; *Argumenty i fakty*, 1990, no. 46, pp. 6–7.

115 *Argumenty i fakty*, 1991, no. 39, p. 1; other polls on Lenin appeared in *Glasnost'*, 1990, no. 22, p. 4, and *Dialog*, 1990, no. 5, pp. 4–7.

116 *Pravda*, 14 October 1990, p. 2; the call for Lenin's reburial came, among others, from Anatolii Sobchak, but his view of the family's own wishes was vigorously contested: see ibid., 24 September 1991, p. 4.

117 Ibid., 26 December 1990, p. 2.

118 Ibid., 26 December 1990, p. 3.

119 Ibid., 1 September 1990, p. 2.

120 *Dialog*, 1990, no. 10, p. 2.

121 Gorbachev, *Izbrannye rechi i stat'i*, vol. 6, p. 382.

122 *Pravda*, 23 March 1989, p. 1, and 15 January 1990, p. 2.

123 *Materialy plenuma Tsentral'nogo komiteta KPSS 8–9 oktyabrya 1990 g.* (Moscow: Politizdat, 1990), p. 201.

124 The new rules are in *Materialy XXVIII s"ezda*, pp. 108–24; Gorbachev's remarks are in ibid., pp. 38–9.

125 *Pravda*, 10 July 1989, p. 2.

126 *Moscow News*, 1989, no. 1, p. 8.

127 *Pravda*, 10 July 1989, p. 2.

128 Ibid., 26 July 1991, p. 2.

129 Ibid., 29 April 1991, p. 4. The playwright Alexander Gel'man was the first Central Committee member to tender his resignation: *Izvestiya TsK KPSS*, 1990, no. 10, p. 47.

130 *Argumenty i fakty*, 1991, no. 12, p. 8.

131 *Dialog*, 1990, no. 17, p. 14.

132 *Pravda*, 6 March 1991, p. 4.

133 Ibid., 21 February 1991, p. 2, and 26 July 1991, p. 2.

134 *Soviet Weekly*, 22 April 1989, p. 14.

135 *Moskovskaya pravda*, 11 July 1989, p. 1.

136 *Pravda*, 18 September 1989, p. 2.

137 Ibid., 26 May 1990, p. 4.

138 As noted in ibid., 18 September 1989, p. 2.

139 Ibid., 23 July 1989, p. 2.

140 Gorbachev, *Izbrannye rechi i stat'i*, vol. 3, p. 259; the views of party delegates were reported in *Izvestiya TsK KPSS*, 1990, no. 8, p. 133.

141 *Perestroika raboty partii*, pp. 45, 51–2, 58–9, 84, 100.

142 On these developments see Stephen White, 'Rethinking the CPSU', *Soviet*

Studies, vol. 43, no. 3 (June 1991), pp. 405–28, and White, 'The politics of the 28th Congress', in E. A. Rees, ed., *The Soviet Communist Party in Disarray* (London: Macmillan, 1992).

143 *Pravda*, 6 March 1991, p. 4. Burlatsky (with others) set out his views in *Literaturnaya gazeta*, 30 January 1991, pp. 1, 5. Andreeva's 'Unity' had been established in May 1989; see the interview in *Argumenty i fakty*, 1990, no. 22, pp. 4–5. Similar views were articulated in the press: see *Kommunist*, 1990, no. 18, p. 3.

144 The Komi party organisation resolved to this effect, and so did the Bashkir: *Pravda*, 20 October 1990, p. 2, and 27 October 1990, p. 2.

145 For the Lithuanian decision see *Sovetskaya Litva*, 21 December 1989, p. 1; for the Georgian decision see *Pravda*, 10 December 1990, p. 3; and for the Moldavian decision see ibid., 10 April 1991, p. 2.

146 See *Izvestiya TsK KPSS*, 1991, no. 4, pp. 69–70.

147 Ibid., no. 1, p. 64. In the summer of 1991 the CPSU again came first, with 19 per cent, followed by Democratic Russia with 7 per cent and the Democratic Party of Russia with 2 per cent, but 69 per cent had no clear party preference of any kind: *Pravda*, 2 July 1991, p. 3.

148 A. A. Protashchik, ed., *Cherez ternii* (Moscow: Progress, 1990), p. 776, *Soviet Weekly*, 2 August 1990, p. 4.

149 *Izvestiya*, 29 November 1990, p. 2.

150 *Izvestiya TsK KPSS*, 1990, no. 4, pp. 157–62 (letters); ibid., 1991, no. 6, p. 91 (visits); and more generally, *Pravda*, 6 March 1991, p. 4.

151 *Perestroika raboty partii*, p. 54, and (for the poll data) *Izvestiya*, 1 October 1991, p. 9. A fuller discussion of the party's final decline based on the Central Committee archives is available in Stephen White, 'Communists and their party in the late Soviet period', *Slavonic and East European Review* (forthcoming).

152 *Obshchestvennoe mnenie v tsifrakh*, issue 1 (1989), p. 15.

153 *Izvestiya*, 29 May 1989, p. 3.

154 *Argumenty i fakty*, 1989, no. 40, p. 1.

155 Ibid., no. 42, p. 3.

156 *Moscow News*, 1990, no. 45, p. 7.

157 *Nezavisimaya gazeta*, 28 February 1991, p. 2.

158 *Dialog*, 1990, no. 11, p. 3; *Pravda*, 12 September 1991, p. 2.

159 *Moscow News*, 1991, no. 15, p. 10 (slightly different results were given in *Nezavisimaya gazeta*, 28 February 1991, p. 1).

160 *Pravda*, 20 December 1990, p. 3.

161 *Arguments and Facts International*, January 1990, pp. 2–3.

162 *Obshchestvennoe mnenie v tsifrakh*, issue 1, p. 7.

163 *Moscow News*, 1991, no. 38, p. 5, and *Izvestiya*, 23 March 1992, p. 3. On political cultural perspectives, see, for instance, Stephen White, *Political Culture and Soviet Politics* (London: Macmillan, 1979). Western scholars, including Jeffrey Hahn and James L. Gibson, have found higher levels of support for multi-party politics in more recent surveys. See for instance Hahn, 'Continuity and change in Russian political culture', *British Journal of Political Science*, vol. 21, no. 4 (October 1991), pp. 393–421, and Arthur H. Miller *et al.*, eds., *Public Opinion and Regime Change: The new politics of post-Soviet societies* (Boulder CO: Westview, 1993).

164 *Pravda*, 10 December 1989, p. 1.
165 Henry L. Roberts, intr., *The Anti-Stalin Campaign and International Communism* (New York: Columbia University Press, 1956), pp. 119–28.
166 See Anatolii Butenko in Yuri Afanas'ev, ed., *Inogo ne dano* (Moscow:
Progress, 1988), pp. 551–2.
167 See the discussion between Ambartsumov, Zdravomyslov and others in
Pravda, 21 January 1990, p. 2.
168 *Pravda*, 26 November 1989, p. 1.
169 A. Tsipko in *Nauka i zhizn'*, 1988, nos. 11 and 12, and 1989, nos. 1 and 2. My
reading of Tsipko owes much to Alec Nove, 'Stalinism, Marxism, Leninism?' (Cologne: Bundesinstitut, mimeo., March 1989).
170 Igor Klyamkin in *Novyi mir*, 1989, no. 2, pp. 204–38. For similar contributions see Klyamkin, ibid., 1987, no. 11, pp. 150–88 ('Kakaya doroga vedet k
khramu?') and Vasilii Selyunin in ibid., 1988, no. 5, pp. 162–89 ('Istoki').
171 V. I. Lenin, *Polnoe sobranie sochinenii*, 55 vols. (Moscow: Politizdat, 1958–65),
vol. 39, pp. 21–2.
172 For Gorbachev's views on this point see, for instance, *Izbrannye rechi i stat'i*,
vol. 5, p. 301.
173 *Izvestiya*, 4 June 1989, p. 2.
174 *Soviet Weekly*, 4 November 1989, p. 15.

8   Towards a New Russia?

1 *Vedomosti S"ezda narodnykh deputatov SSSR i Verkhovnogo Soveta SSSR*, 1991,
no. 37, art. 1083.
2 *Gosudarstvo i pravo*, 1992, no. 4, pp. 4–8; and (for the constitutional
amendments) *Vedomosti S"ezda narodnykh deputatov Rossiiskoi Federatsii i
Verkhovnogo Soveta Rossiiskoi Federatsii*, 1992, no. 20, art. 1084.
3 B. I. Koval', ed., *Rossiya segodnya. Politicheskii portret, 1985–1990 gg.* (Moscow:
Mezhdunarodnye otnosheniya, 1991), p. 405. For an interim biography, see
John Morrison, *Boris Yeltsin: From Bolshevik to Democrat* (Harmondsworth:
Penguin, 1991).
4 Boris Yel'tsin, *Ispoved' na zadannuyu temu* (Leningrad: Chas pik, 1990),
pp. 17–18, 23, 25.
5 *Argumenty i fakty*, 1990, no. 22, p. 2, and (for 'which society is best') *Rossiiskie
vesti*, 21 April 1993, p. 1.
6 See for instance *Izvestiya*, 23 May 1991, p. 3.
7 Ibid., 11 June 1992, p. 3.
8 *Pravda*, 10 June 1991, p. 2.
9 Up to 80 per cent of local functionaries were the same, according to an
investigation reported in *Rossiiskaya gazeta*, 4 March 1992, p. 2. Yel'tsin
noted that there was less continuity at national level: *Izvestiya*, 27 March
1992, p. 7.
10 *Izvestiya*, 5 October 1992, p. 3.
11 For the resolution see *Vedomosti.. Rossiiskoi Federatsii*, 1992, no. 17, art. 899.
12 *Izvestiya*, 13 April 1992, p. 1.
13 *Rossiiskaya gazeta*, 20 April 1992, p. 3.

14 *Vedomosti.. Rossiiskoi Federatsii,* 1992, no. 17, art. 900.
15 *Izvestiya,* 15 June 1992, p. 1. Gaidar had been appointed in November 1991 as first deputy prime minister with responsibility for economic reform: *Nezavisimaya gazeta,* 9 November 1991, p. 1.
16 *Rossiiskaya gazeta,* 2 December 1992, pp. 3–4.
17 Ibid., pp. 3–5.
18 Ibid., 15 December 1992, p. 1.
19 *Pravda,* 16 December 1992, p. 1.
20 *Izvestiya,* 16 December 1992, pp. 1–2.
21 *Komsomol'skaya pravda,* 9 January 1993, p. 1; the decision had subsequently to be modified (*Izvestiya,* 18 January 1993, p. 1).
22 For the list of appointments see *Izvestiya,* 24 December 1992, p. 1.
23 Ibid., 14 December 1992, p. 3.
24 *Rossiiskaya gazeta,* 13 March 1993, p. 1.
25 Ibid., 16 March 1993, p. 1.
26 *Rossiiskie vesti,* 4 March 1993, p. 1.
27 *Federatsiya,* 1993, no. 31, p. 1.
28 *Rossiiskaya gazeta,* 16 March 1993, p. 1.
29 *Delovoi mir,* 23 March 1993, p. 1; or with a critical commentary, *Pravda,* 24 March 1993, pp. 1–2.
30 *Rossiiskaya gazeta,* 23 March 1993, p. 1.
31 Central television, 20 March 1993; the Constitutional Court's formal verdict appeared in *Rossiiskaya gazeta,* 24 March 1993, p. 3. The Supreme Soviet's resolution of 21 March on Yel'tsin's broadcast described it as an 'attack on the constitutional foundations of Russian statehood': *Federatsiya,* 1993, no. 32, p. 1.
32 *Rossiiskaya gazeta,* 25 March 1993, p. 1 (dated 20 March); the decree is also dated 20 March in *Rossiiskie vesti,* 25 March 1993, p. 1, but it is dated 24 March in *Moskovskaya pravda,* 25 March 1993, p. 1, and appears undated in *Rossiiskaya gazeta,* 23 March 1993, p. 4.
33 *Pravda,* 30 March 1993, p. 1.
34 For the decision of 29 March on the referendum see *Rossiiskaya gazeta,* 1 April 1993, p. 3; Yel'tsin's questions are in *Segodnya,* 10 March 1993, p. 1.
35 The ballot papers are themselves illustrated in *Rossiiskaya gazeta,* 9 April 1993, p. 1, and in *Pravda,* 10 April 1993, p. 1. The text of the Russian law on the referendum is in *Rossiiskaya gazeta,* 2 December 1990, pp. 1, 7. For a full study of the April referendum see Marie Mendras, 'Les trois Russie: analyse du référendum du 25 avril 1993', *Revue française de science politique,* vol. 43, no. 6 (December 1993), pp. 897–939.
36 See *Rossiiskaya gazeta,* 6 May 1993, p. 1 (on the third and fourth questions the votes against were 30.2 and 19.3 per cent respectively). For the Constitutional Court's ruling see ibid., 23 April 1993, p. 1.
37 For the draft see *Izvestiya,* 30 April 1993, pp. 3–5.
38 See for instance Khasbulatov in *Rossiiskaya gazeta,* 30 April 1993, pp. 3–4. A 'Burbulis plan' for media coverage, similar in tone to documents of the communist period, aroused particular indignation: see *Rossiiskaya gazeta,* 7 April 1993, p. 1, and *Pravda,* 8 April 1993, p. 2.

39 *Rossiiskaya gazeta*, 23 April 1992, p. 3.

40 Ibid., 8 April 1992, pp. 1, 2–4.

41 *Rossiiskie vesti*, 4 March 1993, p. 1; Yel'tsin made a similar point in an interview in *Argumenty i fakty*, 1992, no. 42, p. 2, and in a speech to his supporters on 28 March 1993 during the ninth session of the Congress of People's Deputies he insisted he would, if necessary, ignore its decisions. Khasbulatov pointed out that more than 70 per cent of the substantive amendments to the constitution had been introduced by the president himself: *Pravda*, 10 April 1993, p. 2.

42 *Izvestiya*, 10 December 1992, p. 1.

43 *Narodnyi deputat*, 1992, no. 12, pp. 7–8, 13–14, and no. 13, pp. 7–8. For an extended statement of his views see Ruslan Khasbulatov, *The Struggle for Russia* (London: Routledge, 1993).

44 *Izvestiya*, 12 March 1993, p. 1.

45 Ibid., 9 February 1993, p. 1, and (for the 'collective Rasputin') 10 April 1993, p. 1.

46 See for instance ibid., 14 December 1992, p. 3.

47 Ibid., 27 March 1993, p. 4.

48 *Izvestiya*, 30 March 1993, p. 1.

49 *Izvestiya*, 30 November 1992, p. 1.

50 *Pravda*, 18 December 1992, p. 2.

51 *Izvestiya*, 16 February 1993, p. 2; for its Programmatic Declaration see *Pravda*, 3 March 1993, p. 2.

52 *Izvestiya*, 11 June 1992, p. 2.

53 *Pravda*, 4 January 1993, p. 1.

54 Institut prikladnoi politologii, 'Politicheskie partii Rossii' (unpublished survey, 1993), based upon interviews with over 1500 respondents in four Russian regions. A brief account appeared in *Moskovskie novosti*, 1993, no. 12, p. 9A.

55 *Izvestiya*, 20 April 1992, p. 2.

56 *Mir mnenii i mneniya o mire*, no. 3(87), November 1993.

57 Richard Rose, Irina Boeva and Viacheslav Shironin, *How Russians are Coping with Transition: New Russian Barometer II* (Glasgow: Centre for the Study of Public Policy, University of Strathclyde, SPP no. 216, 1993), pp. 43–5.

58 See *Sotsiologicheskie issledovaniya*, 1992, no. 2, p. 77.

59 *Mirovaya ekonomika i mezhdunarodyne otnosheniya*, 1992, no. 1, p. 57. A similar view is presented in *Gosudarstvo i pravo*, 1992, no. 9, p. 157.

60 *Izvestiya*, 10 January 1992, p. 3.

61 *Argumenty i fakty*, 1993, no. 7, p. 2 (slightly adapted). Several recent reference guides to Russian parties are available, including R. Medvedev, ed., *Spravochnik: Politicheskie partii, dvizheniya i bloki sovremennoi Rossii* (Nizhnii Novgorod: Leta, 1993), and V. S. Ignonin, ed., *Rossiya: Politicheskie partii i obshchestvennye ob"edineniya*, vol. 1 (Moscow: Ivan, 1993).

62 The decree, soon famous as No. 1400, appeared in *Rossiiskie vesti* and in *Izvestiya*, 22 September 1993, p. 1; the election date was later changed to 12 December and the size of the Duma was increased from 400 to 450 seats (*Izvestiya*, 12 October 1993, p. 1 and *Rossiiskaya gazeta*, 8 October 1993,

pp. 3–5). Arrangements were made for elections to the upper house, the Council of the Federation, on 11 October (*Rossiiskaya gazeta*, 12 October 1993, p. 1). The original decree had indicated that the Federal Council would consider elections to the Russian presidency, and on 23 September elections were declared for 12 June 1994 (*Nezavisimaya gazeta*, 24 September 1993, p. 1); this decision was later reversed and Yel'tsin announced he would serve until the end of his term (*Segodnya*, 9 October 1993, p. 1).

63 Gaidar's reappointment was reported in *Izvestiya*, 23 September 1993, p. 1; the decree on property and the parliamentary newspaper appeared in *Rossiiskaya gazeta*, 25 September 1993, p. 2. The editor of *Rossiiskaya gazeta* was later replaced: ibid., 25 September 1993, p. 1.

64 The Court's decision appeared in *Pravada*, 23 September 1993, p. 1; the texts of the decrees are in *Rossiiskaya gazeta*, 23 September 1993, p. 2.

65 The first appointments were reported in *Rossiiskaya gazeta*, 23 September 1993, p. 3.

66 *Nezavisimaya gazeta*, 29 September 1993, p. 1; for the text of the decree see *Rossiiskaya gazeta*, 1 October 1993, p. 1.

67 *Izvestiya*, 28 September 1993, p. 3 (zero option); Yel'tsin's rejection of simultaneous elections was reported in *Segodnya*, 28 September 1993, p. 1.

68 The army's total commitment was made clear by General Grachev on several occasions (see for instance *Segodnyu*, 23 September 1993, p. 1, and 30 September 1993, p. 1). The reaction in the regions and republics was more qualified and a majority of regional leaders eventually declared themselves opposed to Yel'tsin's decree (ibid., 2 October 1993, p. 2). The talks under church auspices began after Yel'tsin had met the Patriarch: *Nezavisimaya gazeta*, 1 October 1993, p. 2.

69 *Rossiiskie vesti*, 5 October 1993, p. 3.

70 For the amnesty see *Rossiiskie vesti*, 25 February 1994, p. 7.

71 Ibid., 5 January 1993, p. 2.

72 *Izvestiya*, 28 December 1993, p. 1 (a total of 878 had been wounded). A detailed if preliminary chronology of the September–October events is available in *Svobodnaya mysl'*, 1993, no. 15, pp. 12–42.

73 *Izvestiya*, 6 October 1993, p. 2.

74 Ibid., 12 November 1993, p. 2.

75 *Rossiiskaya gazeta*, 15 October 1993, p. 2, and *Izvestiya*, 27 October 1993, p. 2. The election of Viktor Linnik as *Pravda*'s new editor was announced in the paper on 2 November 1993, p. 1.

76 *Rossiiskie vesti*, 5 October 1993, p. 2 (the curfew was first imposed on 3 October at 16.00); *Rossiiskaya gazetu*, 12 October 1993, p. 1.

77 *Rossiiskaya gazeta*, 9 October 1992, p. 1; *Izvestiya*, 7 October 1993, p. 1 (Zor'kin's resignation).

78 *Komsomol'skaya pravda*, 6 October 1993, p. 1.

79 *Izvestiya*, 28 October 1993, p. 1.

80 Ibid., 7 October 1993, p. 2, and 9 October 1993, p. 2.

81 Ibid., 21 October 1993, p. 2.

82 Ibid., 11 November 1993, pp. 1–2. Several helpful surveys of the blocs were published, including ibid., 13 October 1993, p. 4, 14 October 1993, p. 4, and

28 October 1993, p. 4; *Novoe vremya*, 1993, nmo. 48, p. 4; and *Rossiiskie vesti*, 11 November 1993, p. 2 (on which this discussion is primarily based). The legislation governing the December elections is conveniently collected by *Rossiiskaya Federatsiya*, 1993, no. 1(13), pp. 4–28. For a preliminary analysis incorporating original survey data see Matthew Wyman et al., 'The Russian Elections of 12 December 1993', *Electoral Studies* (forthcoming).

83 *Vybor Rossii*'s foundation was reported in *Izvestiya*, 19 October 1993, pp. 1–2. On television coverage see ibid., 25 November 1993, pp. 1 and 4, and 10 December 1993, p. 4.

84 *Megapolis-Express*, 1993, no. 45, p. 17.

85 The Liberal Democratic 'draft constitution' was compared with the official draft in *Nezavisimaya gazeta*, 8 December 1993, p. 5.

86 See particularly the articles by Kronid Lyubarsky in *Novoe vremya*, 1994, no. 7, pp. 8–12, and 9, pp. 10–13, and also *Izvestiya*, 4 May 1994, p. 4. Lyubarsky (himself a candidate) was also interviewed in *Ogonek*, 1994, no. 6–7, pp. 6–7.

87 For the final results see *Segodnya*, 28 December 1993, p. 1. A list of elected deputies appeared in *Rossiiskie vesti*, 28 December 1993 and (a more accurate one) in *Rossiiskaya Federatsiya*, 1994, no. 2, pp. 8–28. *Vybor Rossi* eventually had the largest deputies' fraction in the Duma, with 76 members; a grouping entitled 'New Regional Policy', including local officials as well as enterprise directors and generals, was the second largest with 65; and the Liberal Democratic Party came third with 63 (*Izvestiya*, 14 January 1994, p. 2; see also *Argumenty i fakty*, 1994, no. 4, p. 2). The non-party group in the Duma was however the largest, with 130 members, and the same was true of the Council of the Federation (*Rossiiskaya Federatsiya*, 1994, no. 2, pp. 13–14). On the Liberal Democratic vote see for instance *Izvestiya*, 30 December 1993, p. 4; 'Elektorat Zhirinovskogo', in *Ekonomicheskie i sotsial'nye peremeny: monitoring obshchestvennogo mneniya*, 1994, no. 2, pp. 30–3; and Peter Lentini and Troy McGrath, 'The rise of the Liberal Democratic Party and the 1993 elections', *Harriman Institute Forum*, vol. 7, no. 6 (February 1994).

88 Ibid., 21 December 1993, p. 2. In a contemporary survey, Russians were asked if a worthy candidate had been advanced in their single-member constituency: just 8 per cent answered affirmatively, a resounding 80 per cent negatively (*Argumenty i fakty*, 1993, no. 45, p. 1).

89 *Izvestiya*, 23 December 1993, p. 1.

90 For the draft, see ibid., 10 November 1993, pp. 3–5 (also *Argumenty i fakty*, 1993, no. 45, pp. 7–12); for the final text see *Izvestiya*, 28 December 1993, pp. 4–6, and *Konstitutsiya Rossiiskoi Federatsii* (Moscow: Yuridicheskaya literatura, 1993). Gorbachev was quoted in *The Times* (London), 29 November 1993, p. 16; the comparison with Napoleon III, by Anatolii Luk'yanov, appeared on *Pravda*, 10 November 1993, p. 3.

91 For Yelt'sin's decree see *Rossiiskie vesti*, 19 October 1993, p. 1 (a more detailed *polozhenie* appeared in ibid., 21 October 1993, p. 3); the final results were reported in ibid., 25 December 1993, p. 1.

92 See particularly *Moskovskii komsomolets*, 11 January 1994, p. 1 (in April 1993, for instance, the electorate had been 107.3 million; the first reported figure for the electorate in December was an inexplicable 105.3, which clearly

made it easier to achieve a 50 per cent turnout). Further irregularities were reported in *Izvestiya*, 4 May 1994, p. 4.

93 For the legal challenge see *Segodnya*, 29 December 1993, p. 2. Gorbachev favoured 'more work' on the text (*The Guardian* (London), 30 November 1993, p. 10); Viktor Sheinis thought the constitutional process in Russia was 'just beginning' (for his and other comments see *Nezavisimaya gazeta*, 9 December 1993, pp. 1–5); for the GULag see Georgii Shakhnazarov in *Rabochaya tribuna*, 9 December 1993, pp. 1–3. For further discussion of the merits of the new draft see for instance *Literaturnaya gazeta*, 1993, no. 46, pp. 1–2; *Obshchaya gazeta*, 1993, no. 17, p. 6; and *Novaya ezhednevnaya gazeta*, 12 November 1993, p. 1 (where it was suggested that the people would have the same role in relation to the President that they had earlier enjoyed in relation to the CPSU).

94 *Izvestiya*, 12 March 1993, p. 1.

95 Ibid., 18 March 1992, p. 1 (Moscow) and 11 September 1992, pp. 1–2.

96 Ibid., 5 January 1993, p. 2.

97 See *Argumenty i fakty*, 1993, no. 2, pp. 1–2, and *Moskovskie novosti*, 1993, no. 6, pp. 8A–9A.

98 Article 17 of the Chechen republic declared it an 'independent state' (*Moskovskie novosti*, 1993, no. 6, p. 9A); it had briefly declared 'holy war' on Russia: *Argumenty i fakty*, 1992, no. 40, p. 4.

99 'Politicheskie partii Rossii'. A similar view was reported in *Argumenty i fakty*, 1993, no. 51, p. 2.

100 *Ekonomika i zhizn'*, 1992, no. 6, pp. 13–16. On the background to post-communist economic reform see for instance Anders Aslund, ed., *The Post-Soviet Economy: Soviet and Western Perspectives* (London: Pinter, 1992), and Aslund and Richard Layard, eds., *Changing the Economic System in Russia* (London: Pinter, 1993). Several new data sources are helpful including *Review of the Russian Economy*, two issues annually from 1992, produced by Gaidar's Institute of the Economy in Transition, and the Centre for Economic Reform's *Russian Economic Trends*, quarterly from 1992, as well as the State Statistics Committee's monthly *Ekonomicheskoe polozhenie Rossiiskoi Federatsii*.

101 *Sovetskaya Rossiya*, 29 October 1991, pp. 1, 3.

102 A. V. Ulyukaev and S. V. Kolesnikov, eds., *Ekonomicheskaya politika Pravitel'-stva Rossii: Dokumenty* (Moscow: Respublika, 1992), pp. 4, 9–11, 12–13.

103 Ibid., pp. 15–16.

104 *Izvestiya*, 20 March 1992, p. 1.

105 Ulyukaev and Kolesnikov, *Ekonomicheskaya politika*, pp. 24–28.

106 Ibid., pp. 28–46.

107 See the summary in *Izvestiya*, 28 February 1992, pp. 1–2.

108 *Programma uglubleniya ekonomicheskikh reform v Rossii* (Moscow: Respublika, 1992); it was also carried in full in *Voprosy ekonomiki*, 1992, no. 8.

109 *Ekonomika i zhizn'*, 1993, no. 4, p. 13; for January–March 1993 see *Izvestiya*, 31 March 1993, pp. 1–2.

110 For the 25.4 per cent fall in industrial output in January–April 1994, see *Izvestiya*, 17 May 1994, p. 1; for the fall since 1989, see *Voprosy ekonomiki*, 1994, no. 2, p. 128.

111 *Pravda*, 9 June 1992, p. 1.

112 *Ekonomika i zhizn'*, 1993, no. 4, pp. 13–16.

113 Goskomstat Rossii, *Statisticheskii press-byulleten'*, 1994, no. 1, p. 6 (1993 inflation rate); *Voprosy ekonomiki*, 1994, no. 2, pp. 159, 129–30.

114 Ibid., 26 August 1992, pp. 1–2; for private trading see *Vestnik statistiki*, 1992, no. 9, p. 20.

115 *Izvestiya*, 4 December 1992, p. 2.

116 Ibid., 1 April 1992, p. 2.

117 Ibid., 10 February 1993, p. 1.

118 *Vestnik statistiki*, 1992, no. 9, p. 13 (Gaidar); *Segodnya*, 16 March 1993, p. 22 (Fedorov).

119 *Mirovaya ekonomika i mezhdunarodnye otnosheniya*, 1993, no. 2, p. 140; for changes in the measurement of a subsistence diet see for instance *Trud*, 3 October 1992, p. 1.

120 Alec Nove, personal communication. The adequacy of official statistics is discussed in a special issue of *Voprosy ekonomiki*, 1993, no. 5, and in *Mirovaya ekonomika i mezhdunarodnye otnosheniya*, 1994, no. 1, pp. 19–29.

121 *Pravda*, 6 February 1993, p. 1.

122 Ibid., 9 June 1992, p. 2.

123 *Guardian* (London), 3 March 1993, p. 8.

124 Ibid., 31 August 1992, p. 6.

125 *Voprosy ekonomiki*, 1994, no. 2, p. 127.

126 *Trud*, 18 January 1994, p. 5. See similarly *Svobodnaya mysl'*, 1994, no. 1, pp. 22–3. The deterioration in food quality is discussed more specifically in *Izvestiya*, 11 March 1994, pp. 1, 5. A few, generally government-sponsored reports suggested rising real incomes: see for instance *Segodnya*, 2 November 1993, p. 1, and *Izvestiya*, 17 February 1994, p. 4.

127 Ibid., 23 May 1992, p., 1.

128 Ibid., 24 March 1992, p. 6.

129 *Rossiiskaya gazeta*, 25 March 1993, p. 6.

130 *Kuranty*, 1 October 1992, p. 5 (Moscow). See similarly *Izvestiya*, 8 September 1993, p. 6 (also Moscow).

131 *Pravda*, 15 January 1993, p. 1.

132 *Izvestiya*, 1 October 1992, p. 2.

133 *Pravda*, 8 December 1992, p. 1.

134 Ibid., 5 January 1993, p. 1.

135 *Izvestiya*, 27 January 1993, p. 5. The dimensions of poverty and the attitudes of the poor are discussed in *Sotsiologicheskie issledovaniya*, 1994, no. 3, pp. 54–61 and 66–9.

136 *Guardian* (London), 20 March 1993, p. 23.

137 *The Herald* (Glasgow), 7 December 1992, p. 4.

138 *Statisticheskii press-byulleten'*, 1994, no 1, p. 33. On the new rich see Olga Kryshtanovskaya, 'Rich and poor in postcommunist Russia', *Journal of Communist Studies and Transition Politics*, vol. 10, no. 1 (March 1994), pp. 3–24.

139 *Statisticheskii press-byulleten'*, 1994, n. 1, pp. 6, 35. There was a related increase in the proportion of longterm unemployed (pp. 35–6).

140 *Izvestiya*, 12 February 1993, p. 5; for the 1993 increase see *Argumenty i fakty*, 1994, no. 15, p. 1.

141 *Izvestiya*, 9 February 1994, p. 5, and 14 January 1994, p. 14.

142 Ibid., 5 November 1993, p. 3

143 *Argumenty i fakty*, 1992, no. 22, p. 8.

144 Ibid., 5 August 1992, p. 1, and 6 May 1992, p. 1.

145 *Pravda*, 30 June 1992, p. 4.

146 *Izvestiya*, 5 August 1992, p. 2; *Argumenty i fakty*, 1992, no. 11, p. 8.

147 *Izvestiya*, 10 January 1993, p. 1, and 11 January 1993, p. 1.

148 *Guardian* (London), 30 January 1993, p. 12.

149 *Izvestiya*, 3 June 1992, p. 1; *Moskovskaya pravda*, 24 March 1993, p. 1; and for the 1993 increase, *Izvestiya*, 3 February 1994, p. 2.

150 *Izvestiya*, 30 March 1992, p. 2.

151 *Izvestiya*, 2 February 1993, p. 1; and for the 1993 fall, *Statisticheskii press-byulleten'*, 1994, no. 1, p. 38.

152 Ibid., 31 March 1993, p. 1.

153 *Pravda*, 3 September 1993, Moscow supplement, p. 3; *Nezavisimaya gazeta*, 2 February 1994, p. 1 (infant mortality). Maternal deaths in childbirth were fifteen to twenty times as high as in the developed West: see *Izvestiya*, 2 February 1994, p. 3.

154 Ibid., 7 October 1992, p. 6.

155 *Izvestiya*, 23 January 1993, p. 2, and *Argumenty i fakty*, 1993, no. 7, p. 8.

156 *Izvestiya*, 12 February 1993, p. 4; *Svobodnaya mysl'*, 1992, no. 11, p. 55.

157 *Izvestiya*, 21 December 1992, p. 3, and 25 December 1992, p. 1.

158 Ibid., 18 March 1992, p. 3; *Nezavisimaya gazeta*, 7 October 1992, p. 6. On alcohol consumption see *Izvestiya*, 4 September 1993, p. 15.

159 *Izvestiya*, 31 March 1993, p. 6, and 4 February 1993, p. 4.

160 *Nezavisimaya gazeta*, 25 March 1993, p. 2.,

161 *Izvestiya*, 18 August 1993, p. 5.

162 *Izvestiya*, 22 January 1992, p. 1.

163 *Nezavisimaya gazeta*, 7 October 1992, p. 6. On the broader question of environmental and demographic deterioration see Murray Feshbach and Alfred Friendly, *Ecocide in the USSR: Health and nature under siege* (London: Aurum Press, 1992); a Russian translation appeared in 1993.

164 *Vedomosti .. SSSR*, 1991, no. 32, no. 904; for the law on property see ibid., 1990, no. 11, art. 164.

165 For the July legislation see *Vedomosti.. Rossiiskoi Federatsii*, 1991, no. 27, art. 927; for the 'Basic provisions' see *Ekonomika i zhizn'*, 1992, no. 2, pp. 18–20.

166 *Vedomosti.. Rossiiskoi Federatsii*, 1992, no. 28, art. 1614.

167 *Izvestiya*, 20 August 1992, pp. 1–2. For the privatisation exercise more generally see Lynn D. Nelson, Lilia V. Babaeva and Irina Y. Kuzes, *Property to the People: The struggle for radical economic reform in Russia* (Armonk NY: Sharpe, 1993); Roman Frydman et al., *The Privatization Process in Russia, Ukraine and the Baltic States* (Budapest: Central European University Press, 1993); and Simon Clarke et al., 'The privatisation of industrial enterprises in Russia: four case-studies', *Europe-Asia Studies*, vol. 46, no. 2 (1994), pp. 179–214.

168 Ibid., 12 January 1993, p. 1.

169 *Sotsiologicheskie issledovaniya*, 1993, no. 2, p. 155.

170 *Izvestiya*, 6 January 1993, p. 2.

171 Ibid., 24 December 1992, p. 1.

172 See for instance ibid., 11 March 1993, p. 1 (counterfeits); *Nezavisimaya gazeta*, 8 October 1992, p. 1 (thefts).

173 *Moskovskaya pravda*, 20 March 1993, p. 2.

174 See *Izvestiya*, 20 February 1993, p. 5, and 24 February 1993, p. 2.

175 *Ekonomika i zhizn'*, 1993, no. 4, p. 13.

176 *Financial Times*, 2 April 1993, p. 16; the report in *Izvestiya*, 3 April 1993, p. 2, simply mentioned 'excesses'.

177 *Izvestiya*, 28 April 1992, p. 1.

178 Ibid., 17 June 1992, p. 5 (Russia).

179 Ibid., 30 April 1992, pp. 1–2.

180 Ibid., 16 April 1993, pp. 1, 3.

181 Ibid., 6 April 1993, p. 3.

182 *Pravda*, 7 April 1993, p. 3.

183 *Argumenty i fakty*, 1993, no. 5, p. 1 (interview with Jeffrey Sachs).

184 *Rossiiskaya gazeta*, 20 April 1993, p. 5 (Rutskoi).

185 *Nezavisimaya gazeta*, 21 March 1993, p. 5. Shatalin's memorandum appeared in ibid., 28 February 1992, pp. 1–2.

186 Ibid., 6 March 1992, p. 4. For Petrakov and his colleagues' alternative economic programme see *Pravda*, 9 June 1992, p. 3, and 11 June 1992, p. 3. Grigorii Yavlinsky's critique appeared in ibid., 6 June 1992, p. 1.

187 See *Voprosy ekonomiki*, 1994, no. 2, pp. 126–60 (a somewhat abbreviated version).

188 *Vek*, 1993, no. 8, p. 6. For the critique of the IMF see *Mirovaya ekonomika i mezhdunarodnye otnosheniya*, 1991, no. 17.

189 *Nezavisimaya gazeta*, 26 March 1992, p. 1 (Arbatov); *Rossiiskaya gazeta*, 24 March 1993, p. 1 (Bogmolov).

190 *Izvestiya*, 27 January 1993, p. 5.

191 Ibid., 6 January 1993, p. 1.

192 Ibid., 3 April 1993, p. 2.

193 For 'social orientation', see for instance *Rossiiskie vesti*, 7 May 1993, p. 1. For the poor, see *Izvestiya*, 22 December 1993, p. 2.

194 *Izvestiya*, 23 August 1991, p. 1.

195 Ibid., 22 August 1991, p. 1.

196 *Literaturnaya gazeta*, 28 August 1991, p. 7.

197 Grushin was the author, among others, of *Mneniya o mire i mir mnenii* (Moscow: Politizdat, 1967); his service, based in Moscow, is known as 'Vox Populi'.

198 *Izvestiya*, 30 November 1992, p. 2.

199 'Politicheskie partii Rossii'.

200 *Mir mnenii i mneniya o mire*, no. 2(86), November 1993.

201 Ibid., no. 11, November 1992, pp. 1, 8.

202 Yel'tsin's changing support is considered graphically in *Argumenty i fakty*, 1993, no. 38, p. 2. A survey in *Nezavisimaya gazeta*, 29 July 1992, p. 2, was exceptional in placing Rutskoi first; by early 1994, however, surveys based on expert assessments were generally placing Chernomyrdin ahead of

Yel'tsin (see for instance ibid., 3 March 1994, p. 1). There was greater trust, according to the surveys, in Grigorii Yavlinsky: see *Moskovskie novosti*, 1993, no. 37, pp. 1A, 5A. On Yel'tsin's evaporating support see Stephen White, Ian McAllister and Olga Kryshtanovskaya, 'El'tsin and his voters: popular support in the 1991 Russian presidential elections and after', *Europe-Asia Studies*, vol. 46, no. 2 (1994), pp. 285–303.

203 *Mir mnenii i mneniya o mire*, 1992, no. 9, p. 1.

204 *Izvestiya*, 31 March 1993, p. 4 (Congress) and 14 September 1992, p. 2 (Supreme Soviet).

205 Ibid., 5 October 1992, p. 3, and 27 March 1992, p. 3 (public relations consultant).

206 Ibid., 6 April 1992, p. 2.

207 *Svobodnaya mysl'*, 1992, no. 12, p. 62.

208 *Ekonomicheski i sotsial'nye peremeny: monitoring obshchestvennogo mneniya*, 1993, no. 3, p. 5.

209 *Izvestiya*, 20 August 1993, p. 4.

210 *Moskovskie novosti*, 1993, no. 34, p. 9A.

211 Ibid., 1994, no. 9, p. 7A.

212 *Izvestiya*, 24 July 1993, p. 8

213 *Izvestiya*, 17 August 1992, p. 2.

214 *Etnicheskoe obozrenie*, 1992, no. 3, p. 49 (which noted that the 'process of mythologisation had 'already begun', p. 50).

215 *Izvestiya*, 17 August 1992, p. 2.

216 *Sotsiologicheskie issledovaniya*, 1993, no. 2, p. 153.

217 *Izvestiya*, 15 June 1992, p. 3. In another survey, 51 per cent were 'hostile' towards the Emergency Committee in 1991, but only 39.2 per cent were still hostile in 1992, while 'positive' assessments had increased from 16.3 to 20.4 per cent ('Politicheskie partii Rossii').

218 *Mir mnenii i mneniya o mire*, 1993, no. 3, p. 1.

219 See for instance *Izvestiya*, 12 October 1992, p. 3, and 3 February 1993, p. 5.

220 'Politicheskie partii Rossii'.

221 *Svobodnaya mysl'*, 1992, no. 12, p. 61.

222 *Izvestiya*, 7 September 1992, p. 3.

223 *RFE/RL Research Report*, 19 March 1993, p. 58.

224 'Politicheskie partii Rossii'.

225 *Argumenty i fakty*, 1994, no. 16, p. 1.

226 *Izvestiya*, 3 February 1993, p. 5.

227 Ibid., 18 March 1993, p. 4.

228 Ibid., 17 March 1993, p. 4.

229 Ibid., 28 September 1992, p. 2.

230 Ibid., 3 February 1992, p. 2.

231 *Nezavisimaya gazeta*, 26 March 1992, p. 2.

232 *Argumenty i fakty*, 1992, no. 18, p. 1.

233 *Sotsiologicheskie issledovaniya*, 1992, no. 7, p. ?

234 *Mir mnenii i mneniya o mire*, 1992, no. 1, p. 7.

235 *Izvestiya*, 19 October 1992, p. 3.

236 Rose, Boeva and Shironin, *How Russians are Coping with Transition*, p. 48.

237 *RFE/RL Research Report*, 16 October 1992, p. 65.

238 *Moskovskie novosti*, 1993, no. 39, p. 6A.

239 *Argumenty i fakty*, 1994, no. 16, p. 1.

240 *Obshchestvennoe mnenie v tsifrakh*, 1990, no. 10, pp. 6–7.

241 *Izvestiya*, 27 March 1993, p. 4.

242 See Richard Rose, *Russians at the Start of the Longest Journey* (Glasgow: Centre for the Study of Public Policy, 1992), and related publications.

243 *Moskovskie novosti*, 1993, no. 15, p. 6A.

244 See John Higley and Richard Gunther, eds., *Elites and Democratic Consolidation in Latin America and Southern Europe* (Cambridge: Cambridge University Press, 1992).

245 Burlatsky in *Pravda*, 18 July 1987, p. 3.

Index

9835